Perspectives on Social Group Work Practice

Perspectives on Social Group Work Practice

A Book of Readings

Edited by
ALBERT S. ALISSI

THE FREE PRESS
A Division of Macmillan Publishing Co., Inc.
NEW YORK
Collier Macmillan Publishers
LONDON

The Free Press
A Division of Macmillan Publishing Co., Inc.
866 Third Avenue, New York, N. Y. 10022

Collier Macmillan Canada, Ltd.

Library of Congress Catalog Card Number: 79-7633

Printed in the United States of America

printing number

1 2 3 4 5 6 7 8 9 10

Library of Congress Cataloging in Publication Data

Main entry under title:

Perspectives on social group work practice.

Includes bibliographical references and index.
1. Social group work--Addresses, essays, lectures.
I. Alissi, Albert S.
HV45.P46 1980 361.4 79-7633
ISBN 0-02-900480-2

Contents

Preface

There are many provocative ideas that can be incorporated into the thinking and practice of social group work. This volume seeks to pull together a variety of materials from disparate sources to expand the repertoire of working concepts, which are vital to contemporary practice. The primary aim is to provide a sound basis for examining practice and to encourage the student to develop his or her own philosophy and approach to practice. Relatively little attention is devoted to the "how to do it" aspects of group work. Instead, the readings are intended to provide a broader context for examining practice, whatever the particular method or approach explored. Inasmuch as the content is germane to all levels of study, the readings should be useful to undergraduate and graduate students alike, as well as to practicing social workers.

The readings were compiled to help social group workers compare the most prevalent views and perspectives on practice. Although every effort was made to select the most representative writings from a range of views, doubtless there are many others that would have been equally suitable.

The book is divided into three parts. Part I, "Conceptual Foundations," provides a general framework for understanding the social group work method. Drawing heavily from historical materials, basic definitions, and descriptions, it explores early commitments and orientations to help the reader gain a better understanding of the nature of the method in a historical context. Acquainting the student with the work and ideas of the early founders, it is hoped, will help develop an appreciation for group work's rich heritage and a sense of mission. Part II, "Current Perspectives," contains samples from the literature that depict the perspectives that are most widely influential on contemporary practice. Although there is much that may be regarded as generic in terms of social work commitments, practice principles, and skills, there is no scarcity of conflicting views and positions. The current preoccupation with "models" of practice is reflected in the chapter headings. But the readings are perhaps better seen as an array of distinctive and yet overlapping perspectives from which any number of "models" may be developed, depending upon the categorization principles used. Part III, "Related Applications," presents materials from the early and current literature that focus on group work both as it relates to casework and community organization and as it relates to group methods in the disciplines of medicine, counseling, and psychology.

In the belief that each perspective is more clearly understood and more fully appreciated to the degree that it is critically examined and compared to alternative views, a number of open-ended questions are included at the end of each chapter along with suggested additional readings. The questions by no means anticipate any single right or wrong answer. Their purpose is to stimulate the student to develop an inquisitive attitude about a variety of issues, to compare and contrast methods, and to become an active participant in developing his or her own perspective. Similarly, the suggested readings are in no way meant to cover every topic. They are simply leads to further study. The serious student who picks up on the readings and "chases footnotes" will find the task rewarding.

I wish to thank the publishers and authors for their kind permission to reprint the materials included in this volume. To *The Journal of Sociology and Social Welfare* under Professor Norman Goroff's editorship, I extend special thanks for making an early, more limited version of this reader available to the students at the University of Connecticut School of Social Work. It was the success of that volume that did so much to stimulate this work.

For the students who I hope will find this volume helpful, I can do no more than to encourage them to continue to examine their own practices in light of changing perspectives and to take an active part in thinking, writing, and otherwise advancing the practice of social group work.

PART I
Conceptual Foundations

SECTION A

The Nature of Social Group Work

It should not be assumed that because social group work has been developed and refined as a conscious professional activity, there is conceptual agreement or even clarity regarding its definition, purposes, practice methods, and techniques. While this is not so much a questioning of what group work has to offer as it is a reflection of changing conceptions about where and how best to direct its efforts, nevertheless it would appear that the essence of group work method needs to be continually re-examined and somehow reaffirmed. What, then, is the nature of social group work? What are its underlying assumptions regarding the value of group experiences? What ideas, movements, and activities go to make up its conceptual foundations? What is the nature of its knowledge, basic values and commitments, and major resources?

In addressing these and similar questions, the chapters in this section provide a general framework for understanding the group work method. The first chapter, prepared especially for this volume, traces group work from its earliest commitments through the succeeding periods of formulation, synthesis, growth, and theory-building. Against a background of changing perspectives, the search for definition, function, and unified efforts emerges as the most persistent theme. Attempts to resolve definitional questions and practice issues became particularly intense after the formation of the National Association of Social Workers (NASW) in 1955. The Council on Social Work Education's three-year curriculum study resulted in thirteen volumes dealing with all aspects of social work. The chapters by Grace Coyle and Clara Kaiser were two of the four influential position papers contained in the group work volume of the study. Coyle dealt with the underlying assumptions regarding the basic values of group experiences and the role of group work in realizing the potentials that inhere in such experiences. Kaiser, on the other hand, focused more pointedly on group work's conceptual foundations—the systems of thought, values, goals, group processes, and methods concepts. The "Frame of Reference" statement, produced under Margaret Hartford's editorship, arose out of a four-year effort of the Committee on Practice of the National Group Work Section of

NASW to incorporate the thoughts and ideas of a wide range of group work practitioners and educators to arrive at greater clarity regarding group work purposes, knowledge, and technical skills.

1

Social Group Work: Commitments and Perspectives

Albert S. Alissi

OVERVIEW

As distinct from the related social work methods of casework and community organization, social group work concentrates primarily on providing group experiences to meet normal developmental needs, to help prevent social breakdown, to facilitate corrective and rehabilitative goals, and to encourage citizen involvement and responsible social action. Characteristically, group work services involve small groups of members coming together with a "worker" on a more or less regular basis, usually as participants in a social agency or institution. Groups vary in size and composition. Participants include persons of all ages, races, and social classes joining together in natural as well as formed groups. Professional training in social group work is provided in most graduate and undergraduate schools of social work. Group work methods are also used extensively by a variety of agency workers with differing kinds of preparation and experience.

Group work is based on many conceptual foundations. Its values can be traced to ethical and religious beliefs rooted in the Judeo-Christian tradition; to the Humanitarian movement, which found expression in the early settlement movement; and to the core of social work values and philosophy, which have evolved out of a long tradition of service to people. Its theories and practices were influenced by the democratic ethic of Mary Follett and Eduard Lindeman; the educational philosophy of John Dewey; the sociologies of Durkheim, Simmel, Cooley, and Mead; the group dynamics of Kurt Lewin; the small group processes of Wilber Newstetter and Grace Coyle; the play theories of Neva Boyd; Freudian psychoanalysis; and the group therapies of S. R. Slavson and Fritz Redl. Systems theory, sociobehavioral theory, and existential thought have influenced some of the more recent versions of practice.

The expansion of group work into new directions over the years is reflected in the wide variety of agencies where its methods are now practiced. Beginning with the settlement houses, community centers, religious organizations, and national youth service agencies such as the YMCAs, Boys' Clubs, Scouting programs, camping, and 4-H clubs, the methods were extended to hospitals, psychiatric clinics, and residential treatment centers and other specialized programs for physically, mentally, and socially handicapped, including the fields of correction, probation, and parole. Public schools, welfare departments, public recreation, industry, trade unions, and public housing projects are among the many areas where additional uses are being recognized and developed.

Social group work ranks among the earliest practical efforts to realize the potentials inherent in the small group experience to maximize the well-being of the individual and improve social conditions. Many of its methods were applied long before any efforts were made to systematize and professionalize practice. Early work with groups was fashioned out of the hard-earned experiences of men and women who manned the social agencies and organizations that sought, during an era of social reform, to combat the harmful effects of the Industrial Revolution upon the lives of people. Infused with a strong sense of purpose and dedication to serve society, the early reformers emphasized personal growth and social development, citizen involvement, democratic participation and association, and cultural pluralism—all of which were early influences on the development of social group work.

The widespread use of group work methods in the education-recreation, "leisure-time," and "character-building" agencies influenced practice in other significant ways. During the 1920s and 1930s, group work came to be viewed largely as an educational process where new skills and knowledge were learned through active involvement in voluntary associations. Creative program activities were used as a tool to enhance normal individual growth and personality development. Workers began to recognize that group leadership techniques had important influences on group processes and that these processes in turn affected the attitudes, behaviors, and personalities of the members. Moreover, workers could appreciate the impact of the small group as a socializing influence on participants and began consciously to use the group as a force for inculcating values and for teaching leadership and citizenship responsibilities. The group became the means for bringing about cooperative democratic changes in other aspects of social functioning as well.

The organization of a group work section in the National Conference of Social Work (NCSW) in 1935 marked a turning point in the development of social group work as the progressive education, adult education, and recreation orientations began to be overshadowed by the alignment of group work with the social work profession. The presence of an organized national forum stimulated the exchange of ideas and became the context in which an earnest search for a definition of practice was launched. The chief aim of group work at that point was seen to be the development and adjustment of the individual and the advancement of socially desirable goals and purposes through voluntary group association and activity. There was, even at this early date, beginning disagreement over whether group work should move away from its educational and preventative objectives in pursuit of therapeutic and corrective objectives (Coyle, 1959, p. 79).

The identification of social group work with social work brought about other changes. The broader, more lofty goals of individual development and societal change received less emphasis as casework, which relied so heavily on psychoanalytic theory, came to influence the professionalization process. During the 1940s and 1950s, group work methods were introduced into many new settings. Of particular significance was the development of group work services in a variety of rehabilitation and adjustive programs throughout the country. Attention was focused on the distinctive contributions group work could make in the treatment of psychic disturbances relative to other forms of group therapies. Although the emphasis on group processes and programmed activity remained unique, the development of diagnostic and treatment skills required new psychological insights and understanding on the part of group workers. It was perhaps inevitable that the increased use of group work in clinical settings was accompanied by a heightened interest in individual adjustment and conformity.

In recent years there has been renewed interest in finding ways to institute social change. The need has been underscored by dramatic expressions of economic deprivation and differential opportunities, urban unrest, racial conflict, large-scale alienation, and the repudiation of societal values by large segments of the population. The current emphasis on advocacy and social action seeks to make social work in general more relevant to these needs. Increasingly, distinctive conceptual models are being formulated which stress different perspectives on group work theory and practice.

Many excellent historical accounts have been written about group work dealing with both the general and the specific aspects of its development (Coyle, 1959; Schwartz, 1959; Middleman, 1968; Konopka, 1963; Hartford, 1964; Wilson, 1976; Somers, 1976). This review will only highlight some of the changing events, practices, and ideas that are essential to an understanding of the various perspectives on social group work. Although it is concerned primarily with the changing ideas and systems of thought and only incidentally with changing events and practices, obviously all have influenced the development of group work and need to be considered. The developments will be discussed in terms of the following stages: *early commitment*—from the turn of the century to the middle 1930s; *period of formulation*—taking place in the middle 1930s; *synthesis and extensions*—which occurred in the 1940s and 1950s; and the *proliferation of formulations*—which characterized the 1960s and 1970s.

EARLY COMMITMENT: UP TO 1935

First and foremost, the early group workers were activists. While the Industrial Revolution, in advancing special interests and personal profits, continued to take its toll in exploiting human potential, a growing number of men and women moved mostly by religious or personal conviction joined emerging self-help causes. Those early volunteers and workers were endowed with a spirit of inquiry and experimentation and a dedication to making things better. Working out of the settlement houses and the character-building and leisure-time agencies, they identified and began responding to human needs. They reached out to the underprivileged, to newcomers, and to youth to engage them in mutual fellowship. They focused early on children to rescue them from the throes of a materialistic environment and to help them grow and develop socially through group association. They sought ways to improve and modify the environment to deal with pressing social problems. Underlying all of these efforts was the belief that they would somehow make democracy work.

Early Club Work

From the start, the small group or "club" was taken to be the most useful medium for advancing the work of the YMCA, YWCA, settlements and related agencies. One of the earliest successful group approaches was the prayer and Bible-reading groups composed of city clerks in London organized by George Williams in the founding of the YMCA in 1844. Both Miss Emma Robarts's Prayer Union and Mrs. Arthur Kinnaird's "General Female Training Institute" were early group-centered programs that caught on and spread rapidly throughout England, eventually combining to form the YWCA in 1877. Meanwhile, in New York a rented room turned into a clubhouse for women wage-earners symbolized the importance of small group association in the development of the YWCA program in America. The first American settlement, the Neighborhood Guild, which was established by Stanton Coit in 1886, was organized around the club idea. Group activities and clubs were ideal for "cultivating neighborly acquaintance" and building "personal ties." "Stanton Coit," wrote Jane Robbins, thinking back on early club work with youth, "had been really eloquent on the subject of forming close friendships and of grappling these young people to us with hoops of steel. We caught the idea" (Woods and Kennedy, 1922, p. 73; Robbins, 1912, p. 1,800).

Arthur Holden reported in 1922 that the average settlement was bound up with the administration of its "club system," the club being the most typical unit of individuals served. Unlike classes, clubs were more closely knit and were bound together by particular friendship ties and common interests. Such clubs were quite autonomous, having their own constitutions and elective memberships. Often an older, more experienced person representing the settlement met with the club in the capacity of a "director" to see that the club received the benefits and advantages the settlement had to offer. This position, Holden pointed out,

> . . . is exceedingly delicate and is one which calls for great tact and forebearance. Club work to be effective should be a natural expression of the members themselves. The director must exercise a nice balance. He can lead but he cannot push. He can point to errors, he can warn of mistakes. He should not, however, insist upon definite or specific action. The ideal director is hard to find [Holden, 1922, p. 65].

Observers found clubs, with their autonomy and freedom, strangely different from other adult-directed activities. More than simply promoting interest in art, crafts, music, drama, or discussion, the clubs demonstrated the value of "the actual interplay of association" (Clarke, 1947). Visitors to the settlement were not accustomed to the climate of openness and the spirit of confrontation and inquiry that permeated so much of the club experience. To witness, for example, a group of working-class adolescents arguing the merits of socialism in a free and open debate was quite out of the ordinary.

The personal influence of the leader on group members was seen to be more directive and influential in other clubs formed by the settlements. In their detailed study of settlement practices, Robert Woods and Albert Kennedy (1922) pointed out, for example, that although much of the early work with boys sought to "get the boys off the streets," as did most of the mass programs characteristic of the times, once admitted, boys were assigned to groups in the conviction that it was better to work intimately with a few rather than superficially with many. "The successful leader," they said, "steeps himself in the activities, hopes, fears, dreams, and endless conversation of his charges, and is thus prepared to encourage each one in the several most vital aspects of his life" (Woods and Kennedy, 1922, p. 77).

By the 1920s, it was generally recognized that small group associations were vital in promoting the developmental, adjustment, and enrichment aspects of individual growth and the democratic participation of social responsibility. Groups were also seen to be useful in treating antisocial behavior and maladjustment and for "preventative work" as well (Konopka, 1956).

The Search for Commonality

Although it was increasingly clear that a beginning expertise in work with small groups was being developed by workers in the various settings, the development of a common framework of practice was impeded by dissimilar organizations and agency structures in which practice was conducted. Margaret Hartford (1966, pp. 132-134) enumerated some of the differing orientations: some were building-centered, others used the facilities of other institutions; some had nationally developed programs, others developed local indigenous services; some used volunteer group leaders, others used paid professional group leaders; some favored formed groups, others responded to natural autonomous groups; some served the socially, economically, and culturally deprived, others served the middle class; some aimed at specific ethnic, racial, or religious groups, others were for all groups; some focused exclusively on small club groups, others offered a range of recreational, informal education, physical education, and mass program activities; some served special age groups, others served all ages; and finally, some held strongly to serving the relatively healthy "normal" population while others sought out those with identified problems for treatment.

It was to be expected that the meaning of group work reflected these differences. For example, a leading textbook by Warner, Queen, and Harper (1930) classified group work along with casework, institutional work and organization, and administration as the four major types of social work. The meaning of group work was intertwined with a range of methods, functions, and fields of service. The subvarieties, for example, included "direction of leisure time," "club work with small groups," "neighborhood work," and "community organization." The concept was used interchangeably with education/recreation and had different referents to social work. The confusion is perhaps best illustrated in the following passage dealing with the relation of recreation to social work:

> Recreation as a type of group social work is intimately related to the other phases of the profession, particularly to case work, and should accomplish more than simply to consume leisure time. Recreation is

> frequently employed as a method in individual cases, and proper "recreational placement" requires a careful analysis of the needs and abilities of the child or adult, and a study of his play history [Warner, Queen, and Harper, 1930, pp. 499–500].

In spite of the definitional and conceptual difficulties, efforts to develop a common framework became more intense toward the end of this period. A common terminology was beginning to develop from common experiences prior to the 1930s. The terms "purposes," "structures," "social process," "status and role," and "stages of group development" became part of the worker's vocabulary. As social psychologists gained influence, additional expressions became familiar, such as "interpersonal relationships," "acceptance-rejection patterns," "conflict," and "social control." And in some cases psychoanalytical concepts found their way into the worker's vocabulary as well (Wilson, 1976, p. 17).

The first course on group work was introduced at Western Reserve University in 1923, and by 1927 the first group work curriculum was established there under Wilber Newstetter's direction. The New York School introduced group work courses in 1934, followed by the School of Social Work in Pittsburgh a few years later. By 1937 there were thirteen educational institutions offering courses in group work, ten of which were in schools of social work (Coyle, 1959).

Although practices were being developed in the field, the professional status of group work remained obscured. Mary Sims (1935) reported, for example, that the YWCA was involved in extensive "experimental" work with informal groups to encourage individual growth and development. Record-keeping procedures were being developed to help judge the success of the work. The focus was also being turned away from exclusive attention to "content" of program activities to the individuals participating in the groups. At the same time she had to acknowledge:

> The Young Women's Christian Association seems to have suffered at various times from an inferiority complex through the failure of social work in general to recognize the techniques of group work as legitimate professional equipment for social workers [Sims, 1935, p. 222].

Ideological and Conceptual Influences

Certain ideologies or systems of thought have been generally recognized as significant in giving direction and content to group work (Kaiser, 1958), and some of them were particularly influential during the period of commitment. The ethical, social, and theistic beliefs embodied in the Judeo-Christian tradition were deeply rooted and formed the basis for commitment. The humanitarianism of the late nineteenth century, which found expression in the settlement house movement, the progressive education philosophy of John Dewey, and the recreational movement all provided direction for action. The study of small groups by certain sociologists contributed new insights regarding group functioning. And finally, the beliefs in democratic values and participatory democracy provided the context in which much of the practice of group work developed.

Doubtless much of the motivation for organizing clubs in England and America at the turn of the century were based on the desire to strengthen character through inculcating Christian principles and values. Often, however, goals reflected either a class bias or a preoccupation with rescuing people from sin. The Society of Parochial Mission Women, for example, "plotted to improve," through the use of soap, thrift, and sanitation, "the very lowest and least thrifty among the wives and mothers of the poorest class" (Woodroofe, 1968, p. 61; Hamilton, 1884). The Girl's Friendly Society sought to bind together working girls and young women as members "to make virtue easier, and to act as a fence between them and the pitfalls of vice" (Woodroofe, 1968, p. 61; "Prevention," 1885).

Humanitarianism represented the collective efforts of a wide range of agencies, personalities, and programs devoted to advancing the welfare of human beings. It gave rise to the settlement movement, which was most influential in giving form and substance to group work. According to Canon Samuel Barnett (Davis, 1967), founder of Toynbee Hall, the aim of the settlement was to bridge the gulf that had been created between the rich and the poor during the industrialization process. By living in the settlement, university men would make the slums an outpost for education and culture. It was, in the words of Lord Beveridge, the distinguished writer and former resident at Toynbee Hall, "a school of post graduate education in humanity" (Spencer, 1954, p. 36). Although religious motivations were ever present in the settlements, often the founders rejected sectarian and evangelical themes in favor of a more practical focus on dealing with such problems as unsanitary factories, crowded homes, long working hours, low wages, employment of women and children, unemployment, and discrimination against immigrant and minority groups.

The self-help emphasis of the settlement differed significantly from the philosophy of the Charity Organization Society (COS) which caused considerable initial antagonism between the two movements around the turn of the century. Basically the charity organization stressed individual causation of poverty, while the settlements were inclined to blame social and economic conditions. While the COS sought primarily to help the poor, unemployed, and downtrodden, the settlements aimed their efforts at the working classes, being more concerned with the "poverty of opportunity" than with the "poverty of clothes." Charity workers were inclined to dismiss the settlement as being too sentimental, radical, unscientific, and vague in direction and purpose. Settlement workers meanwhile tried to dissociate their movement from charity in the public's mind. While the COS held that it was the responsibility of the upper classes to extend help to the lower classes, the settlement stressed the reciprocal and mutual dependence of the classes on each other. But changing practices and the widespread exchange of personnel engaged in philanthropic and reform activities brought about new attitudes and closer cooperation. The merging of interests was perhaps best symbolized by the election of Jane Addams in 1909 to the presidency of the National Conference of Charities (Davis, 1967).

The influence of the settlement movement was felt in innumerable ways. In education, the settlements initiated educational experiments in developing child care, kindergarten programs, and vocational training all aimed at relating education to real world experience. In the field of recreation, they were successful in establishing the first public playgrounds and recreation programs. Many summer camps and "fresh air" programs were started by settlements. Public schools were influenced to develop "school social centers" for clubhouse and recreational purposes. Workers were also active in their support of the labor movement. Ellen Star, for example, joined in picketing, raising money, and making speeches in support of labor. Through the efforts of such workers as Florence Kelly, settlements did much to eliminate child labor and unionize women. The influence of the settlement was also felt in other areas such as housing reform, intercultural and interracial relations, immigration, health, sanitation, political reform, etc. (Davis, 1967).

The philosophical and educational theories and practices of John Dewey, which found expression in the progressive educational movement, had a most direct influence on group work. Dewey held that education, to achieve its fullest potential, must reflect the needs of the learner and take into account the "total" person, including social and emotional as well as intellectual factors. In contrast to the traditional classroom methods of "rote" teaching, the new emphasis was on "learning by doing." The role of interaction in the learning process placed a new importance on the teacher-child relationship and on the small group as a primary resource for learning. Dewey, a member of the first board of trustees at Hull House and a frequent visitor to the settlement, was influential in seeing his ideas experimentally applied in practice. Group workers placed great emphasis on education for democratic living; with Dewey they held, at base, the belief that unless education was tied to a larger democratic frame of reference it would be "aimless and lacking in unified objective" (Dewey, 1939, p. 25).

Group workers were influenced by still another movement that arose to provide release from the drudgery and monotony of life in an industrialized climate, where the worker seemed to lose all but his capacity to work. The recreation movement transformed early negative attitudes toward free and spontaneous use of free time and the utility of play especially for children to a positive recognition of the values of recreation as a vital necessity to the well being of all. Activities were of course central to the concepts of play and recreation. In time the emphasis on the play life of children, games, sports, arts, and crafts, including a variety of other leisure-time pursuits, was on "the proper use of leisure," which was not only enjoyable but "constructive" as well (Slavson, 1948).

A variety of theories of play were drawn upon including Spencer's (1873) "surplus energy," Groos's (1901) "preparation for life" theory, Hall's (1904) inheritance or recapitulation theory, William James's (1890) "instinct" theory. In their sociological study of leisure and recreation, Neumeyer and Neumeyer (1949) noted the importance of groups in recreation. Most recreation groups were seen to be primary in nature, in that they were based on intimate face-to-face contacts and cooperative associations. The mutual identification, feelings of "we-ness," and *esprit de corps* were prominent and taken to be a most important influence on behavior.

Neva Boyd, who had prior training and experience as a kindergarten worker, was a strong advocate of the play movement and continually urged group workers to appreciate the social values to be derived from spontaneous play and recreation throughout all stages of life. She and her associates began an experimental school in training professional recreation and play leaders, which eventually became part of the Group Work Division in the Department of Sociology at Northwestern University (Simon, 1971).

Although much of early practice was being developed by practitioners who relied primarily on their own insights from their day-to-day experiences, the beginning or early theoretical framework for group work was being shaped by such early sociologists as Emile Durkheim, Georg Simmel, Charles H. Cooley, George Herbert Mead, and William McDougall. Durkheim's (1951: 1964) emphasis on the reality of social phenomena contributed to the view that the group was in fact greater than the sum of its parts. The significance of attachments and belonging, alienation and isolation were highlighted in his concepts of "organic" and "mechanical" societies, social solidarity and anomie. The work of Simmel (1950) focused attention on structure or "forms" of association and reciprocal relationships as strong determinants of behavior. His many insightful observations regarding the dyad, triad, and subgroup formations stimulated interest in analyzing further interactional processes within small groups. Cooley's (1909) concept of the primary group made it clear that small, cohesive, intimate, face-to-face groups such as the family, play group, or neighborhood have the earliest and most fundamental impact on individual socialization and personality development and play a major role in preparing for participation in the larger society. The concept of the "looking glass self" or "reflected self" (Cooley, 1902) called attention to the role others play in the development of the conception of the self. Mead (1934) was later to distinguish the "I" and "me" parts of the self, which provided a framework for relating the impact of the group experience to the individual and social development of its members. And finally, McDougall's (1920) concept of the "group mind" as a collective spirit independent from the individual, although seen to be fallacious, did point out how mutual influences within groups contribute to a sense of togetherness and semblance of a unified single entity that could be treated as a whole.

Group workers were strongly influenced by the social and political philosophies of Mary Parker Follett, Eduard Lindeman, and Harrison Elliott, who did much to operationalize the democratic ethic upon which group work was founded. In their view, democracy went far beyond political action and permeated all social relationships. Follett's book *The New State* (1926) made it clear that democracy was not to be achieved through political parties and the ballot box but rather through active group participation. As an active settlement worker she went further to put her ideas to work by organizing small groups for enlightened political action. Citizenship participation was also emphasized in the social philosophy of Lindeman (1925). Participation was important because it contributed to the strengthening of society as well as to individual and social development. Elliott, in his book *The Process of Group Thinking* (1928), provided a practical analysis of how the give-and-take of individual ideas within the small group provided the most effective means for developing creative growth and democratic solutions.

THE PERIOD OF FORMULATION: THE MID-THIRTIES

The 1930s represents a period of formulation and organization in the development of group work. Although the sequence of events produced movement toward a common identity with the profession of social work, the search for a definition, which occupied so much attention during this period, failed to produce widespread agreement. Instead, it merely seemed to highlight issues, many of which have persisted in one form or another throughout the history of social group work.

Interest in formulating practice was stimulated by the appearance of a number of small study and training groups of professionals in the early 1930s. Grace Coyle, for example, organized a two-week institute on group work, which was given in the summer of 1934 at Fletcher Farm in Vermont and was attended by forty YWCA and settlement house workers. Hedley Dimock and Paul Limbert at the YMCA schools at George Williams College and Springfield College, respectively, similarly offered institutes and seminars to train group workers. The New York Conference on Education in Group Work sent representatives to meet with group workers from Western Reserve, Ohio State, and Chicago's Committee on Group Work to consider ways to consolidate thinking about group work further (Wilson, 1976; Hendry, 1947).

Following the request of a number of group workers who had gathered two years earlier at the National Conference of Social Work (NCSW) in Detroit, a group work section of the Conference was created in 1935, which became a landmark year in group work's history. By 1936, the American Association for the Study of Group Work (AASGW) was formed. The membership of the AASGW grew to 400 by 1938. In a two-year period from 1937 to 1939 the number of institutions providing group work training grew from thirteen to twenty-one (Coyle, 1959). Recognizing the need to develop the group work literature on practice, the AASGW established a bulletin entitled *The Group—in Education, Recreation, Social Work*, which served as a principal means of communication from 1939 to 1955 (Trecker, 1955).

Wilber I. Newstetter and Grace L. Coyle did much to point up the value of social scientific understanding of small group processes. In research conducted at the Wawokiye Camp Project, Newstetter and his associates (1938) utilized sociometric data to measure group interaction and to further the understanding of individual and group adjustment. The presence of a large number of "problem" boys referred to the camp by the Child Guidance Clinic focused early attention on the use of group work as a diagnostic and treatment resource and demonstrated "by practical results" the value of adjustment through group association. In her book *Social Process in Organized Groups*, Grace Coyle (1930) drew heavily from the social sciences in presenting a frame of reference for analyzing the universal processes that occur in small face-to-face groups. Such knowledge was to become standard equipment for social group work practice in the years ahead.

Later, she edited a collection of case studies (Coyle, 1937) based on records kept by students at the School of Applied Social Sciences, Western Reserve University, analyzing their group work practice with community-based groups.

Throughout the period, educational and recreational goals were stressed. Generally the small group experience was seen to be an important vehicle for assisting the normal growth and development process and for promoting citizen and social responsibility and action. In her early study of group work positions in twelve different types of organizations, Maragetha Williamson (1929) found that although there was no clearly defined unified "field" of practice, there was a certain commonality among workers based on the recognition of similar philosophies, practice methods, and training techniques. Group work, she pointed out, was viewed as a service for individuals who, through normal satisfying group activities, are encouraged to grow and develop socially and emotionally and to participate responsibly in society.

A review of some conceptions of group work during this period of formulation reflected many variations on these personal development, adjustment, and social responsibility themes. Henry Bush (Hartford, 1964; Bush, 1932) emphasized the recreational and educational aspects of group work and the value of the small voluntary club in developing members' personalities. Helen Hart (Hartford, 1964; Hart, 1933) saw group work to be an educational task, the special function of which was the development of personality through group experience. Coyle (1935a) wrote that group work was an "educational procedure" that relied on face-to-face interaction of people bound together by common interests in voluntary group associations to bring about individual and group adjustment. And in her prize-winning NCSW paper "Group Work and Social Change" (1935b), she stressed the importance of group process as a mode of social action to bring about social change. Individuals were seen to be responsible to help improve, through participation, the democratic social order. There was still much confusion, however, about the meaning of group work. Newstetter's paper, *What Is Social Group Work?* (1935), outlined three differing conceptions: group work viewed as a field, as a process, and as a set of techniques.

The close relationship between group work and education, recreation, and camping naturally reinforced the view that activities and programming in groups was essential. However, as Middleman (1968) observed, group workers tended to play down the importance of activities in their definitions for fear that groups would somehow become activity-centered rather than person-centered. To some, like Neva Boyd (1937), there was little doubt about the utilization of play and the arts in group work. Being satisfied that the efficacy of directed play and program activities in the socialization process had been demonstrated, she and her associates introduced group work as an experimental treatment modality at the Chicago State Hospital for the Insane as early as 1918 (Boyd, 1935).

Elise Campbell (1938) reported in her study of group work practice that loosely organized group club programs and the use of volunteers limited the capacity of the group work agency to improve individual adjustment and solve personal problems. Better training was needed if workers were to be expected to promote personal growth and adequately counsel individuals with personal problems in the group. On the other hand, Joshua Lieberman (1938), believing that the responsibility for individual development and adjustment was shared by the home and other educational institutions, insisted that group work's main emphasis should be on training for social responsibility and citizen participation through voluntary purposeful group experiences. The view was echoed by S. R. Slavson (1938), who pointed out that the first objective of group work was the preservation and extension of democracy. Meanwhile Nathaniel Cantor (1939, p. 17) argued that all group work programs were based on some form of social action. The issue was not group work and social action; "group work *is* social action."

Although some common denominators were evident as the decade came to an end, the search for a definition served to highlight emerging differences that were far from settled. While there was agreement that group work represented a conscious, disciplined approach to groups, which required specialized training in group work principles and practices, there was much disagreement over purposes and functions. Some workers were beginning to see group work as a means of helping people work with problems of social relationships. Others maintained the focus on work with "normal" people. Many viewed group work as an educational learning process. Some emphasized the leisure-time recreational aspects. In addition, there were considerable differences regarding the emphasis to be given to social action and social change. In general, workers seemed to have differing conceptions of what was meant by personal growth, social adjustment, and social development (Hartford, 1964).

SYNTHESIS AND EXPANSION: 1940s-1950s

As the threat of totalitarianism took on new meaning during the war years, interest in democratic philosophy and principles was heightened. The advent of war services brought caseworkers and group workers together and hastened the identification with social work. Increasingly, attention was being given to the use of group work for therapeutic purposes, working with formed nonvoluntary groups, developing interracial and intercultural programs, and working on professional issues related to identification, knowledge building, and improving the quality of practice. The cold war and McCarthyism of the 1950s hindered the activities of those who would advance social goals. For the most part, practice concerns continued to center on the use of groups for therapeutic purposes. Attention also turned to developing outreach services for "hard-to-reach" youths. Throughout the period there was active interest in developing technical knowledge and skills, as well as a beginning interest in defining group work practice in research terms. And finally there was increased collaboration between casework and group work in providing services to individuals (Somers, 1976).

Although the definitional and identification issues that characterized the 1930s continued into the 1940s, there was some synthesis of ideas, as reflected in the first official 1949 definition. Subsequently, there was a period of expansion as group work was introduced into a variety of new settings, including the psychiatric clinics and hospitals, specialized treatment and correctional institutions and programs, public schools, public recreation programs, and public welfare departments (Wilson, 1976). This in turn led to some re-examination of roles and functions and further work on defining the relation of group work to other methods, such as group therapy, group psychotherapy, and group dynamics.

Identification with Social Work

Questions regarding whether group work should take on varying identifications with social work, education, or recreation or continue to develop as a distinctive profession based on its own small group expertise continued into the 1940s. William Heard Kilpatrick (1940, p. vii) who had long advocated an education identification, argued that group work was not a separate field but rather "a method to be used in all kinds of educational effort." Charles E. Hendry (Dimock, Hendry, and Zerfoss, 1938), one of group work's early pioneers, was less committed, holding that group work was not yet in a position to decide between the professional classifications. Whether it was independent or part of a larger existing profession remained to be determined. LeRoy Bowman (1935) was strong in his opposition to linking group work with social services. Group work, he said, was not primarily a service for those seeking help but a "social mechanism perfectly competent people utilize to achieve their own ends" (p. 385).

But the movement toward social work that began in the mid-1930s was well under way as group work agencies were increasingly identified with social welfare agencies and programs. Any remaining questions were largely dispelled in the wake of Grace Coyle's (1955a) influential paper "On Becoming Professional," presented to members of AASGW at the NCSW in Buffalo in 1946. Referring to the professional identification dilemma, she commented, "We must, it seems, be either educators or social workers" (p. 338). To her, the move toward social work represented changing perspectives regarding the nature of social work itself. As she put it:

> My own hope is that the emerging definition of social work may define it as involving the conscious use of social relations in performing certain community functions, such as child welfare, family welfare or health services, recreation, and informal education. Case work, group work, and community organization have this common factor, that they are all based on understanding human relations. While the specific relations used in each are different, the underlying philosophy and approach are the same: a respect for personality and a belief in democracy. This we share with case workers and expert community organization people. It is for this reason that I believe group work as a method falls within the larger scope of social work *as a method* and as defined above [p. 340].

At a group work section meeting, she presented a second paper, "Social Group Work in Recreation," in which she distinguished group work from the field of recreation. "Recreation," she wrote, "is a function to be performed; social group work is one method of fulfilling that function" (Coyle, 1947, p. 202). Acknowledging that program and relationships were "inextricably intertwined," she pointed out that a distinctive social group work method emerged with the increased recognition that the human relations aspects of group experiences were as important as understanding various types of programs.

The process of synthesis and expansion was reflected in the events taking place. Ten years after its formation, the AASGW membership voted to become a professional organization, and the American Association of Group Workers (AAGW) was formed in 1946 with 2,300 members on its rolls. As Wilson (1976) points out, some of the early leaders who were more identified with group work as a movement turned elsewhere as professionalization approached. Some group workers, for example, who were more interested in planning and social action moved toward the newly formed American Association for the Study of Community Organization. The AAGW was concentrated over the next ten years on building and developing group work into a recognized professional activity. The eventual merger of AAGW with six other organizations to form the

National Association of Social Work in 1955 was the final step in the process of identification. Group work was clearly established as one of the methods of social work.

A number of volumes appeared during this period that served to pull together some of the thinking about group work practice. Grace Coyle's *Group Experience and Democratic Values* appeared in 1947, and in it she continued to emphasize small group approaches within a democratic framework. *Group Work with American Youth* (1948) followed, with much illustrative material regarding group leadership in recreation and voluntary education in leisure-time community service settings. Harleigh Trecker (1972) provided one of the first textbooks in group work in 1948, *Social Group Work: Principles and Practices*, which was updated and revised in 1955 and again in 1972. Gertrude Wilson's and Gladys Ryland's major textbook (1949) dealt with all aspects of theory and practice. It contained a thorough analysis of program media, illustrations of practice with differing groups, and material on supervision and administrative processes. Helen Phillips's *Essentials of Social Group Work Skill* (1951) emphasized how the worker's skills serve as a primary vehicle for fulfilling social values and purposes. Alan Klein's (1953) volume reasserted the democratic underpinnings of group work and stressed the importance of helping groups deal with problems as responsible citizens. And finally, a volume prepared by Marjorie Murphy (1959) as part of the Council on Social Work Education's curriculum study pulled together the current thinking about group work based on a thorough review of the literature, visits to social work schools, and contributions of major position papers by leading group work educators.

Social and Behavioral Science Influences

The desire to develop knowledge and practice led group work educators and practitioners to look more carefully to social psychology, sociology, and anthropology and to small group researchers and theorists for help. For example, Dorothea Sullivan's (1952) well-known group work reader contained works by Bradford, Benne, Lippitt, and Nylen; Cattell; Clinard; Lewin; and Jenkins and Zander. Workers were also familiar with Lewin, Lippitt, and White's (1939) study of the influence of leadership styles on group climate; Moreno's (1934) and Jennings's (1943) sociometric and near-sociometric conceptions of structural relationships; Bales's (1950) interaction process analysis; Cattell's (1951) group syntality; the Sherifs' (1953) studies on intergroup relations; Asch's (1956) studies of group norms; and Hemphill's (1956) study of group dimensions. Generally, practitioners immersed in practice were not inclined to engage in research, although some studies in agency and camp settings were done by Maas (1954), Lowy (1952), Gump and Sutton-Smith (1955), and Polansky, Lippitt, and Redl (1950), among others.

The work of certain social theorists provided additional concepts with relevance to group work. Drawing on empirical studies of small task-centered groups, Parsons and Bales (1955) provided a structural analysis of the family, which stressed the differential impact of instrumental and expressive functions of interacting statuses and roles on the socialization of the child and provided a group dimensional view of the family to supplement the parent-child emphasis of psychoanalytic theories. Robert Merton (1957) called attention to latent and manifest functions in his functional analysis of social phenomena. His concepts regarding reference group behavior and group properties were particularly relevant to practice. George Homans's (1950) interaction theory of small groups, which stressed the interdependence of activity, interaction, and sentiment in group functioning, provided still another framework for consideration in practice.

Some of the small group research conducted during this period raised questions regarding the application of research to practice. There was, for example, disagreement concerning the relationship of group work to the developing field of social psychology known as group dynamics (Cartwright and Zander, 1968). The controversy between group workers and advocates of group dynamics was based largely on differing values and ethical positions stemming from the contrasting emphasis of group work on service and of group dynamics on research. Wilson (1976) reported that in the early 1940s she raised ethical questions and objected to a proposal by Kurt Lewin and Gordon Hearn to apply their experimental methods to groups led by students at the University of Pittsburgh School of Social Work. Although she agreed that there could be some shared learning, Grace Coyle (1949) raised questions concerning the underlying philosophy and tactics often employed by group dynamists.

The influence of psychoanalytical thought and psychodynamic concepts, which had been so apparent in casework, began during this period to influence group workers as well. Freud's *Group Psychology and the Analysis of the Ego* (1922) focused on individual motivation and defensive processes, which found expression in groups. Psychoanalytic concepts and hypotheses appeared in the literature in the writings of S. R. Slavson, Margaret Svendsen, Fritz Redl, Saul Scheidlinger, Gertrude Wilson, Susanne Schulze, Gisela Konopka, Raymond Fisher, and others. Departing from Freud, Otto Rank gave primary emphasis to the birth trauma as a cause of psychoneurosis and stressed the human will as a creative organizing force that could be used by the individual for his own growth and development

(Ryder, 1976). Reflecting such thinking, Helen Phillips (1951) contributed much to an understanding of how to help individuals and groups choose their own directions for growth and change. Her discussion of worker skills, use of time, and agency functions and purposes influenced group work practices in varied settings.

Expansion into Therapeutic Settings

Although there had been some early applications of group work in therapeutic settings before group work had come to be identified as a method (Konopka, 1956; Coyle, 1959) the trend seems to have begun in 1938 when Gisela Konopka began treating parents and children at the Pittsburgh Guidance Center, first as a second-year graduate student and then as a full-time staff member. Similarly, the work of Fritz Redl (1944) and the Detroit Group Project initiated in 1942 used trained group workers to provide diagnostic services and specialized group treatment for emotionally disturbed children. Such practices caught on rapidly, and soon group workers were sought after by hospitals, clinics, and rehabilitation centers throughout the country. The development of these services seemed to be limited only by the inability of the schools of social work to meet the new demand.

The introduction of group work into therapeutic settings caused mixed reactions and raised new questions. A number of volumes dealing with therapeutic group work in psychiatric settings appeared (Konopka, 1949, 1954; Schulze, 1951; Trecker, 1956). Interest was being generated at the National Conference to provide forums for exchanging experiences and clarifying the role of group work in relation to other methods such as group therapy and group psychotherapy (Konopka, 1951).

Questions were also raised regarding group work's relation to casework and other specialized treatment programs within therapeutic settings (Fisher, 1949). Meanwhile, some caseworkers found it difficult to accept the activity focus of group work. As Wilson (1976) pointed out, not until psychiatrists and analysts began consulting on the therapeutic values of games, dancing, and crafts did some caseworkers begin to explore their uses in practice. And even then, services were conceived in terms of "group therapy" or "group casework" rather than group work.

In keeping with these trends, conceptions about group work practice were subject to revision. In 1949 the AAGW published its official definition of group work, which asserted:

> The group worker enables various types of groups to function in such a way that both group interaction and program activities contribute to

> the growth of the individual and the achievement of desirable goals [Coyle, 1955b, pp. 61-62].

The objectives were in keeping with the wide range of interests: The emphasis was on personal growth, adjusting individuals to other individuals, groups, and society; motivating individuals toward the improvement of society; and recognition by the individual of his own rights and abilities and the differences of others.

But by 1956 a different definition was to be issued by the Commission of Social Work Practice of the newly created NASW, which clearly reflected the expanded interest in the treatment aspects of practice. Group work was defined in this way:

> A service to groups where the primary purpose is to help members improve their social adjustment, and the secondary purpose is to help the group achieve objectives approved by society. . . . The definition assumes that the members of groups receiving social group work services *have* adjustment problems. It further assumes that there is a diagnostic process through which the worker is aware of the nature of the problems of the members, and that the programming in the group is determined by the findings of the diagnosis. . . . The skills used in this process are acquired through application of a wide variety of knowledge in clinical training of social group work field instruction [Hartford, 1964, pp. 75-76; Wilson, 1956].

Less than one-fifth of the membership of the group work section agreed with the narrowness of this statement. The University of Pittsburgh group work faculty, responding to the changing emphasis, was later moved to develop its position paper reaffirming social action as an essential component in group work.

The lack of group work personnel to meet the new demands for providing group work services in treatment settings added to the controversy. In 1959, Robert Vinter wrote that group work was in a "near crisis situation" stemming from a shortage of trained workers. The overcommitment of the profession to "socialization" and "consumption" functions needed, he argued, to be redirected toward "integrative" functions dealing with problems of adjustment in personal and social relations. In a similar vein, Raymond Fisher (1959) argued that group work had ceased to be practiced directly in most group service agencies and that the direct application of group treatment skills used in treatment settings required that group work become treatment-focused.

And so as group work entered the 1960s and 1970s, it was clear that it had dropped the emphasis on education and had become identified with social work with a concomitant emphasis on treatment and rehabilitation. Democratic participation and social change remained somewhat in the background as attention was fixed on social development, growth, and adjustment through selected group experiences. The varying perspectives persisted, however, and set the stage for the proliferation of formulations that followed.

RECENT TRENDS AND PERSPECTIVES: 1960s AND 1970s

The most recent period in the history of group work is characterized by the development and refinement of differing conceptual models of practice. Some reflect increased interest in methods and techniques, developing specific treatment goals, systematizing worker interventions, and evaluating outcomes; others place less emphasis on techniques and empirical testing, and instead advance humanistic commitments to personal growth and self-actualization.

Assessing Purposes and Functions

Although by this time the search for an identity had slackened, it had not ended, and questions regarding purposes and functions remained. The effort to define a unitary practice continued for a period largely through the efforts of the Group Work Section of the NASW. Acting on a recommendation of the retiring AAGW board, a major statistical study of the membership was conducted to get an accurate picture of actual practice in the field. The findings, not unexpectedly, revealed that there was still little agreement about the purposes of group work; questions were still being raised about how it fitted into the larger social work picture. Subsequently, the Committee on Practice of the Group Work Section (Hartford, 1964) worked on developing a frame of reference that drew materials largely from individual position papers. There was some agreement for each of the following major purposes: (1) *corrective*—to provide restorative or remedial experiences in instances where there has been social and personal dysfunction or breakdown of individuals or within social situations; (2) *preventive*—to prevent personal and social breakdown where there is danger of deterioration; (3) *normal growth and development*—to facilitate the normal growth and development processes of individual members, particularly during certain stressful periods in the life cycle; (4) *personal enhancement*—to achieve a greater measure of self-fulfillment and personal enhancement through meaningful and stimulating interpersonal relations; and (5) *citizen responsibility and participation*—to inculcate democratic values among group members as they are helped to become responsibly involved as individuals and members of groups, as active participants in society.

The statement called attention to many ideological differences that continued to exist between those who would limit group work services to normal individuals and groups and those who would limit it to those in need of corrective or treatment services. In reflecting on the frustrating process, Gertrude Wilson (1976) voiced this opinion:

> To date, no one has succeeded in formulating a mutually agreed-upon statement of the purpose and function of group work . . . progress is not made by the formulation of ideal definitions into which bits of practice are to be fitted. Perhaps greater progress could be made by studying and analyzing the actual behavior of social workers in group situations; from this it might be possible to identify the elements of social work methods in serving groups [p. 39].

The impact of group work's identification with social work was also seen as a mixed blessing. In his assessment, Schwartz (1959) pointed out how it lent strength and discipline by providing a professional identity that went beyond any single agency or movement and offered a clearer and more distinct sense of function and purpose. It strengthened the movement toward developing a more conscious method of working, supervising, and recording practice. It also added to the awareness of psychodynamic concepts of human behavior. On the other hand, the identification tended, Schwartz pointed out, gradually to disengage group workers from "some of their most fruitful professional and theoretical connections." Following casework in embracing the Freudian orientation led to a dampening of "the spirit of inquiry" that characterized early efforts to seek many sources of knowledge and insight and resulted in many instances in an "uncritical acceptance of a single explanation of human behavior" (p. 124).

Recent Behavioral Science Influences

Recently, group work, like social work as a whole, has renewed the quest for additional sources of knowledge in developing effective practice models. The influence of systems theory, behavioralism, and existentialism were particularly apparent. Drawing from general systems theory (Bertalanffy, 1968; Hearn, 1969), as well as from the more familiar social system theories (Parsons, 1951), writers have looked for generalized principles to help cut across the specialized traditional domains and have added to an understanding of the essential sameness of phenomena, whether they be physical, biological, or social in nature. The system perspective called attention to the ways interactions are patterned, taking on varying forms as subparts and larger wholes within a network of mutually influencing relationships. The view increased an appreciation for the creative and adaptive potential of individuals within functioning, changing systems. For, contrary to the belief that social systems represented closed stable entities, they were seen more accurately to "thrive on change"—to generate, elaborate, and reconstruct patterns of meanings and actions and interactions (Buckley, 1967).

There is growing interest, particularly in the problem-oriented approaches, in applying behavioral concepts and sociobehavioral theories in group work. Focusing primarily on observable responses, behavioralists maintain that all behavior can be explained in terms of conditioning, which is viewed simply as a teaching-learning process whether stemming from Skinner's operant conditioning, the classical conditioning of Pavlov, or the counter-conditioning procedures of Wolpe (Bruck, 1968). The sociobehavioral approach (Thomas, 1977) is seen to be particularly promising, inasmuch as it combines experiences from social work practice and other helping professions with empirically tested knowledge and techniques from behavioral modification, social psychology, and other behavioral sciences. The focus in group treatment continues to be on developing practice techniques that manipulate reinforcing or aversive stimuli in group sessions, characteristically aimed at helping group members behave differently in specific problematic situations (Frankel and Glasser, 1974).

Existentialism constitutes still another area of developing interest. Unlike psychoanalysis, which constitutes a more or less united school, existentialism is rather a way of thinking with broad applicability. In its widest sense it is concerned not with formulating and achieving goals but with the essence of man's existence, the meaning of life's purposes and goals. Insofar as it stresses the achievement of the fullest potential in man, it certainly is not new to group work, although the renewed emphasis it places on human freedoms, choice, and individual responsibility takes on new significance with the development of group work models. In contrast to other approaches, existential thinking holds that human behavior cannot be understood in quantifiable, formalistic terms and that human interaction is not predictable but emerges as individuals are freed to "become" themselves.

On the occasion of the Tenth Anniversary Symposium of NASW in 1965, Margaret Hartford (1966) summarized certain trends that had taken place in group work over the decade. Interest in pursuing treatment and rehabilitative objectives continued to spread as group work moved into correctional and therapeutic settings and into programs that had traditionally been reserved for casework and individual counseling. Group work was increasingly seen as a distinctive method, with a developing theory of its own, separate from agency settings, organizations, and fields of service. In addition, some group work tools, such as "professional relationships," "program media," and "verbalization," were beginning to be seen as separate from the group work method itself. Although the main thrust had been in concept development and theory building, Hartford noted that only "bits and pieces of work" were under way, which was not nearly enough.

During this period a number of textbooks dealing with both the general and specific aspects of practice appeared. Konopka (1963) sought to pull together existing knowledge about group work and present it as "a whole piece of cloth." Northen (1969) provided a "psychosocial" view of group work and emphasized the need for a unified theory of social work practice. Alan Klein (1970), on the other hand, offered his book as a supplement to existing literature to counteract monolithic theories. Uniquely, Ruth Middleman (1968) called attention to the importance of programming in group work and contributed to the development of a theoretical base for using nonverbal media with groups. And finally, Hartford's *Groups in Social Work* (1972) continued the process of integrating social science knowledge of small group processes with changing practices begun years before by Grace Coyle.

Collections of papers were also beginning to appear which contributed to theory-building by stressing differing formulations of practice. Faculty members at the Boston University School of Social Work published two volumes under Saul Bernstein's (1965; 1970) editorship, which explored theories dealing with group development, group composition, goal setting, decision-making, and so forth. Robert Vinter and his associates (1967) at the University of Michigan School of Social Work, representing a problem-oriented approach, published a series of papers that relied heavily on use of scientific methods in diagnosing, assessing, and systematizing intervention in selectively identified problem areas. A more comprehensive volume (Glasser, Sarri, and Vinter, 1974) expanded on the use of social and behavioral sciences in the continuing effort to systematize socio-behavioral treatment methods. Similarly, Sheldon Rose (1973; 1977) developed a fairly comprehensive behavioral approach to group treatment based on a combination of group dynamics, learning theory, and behavioral modification techniques. Using a humanistic framework, Tropp (1969) offered a collection of papers that emphasized the use of groups in normal growth and development for self-actualization for democratic responsibility. William Schwartz and Serapio Zalba (1971) edited a collection of papers dealing with theory and practice within both an existential and systems-theory framework.

It was perhaps inevitable that the proliferation of formulations would stimulate interest in identifying and classifying the varying models and approaches. Schwartz (1964) identified the medical, scientific and organic approaches. Vinter (1965) noted the successive emphasis given to democratic decentralization; to educational and socialization goals; and to treatment or rehabilitative approaches. Papell and Rothman (1966) later distinguished between the "social goals," "remedial," and "reciprocal" models. Inspired by an earlier volume that sought to codify case work theory, Robert Roberts and Helen Northen (1976) edited a collection of no less than ten distinctive theoretical orientations variously labeled generic, organization, psychosocial, functional, mediating, development, task-centered, socialization, crisis-intervention and problem-solving.

Ever since the *Group*, which had done so much to disseminate knowledge about group work practice, was discontinued in 1955, the lack of an adequate organ of communication for group workers has been sorely felt. There is some hope, however, that a new journal, *Social Work with Groups: A Journal of Community and Clinical Practice*, will help to fill the void. The trend continues in the direction of developing generic approaches. Interestingly enough, the editorial policy statement takes little notice of social group work as such. The *Journal* is to be used "as a vehicle of communication for the several sectors of our profession wherein the small group heritage and the building of knowledge and skills of group practice are embodied" (Papell and Rothman, 1978, p. 4).

But the forces for reversing this trend may already be at work. In fact, in the very same issue of the *Journal*, Emmanuel Tropp raises the persistent question: "Whatever Happened to Group Work?"

REFERENCES

ASCH, S. E., 1956. "Studies of Independence and Conformity: I. A Minority of One Against a Unanimous Majority," *Psychological Monographs*, Vol. 70.

BALES, R. F., 1950. *Interaction Process Analysis: A Method For the Study of Small Groups.* Cambridge, Mass.: Addison-Wesley.

BERNSTEIN, S., ed., 1965. *Explorations in Group Work: Essays in Theory and Practice.* Boston: Boston University School of Social Work.

——, ed., 1970. *Further Exploration in Group Work.* Boston: Boston University School of Social Work.

BERTALANFFY, L. V., 1968. *General Systems Theory: Foundations, Development, Application.* New York: Braziller.

BOWMAN, L., 1935. "Dictatorship, Democracy, and Group Work in America," *Proceedings of the National Conference of Social Work.* Chicago: University of Chicago Press.

BOYD, N. L., 1935. "Group Work Experiments in State Institutions in Illinois," *Proceedings of the National Conference on Social Work, 1935.* Chicago: University of Chicago Press.

——, 1937. "Social Group Work: A Definition with a Methodological Note," *Northwestern University*, Vol. 1, Bulletin No. 1.

BRUCK, M., 1968. "Behavioral Modification Theory and Practice: A Critical Review," *Social Work*, Vol. 13, No. 2.

BUCKLEY, W., 1967. *Sociology and Modern Systems Theory*. Englewood Cliffs, N.J.: Prentice-Hall, Inc.

BUSH, H. M., 1932. "Rebuilding the Group Club," Summary of Round Table 20th Conference of the National Federation of Settlements, Inc., Philadelphia, Pa. (mimeo).

CAMPBELL, E., 1938. "Gauging Group Work: An Evaluation of a Settlement Boys Work Program," National Youth Administration, Detroit, Michigan.

CANTOR, N., 1939. "Group Work and Social Science," *Group Work, 1939*. New York: American Association for the Study of Group Work.

CARTWRIGHT, D., and A. ZANDER, eds., 1968. *Group Dynamics Research and Theory*. New York: Harper & Row.

CATTELL, R. B., 1951. "New Concepts for Measuring Leadership in Terms of Group Syntality," *Human Relations*, Vol. 4, No. 2.

CLARKE, H. I. 1947. *Principles and Practice of Social Work*. New York: Appleton-Century.

COOLEY, C. H., 1902. *Human Nature and the Social Order*. New York: Scribner's.

——, 1909. *Social Organizations: A Study of the Larger Mind*. New York: Scribner's.

COYLE, G. L., 1930. *Social Process in Organized Groups*. New York: Richard R. Smith.

——, 1935a. "What Is This Social Group Work?" *Survey*, Vol. 71, No. 5.

——, 1935b. "Group Work and Social Change," *Proceedings of the National Conference of Social Work, 1935*. Chicago: University of Chicago Press.

——, ed., 1937. *Studies in Group Behavior*. New York: Harper.

——, 1947. *Group Experience and Democratic Values*. New York: Women's Press.

——, 1948. *Group Work with American Youth*. New York: Harper & Brothers.

——, 1949. "The Relation of Group Dynamics to Group Work, *Journal of the National Association of Deans of Women*, Vol. 12, No. 3.

——, 1955a. "On Becoming Professional," in *Group Work: Foundations and Frontiers*, H. Trecker, ed. New York: Whiteside, William Morrow.

——, 1955b. "Definition of the Function of the Group Worker," in *Group Work: Foundations and Frontiers*, H. Trecker, ed. New York: Whiteside, William Morrow.

——, 1959. "Group Work in Psychiatric Settings: Its Roots and Branches," *Social Work*, Vol. 4, No. 1.

DAVIS, A. F., 1967. *Spearheads for Reform: The Social Settlements and the Progressive Movement 1890–1914*. New York: Oxford University Press.

DEWEY, J., 1939. "Education and Social Change," in *New Trends in Group Work*, J. Lieberman, ed. New York: Association Press.

DIMOCK, H. S., C. E. HENRY, and K. P. ZERFOSS, 1938. *A Professional Outlook on Group Education.* New York: Association Press.

DURKHEIM, E., 1951. *Suicide: A Study in Sociology*, G. Simpson, ed. Glencoe, Ill: Free Press.

——, 1964. *The Rules of Sociological Method*, G. E. G. Catlin, ed. New York: Free Press of Glencoe.

ELLIOTT, H., 1928. *Process of Group Thinking.* New York: Association Press.

FISHER, R., 1949. "Contributions of Group Work in Psychiatric Hospitals," *The Group*, Vol. 12, No. 1.

——, 1959. "Social Group Work in Group Service Agencies," *Social Work With Groups, 1959.* New York: National Association of Social Workers.

FOLLETT, M. P., 1926. *The New State: Group Organization, the Solution of Popular Government.* New York: Longmans, Green.

FRANKEL, A. J. and P. H. GLASSER, 1974. "Behavioral Approaches to Group Work," *Social Work*, Vol. 19, No. 2.

FREUD, S., 1922. *Group Psychology and the Analysis of the Ego.* London and Vienna: The International Psychoanalytical Press.

GLASSER, P., R. SARRI, and R. VINTER, eds., 1974. *Individual Change Through Small Groups.* New York: Free Press.

GROOS, K., 1901. *The Play of Man.* New York: Appleton.

GUMP, P., and B. SUTTON-SMITH, 1955. "The 'It' Role in Children's Games," *The Group*, Vol. 17, No. 3.

HALL, G. S., 1904. *Adolescence.* New York: Appleton.

HAMILTON, M. C., 1884. "Mission Women," *The Nineteenth Century*, Vol. 16, No. 94.

HART, H., 1933. "Criteria for Evaluating the Group Work Method: Results with Individuals," National Conference of Social Work (mimeo).

HARTFORD, M., 1964. "Social Group Work 1930 to 1960: The Search for a Definition," in *Working Papers Toward a Frame of Reference for Social Group Work*, M. Hartford, ed. New York: National Association of Social Workers.

——, 1966. "Changing Approaches in Practice Theory and Techniques," in *Trends in Social Work Practice and Knowledge: NASW Tenth Anniversary Symposium, 1965.* New York: National Association of Social Workers, 1966.

——, 1972. *Groups in Social Work.* New York: Columbia University Press.

HEARN, G., ed., 1969. *The General Systems Approach.* New York: Council on Social Work Education.

HEMPHILL, J. K., 1956. *Group Dimensions: A Manual for Their Measurment*, Columbus: Ohio State University, Bureau of Business Research.

HENDRY, C. E., 1947. "All Past Is Prologue," in *Toward Professional Standards, A.A.G.W. 1945-46.* New York: Association Press.

HOLDEN, A. C., 1922. *The Settlement Idea.* New York: Macmillan.

HOMANS, G. C., 1950. *The Human Group.* New York: Harcourt, Brace.

JAMES, W., 1890. *Psychology.* New York: Holt.

JENNINGS, H. H., 1943. *Leadership and Isolation.* New York: Longmans, Green.

KAISER, C., 1958. "The Social Group Work Process," *Social Work*, Vol. 3, No. 2.

KILPATRICK, W. H., 1940. *Group Education for a Democracy.* New York: Association Press.

KLEIN, A. F., 1953. *Society-Democracy and the Group.* New York: Whiteside.

——, 1970. *Social Work Through Group Process.* Albany: School of Social Welfare, State University of New York at Albany.

KONOPKA, G., 1951. "Similarities and Differences Between Group Work and Group Therapy," *Proceedings: National Conference on Social Work, 1951.* New York: Columbia University Press.

——, 1949. *Therapeutic Group Work with Children.* Minneapolis: University of Minnesota Press.

——, 1954. *Group Work in the Institution.* New York: Association Press.

——, 1956. "The Generic and Specific in Group Work Practice in the Psychiatric Setting," *Social Work*, Vol. 1, No. 1.

——, 1963. *Social Group Work: A Helping Process.* Englewood Cliffs, N.J.: Prentice-Hall.

LEWIN, K., R. LIPPITT, and R. K. WHITE, 1939. "Patterns of Aggressive Behavior in Experimentally Created Social Climates," *The Journal of Social Psychology*, Vol. 10, No. 2.

LIEBERMAN, J., 1938. "Group Leadership and Democracy," *Proceedings of the Connecticut Conference on Group Work*, New Haven, Connecticut.

LINDEMAN, E., 1925. *Social Discovery: An Approach to the Study of Functional Groups.* New York: Republic.

LOWY, L., 1952. "Indigenous Leadership in Teen-Age Groups," *Jewish Center Worker*, Vol. 13, No. 1.

MASS, H. S., 1954. "The Role of Member in Clubs of Lower-Class and Middle-Class Adolescents," *Child Development*, Vol. 25, No. 4.

McDOUGALL, W., 1920. *The Group Mind.* New York: Putnam.

MEAD, G. H., 1934. *Mind, Self and Society.* Chicago: University of Chicago Press.

MERTON, R. K., 1957. *Social Theory and Social Structure.* Glencoe, Ill.: Free Press.

MIDDLEMAN, R. R., 1968. *The Non-Verbal Method in Working with Groups.* New York: Association Press.

MORENO, J. L., 1934. *Who Shall Survive?* Washington, D.C.: Nervous and Mental Diseases Publishing Co.

MURPHY, M., 1959. *The Social Group Work Method in Social Work Education.* New York: Council on Social Work Education.

NEUMEYER, M., and E. NEUMEYER, 1949. *Leisure and Recreation.* New York: Barnes.

NEWSTETTER, W. I., 1935. "What Is Social Group Work?" *Proceedings of the National Conference of Social Work, 1935.* Chicago: University of Chicago Press.

——, M. J. FELDSTEIN, and T. M. NEWCOMB, 1938. *Group Adjustment A Study in Experimental Sociology.* Cleveland: School of Applied Social Sciences, Western Reserve University.

NORTHEN, H., 1969. *Social Work with Groups.* New York: Columbia University Press.

PAPELL, C. P., and B. ROTHMAN, 1966. "Social Group Work Models: Possession and Heritage," *Education for Social Work,* Vol. 2, No. 2.

——, eds., 1978. "Editorial Policy Statement," *Social Work with Groups,* Vol. 1, No. 1.

PARSONS, T., 1951. *The Social System.* Glencoe, Ill.: Free Press.

—— and R. F. BALES, 1955. *Family: Socialization and Interaction Process.* Glencoe, Ill.: The Free Press.

PHILLIPS, H., 1951. *Essentials of Social Group Work Skill.* New York: Association Press.

POLANSKY, N. A., R. LIPPITT, and F. REDL, 1950. "An Investigation of Behavioral Contagion in Groups," *Human Relations,* Vol. 3, No. 4.

"Prevention," 1885. *The Nineteenth Century,* Vol. 18, No. 106.

REDL, F., 1944. "Diagnostic Group Work," *American Journal of Orthopsychiatry,* Vol. 14, No. 1.

ROBBINS, J. E. 1912. "First Year at the College Settlement," *Survey,* Vol. 27.

ROBERTS, R., and H. NORTHEN, eds., 1976. *Theories of Social Work with Groups.* New York: Columbia University Press.

ROSE, S. D., 1973. *Treating Children in Groups.* San Francisco: Jossey-Bass.

——, 1977. *Group Therapy: A Behavioral Approach.* Englewood Cliffs, N.J.: Prentice-Hall.

RYDER, E. L., 1976. "A Functional Approach," in *Theories of Social Work with Groups,* R. W. Roberts and H. Northen, eds. New York: Columbia University Press.

SCHULZE, S., ed., 1951. *Creative Group Living in a Children's Institution.* New York: Association Press.

SCHWARTZ, W., 1959. "Group Work and the Social Scene," in *Issues in American Social Work,* A. J. Kahn, ed. New York: Columbia University Press.

——, 1964. "Analysis of Papers," in *Working Papers Toward a Frame of Reference for Social Group Work,* M. Hartford, ed. New York: National Association of Social Workers.

—— and S. Zalba, eds., 1971. *The Practice of Group Work.* New York: Columbia University Press.

SHERIF, M., and C. W. SHERIF, 1953. *Groups in Harmony and Tension: An Integration of Studies on Intergroup Relations.* New York: Harper & Brothers.

SIMMEL, G., 1950. *The Sociology of Georg Simmel*, K. H. Wolff, ed. Glencoe, Ill.: Free Press.

SIMON, P., ed., 1971. *Play and Game Theory in Group Work: A Collection of Papers by Neva Boyd.* Chicago: Jane Addams Graduate School of Social Work.

SIMS, M. S., 1935. *The Natural History of a Social Institution: The Young Women's Christian Association.* New York: Women's Press.

SLAVSON, S. R., 1938. "Changing Objectives in Group Work," *Proceedings of the Connecticut Conference on Group Work*, New Haven, Connecticut.

——, 1948. *Recreation and the Total Personality.* New York: Association Press.

SOMERS, M. L., 1976. "Problem-Solving in Small Groups," in *Theories of Social Work with Groups*, R. W. Roberts and H. Northen, eds. New York: Columbia University Press.

SPENCER, H., 1873. *The Principles of Psychology.* New York: Appleton.

SPENCER, J., 1954. "Historical Development," in *Social Group Work in Britain*, P. Kuenstler, ed. London: Faber & Faber.

SULLIVAN, D. F., ed., 1952. *Readings in Group Work.* New York: Association Press.

THOMAS, E. J., 1977. "Social Casework and Social Group Work: The Behavioral Approach," *Encylopedia of Social Work, 1977*, Seventeenth Issue, Vol. II. New York: National Association of Social Workers.

TRECKER, H., ed., 1955. *Group Work Foundations and Frontiers.* New York: Whiteside.

——, 1956. *Group Work in the Psychiatric Setting.* New York: Whiteside, William Morrow.

——, 1972. *Social Group Work: Principles and Practices*, New York: Association Press.

TROPP, E., 1969. *A Humanistic Foundation for Group Work Practice.* New York: Associated Educational Services Corporation.

——, 1978. "Whatever Happened to Group Work?" *Social Work with Groups*, Vol. 1, No. 1.

VINTER, R. D., 1959. "Group Work: Perspectives and Prospects," *Social Work with Groups, 1959.* New York: National Association of Social Workers.

——, 1965. "Social Group Work," *Encylopedia of Social Work*, New York: National Association of Social Workers.

——, ed., 1967. *Readings in Group Work Practice.* Ann Arbor, Mich: Campus Publishers.

WARNER, A. E., S. A. QUEEN, and E. B. HARPER, 1930. *American Charities and Social Work.* New York: Crowell.

WILLIAMSON, M., 1929. *Social Worker in Group Work.* New York: Harper & Brothers.

WILSON, G., 1956. *The Practice of Social Group Work*, Summary of the Report, the Committee on Practice, Group Work Section. New York: National Association of Social Workers (mimeographed).

——, 1976. "From Practice to Theory: A Personalized History," in *Theories of Social Work with Groups*, R. W. Roberts and H. Northen, eds. New York: Columbia University Press.

WILSON, G., and G. RYLAND, 1949. *Social Group Work Practice.* Cambridge: Riverside Press.

WOODROOFE, K., 1968. *From Charity to Social Work in England and the United States.* London: Routledge & Kegan Paul.

WOODS, R. A., and A. J. KENNEDY, 1922. *The Settlement Horizon: A National Estimate.* New York: Russell Sage Foundation.

2

Some Basic Assumptions About Social Group Work

Prior to her death in 1962, Grace L. Coyle was Professor of Social Work at the School of Applied Social Science, Western Reserve University, Cleveland, Ohio.

Grace L. Coyle

Social group work as one of the types of social work practice grows out of a certain recognition of the needs of people in our society and some experience with the ways of meeting them. It is necessary to make a distinction between the functions of the social services and the development of the practice of social work as one and probably the most essential method involved in their administration.

Among the functions of the social services are included the provision of income maintenance by a variety of relief services, the family and child welfare services, institutional care for dependent children, old people, the chronically ill and others, social services for the physically and mentally ill or handicapped and the provision under community auspices, public and private, of recreation and informal education aimed at the constructive use of our increasing leisure time. Some of the latter services have grown up especially in low income or disorganized areas which provided few physical facilities or opportunities for leisure time activities and some have been centered primarily on the needs of particular age groups—children and youth, for example, or more recently old people.

Social group work as a defined method developed first in settlements and community centers in low income areas and in the youth serving agencies. As the method has grown, especially in the last ten years, social group workers have been employed in the social service departments of hospitals and clinics and in a variety of institutions for the ill, for dependent children or old people and in therapeutic camps and similar situations.

From Marjorie Murphy, *The Social Group Work Method in Social Work Education*, vol. 11 of the Curriculum Study (New York: Council on Social Work Education, 1959), pp. 88–105. Reprinted with permission.

All such social services are rooted in the sense of responsibility which a democratic society has for making provision by collective effort for the needs which the society itself produces or which it comes to recognize. The development of social work as a professional practice grew up out of an increasing recognition that the needs creating the social services were not only needs for more income, for food, shelter and clothing, or for medical or custodial care. The turning point in the development of social work came with the recognition that accompanying such needs, sometimes as cause and sometimes as effect, were problems in psychosocial relations.[1] It became clear that the major skill in addition to the organization and administration of the services themselves lay in an understanding of these psychosocial relations and in the ability of the worker to use his relationship to the client in ways which contributed to psychological health as well as to efficient administration. Improvement came to be seen both in movement toward self maintenance and independence and also in a socially acceptable relation to others and to society itself. Obviously the values so defined and their evolution into the professional goals of the social worker are beyond the compass of this paper, but it seems clear that social work practice has always these two dimensions—the provision of some type of social service, usually defined as the function of an agency, and secondly the "helping process" so called, by which the worker administers the service in part through the relationship he establishes with the client.

This basis of social work as a professional practice is introduced here because it will, I believe, clarify the development and function of social group work. Case work as a definable practice grew up entangled in the functions of the various social services which social workers administered, particularly in public assistance, family and child welfare, medical and psychiatric social service. The significance of the Milford Conference lies in the recognition it brought that although the functions of the agencies differed, the practice itself had common characteristics and that those characteristics focused around relationships between client and worker.[2]

About a decade after this development of casework, *i.e.*, in the early 1920's, a similar recognition appeared among workers in settlements, community centers and youth serving agencies that while the services and the programs of these agencies differed, there were in fact many and basic similarities in the skills and goals of such workers which were visible and definable. This sprang up simultaneously in several centers (especially New York, Cleveland and Chicago) and, so far as I know, in large part independently of developments in casework.

The similarity consisted of the realization that significant relations existed between members of the agency groups and between leaders of such groups and their members. The attempt to discover and define these relationships and to examine how professional workers should be trained for such services led, during the 1920's and 1930's, to the development of group work as a part of social work and the decision in the 1940's that training for it should be in schools of social work. Here too the function of agencies and programs had to be disentangled from the relationships involved, and both function and relationships had to be defined in terms of the skills, goals and values which should guide the behavior of such professional workers.

Since that early recognition of this common element in work with groups in these agencies, there has been over the last twenty-five years an examination of records of such groups, an attempt to formulate the function of workers with them and some attempt to put to use concepts and theory about group behavior drawn from the underlying social sciences. Such formulation is still rudimentary, in part because of the partially developed state of these sciences and the lack of integration between personality theory and small group theory. In part its rudimentary state may be laid to the pressure of practice itself and the inadequate research in social work which hampers all our development. In spite of these handicaps and shortcomings there do exist certain defined assumptions upon which group work rests. I shall define these in three sections. (1) Some assumptions on the potential significance to individuals of group experience of the kinds available through social agencies. (2) Some assumptions as to the role of the group worker including the skills, attitudes, goals and values essential to such practice as a part of social work. (3) Some implications for social work education. Within the scope of this paper it will obviously not be possible to provide all the bases for these assumptions but such could, I believe, be provided to a reasonable extent if time and space permitted. (I have omitted as not essential to the purpose of this paper the footnote references which could have been given to back up some of the statements made.)

SOME ASSUMPTIONS ON THE POTENTIAL SIGNIFICANCE OF GROUP EXPERIENCE TO INDIVIDUALS

The practice of social group work rests obviously on the assumption that group experience of various kinds under the auspices of public or private agencies has potential value for its participants. Since such groups provide both program experience usually in recreation or informal education activities and opportunity for social relationships among members and with a leader, we shall consider both program and relationships as equally the concern of the group worker. Our experience with the provision of such services leads us to define their potential value in terms of several basic needs.

Group Experience and the Maturing Process

In the first place it seems clear that experience in small face-to-face groups affording opportunity for intimate relationships plays an essential part in the process of human maturation. During the early stages of maturation from the time the child steps out of the family into the world of his peers in school and on the playground or the streets until he establishes a family of his own, usually in his early twenties, there is observable a common pattern of group relations found among most children. These include such familiar groups as the loosely organized play groups usually of one sex found in the latency period before puberty, the close-knit clique or gang of five to fifteen intimates customary in early adolescence, the dating courtship groups of pairs often arising out of larger recreation activities and functioning within them. Such groups seem to meet certain psychological needs including the development of independence from the parental family, the identification of sex role in company with others of the same sex and then with those of the opposite sex, the attainment of the social skills and attitudes acceptable to one's peers as, for example, in athletics for boys, the exploration and incorporation of the changing social values needed as the individual grows from child to adult.

For many of our youth, such experience with groups of their peers will be maintained throughout their young adult years in which they are finding and adjusting to jobs and/or marriage, needing satisfying companionship in recreation and finding their place in the adult community.

While there is some differentiation among social class or ethnic groups in their pattern of group affiliation among the children and youth of our society, it follows so much the same progression and evidently meets so much the same basic psychological needs in the maturing process that one is tempted to define it as the normal. Whether it represents a response to societal conditions or to the intrapsychic needs of the developing ego, yet remains to be investigated. The unhappy fate of those who deviate from its seems to be further proof of its deep significance to the individual. The sissy or tomboy of the pre-adolescent play group, the outcast who never finds his intimates in early adolescence, the isolate who is not acceptable as the courtship period comes on, the cry baby, the bully, the sex deviant, all give evidence of maladjustments in the psychosocial maturing process. For the majority who mature to an acceptable degree of adjustment, it appears that the gaining of acceptance and achievement with one's peers in intimate small groups, the learning to establish satisfying relations and to acquire the necessary social skills all go on through a succession of changing group memberships.

If this is a "normal" process unfolding, as it were, out of an inner necessity or a social demand, it might well be asked why should society need to establish social service to provide for it or train workers capable of facilitating it. It is true that many individuals and, perhaps in certain social groupings, most children and youth find in their environment the social nourishment for this growth. However, there is some evidence that one of the problems of our society is that as an unexpected and unwanted by-product of our technological economy and our highly urban mobile and impersonal society we tend to produce an unusual number of unhappy individuals and hostile groups. As Elton Mayo pointed out some years ago our society does not of itself train us in the social skills[3] which its complex relations require. Since this is, I believe, the case, it is inevitable that society should undertake to meet these inadequacies by setting up planned means to train its new members.

It is a curious and significant fact that the so-called youth services, usually in the form of adult led groups of youth between ten and eighteen years of age, have sprung up in every industrialized society. In the decade between 1910 and 1920, for example, our four major youth programs originated (Boy and Girl Scouts, Campfire Girls and 4H Clubs) along with innumerable smaller programs under all kinds of auspices. Their spread and acceptance in this country is paralleled by a similar growth in England and on the continent. The major part played by government controlled youth programs in totalitarian states is proof also of the potency of its newly devised social instrument.

One is led by this fact into some speculation as to whether our complex society is in fact attempting to deal by such means with the same basic psychological and social problems of transition which gave rise in primitive societies to the so-called "rites of passage" between childhood and adulthood. We live in a society whose technology requires a long educational period involving economic dependence on parents; the learning of complicated job skills and relationships in a highly structured occupational system; the restraint of sexual capacities by delaying marriage eight to ten years after physical maturation and a capacity to participate as citizens with a combination of conformity to necessary authority and independent responsible judgment. It seems possible that these youth programs are the spontaneous, largely unconscious response of the society in search of a means to retard full sexual satisfactions and then to provide sanctioned relationships under certain controls, to teach self government through a simple form of democratic experience, to develop capacities for human relations with adults, to teach the young how to act as representatives of groups in larger intergroup activities, to train youth in discussion of issues vital to them, to give opportunity for exercise of physical powers not used in actual productive work (it is interesting that athletics is often referred to as a "work-out"). I cannot help suspecting that there is some kind of a deep social and psychological significance to the creation and spread of this new social device and that its true meaning lies in its use as a training in the adaptive social skills in preparation for adulthood in our kind of society. The practically universal falling away from such activities at about sixteen and the inability of agencies to engage the interest of many youth from the beginning of courtship until after marriage further strengthens my suspicion that these services are becoming such an adaptive instrument, as essential as our public schools to the rising generation. If I am correct in this speculation it becomes obvious that the leadership of such activities is important to our youth and to society and that since much of the training needed is in the skills of relationships of various kinds that in time such leadership should be knowledgeable in both the psychological and the social significance of this transition period.

Group Experience as a Supplement to Other Relationships

While the great bulk of the social services that use the group work method is to be found in programs for children and youth there is evidence that certain kinds of group experience can be provided which give support and enrichment to people whose other primary relations are not proving to be entirely satisfying. These might be regarded as supplemental social nourishment as it were for those whose lives are for some reasons meager or lacking in intimate social relations.

Perhaps the place where this use can be most clearly seen is in the programs for older people who through the loss of friends and family are impoverished socially. The rise and spread of centers and clubs for older people and their expansion under a great variety of auspices seems to give evidence that such services meet essential needs either not present or not recognized in earlier times. They serve not only to fill vacant time after retirement. They also give support against natural anxiety as to illness and death; they provide new interests through activities for the lost job interests and they often lead to establishing of both meaningful friendships and in fact a considerable number of marriages.

A somewhat similar supplementary function is served by daytime programs for young married women with small children. The confusion in the role of women created by our conflicting demands on them relating to marriage and job competence often leads to certain kinds of maladjustment when competent women used, for example, to office positions, marry and shift to housework and the care of small children. Group programs for such young women often can provide the chance for companionship with others going through the same experience, for appropriate training in the understanding and care of young children and in the development of avocational interests which replace to some extent lost job opportunities.

These are perhaps enough to illustrate what is meant by the use of varieties of group experience to supplement other relations. Here, too, as in the earlier section it should be evident that where possible leadership should be equipped to understand what the basic psychological needs are and equally what kinds of program and group experience can best meet them. Such programs must, of course, be seen as supplemental and be planned to fit into the life situations of participants in helpful ways.

The Use of Group Experience as Preparation for Active Citizenship in a Democracy

Group workers have from the beginning been interested in the use of group experience as a preparation for responsible participation of members of groups as citizens and often as neighbors in areas of social tension and disorganization.

This aspect of the goal of group work manifests itself chiefly in three ways. Experience in the small face-to-face self-governing group, especially the club, provides experience in the development and pursuit of common goals, in the control of impulsive behavior for the accomplishment of deferred common ends, in the creation and acceptance of self-imposed authority in the learning of leadership skills, *i.e.*, in the experience of the democratic process. There are plenty of group records which describe this learning process and its value is indicated in the use of the self-governing club and of representative councils by many organizations as the most acceptable and most effective instrument for preparing children for active participation in our communities. The essential and dominating function of organized groups such as churches, unions, boards, committees to fulfill many social needs is widely recognized. Children grow up into more responsible and more important self-governing groups by experience in dealing with and solving the major concerns natural to childhood and adolescence. Programs, of course, must be adapted to the age range of members and for the young are largely athletic or social or related to avocational interests, but what can be learned in relationships through planning and executing such activities has value in training for other kinds of self-governing organizations into which they will go as adults. The contrast between these goals and the habits of obedience and subservience taught in Nazi or Communist youth groups makes clear the social function of such groups as preparation for participation in the adult society of a democracy.

A second way in which group workers use group experience as preparation for citizenship is by the introduction as program in certain groups of the discussion of various kinds of social issues. Discussion may range from the concern of a group of teen-agers for more adequate city playgrounds to a discussion of international questions in a group of young married women. An interesting example of this occurred last fall in a home for older women when the group worker introduced discussion of the current political campaign, encouraged members who had not voted for years to register and vote, and enlisted the League of Women Voters to present campaign issues. The results for many of the women were not only a more intelligent and active interest in the election itself but also a concomitant change in attitude from inertia and the hopeless waiting for death to a sense of usefulness and a renewed belief in their own potentials.

A third way in which group work services have been used to contribute to socially desirable attitudes lies in the area of the use of planned group experience to deal with neighborhood tensions especially in interracial or interethnic group situations. This takes great understanding of the social situation and of the effects of various types of programs and group relations. It is, however, quite widely regarded as one of the major goals of agencies using group work methods.

This particular function of the group worker seems to be more fully developed than any similar goal found in casework, I believe, because group work does not deal as frequently with the physically and emotionally ill or the economically distressed. The ability and the means to extend one's interest to others and to social concerns is probably more possible when some degree of normal personal adjustment is present. However, if one sees such programs as related to the maturing process mentioned above, they are clearly a part of what a democratic society needs for its youth. They have, I believe, also a wider social significance as one way to combat the sense of anomy, uselessness or submergence which our society tends to produce for many.[4]

Group Experience as a Corrective for Social Disorganization

Within the last ten years, especially, there has begun a use of group work to deal with the delinquent gang situation in areas of social decay and disorganization. This is illustrated by the work of the New York City Youth Board and similar programs in Los Angeles, Cleveland and elsewhere. Its major characteristic is the use of group leaders detached from agencies who establish contact with groups of youth in the natural hangout spots and provide leadership and often needed athletic and social facilities for groups of youth who are engaged in or on the verge of delinquent behavior.

It is obviously not possible either to describe or to evaluate such programs. There is an increased demand for trained group workers to direct and work in them and there is a recognition of the need for research as to results. At this point of their development, their significance for social work lies in the fact that they indicate the recognition of the social as well as psychological causes of delinquency and therefore the necessity to counter it with measures that act upon a social rather than an intrapsychic treatment base. It seems obvious that while clearly these close-knit groups of adolescents which we call anti-social gangs are only a perverted form of the normal maturing process, that their perversion is produced in large part by the action of their anti-social environment.

The highly structured youth gang society of the areas of most social disorganization is found in various forms the country over and apparently to some extent in other countries. Certainly the answer cannot be found in multiplying child guidance centers even if this were feasible. The social origins of this perversion of the natural social-psychological needs of young people lie in an environment filled with intergroup tensions, poverty, lack of vocational opportunity, especially for minority groups, broken families, and anti-social mores of the adult population. The attempt to penetrate the peer culture which this environment produces, through carefully selected adults who can modify the anti-social norms of these groups and provide socially desirable outlets for their dominant interests and needs seems to be the most promising device at present being tried.

A second type of planned group activity as related to social disorganization is that developed in certain types of changing areas. It has been mentioned above that intergroup tensions between racial, ethnic or religious groupings have often been dealt with through discussion and joint activity in a variety of agencies. There are, however, other situations in which a changing neighborhood may be helped by planned group activity. Suburban areas, for example, into which have moved people from widely different cultural backgrounds, often present chasms of social difference and misunderstanding. Group work with both adults and children can be the means of increased acquaintance and the development of common interests upon which a healthy community life can rest. The same kind of problem often arises in public housing estates or newly settled industrial areas, which have sprung up around new industrial plans. Some experience exists which would indicate the usefulness of group work skills for such situations.

A similar use of groups to counteract unwholesome elements in the social environment is being developed in the use of group workers in institutions of various kinds. The institutional setting, whether it be the hospital ward, the home for dependent children or old people, or some similar setting produces psychological reactions in the form of anxiety, of the sense of guilt or desertion, or the tendency to withdraw into seclusion. Planned group activity of various kinds can be used to establish helpful social relations, to provide programs which aid in dealing with the psychological effects, and to help through a carefully selected leader in dealing with the unfamiliar, often frightening and sometimes repressive character of the institutional life. Such use of group workers is only beginning and the increase would be more rapid if trained staff were available.

The Use of Group Experience in the Treatment of Intrapsychic Maladjustments

There is no intention here to draw a sharp line between those personal maladjustments which are intrapsychic in origin and those caused chiefly by social factors in the environment. Of course the causal factors are constantly intertwined and interact on each other.

However, for purposes of sharper delineation of functions it is perhaps useful to mention the functions of the group worker in mental hospitals, clinics and other treatment centers for the physically or emotionally disturbed or physically handicapped. In such cases the group worker is a part of a treatment team in which his observation of the behavior of patients is used for diagnostic purposes and groups activities and relationships are used as a part of treatment. Considerable experience is now accumulating as to the value to individuals which can be found in guided group experience under adequate leadership.

The above analysis of the values which our experience leads us to believe are available through properly trained group work leadership shows two interacting functions, one related to the meeting of individual need through a variety of group experience, the other a contribution to society itself through developing habits and skill in democratic participation and the social attitudes and concerns which make for healthy community life.

In terms of the individual, the group worker discovers needs and interests both by his participation with the group in planning their own programs and by his generalized knowledge of what may be expected in working with people of various ages or social backgrounds. He often has to infer needs and interests from behavior in the group supplemented by greater contact with some individuals. Where the behavior of individuals in the group indicates it, he should, of course, be able to establish contact outside the group itself and if necessary help the person to secure other services which he may require.

It has also been evident from the above that I believe such group experience under proper leadership can make various contributions to society itself, both in providing a more wholesome social milieu for the individual, in preparing for and encouraging participation as responsible citizens and as counteracting anti-social influences frequently found in the environment.

If I am making too large claims here I wish to point out that I am talking about potential values. Some of these our experience with group work has shown us can be realized; some are still experimental and untested; some we are only beginning to glimpse. In all cases our present stage of development must be seen as only in its infancy. We shall then turn to the second section.

SOME ASSUMPTIONS AS TO THE ROLE OF THE GROUP WORKER

If these potentials are to be realized within the agencies providing social services, we need a type of social worker with particular skills and attitudes. What are the most essential skills of the social group worker?

It seems to me that the primary skill is the ability to establish a relationship with a group as a group. This involves the capacity to feel at ease and, in fact, to enjoy the social interplay among members and to be able to perceive both individual behavior and its collective manifestations (for example, to be aware of the morale of the group or its network of interpersonal relations) as well as to become a part of the relationships and to affect them. The worker must have inevitably as the recognized agent of the agency a position of a certain kind of authority or leadership in relation to the group. He uses this role to encourage the group to locate its own goals and to work effectively toward them, to encourage wholesome relationships developing to the members and within socially acceptable values, to discover interests and the program activities to fulfill them. It requires of a worker, as all social work functions do, a self-awareness and the devotion of his abilities and efforts to the growth of the members into the fuller use of their powers.

This establishment of a relationship with the group rests in part on an intellectual understanding of the dynamics of individual behavior and a rational system of ideas for the diagnosis of group behavior within its social setting. More than that, however, it requires that sympathetic apprehension of each situation in its uniqueness which enables him to enter into it, at the same time maintaining his professional function.

Among the essential skills of the group worker is the necessary knowledge about program activities likely to be of interest to a particular group. This does not mean, of course, that he has to have all the recreation or education skills which may be required but that he must have enough familiarity with program to help a group to develop their own and to find specialized leadership if required.

He should be similarly at home with the various types of groups likely to be useful. This should include not only the use of clubs or close-knit friendship groups but also the use of interest groups or classes, teams, committees, intergroup councils, and large activities such as dances or forums. The basic skill here rests on the recognition that various group experiences have different values to particular individuals or at particular times in life.

In the diagnostic and planning process with the group, both program activities and the varieties of group experiences become the tools of the group worker by which he enables a group to develop fruitfully. It is a serious mistake to regard clubs or intimate friendship groups, formerly called "natural groups," as the only or even the most important tool. A learning experience for one person in a creative dramatics group, or a responsible position for another in a task centered group such as a club council are equally within the scope of the group work function. A worker should be able to use as tools a great variety of kinds of groups.

A third major aspect of the group worker's role lies in his ability to deal with values and the conflicts of values he may encounter. As a representative of a social agency and as a professional social worker he is committed to certain social values. These include the respect for individuals and the desire to have them develop into socially useful, self-maintaining and growing personalities. However, he must also deal with some of the concrete conflicts which such a value will precipitate. He obviously does not go along with the delinquent behavior of the gang group with which he is working nor does he necessarily accept and promote the social snobbishness of a group of "overprivileged" adolescents in a wealthy suburb or the racial intolerance of a group of second generation parents in a changing area. Such conflicts are an inevitable part of social work practice. We cannot escape them by being "nonjudgmental." The mistaken use of this valuable concept in some cases and an equally mistaken appeal to democracy can combine to leave the social worker himself in a state of value confusion and helplessness. As a professional worker he must have his own values one of which, I should hope, would be a larger degree of flexibility and the imagination to enter into the experience of others, combined, however, with strength and personal security. A large order!

The group worker needs also certain knowledge and skills which are common to all social workers. He must know how to establish contact with individuals in his group who need more help than the group can provide. This requires the ability to recognize symptomatic behavior, and to establish a relation with the individual. In most instances, except in the therapeutic groups mentioned above, the group worker cannot himself undertake an individual relationship of the casework variety. This is not because he may not be equipped or able to do so but because to do so would confuse his role with the group and often make it impossible for him to fulfill it. In this, the group worker, like the teacher, has other functions which will be hampered if he embarks on intensive individual relationships. He should, however, be able to recognize need for personal help, to know available resources in casework or other services and to be able to make the necessary referrals. He should also be able, of course, to receive referrals and to place individuals in helpful group situations. In this he uses largely the diagnosis of others but applies to treatment his special tools available through program and relationships in groups.

We have proceeded so far on the assumption that group workers in their professional capacities actually lead groups. This we know from practical experience and from recent studies is in fact often not the case. The group worker's time is often used for administrative or supervisory functions or he is drawn into community organization in neighborhoods or into community planning on a citywide basis. So it is sometimes said what is the use of his being trained in the direct practice of group work. By some it is inferred from this that group work is dead or has never been born. As I see it, this situation requires careful attention. There are several aspects which group workers should consider.

In the first place, in my experience the number of situations in which group workers do lead groups is increasing though slowly. It is true that this is occurring more often in the therapeutic settings than elsewhere or in situations like the programs with so-called hard-to-reach youth where it is recognized that special skill is required. It is this fact that makes such positions especially desirable to some. There seems to me to be some recognition, though not as much as I would wish, in the regular leisure time agencies that group workers should be employed to lead groups and not pushed into supervisory positions too soon or for too much of their time. I doubt if the supply of group workers is likely in the foreseeable future to be sufficient to staff the agencies completely with trained workers, although the percentage is noticeably higher in some agencies which really attempt it than in others who give only halfhearted support to the effort. Where insufficient group work staff is available, they are almost inevitably used for supervision. We need to recognize, however, that this is one aspect of scarcity. Exactly the same thing is true of caseworkers in our public assistance programs. The long range answer may be to increase the supply. The short range answer seems to me to lie in two measures—a more thorough and adequate system of in-service training of the volunteer or less trained staff by the available trained staff. Group work has never developed its supervision as fully as in casework and it is even more needed. A second answer lies in a careful study of groups to be led in an agency to locate those which can best be led by less skilled workers and those requiring the greatest expertness available. If this were done, a certain amount of every group worker's time could be set aside for direct practice and his skill used directly where it was most needed and indirectly where he supervised other leaders.

The fact that, for the present at least, group workers are likely to be used in supervisory positions to a large extent and within a few years after training, means we must prepare them in how to supervise and how to pass on their knowledge in an appropriate form to the others who will be doing direct leading. Inevitably knowledge and skill learned in professional education suffer from dilution in these circumstances, but, from my experience with a considerable number of highly skilled and knowledgeable workers in local agencies, professional knowledge enables them to diagnose and work with groups even when done through others at an entirely different level of competence from that of untrained workers. Though there is no doubt some seepage, the stream of understanding and skill still flows through to the clientele with considerable strength and usefulness. This leads me to believe that we must tackle this issue of the lack of opportunity for workers to do direct practice with all the means in our power. However, I believe, the situation is on the whole improving.

Like other social workers the group worker has a responsibility for helping in community planning and the provision of necessary social services. His particular contribution may be in the area of services for recreation and informal education. Increasingly as practice develops in some of the newer uses of group work, he should also work on getting group work introduced as it proves valuable into new settings in hospitals, clinics, institutions and other situations. While he inevitably will have a special interest in those agencies or situations where group work is used or should be introduced, the group worker should have an identification with the profession of social work. He will, therefore, share in the profession's concerns on social policy and the prevention of the social ills with which the social services deal.

SOME IMPLICATIONS FOR THE EDUCATION OF GROUP WORKERS

It is obvious from the above that the group worker needs professional training in social work, which he uses in somewhat different ways than does the caseworker or the community organization worker. There are, however, certain special requirements within the general training which he must have.

He must have as a central part of his body of knowledge an understanding of the group process.[5] His practice courses in group work and his field work center on his learning how to use such knowledge in his role as group worker.

He needs a body of knowledge on individual behavior and also on the community in order to understand both the members of his groups and the interaction of his groups with their social setting. Again he applies this in line with his function.

He requires the usual background knowledge of the social services, and their history, and the teaching of professional values and ethics required for all social workers. There are, I think, some problems of professional goals and ethics peculiar to group workers and related to their function of leadership which need to be defined in field work and in the courses on group work practice.

It seems evident that the social work curriculum, where it includes content on group and community process, has in it the ingredients for the training of group workers. We need, however, to be free from any pressure to eliminate the basic differentials between casework and group work. It is true that there are generic elements common to all social work but it is also true that there are specific aspects of the group worker's function which need recognition, discriminating judgments and freedom to develop. The pressure toward conformity which has appeared at points in an emphasis on the generic should not be followed to eliminate the essential features of a group worker's education to fulfill a function in part the same, but in part different, from that of other social workers.

NOTES

1. The term psychosocial relations frequently used in defining social work is understood by the author to mean not only the intrapsychic reactions of individuals in their relations with others but also the social conditions or situations such as migration or unemployment or those lacks in social relations for example in the case of dependent children, or isolated old people, which produce unhappiness, or social dysfunctioning. For further explanation of this interpretation of psychosocial relations, see author's "The Social Worker and His Society," *Social Service Review,* XXX (December, 1956), 387-399.
2. It is possible that the rise of the emphasis on function in the Pennsylvania School of Social Work and on relationship as a major element in casework developed out of this necessity to disentangle services and the relationship necessary to their administration. This process of disentangling two distinct and different aspects of experience in the practice of social work seems to recur. It may be a necessary step in clarification.
3. I am using social skills here as defined in Elton Mayo, *Social Problems of an Industrial Civilization* (Graduate School of Business Administration, Harvard University, 1945).
4. It is not possible here to deal adequately with this question but it is interesting to note that many writers from Durkheim to Fromm who point out the anomy and rootlessness of much of our population often wind up with a proposed solution in the form of vitalizing small group life to give meaningful personal relations and to encourage participation in the solution of social issues nearest to those involved. In fact so far as I know no one who has tried to find an answer to this problem has ever proposed anything else.
5. For an outline of concepts needed here, see "A Study of Group Process" in Margaret E. Hartford and Grace L. Coyle, *Social Process in the Community and the Group* (New York: Council on Social Work Education, 1958).

3

The Social Group Work Process

Clara A. Kaiser is Professor Emeritus, Columbia University School of Social Work, New York.

Clara A. Kaiser

The actual birthdate of social group work has never been certainly determined, nor is there full agreement on its progenitors. In attempting to delineate social group work as a purposive and disciplined way of affecting group process it seems to me important to look back into the ideas, movements, and activities which played a part in bringing it into being. In doing so we must distinguish between those which had an influence on the ideas and purposes of social group work and those which acted to bring it into being as distinct from other forms of endeavors to influence group life. Group work neither emerged full blown from the minds of one or more individuals, nor did it just grow like Topsy. In contrast to the Elder Sister discipline of social casework, group work had no Mary Richmond to systematize the principles which had been derived from experience. Group work evolved from the recognition by a number of persons engaged in a variety of educational, recreational, and social service activities that they had common interests and concerns because they were all, to some extent, working with groups of people. They were not mainly concerned with sharing their knowledge of what group process and group behavior consisted, but with ways in which the goals of the programs and services of their respective agencies could be more effectively achieved. These agencies included schools, social settlements, youth-serving agencies, recreational centers, and camps. In other words, it was to improve services and the quality of leadership offered to groups that motivated the early efforts to formulate principles which could guide agencies in developing their programs and in training the workers who served as group leaders. The history of this movement to develop a common body of knowledge and skill for practice in a variety of group-serving agencies mainly concerned with leisure-time programs for children and youth has never been fully compiled, but it is not within the scope of this paper to do so. Two articles contained in *Group Work—Foundations and Frontiers* (Coyle, 1953; Kaiser, 1953) give some historical perspective of the developments in the formulation of group work as a professional discipline in social work. More recently, Charles Levy has provided a well-documented historical summary of the main organized efforts to delineate the objectives, forms, and methods of social group work as an aspect of social work practice and the body of knowledge and skill forming the basis for professional education (Levy, 1958a, 1958b).

The ideological forebears of group work as a distinctive process in work with groups are numerous and their influence on its value system and methodology are sometimes more implicit than explicit. I shall attempt, however, to identify what seem to be the most significant systems of thought which have given direction and content to the conceptual framework of social group work.

1. The ethical, social, and theistic beliefs embodied in the Judeo-Christian religions.
2. The humanitarian movement of the late nineteenth century which found expression in the social settlement movement in England and later in the United States.
3. The educational philosophy of John Dewey and his followers who formulated the theories of progressive education.
4. The theories of certain early sociologists who saw in the small group the key to studying the relation of the individual to society, especially Durkheim, Simmel, Cooley, Mead.
5. Recent basic research in small group theory by social scientists, such as Kurt Lewin, Moreno, Elton Mayo, and Merton.
6. The democratic ethic not only as it applies to a political system, but as it permeates all forms of social relationships, and as expressed in the writings of such authors as Mary Follett and Eduard C. Lindeman.
7. The psychoanalytic school of psychiatry.
8. The values, principles, and methods of social work as the profession within which social group work has developed.

I shall not attempt to trace what and how each of these ideological systems contributed to the philosophy and methodology of social group work, but in delineating what seems to me specific and, to some extent, distinctive to this process, I shall indicate what bearing they seem to have had on its theory and practice.

Social group work is not a separate profession, but a discipline within the profession of social work. Its major distinctiveness from the other methods in social work practice lies in the fact that its unit of service to people is the group. This has a different connotation than if we were to designate the unit of service as the individual in the group. Both social casework and community organization are concerned with group relations, but their units of service are respectively the individual and the community. This does not mean that the values to be derived from any helping process must not be measured in terms of the impact it has on the well-being of the individual human being, which is the ultimate goal in a democratic society. It does mean that group work is a means for serving the individual *through* the medium of the group. An understanding of and the ability to work purposively with groups are at the core of the social group work process.

Social work is not by any means the only professional service concerned with a purposive method of working with groups. Educators, clergy, physicians, industrial managers, social science researchers, among others, make conscious use of the group process as a means for achieving the ends of their professional disciplines. The elements which distinguish the social group work process from those pertinent to other disciplines will not be discussed in this paper, since consideration has been given to this question in other papers (Lerner and Kelman, 1952; Peck et al., 1954; Kaiser, 1957, p. 158).

The conceptual framework of social group work as a means for affecting the group process must be examined in relation to three major categories of concepts. These categories are concepts pertaining to: (1) the basic values underlying practice and the goals sought by the social group worker; (2) the nature of the group process and its significance for the individual and for society; (3) the methodology of the social group work process.

VALUES AND GOAL CONCEPTS

The value system on which social group work rests is fundamentally that on which all social work endeavor is based. This is attested to very generally in the literature of social group work. The definition of the function of the group worker formulated in 1949 by a committee of the American Association of Group Workers embodies in it this value system (Coyle, 1949). These basic value concepts have been admirably stated by Gordon Hamilton in a paper entitled "Helping People—The Growth of a Profession" (Kasius, 1949). She enumerates the following as the "key concepts of social casework today":

1. Any ability to help others effectively rests on respect for the human personality—on the person's right to make his own life, to

enjoy personal and civil liberties, and to pursue happiness and spiritual goals in his own way.

2. Help is most effective if the recipient participates actively and responsibly in the process.

3. Respect for others, acceptance of others as they are, and as potentially they can be, tends to induce between worker and client, between the one who seeks and the one who offers help, a relationship which is not only the medium for educational counseling, but for a therapeutic process.

4. Respect for others includes respect for their difference.

5. Self-awareness is essential in understanding others.

6. The individual has responsibility not only for himself but toward the society in which he lives.

These concepts are as pertinent to the helping process when afforded to groups of people as they are in casework. In them we find explicit expression of the beliefs implicit in the Judeo-Christian religions and in the democratic ethos.

Concepts with respect to the goals and objectives of the social group worker as he relates himself purposively to groups fall within a realm in which there is less agreement than in that of the value system. The goals of the group worker must be related to the many variables present in every group situation. The specific needs of individual members, the purpose for which the group exists, the purposes and policies of the agency, the social sanctions of the community, all are factors which must affect the objectives of the social group worker with respect to his function as a helping person. However, there are at least three issues with regard to the goals of the worker seeking to meet needs of human beings through group experience which pertain generally to the social group work process in distinction to other purposive ways of working with groups. The first of these concerns whether the objectives of the worker are directed primarily to contributing to the adjustment and growth of the individual member or whether they are *also* directed toward the development of the group as an instrument for achieving common goals consonant with the values of human relations discussed above. If the objectives of the social group worker are equally directed toward individual and group movement, it profoundly affects the basis on which the group worker uses himself and his knowledge and skill in determining his goals with respect to a specific social situation. In my opinion this dual concern for the individual's needs and those of the group as a network of interrelationships is a concept which differentiates social group work from other helping disciplines.

The second issue related to goal concepts in social group work has to do with the relative importance to be attached to the quality of the content of group program and the quality of the social interaction processes in group life. John Dewey's definition of education as "any change wrought in an individual as a result of experience" (Childs, 1939) has often been interpreted to mean that substantive knowledge is less important in the educational process than the feelings resulting from a learning experience. The psychological and emotional factors in the growth process are also emphasized in psychoanalytical theory. The definition of the function of the group worker begins with the following sentence: "The group worker enables various types of groups to function in such a way that both *group interaction* and *program activities* contribute to the growth of the individual and the achievement of desirable goals" (Coyle, 1949). In spite of this affirmation of the indivisibility of the significance of the quality of the social processes engendered in group life and the intrinsic values of the group's activities, there has been some tendency to subordinate the latter to the former ingredient in pursuing the objectives of the social group work process. Perhaps it is necessary to rethink the concept of program activities as *tools* or *media* rather than as ends in the process of developing the intellectual, social, and emotional potentials of the individual and the effectiveness of the group in accomplishing a progressively more meaningful and significant task. These tasks should include the development of socially aware and effective citizens and the achievement of socially useful group actions if group work is to fulfill its stated objectives. This focus in the objectives of social group work was ably set forth by Grace Coyle when she says:

> One of the primary functions of group work is the attempt to build on the inevitably social interests both of children and adults a type of group experience which will be individually developing and socially useful. By providing within the group work agency for experience in group management, in cooperation for a common interest, in collective behavior, the agency can help its members to discover how to take their place in this organizational life of the community [Coyle, 1935, pp. 395-396].

With respect to this aspect of the objectives of social group work, we can trace the influence of the social settlement movement with its strong emphasis on the need for concerted action to eliminate and alleviate the social conditions which were causing human deprivation and suffering.

The third issue with respect to goal or objective concepts in social group work has been sharpened by the increasing use of social group work in medical, psychiatric, and rehabilitation services. Are the goals of social group work oriented to therapy or treatment of dysfunctioning of individuals or groups or to the development of potentials for growth, or are both within the sphere of this discipline? My answer to this question is that social group work has both therapeutic and developmental goals, but its processes are educative rather than clinical in nature. Saul Scheidlinger has defined this distinction as follows:

> It is useful to differentiate between therapeutic effects accruing from a variety of mental hygiene-based group measures, and therapy in the sense of a psychological process where specific techniques are applied by trained practitioners to deal with recognized areas of pathology [1956, p. 37].

Not all members of our professional family would make this distinction so sharp. My reason for doing so is not for the purpose of drawing fine lines between group therapy and group work, but because I feel that social group work has its major contribution to make in focusing on building on the ego strengths of individuals and on the social health of groups.

CONCEPTS WITH RESPECT TO GROUP PROCESSES

Since we have defined the social group work process as a purposive and disciplined way of affecting the group process, there must be some conceptual framework as to the nature and forms of group life to which this process is pertinent. The small face-to-face group is increasingly becoming the subject of study and research by both the applied and the theoretical social sciences. We can know much more about the sociological and psychological properties and behavior of groups than we could have ten years ago. How fully or meaningfully this new knowledge about the dynamics of group life has been incorporated into the concepts about how social group work aims can be more effectively attained is far from clear. Is the answer to this problem that the social scientist researcher on small groups is oriented to examining the group process as it functions, and the social group worker on methods to bring about change in groups values and behavior? This difference in purpose of the social scientist and the social group worker has served as a barrier in communication between them. There are signs that this barrier is less formidable than it was and that we can look forward to greater demonstration research that can be used for action purposes.

In the development of principles and methods of guiding and enabling groups to achieve the objectives discussed above, it has been recognized that the social group work process is not applicable to all forms of group life. There was a tendency in the earlier stages of the development of the theoretical framework of group work to delimit its application to groups with very specific attributes and purposes.

More recently the scope of social group work with respect to the kinds of groups it serves has been greatly expanded. On the other hand, in defining the role of the professional group worker a distinction is now being drawn between "working with groups" and engaging in the "process of social group work." This distinction seems to me to be sound provided that it is based on the methodology of the worker and not on the characteristics of the group.

To be sure, social group work, like the other social work methods, is practiced within the institutional context of social welfare, health, and educational agencies. The number and variety of agencies which now afford group work services is increasing rapidly. Many types of groups are served in these agencies and by no means all of them are served through the medium of social group work. The reasons for this fact are manifold and they lie to a large extent in the still uncharted realm of determining what kinds of individual and group needs can best be met through the use of the professional disciplines of the social group worker. They also lie in institutional conditions which sharply limit the availability of trained social group workers for direct service to groups. This is an area in which there is an urgent need for research as was evidenced in the pilot study of social group work practice undertaken by the Group Work Section of the National Association of Social Workers in 1956 (Wilson, 1957).

The concepts of social group work regarding the meaning of group life for the individual and for society are to some extent implicit in its objectives. Since the group is the unit of service, there is an assumption that groups provide a medium for the satisfaction of basic needs of the individual and as a channel for affecting the social structure. Group life is a pervasive aspect of all human experience. The individual personality is an abstraction outside of the social groups to which he belongs; society does not exist apart from the groups which compose it. Any deliberate effort to influence group life must of necessity be limited to those groups which accept and utilize the role and function of a helping person. The agency is the social structure within which such groups are formed and function.

In recent years emphasis has been placed on servicing groups not affiliated with agencies. The workers with such groups have been designated "detached workers." This is probably a misnomer since the worker is not detached from the purpose of the agency in affording services to these groups but only from the physical or operational aspects of the agency. In general, social group work is a process which is applied in agency practice. The purposes and structure of the agency are therefore major factors in determining the kinds of groups with which social group work is employed. But individuals and groups have many different purposes in identifying themselves with an agency. The groups within this structure will take many different forms, as to their specific purposes, as to their structure, and as to the meaning they have for their members. Helen Phillips has defined the agency's function with regard to the groups within it clearly:

> The function of the group work agency is to provide group experiences—the kind of experience that, through appropriate structures and enabling leadership, will contribute to the agency's purposes of effecting the social growth of the group's participants and the development of group units in the direction of social usefulness. The constant demand on the worker as he helps the members to develop both themselves as individuals and their groups is that he focus his attention on the group relations which the agency provides by its very function. The group unit is the primary working base for the worker's contribution to the fulfillment of agency purpose [1957, pp. 51-52].

The concepts of social group work regarding the nature of the group process are derived both from the accumulated experience in practice and from the social and behavioral sciences. Some principles or assumptions with respect to group process and behavior have been formulated and incorporated into the body of knowledge underlying practice. These have to do with attributes of groups which seem most conducive to achieving the goals of the group work process. These attributes include how groups are formed, size of groups, degree of homogeneity with respect to age, sex, interests, cultural background, expressed or implicit purposes the group has for its members, nature of interests for group activity, group structure and controls, quality of interpersonal relations, *esprit de corps* or group feeling. Although social group work has become much more aware of the essential elements in group life, little or no empirical research has been undertaken to test our assumptions or predilections for certain qualities of groups in relation to goals which have been fairly clearly delineated. That the need for such research is clearly indicated may be seen in the increasing concern which practitioners, agencies, and professional educators have with what seems to be the gap between theory and practice in social group work. Could this gap be bridged by closer and more effective collaboration between the social scientists and social group workers in not only increasing knowledge of group phenomena but in improving our methods for enriching and repairing individual and group life? We have already taken much from the sociologists, psychiatrists, and social psychologists. Perhaps it is time to give as well as take in this vital task of advancing the art of human relations.

METHODOLOGY

It is beyond the scope of this paper to examine fully the concepts which underlie the methods and techniques of the social group work process. Within the last few years a substantial number of books and articles dealing with social group work theory and practice have contributed richly to the methodological basis for practice. This fact is especially remarkable since prior to the 1930's there was scarcely any literature in the field and it testifies to the vitality of this professional discipline.

Concepts pertinent to the methodology of the social group work process have been succinctly and usefully set forth by Gisela Konopka in a paper presented at the Institute on Group Work in the Psychiatric Setting in July 1955 as follows by what she describes as "guidelines and essential parts of the generic group work method" (Konopka, 1956, pp. 21-22):

1. The function of the social group worker is a helping or enabling function: This means that his goal is to help the members of the group and the group as a whole to move toward greater independence and capacity for self-help.

2. In determining his way of helping, the group worker uses the scientific method; factfinding (observation), analyzing, diagnosis in relation to the individual, the group and the social environment.

3. The group work method includes the worker forming purposeful relationships to group members and the group: This includes a conscious focusing on the needs of the members, on the purpose of the group as expressed by the members, as expected by the sponsoring agency and as implied in the members' behavior. It is differentiated from a casual unfocused relationship.

4. One of the main tools in achieving such a relationship is the conscious use of self. This includes self-knowledge and discipline in relationships without the loss of warmth and spontaneity.

5. There should be acceptance of people without accepting all their behavior: This involves the capacity for "empathy" as well as the incorporation of societal demands. It is the part of the method that is most closely intertwined with a high flexibility and abudance of warmth in the social group worker as well as identification with values and knowledge.

6. Starting where the group is: The capacity to let groups develop from their own point of departure, of capacity, without immediately imposing outside demands.

7. The constructive use of limitations: Limitations must be used judiciously in relation to individual and group needs and agency function. The forms will vary greatly. The group worker will mainly use himself, program materials, interaction of the group and awakening of insight in the group members.

8. Individualization: It is one of the specifics of the group work method that the individual is not lost in the whole, but that he is helped to feel as a unique person who can contribute to the whole.

9. Use of the interacting process: The capacity to help balance the group, to allow for conflict when necessary and to prevent it when harmful; the help

given to the isolate not only through individual attention by the group worker alone but also by relating him to other members.

10. The understanding and conscious use of nonverbal as well as verbal material: I especially put nonverbal material first, since the group worker deals a great deal with this, especially in work with children. His capacity to use program materials, which do not demand verbal expression and yet are helpful, should be very wide.

This delineation of principles guiding social group work practice indicates how deeply they are imbedded in the principles guiding all social work practice. It also reflects the body of knowledge which is essential for the social worker who seeks to serve needs of people through group experience. That group life can only be influenced by an understanding of the psychosocial factors which affect it is a fundamental principle in social group work. The diagnostic process so basic to all social work methods must in group work encompass the group as a unit of social relationships within the context of its social environment as well as the individuals who compose its membership. This involves for the group worker basic knowledge of the psychodynamics of both individual and group behavior and of social processes and institutions. This knowledge must be incorporated into the worker's use of himself as a helping person. Self-awareness and a clear conception of his role in dealing with group and individual needs are essential ingredients in social group work practice. Understanding of educational theories and methods are also important elements in the group work process particularly with respect to the selection and development of program content.

Although there are many areas of social group work methodology which need further formulation and scientific validation, this is not the most urgent problem confronting the field. The chief problem lies in bringing about a closer integration of the avowed goals of social group work process with the scientific knowledge now available about group life, and the formulated methods and techniques for the purposive development of group processes and relationships in practice in the ever expanding number and types of settings in which groups of people are being served. Group life has potentialities for stultifying and restricting individual growth into patterns of rigid conformity or dependence as well as for releasing and strengthening the capacities of individuals. Group life may have a regressive and even destructive effect in our societal structure. In furthering social and mental health, we must become as knowledgeable and concerned with the causes of dysfunctioning of groups as we are with those of individuals and of our basic institutions. The increase in the number of antisocial groups among youth and adults bears witness to this fact. The protest of such writers as William H.

Whyte (1956), against the trend toward subordinating individual creativity and initiative to group thinking and action in an increasingly bureaucratized society must be scrutinized by the social group workers as well as by the social psychologists. More than any other applied social science, social group work has a responsibility to afford demonstrable and discriminating evidence of how human society can be bettered through services which enhance the meaning of group experience to individuals and which contribute to the achievement of the goals of a democratic society.

Social group work is still a new and evolving discipline. Professional education for this area of social work practice has existed for barely three decades. The responsibility for preparing creative and effective practitioners for professional service rests not only with the schools of social work but also with the agencies and the bodies of professional workers. In summarizing, I would like to suggest the following tasks which these groups must undertake if social group work practice and professional education for it are to attain the stature necessary to achieve their avowed goals.

1. There must be a clearer delineation of the focus of social group work objectives. Is it a process directed to working with individuals in groups or one working with groups of individuals?

2. The scientific basis of practice must be broadened and deepened through better integration of relevant knowledge from the social and behavorial sciences.

3. Research techniques should be applied to the problems encountered in practice and to the measurement of movement toward goals for groups and individuals.

4. Recording as a tool in practice and for professional education should be more fully and effectively developed.

5. The impact of differentials in agency settings on practice should be analyzed so that both generic and specific elements in professional education may be incorporated into the curriculum.

6. The content and emphasis in professional education curricula should be examined in view of the preponderance of supervisory and administrative functions carried by the great majority of trained social group workers.

7. Relationships of social group work with other professional disciplines within social work and in related fields should be more clearly defined and developed.

Social group work as a purposive process for influencing the group process derives its body of knowledge from multiple sources. The most important responsibility practitioners and educators have is to integrate and synthesize this knowledge as a means for effective service to human beings.

REFERENCES

CHILDS, J. L., 1939. "Educational Philosophy of John Dewey," in *John Dewey As Educator*, J. L. Childs and W. H. Kilpatrick, eds. New York: Progressive Education Association.

COYLE, G. L., 1935. "Group Work and Social Change," *Proceedings of the National Conference of Social Work, 1935.* Chicago: University of Chicago Press.

——, 1949. "Definition of the Function of the Group Worker," *The Group*, Vol. 11, No. 3.

——, 1953. "On Becoming Professional," in *Group Work—Foundations and Frontiers*, H. Trecker, ed. New York: Whitside, William Morrow.

KAISER, C. A., 1953. "Group Work Education in the Last Decade," in *Group Work—Foundations and Frontiers*, H. Trecker, ed. New York: Whitside, William Morrow.

——, 1957. "Characteristics of Social Group Work." *The Social Welfare Forum, 1957.* New York: Columbia University Press.

KASIUS, C., ed., 1949. *Social Work as Human Relations.* New York: Columbia University Press.

KONOPKA, G., 1956. "The Generic and the Specific in Group Work Practice in the Psychiatric Setting," in *Group Work in the Psychiatric Setting*, H. Trecker, ed. New York: Whitside, William Morrow.

LERNER, H. H., and H. C. KELMAN, eds., 1952. "Group Method in Psychotherapy, Social Work and Adult Education," *The Journal of Social Issues*, Vol. 8, No. 2.

LEVY, C. S., 1958a. "Is Social Group Work Standing Still?" *Social Work*, Vol. 3, No. 1.

——, 1958b. "From Education to Practice in Social Group Work," unpublished doctoral dissertation, New York School of Social Work, Columbia University.

PECK, H. B., et al., 1954. "The Group in Education, Group Work and Psychotherapy," *American Journal of Orthopsychiatry*, Vol. 24, No. 1.

PHILLIPS, H. V., 1957. *Essentials of Social Group Work Skill.* New York: Association Press.

SCHEIDLINGER, S., 1956. "Social Group Work and Group Psychotherapy," *Social Work*, Vol. 1, No. 3.

WHYTE, W. H., 1956. *The Organization Man.* New York: Simon & Schuster.

WILSON, G., 1957. "The Practice of Social Group Work," in *Practice Committee, Group Work Section.* New York: National Association of Social Workers (mimeo).

4

Frame of Reference for Social Group Work

Margaret E. Hartford is Professor of Gerontology and Social Work at the Leonard Davis School of Gerontology, University of Southern California, Los Angeles.

Margaret E. Hartford

Social group work is that method of social work in which the group experience is utilized by the worker as the primary medium of practice, for the purpose of effecting the social functioning, growth, or change of the group members. The social group worker's practice includes a number of different activities depending on agency setting and job definition. The group worker's functions may include services to groups and individuals, administration, supervision, organization, program planning, and coordination, intake and group placement, record keeping, or community and public relations. All of these activities and others are considered aspects of social work practice. The social group work *method* may be distinguished as those specific activities of the worker with or in behalf of the group in which the group experience is used for the benefit of the members.

Within the context of professional social work, social group work incorporates values, purposes, knowledge, and sanctions common to all of social work. The difference between social group work and other methods of social work lies

1. in its methodology
   The social group worker functions primarily with the group as his major method of helping. His use of individual methods or intergroup methods, although vital to his practice, are secondary.

Reprinted with permission. From *Working Papers Toward a Frame of Reference for Social Group Work*, pp. 4–10. Published 1964, National Association of Social Workers, Inc.

2. in differential use of common bodies of knowledge
   The social group worker draws heavily upon individual personality theory, sociocultural theory of society and personality, interactional theory, and he may draw upon social psychology and group dynamics more than the other methods of social work.
3. in different emphasis of some of the purposes toward which social group work is directed
   He uses his method toward the restoration of personal and social dysfunctioning and the prevention of social and personal breakdown, but also toward the promotion of normal social growth especially in stress periods, and to provide opportunity for personal enhancement and to develop citizen participation. In these three latter purposes social group work may differ in some degree from other methods of social work practice.

SETTINGS

The social group work method is employed in a variety of settings or types of agencies and organizations. These include neighborhood and community services, group services, youth services, hospitals and clinics, correctional institutions, schools, residential treatment centers, institutions for aged, ill, or people with special problems, churches, family and child welfare services, public assistance, and camps. Though the purpose, focus, goals and the sanctions of the services are conditioned by the setting and the clientele, the group work method is practiced in essentially the same form regardless of setting.

FOCUS

The social group worker, in providing service, gives simultaneous attention to the group processes, and to the functioning of the individual members. He draws upon knowledge and skill in understanding and affecting group processes as well as knowledge and skill in working with individuals within the group. This dual focus is a particular characteristic of social group work practice. The social group worker may organize the group or may intervene in an already existent group in such a way that the group experience will provide a helping milieu for the individual members in accordance with their social needs. In group work practice the group development is sometimes seen as an end in itself.

PURPOSES

The social group work method is used to maintain or improve the personal and social functioning of group members within a range of purposes. Groups may be served for corrective purposes when the problem is in the person of group members or in the social situation or both, for prevention where group members are in danger of dysfunction, for normal growth purposes particularly at critical growth periods, for enhancement of the person and for the purpose of education and citizen participation. Any group may be served for any one or all of these purposes simultaneously, and the purposes of the service may change through time, but are related to the social functioning needs of the particular group members within their social context and within agency focus and goal.

1. Corrective Purposes

In instances where there is or has been social or personal dysfunctioning or breakdown within individual members, or within their social situations, the group experience may be utilized to provide corrective experiences. In these instances something may have gone wrong or never developed within the person or within the social situation. A group of people may have similar problems or be affected adversely by their social situation. Examples of such problems include delinquents, emotionally retarded people who need social experiences guided by a strong adult, people suffering from physical or emotional breakdown or social isolation, or people who are demoralized by socially, economically, and culturally deprived social situations.* In these examples the group with the group worker may provide the necessary corrective experiences to provide growth or change.

2. Preventive Purposes

In instances where individual group members or the group as a whole may exist in circumstances where there is danger of deterioration in personal or social functioning, the group experience may be used to maintain current level of functioning to prevent personal and social breakdown. Under these circumstances the group with the social group worker may provide a constructive program of mental health, provide alternatives from the surrounding delinquency or other social problems, present alternative values, provide motivation for change from prevailing cultural trends, provide an opportunity

*Examples are not intended to be exhaustive, but merely illustrative.

for early detection of potential emotional problems and offer alternative resolution to personal pressures, or provide supports for people thought to be under stress and in danger of deterioration.

3. Normal Social Growth

The group experience guided by the worker may help to facilitate the normal social growth process and the extension of effective social functioning, particularly for people in stress periods. The social group worker through his interventions helps the group to provide preparation for the adaptation to new situations such as occur in migration or immigration, approach to marriage or parenthood, and growth into new age roles such as adolescence, young adulthood, or old age. The guided group experience may provide social associations and peer relations necessary to facilitate the progression through the normal developmental periods, and to extend the range and quality of social relationships.

4. Personal Enhancement

Through collective experience and interpersonal exchange the individual develops skills, expresses latent talent, fulfills potential for growth, and finds enrichment of life which could not be achieved as adequately through individual experience. Such groups would include some of the creative arts, interests, intellectual and philosophical discussions, or action groups in which the individual member grows and finds a fuller life experience through the group, not available to him through individual activities. The social group worker may facilitate the group processes so that such experiences may be found by the individual members.

5. Citizenship Responsibility and Participation

The social group worker guides the group toward experiences which provide for the members the incorporation of democratic values for themselves for the group as a whole, and for the wider society. The emphasis in this purpose is on the value development and change within the members that incorporates belief in rights and dignity of all human beings, not just practice in democratic procedures. By being helped to participate actively in group life, individuals may learn to lead and to follow, to take part in the decision making process, to assume responsibility for themselves and others, to delegate, to think independently and collectively, to abide by decisions to which one has agreed in the group, and to assume some responsibility for society.

KNOWLEDGE

The social group worker draws upon, integrates, and applies several bodies of knowledge including personality theory, group theory, sociocultural theory, knowledge of social welfare organization, knowledge of program media, and theory of group work method.

1. Personality Theory

The social group worker uses dynamic theories of personality by which he can understand the meaning of individual behavior from an intrapsychic and interpersonal or social view. The social group worker uses generalized knowledge about expectations of personal and social behavior at various stages of development within the cultural context. Knowledge is also used of the effects of the sociocultural and group experience on personality development. The social group worker employs this knowledge in his activity with the group in order to provide the opportunity for helping the individual members to grow, change, or correct their social functioning. This knowledge is drawn from biology, physiology, psychology, psychiatry, social psychology, anthropology, and education.

2. Group Theory

The social group worker uses theory and concepts about groups by which he can understand and also intervene effectively in the processes of groups. Some of the elements or processes he needs to understand are: the group formation, continuity, and dissolution processes, the elements of group composition, goals, structure and functioning, patterning of relationships, group influences and controls, deliberative process and decision making, the nature of group cohesion and morale, and the cultural properties of groups. The social group worker draws his group theory from social psychology, sociology, anthropology, psychiatry, and to some extent theory about groups that have developed within the practice of group work itself.

3. Sociocultural Theory

The social group worker draws upon knowledge of the nature, function and structure of society and culture, subcultures and substructures including reference groups, social, ethnic, social class, family, geographical, and occupational organization. He uses systems theory, social change theory, and organizational theory and some of the theoretical formulations of social dysfunction, such as anomie, disengagement, minority status, economic depression, etc. He draws this knowledge of social theory from sociology, anthropology, economics, social psychology, and political science.

4. Knowledge of Social Welfare Systems

The social group worker uses a body of knowledge about the organization of social welfare systems, public and private, the nature and function of resources, and the interrelatedness of the social welfare services. The worker uses knowledge of the need systems and the various approaches to need meeting and problem solution at the community level. This knowledge stems from social work and social welfare organization, social sciences, and some knowledge developed within community organization practice.

5. Knowledge of Program Media

The social group worker uses knowledge about the nature and functions of various program media for personality development, for facilitating social, intellectual, and physical growth, for stimulating motivation for change and for facilitating group development or change. Program media used in social group work may be verbal and nonverbal and includes arts and crafts, dramatics, music, sports and games, discussion, camping and camp crafts, dancing, and trips (among others). The sources of this knowledge beyond social group work itself are education, physical education, recreation, adult education, and the arts. The social group worker needs enough knowledge about the uses of the various media to be able to be selective in the program which he introduces or facilitates from the suggestions of members, appropriate for the particular members in the specific group.

6. Practice Theory

Specific practice theory relative to the use of social group work remains to be fully developed and tested. However, practicing group workers and educators do use theoretical formulations based on the accumulation of widom, knowledge, and clinical experience, and the integration and application of knowledge from the basic sciences and other professions.

Some of the elements of practice theory follow: The Group is the means for providing social group work service. The worker gives attention to the growth of members in the development of themselves and their group through their interactions and activities with each other and with the worker. As part of the service the worker may find it necessary or deem it important to engage in individual conferences with members or in behalf of members, but this is related to the use of the group as the major medium of service.

Service is provided to groups and individuals by the social group worker on the basis of diagnostic thinking about and feeling for the particular people in the specific group in their circumstances and within the defined service area or agency framework. Decisions about service are made at the administrative, programming, and staffing levels as well as with individuals and in the group, based on an assessment of need in light of focus, goal, and resources. Diagnostic thinking includes an awareness of the differential social functioning needs and strengths of the particular individuals which may be amenable to growth or change within the group experience. Diagnostic thinking also includes an assessment of the group as an entity in light of a theoretical formulation of the nature of groups.

The social group worker's interventions take the form of interaction or relationship with members and group, the facilitation of interpersonal relationships among members and promotion of group action through various group activities or program media toward the end of growth or change of the group and the individual members in accordance with members' and workers' goals determined in the diagnostic process.

The social group worker's constant evaluation of the process of growth and change taking place within the group and with the individual affect his intervention and methods of procedure.

TECHNICAL SKILLS

The technical skills of the social group worker exist in practice and are developed from clinical experience and the application of existent theory. The social group worker uses his knowledge, makes an assessment of the needs and strengths of the members and of the group, and intervenes with the group using a range of technical skills. Most of these technical skills remain to be described, elaborated, and operationalized, while others need to be tested for further theoretical support. Some of the technical skills of the social group worker which have been identified are as follows:

1. skill in relationship with members and in the facilitation of relationship between and among members
2. skill in diagnosis or assessment of the social functioning needs of individuals and of the group, using an integration of the several bodies of knowledge
3. skill in systematic observation and assessment of individuals, groups, social situations, and problems to determine need for service

4. skill in forming, continuing, and terminating groups
5. skill in intervention in group processes
6. skill in leadership in handling structure and authority, facilitating and guiding the group
7. skill in involvement of group members in planning and group activity
8. skill in analysis of program media and in use of program media with group
9. skill in recording
10. skill in use of agency resources
11. skill in facilitating the use of community resources
12. skill in use of professional judgment in choice of actions related to individuals and groups
13. skill in evaluation of professional activity and of individual and group movement
14. skill in communication of attitudes, feelings, and opinions

VALUES

Social group work practice as one of the methods of social work is influenced and bound by the philosophy, values, and ethics of the profession. It rests upon a belief in the dignity of all men and the social responsibility of men for their fellow men. The social group worker, therefore, accepts the specific responsibility to perform professional practice for the benefit of the group members and the welfare of society and works toward the extension of the democratic ideal.

Study Questions

1. Suppose group work had not become part of social work at the time that it did. How might social work with groups be different today? How would social group work be different had it identified more strongly with education? With recreation?

2. During an early controversy over purposes and direction, Vinter (1959) warned that group work was retreating from the "profession's historic mission of serving those most in need" and argued that group work resources should be redirected into rehabilitative and treatment areas. What do you see as the central mission of social work? Are the historic missions of social work and group work the same? Are they complementary or incompatible? Under what conditions should one give way to another. When should a mission be abandoned altogether? (See Sirls et al., Chapter 14, below.)

3. Which concepts and systems of thought derived from the early development of group work have particular significance in present-day practice? Which concepts do you think have the greatest potential for addressing future problems?

4. To what degree has social group work been used in realizing the potential values of group experience as outlined by Coyle? What progress, if any, has been made in providing professional group work services to assist in the maturation process? As a supplement to other relationships? In preparation for active citizenship? As a correction in social disorganization? In the treatment of intrapsychic maladjustments?

5. Coyle points out that in addition to the generic elements common to all social work, there are specific aspects of the group worker's function which need nurturing and development. What are the generic elements shared with casework, and community organization? What are the specifics unique to group work?

6. Thirty years ago, Newstetter (1948, p. 206) wrote, "Only a person with professional qualifications for social work practice would be able to use methods which would permit us to identify the resulting process as a social work process." Do you agree? Is a group worker engaged in casework whenever he/she works individually with one of the group members? Is a caseworker engaged in group work whenever he/she works with clients in a group? Is the method to be defined in terms of professional preparation and/or by the character of the activity? What, then, is the essence of the method?

7. Kaiser makes reference to certain elements that distinguish social group work processes from other disciplines. Do the same distinctions hold today? (See Alissi, Chapter 24, below.)

8. How do we stand today in regard to the goals issues outlined by Kaiser? What is the relative weight given to individuals versus groups; programming versus interaction; therapy versus development? In your view, does the "frame of reference" statement clarify any of the issues?

9. Has there been any significant progress made toward accomplishing the tasks suggested by Kaiser? Has there been a clearer delineation of social group work objectives? In what areas has the scientific basis of practice been broadened and deepened? Can you identify specific instances where research techniques have been applied to practice problems? How is recording used as a tool in practice today? To what extent are the generic as well as the specific elements of practice incorporated into professional education? Are students being adequately prepared to take on supervisory and administrative functions? Has there been a clearer definition of social group work relative to other professional disciplines?

10. The frame of reference statement makes it clear that the social group work method is influenced and bound by social work values. Are these values any different from those of "any good person" in our culture? Are there any differences between social work values and those of any of the related helping professions?

11. How would you go about updating the frame of reference statement? Do the basic purposes adequately cover the range of group work functions? Is there any significance to the order—correctional purposes being first and citizenship responsibility and participation being last? How would you update and make more specific the statement on knowledge? Which of the technical skills remain to be described, elaborated, and operationalized? Which need further theoretical support? Which skills would you consider to be at the core of practice? Which, if any, are unique to social group work?

Suggested Readings

DEAN, W. R., 1977. "Back to Activism," *Social Work*, Vol. 22, No. 5.

FELDMAN, R. A., and H. SPECHT, 1968. "The World of Social Group Work," *Social Work Practice, 1968.* Selected Papers 95th Annual Forum NCSW. New York: Columbia University Press.

KONOPKA, G., 1978. "The Significance of Social Group Work Based on Ethical Values," *Social Work with Groups*, Vol. 1, No. 2.

LANG, N. C., 1978. "The Selection of the Small Group for Service Delivery," *Social Work with Groups*, Vol. 1, No. 3.

LEVINSON, H. M., 1973. "Use and Misuse of Groups," *Social Work*, Vol. 18, No. 1.

LEVY, C. S., 1958. "Is Social Group Work Practice Standing Still?" *Social Work*, Vol. 3, No. 1.

——, 1976. *Social Work Ethics.* New York: Human Sciences Press.

MIDDLEMAN, R. R., 1978. "Returning Group Process to Group Work," *Social Work with Groups*, Vol. 1, No. 1.

NEWSTETTER, W. I., 1948. "The Social Intergroup Work Process," *Proceedings of National Conference on Social Work, Selected Papers, 1947.* New York: Columbia University Press.

PERNELL, R. B., 1973. "Social Group Work," *Goals for Social Welfare, 1973-1993*, H. B. Trecker, ed. New York: Association Press.

PUMPHREY, M., ed., 1959. *The Teachings of Values and Ethics in Social Work Education.* New York: Council on Social Work Education.

REID, W. J., 1977. "Social Work for Social Problems," *Social Work*, Vol. 22, No. 5.

ROSENTHAL, W. A., 1973. "Social Group Work Theory," *Social Work*, Vol 18, No. 5.

SHULMAN, L., 1969. "Social Work Skill: The Anatomy of a Helping Act," *Social Work Practice, 1969.* Selected Papers 96th Annual Forum of the National Conference on Social Welfare.

——, 1978. "A Study of Practice Skills," *Social Work*, Vol. 23, No. 4.

SPECHT, H., and A. VICKERY, eds., 1977. *Integrating Social Work Methods.* London: George Allen & Unwin.

TROPP, E., 1966. "The Further Development of Group Work as a Separate Method," *Social Work Practice, 1966.*

——, 1968. "The Group: In Life and in Social Work," *Social Casework*, Vol. 49.

VINTER, R., 1959. "Group Work: Perspectives and Prospects," *Social Work with Groups, 1959.* Selected Papers from the National Conference on Social Welfare. New York: National Association of Social Workers.

SECTION B

Early Orientations

The early writers had high expectations and few doubts about the value of group work in American society. Group work's greatest contribution was broadly conceived to be the experience it provided in social living. Recognizing that effective participation in a democratic society did not come about automatically, they believed that a good share of the responsibility for training for social participation rested with social group work. It was through the group that individuals could be helped to deal with the complexities of modern community life and to overcome the social obstacles that threatened social progress and, for that matter, civilization itself. This view did not, as some thought, divorce an interest in advancing social goals from a concern for promoting individuals growth and change. Indeed, it was the emphasis on developing "well-balanced personalities" as essential to good citizenship and social living that made group work unique among the helping professions. In the strong belief that the individual could not be separated from society, the small group experience was taken to be the most creative resource for advancing the well-being of both.

Drawing from many intellectual and ideological sources, the early orientations centered on such key concepts as democracy, social action, education, play, and individual and group adjustment. The articles contained in this section, written during group work's formative years, reflect these basic conceptions.

In his philosophical note, Lindeman emphasizes the value of group experiences in making democracy work. "Democracy" he declares, "becomes a farce, not because it has lost its ideal force, but because its devotees are, democratically speaking, illiterate; they do not know how to operate in and through groups." In the same vein, Grace Coyle searches for a practical frame of reference for educating people, whatever their level of functioning, to engage in meaningful social action. The educational emphasis was complemented by other conceptions, which stressed values of recreation, therapy, and related group experiences as important forms of adjustment. Neva Boyd's classic paper on play as a means of adjustment turned attention from instructive activities and competition in organized recreation to the social, psychological, and physiological benefits to be derived from meaningful involvement in planned but spontaneous play. How all of these ideas were integrated into workable principles to guide early practice is well illustrated in the chapter by Wilber Newstetter.

5

Group Work and Democracy—A Philosophical Note

Eduard C. Lindeman died in 1953, a few years after retiring from the faculty of the Columbia University School of Social Work, New York.

Eduard C. Lindeman

Those who sense the need for a democratic discipline, a social method for achieving social goals, find themselves involved in annoying polemical discussions. This annoyance arises from the fact that they themselves see so clearly that survival in a technological society depends upon our capacity to develop habits of collaboration, facilities for working in and through groups, and hence they cannot understand why others, and particularly those who seem to share their ultimate goals, remain so obtuse. But there are various ways in which this understanding of the essential nature of groupness arises in people's minds. In some cases this "sensing" of the group compulsion is a derivative of feelings and emotions; frequently it comes about as a consequence of logical reasoning and has little or nothing to do with the theorist's own social behavior; and, occasionally this conviction comes into consciousness as a result of functional experience. Psychologically, it would be preferable, of course, if the foregoing sequence were always reversed—that is, if advocates of group method could first learn its functional foundations, then proceed to evolve a rational framework, and finally enjoy the corroborative fulfillment of feelings. In actual experience it matters little, presumably, what point of departure leads one to social awareness so long as feelings, intelligence, and actions are ultimately integrated within the personality pattern.

It has been a growing notion on my part that the advocates of group work were weakest at the functional point. What the unconvinced really want to know is whether group work can be made efficient, and for what ends. The question that seems to disturb them

From *New Trends in Group Work*, edited by Joshua Lieberman. New York: Association Press, 1939, with permission of Follett Publishing Company.

most is: What functions are groups supposed to perform? Or stated otherwise, what can groups do that cannot be done better by means of individual initiative and energy? In André Maurois' exciting dialogue between an army lieutenant and a professor of philosophy,[1] the lieutenant in a testy tone says to his companion: " . . . a group is never capable of giving orders, not even for a luncheon. Do not forget that, had it not been for a few choice spirits, the Third Republic would undoubtedly be today the appanage of the German Empire. . . ." We may dismiss the last portion of this colloquy with a wry thought for the present dilemma of France and concentrate only on the lieutenant's assumption that giving commands or orders is considered by some to be the proper function of a group.

A moment's reflection focused upon the lieutenant's pronouncement will reveal that he has grossly oversimplified the situation. His experiences in the army—which is a mechanistic collection of individuals operating on behalf of goals and purposes with which they have had nothing to do—have no meaning for the processes of a civil democratic society. In the affairs of civil societies, except dictatorships, we must begin with an antithetical assumption—namely, that all valid leadership (a) exercises its functions as a response to group purposes, or (b) is a directional force that flows through the group and is hence qualified by the degree of friction there encountered, or (c) is a function performed through the group's coercive power. A leader can perform his appropriate functions for a group only when he is fully aware of the fact that coerciveness inheres in the group and not in him. "Every association, by the mere fact of its existence, is endowed with some coercive power, and actually exercises some such power in the course of pursuing its object."[2] Herein lies the essence of democratic theory—namely, that ultimate power resides in the people, in the collectivity. The people may, of course, delegate this power, but they can never forfeit it, because at that moment they cease to exist as a free society or an association of equals. Herein lies also the fatefulness of the problem of democratic methods and disciplines, because it now appears that people do not lose their sovereign power always by usurpation but also by reason of the fact that they use it so badly in crises. The non-democratic dominator can succeed only after the democratic process has broken down, after it has ceased to be an efficient instrument for satisfying human needs.

Those who advocate group methods find themselves in much the same dilemma as that of many so-called progressive educators: they become absorbed in the means and tend to become increasingly vague concerning the ends. What they do seems exciting enough, but the layman's straightforward question is: Toward what does it progress? This difficulty is probably not so serious as the second, which comes about when these enthusiasts attempt to construct an end out of what is essentially a means. If group work is another name for democratic process, then it should never be discussed as though it were an end, because democracy is not an end. When a method is transmuted into a goal, its reality tends to disappear. Thus, it is possible to cling to democracy as a goal and at the same time to develop behavior-patterns that are not merely undemocratic but which actually tend to destroy democracy at its core. Thus it happens in our time that one must be extremely critical toward those who repeat the word democracy, and especially toward those who extol its central value—namely, freedom. When one observes the tactics now being employed by those who are struggling against a further democratization of our economic system and at the same time base their reactionary claims upon freedom, one is tempted to paraphrase Madame Roland's famous cry of despair over Liberty. "O Democracy! O Democracy! how many crimes are committed in thy name!" From my point of view, the greatest of these crimes is not hypocrisy but the prevailing lazy attitude that prevents sentimental adherents of democracy from developing scientific methods for its realization. Democracy is neither a goal nor a gift. On the contrary, it is an exceedingly difficult mode of life that emerges as a result of certain kinds of experience and which places upon its participants an unusual form of responsibility.

As I observe varieties of contemporary experience, it appears to me that group work, either by design or by "accident," is utilized primarily in recreation, education, and in social organization—that is, in playing, learning, and administering. If a considerable proportion of those experiences which may be labeled as enjoyment, as learning, and as functional achievement were operating under a group-work discipline, I should have no further fears concerning the future of democracy; but unhappily, the examples that have come to my attention are characterized by scarcity. Now, one should not expect that a democratic culture will be democratic throughout; on the contrary, it would perhaps be healthier if there were obverse examples of non-democratic behavior. The real question is: how many non-democratic "lumps" can be tolerated in a democratic society? Playing, learning, and administering are merely three of the many zones of experience, but they happen to be the three upon which differentiated cultures mainly subsist. If those behavior patterns that result from leisure, learning, and social organization were all founded upon social methods, the democratic process would come about as a natural by-product of experience. However, another perplexity arises at this point.

The price we are obliged to pay for an ever-widening use of science and technology is increased conscious control over all the affairs of life. Secondary groups tend to supplant primary groups; and a secondary group comes into existence only through conscious organization. Organized recreation takes the place of undirected leisure, and each step in this direction elevates our consciousness with respect to leisure as a problem to be approached collectively. Concerning education, it may already be said that its organization and administration represent one of the major responsibilities of an orderly society. Each step in the increase of consciousness directed toward social control in these areas, as well as elsewhere, is likely to lead to a quick resort to the process known as "fixing authority." To fix authority means in most instances to centralize control. Thus it happens that our social compulsions lead us to utilize administrative devices that are the antithesis of social method. Once this process of fixing authority through centralization begins, one observes that all administrative units tend to become strata in various hierarchies of control. Thenceforward, the "front office" comes to have a symbolic meaning that is no longer functional but hierarchical. In fact, the "front office" may be said to be the symbol of non-democratic authority and methodology, and, alas, these front offices now exist in most of our enterprises, even those which, unlike business, aim to perform social functions.

Wherever there exists a "front office" and a front-office psychology, group method meets its nemesis. The principal difficulty with hierarchical authority is that it makes communication first difficult and later impossible. Group method can become an administrative facility only when communication is being enhanced and expanded. Many careless thinkers seem to believe that centralized authority and administrative hierarchies are necessary, or pardonable, on the grounds of expeditiousness or efficiency. They still allow for communication on the level of end-actions but they exclude communicativeness from policy-making. This means that an ever-increasing number of citizens will be expected to perform functions that they do not understand and to carry out policies for which the goals remain obscure. This procedure obviously excludes the masses from the most meaningful of all human activities—namely, the discussion and formulation of ends, goals, purposes, and values. Ultimately, it means, of course, that they will lose this capacity altogether, at which point they will not merely submit to dictatorial authority but will actually demand to be ruled.

Historically, it has been assumed that one sign of Anglo-Saxon genius is to be found in our habit of finding ways of delegating authority and of dispersing power. If this be genius, then it suffers as genius invariably does from lack of perspective. If power is to be dispersed, then everybody must be trained to exercise it. Our neglect with respect to the necessary training for democratic living is the chief factor in our present and shameful dilemma. Democracy becomes a farce, not because it has lost its ideal force but because its devotees are, democratically speaking, illiterate; they do not know how to operate in and through groups. And, precisely because we have neglected to train people for group life it now happens that much of our social activity is shot through and through with latent or overt elements of pathology. It is extremely difficult to adapt individuals to group life if they are incapable of comprehending the social realities of our time, if their experience is characterized by both inner and outer insecurities, and if they cling to a child's inexperienced attitude toward authority as such. A group is actually a threat to such individuals; they approach groupness with trepidations and fears; once in the group, their chief preoccupation is to maintain individual autonomy; every exercise of authority appears to them as a denial of freedom rather than a step toward order. Consequently, such individuals are not renewed and refreshed by group activity; on the contrary, it wearies and fatigues them, and at the first signal of release they hurry back to what seems to them to be independence, but which is in reality a most damaging form of insulation.

Still another remaining difficulty troubles me: the constant reference to quantity among the advocates of group work. They seem to me to be constantly worried about such matters as the number of groups in existence, the number of members in such groups, and the number of active participants. A preoccupation with quantity is likely to be a sign of insensitiveness concerning quality. Whenever democracy is reduced to quantitative levels, one may be certain that it has already lost its appeal as a mode of life. But, one must repeat over and over again, democracy is neither a goal nor a mechanical device for attaining a preconceived goal. It is at bottom a mode of life founded upon the assumption that goals and methods, means and ends, must be compatible and complementary if experience is to bear creative consequences. Whoever holds to this assumption must be essentially a "quality" person. Group work will not satisfy basic human needs if it merely quantifies and facilitates the democratic procedure; its major mission is to intensify the quality of life. Neither the "hard-boiled" administrator nor the sentimental group worshiper represents desirable qualities of personality, and ultimately group work must be measured in terms of its reflection in human personality. In one sense, it may be said that the function of group work is to determine whether or not we can produce persons who are both worthy of freedom and capable of utilizing its discipline in ministering to the common needs of their fellows.

NOTES

1. *Captains and Kings.*
2. G. D. H. Cole in *Social Theory*, Chapter VIII, "Coercion and Co-ordination."

6

Education for Social Action

Grace L. Coyle

In order to make clear exactly what we are discussing, I wish to begin by offering a definition of social action as it will be used in the following presentation. By social action, I mean collective action by a group directed toward some social or, perhaps better, societal end. In this sense not all group action is social action, although in one sense of the term it might be called such. The common practice, however, as it is developing in social work and elsewhere, is to reserve the term for action that is both done *by* a group and *for* social ends.

The significance of such action in the program of the group work agency rests fundamentally upon certain educational and social preconceptions that perhaps should here be made explicit. I am sure we are all agreed upon them, though we may differ as to their practical implications for program.

From an educational viewpoint, we, I assume, would agree (1) that one of our purposes is to contribute to the creation of a socially awakened and socially intelligent body of citizens; (2) that such a result can only be attained by an educational method that starts within the actual experience of the group and encourages the growth of a sense of social responsibility to the larger whole; (3) that such education cannot be a matter of words or ideas alone but must involve actual realistic experimentation and participation in social action—i.e., the use of social materials, just as we use other materials for other program purposes.

Behind such an educational philosophy, of course, lies a belief in democracy rather than dictatorship. (There seems to be no other choice.) And, further, a belief that our society could well be improved by various changes in laws, institutions, and customs, in order to provide adequately for the physical well being and personality growth of all its members. These two convictions taken together mean that one of the functions of a citizen in our democracy is to contribute to the progressive improvement of our social life through

From *New Trends in Group Work*, edited by Joshua Lieberman. New York: Association Press, 1939, with permission of Follett Publishing Company.

social change democratically determined upon and brought about by rational non-violent means.

If we believe vividly and whole-heartedly in these propositions, it is inevitable that as group workers we should aim to provide for the children and young people within our agency experience in social participation *at the level* at which they wish to and are capable of participating. We shall do this both because we believe the preservation and growth of our democratic society depends upon the development of such citizens and also because we believe the individual will find mature fulfillment in the identification of himself with a social whole to which he can worthily devote his powers. This implies no sacrifice of the individual to a mystic state, but merely that balance of individual liberty to develop, with the voluntary, critical, and intelligent participation in government upon which the social cohesion of a democracy depends.

Starting with this agreement on principle, I wish to devote this paper to certain practical aspects relating to how we can do this. Our chief problems in regard to methods within group work seem to me to lie in the areas of:

What are the places where the group touches some social issue?
How can we build an educational experience out of that contact?
What are the tests of success in this area?

The answers to these questions seem to me to differ so widely at different ages that I am going to discuss them in terms of three age groups—programs with young children under twelve, with adolescents up to twenty-one, and with young adults.

A program directed toward the ultimate purposes of social action which begins with young children must, to be sound educationally, rest firmly upon their emotional needs and intellectual development. We must be careful not to superimpose upon them adult motivations beyond their comprehension or expose them to severe emotional strains for which they are not equipped. There are certain characteristics of the child's experience that we must take into consideration in thinking of such a program. He is just emerging from the shelter of the family into the group life of the school and playground, his capacities for socialized contacts with others are just developing—i.e., he is just learning to give as well as take. His only experience with authority is that which comes from parents or parent substitutes. His imagination is often vivid, and imaginative play is at its height. His group relations usually are unstable, shifting, and undefined. He is usually less aware of the social barriers common to the community, nationality, economic class, etc., than he will become in adolescence. He is primarily interested in those of his own sex. (For corroboration of the last three statements I should like to refer to Moreno's studies in group relations in *Who Shall Survive.*) On such a basis, what kind of group activities can be developed that will start the process of creating the socialized citizen?

His need for socializing contacts, for broadening his ability to make social contacts with his peers can and is met through many forms of group experience in the open-club group or interest group. The first step toward wider social interests is often that which he makes in the play group and the club. Those experiences, I am assuming, will have certain ultimate outcomes related to his wider social attitudes. More specifically and directly, however, the agency may provide the basis for a gradual socializing process. This seems to be done, where it is being done at present, in two ways—either through imaginative experience in make-believe communities or in actual experimentation in some very elementary experiences in social action.

The imaginative experience is best illustrated by the type of program used, for example, in the Children's Village of the Smith Memorial Playgrounds in Philadelphia. Here a group of about 120 children with the assistance of about eight adults set up on two afternoons a week a make-believe community with its homes, schools, theatre, streets, bank, post office, hospital, etc. A wide range of functions have to be performed. Mothers, nurses, postmasters, bankers, teachers, waitresses, etc., assume the responsibilities required. The adult assistants help where they are needed, and, in discussion with groups of mothers, nurses, teachers, storekeepers, etc., provide some guidance. The genius of the plan lies, however, in its being motivated by the children's, not the adults', imagination. Its flexibility and freedom to change about frequently allow for the unstable group relations and short interest span of that period. Its situations provide excellent opportunity for learning to perform community functions graded to the ability of the group. One interesting question is raised in this connection. The psychological age of these children in the so-called latency period creates an inability to dramatize the complete family, so that all the families have mothers only, the boys appearing as policemen, storekeepers, officials, etc., but practically never as fathers. Its necessary incompleteness at this point raises certain questions but it does not vitiate its value, I believe, in much that can be taught through it of the first steps toward social responsibility.

Even young children however can under some circumstances play some part in the actual community as well. A recent report from one settlement describes a children's club that undertook to reform its neighborhood, concentrating at the children's suggestion on its cleanliness, health, and safety. Their activities began with a survey and the making of a map showing points needing improvement. The city health officer was invited to talk with them, and the Street Commissioner and the Chief of Police gave them advice. As a result, definite proposals emerged, including more refuse cans, better garbage collection, policemen on dangerous corners. Incidentally, a good deal of education was secured on dangerous habits of play. The chief value of the project lay in the experience it provided the children in actually fashioning their environment nearer to their desire and in doing so by a real dealing with the authorities involved.

Other groups have made play spaces out of unsightly vacant lots, planned and carried through safety campaigns among children, work on insect control and many similar projects.

In my first year in settlement work in the Old College Settlement on Rivington Street, I remember the heroic if sometime ineffective work of the Civic League of small boys who braved the heavy-handed mothers of the neighborhood in their attempts to enforce the tenement house laws on lighting and fire escapes. There was, I believe, sound education in that idea. Certainly, if we can do anything to shape social attitudes in this period, it lies in diverting to actual social purposes some of the energy of childhood and also in using at points the imaginary and therefore more controllable element of play. Many opportunities for such improvement lie about us certainly, and in some of these, the interest and enthusiasm for activity of some of our children's groups could be turned to account. If such activity really struck down roots into the children's own motivations and if their experience with it is successful enough to encourage further experiment, we may have started the sprouts of intelligent social action.

All of these suggestions may seem exceedingly mild to be called social action. They are merely seed beds for social rather than an anti-social attitude. They do not bring children into contact with major social evils or enlist them in social causes. We know, however, that a large number of our children are themselves drawn into the more violent or more vicious aspects of our social life. Their parents are on strike; they watch the picket lines, or sometimes walk in them; they see the police in action; on such occasions they know what unemployment means in overcrowding and underfeeding; they meet race prejudice when they step out of the door. We do not yet know what distortions in personality are caused by such experience with social violence and group hostility in the early years. It is a field yet to be explored by the psychiatrists and for which, in its extreme forms, only careful individual care can perhaps deal with the results. But while we wait for more expert help, we must deal with the situation as best we can. We can perhaps interpret the conflict in understandable terms where possible, directing emotions to helpful and positive outlets where we can and providing harmless outlets for the hostilities engendered if nothing else is possible. We can provide within the agency at least an experience of friendly acceptance and appreciative understanding that may serve to counteract a little bitterness of the social struggle which is too intense for children to endure without injury.

When we are dealing with the adolescent age, we have obviously a very different situation. Adolescents are themselves consciously facing problems that are rooted in the social scene. They are trying to get jobs, often unsuccessfully. They are terribly conscious of their own need for more clothes, more space, better homes, more money for recreation. They are at the same time surging with new and upsetting emotions. They are beginning to be absorbed in the opposite sex. They are freeing themselves from parental control. As Dr. Redl, director of the Guidance Clinic in Vienna, recently pointed out to the Conference of the Progressive Education Association, it is normal for adolescents to form together in groups and to develop intense group emotions. They are seeking emotional security through intensive group satisfaction. Such groups easily fall a prey to dictators who use them for their own social purposes. Their great potentiality needs to be recognized by educators, in order that this perfectly normal need for group experience can be met in *socially* constructive ways. As one looks at what we are offering to such adolescents in the group work agency to meet their need for group experience and to tie up their incipient social idealism to worth-while ends, one is inclined to feel discouraged. In some places we provide a program chiefly of games and sports plus arts, crafts, and social clubs, but I have often asked in vain when I inquired for any activities that encourage wider social attitudes. I am not, of course, talking about the old fashioned "service" project that runs from Christmas baskets to entertaining the old ladies or the orphans in a nearby institution. The contribution of such programs to vital social understanding or to democratic attitudes is questionable to say the least. They date back to a period of noblesse oblige rather than to a conception of a democratic community. Nor am I referring to the familiar "citizenship" programs, carried out with flags and ceremonies, which teach loyalty and conformity rather than critical judgment and active participation.

What we must find rather is opportunities for young people of the adolescent age to take hold of problems in the community closely related to their interests, within their range, and providing them with satisfying experience in actually getting things done. Such opportunities lie about us, I believe, all the time. We need chiefly an awareness of the young person's own needs, his reaction to his social situation, and an ingenuity in following the leads he gives us. I remember a leader of a group of adolescent girls who told me about a discussion in her club where a strike occurred in the neighborhood. Some of the girls were the children of workers, some of foremen, so the strike re-appeared within the club meeting. When I asked her how she dealt with it, she said, "Oh, we went for a nature walk that day." A similar opportunity occurred last year in a club of newsboys, led by one of our students, in which the question of organization came up. The boys had been told by a union representative they had to give $5.00 to the union. The club at its next meeting burst into violent debate. I asked the leader what he did, and he replied, "Well I told them it was probably just a racket, and let it go at that." Innumerable instances like this will occur to all of us. Here are the openings. Here is the group ready for leadership. What can we do to turn these opportunities to account? It is not by any means impossible.

I talked last summer with a boy's worker in a neighborhood where the tense racial feeling culminated some years ago in a serious race riot. Community attitudes are reflected within the settlement in a drawing apart of colored and white children, as soon as they reach adolescence, into separate clubs between which bad feeling has been common. He has set out to redirect that feeling into constructive channels, to develop a *common* concern in the *common* property of the house, instead of allowing one group to usurp the game room and the other the gym, as has been the case. He has built a club council which is inter-racial and which last winter spent much time in discussing current social questions, such as unemployment, which they were all—both colored and white—facing. Racial attitudes have changed imperceptibly through common enterprises, so that a council supper finally became possible, which symbolized a remarkable shift from previous community attitudes. This is simple but basic. It is familiar talk to most of us, but not yet current practice, so far as I can discover, in many neighborhoods facing racial conflicts. It takes sensitivity, persistence, imagination, but the adolescent is able and willing to co-operate if we know how to use our group contacts for educational ends.

Other instances, of course, can be quoted, in which more direct action was involved. An account recently published of an incident in New York City gives an instance perhaps familiar to many of you. A tenement house fire had cost the lives of several children in the neighborhood. As a result, the children gathered in the settlement to discuss what might be done to prevent such occurrences. Out of it grew a protest parade of 700 children to the City Hall. A housing committee of 15- to 19-year-olds was organized, who studied housing, sent representation for a hearing to Albany, circularized the community, reported violations of the tenement house law, and in other ways organized public opinion. The results apparently were not only valuable education for the children but actually had some results in improved protection. I presume all of us here could cite some similar illustrations of social action program with adolescent groups.

What are the characteristics of a successful program of this sort with adolescents? The first necessity of course is to begin at the point where the first sprout of social interest is evident and to cultivate that. Such projects must allow for activity—the doing of things—not simply talking. They must contain experiences within the range of the group and they must result in observable improvement, if possible, so that further action is encouraged.

The social idealism of the callow years, when it appears, needs to be recognized and met, not ridiculed or suppressed. But it should be encouraged to try itself out on tough reality, not spend itself in sentimentalism. The expenditure of emotion without the invigorating necessity of dealing with the facts as they are is especially dangerous and is good preparation for the emotionalized appeals of the mass movements of youth like those in the totalitarian states. That is why action—experience in doing—is so essential a part of social education at this period. Otherwise it is likely to evaporate in many instances in candlelight ceremonies and pink cheesecloth figures representing Peace or in semi-military maneuvers with a superpatriotic flavor, equally ungeared to what is happening down the street. An ounce of realistic experience is worth a pound of sentimentality.

The attitude toward authority during this period is of particular importance both to individual growth and to attitudes toward society. Society and its good comes to stand in the role of parent, controlling and directing. Some adolescents react to the social problems they face by an assumption that some remote "they" are responsible. This reflects the absent but controlling parent some of us never give up. This attitude can well become the basis for later dependency and social inertia. Others adopt a blind following of some idolized leader. This is the seed bed for dictatorship. Others for various emotional reasons revolt against all authority. This is a good root for delinquency. If they are to become responsible citizens, the attitudes toward authority must gradually shift during adolescence until they themselves become identified with the society, in which authority rests. Projects and programs, therefore, which provide active experience in protecting safety, or health, building playgrounds, enforcing laws, formulating improvements, instead of their opposites, may help to produce the identification with the creative and constructive authorities. This is both socially useful in what is actually accomplished and individually developing. As they develop through adolescence, the projects can become more difficult, the action more socially significant. The important thing is that we help them to find their way toward an alignment with the constructive forces in realistic experience emotionally satisfying and intellectually developing.

With the third group, the young adult over twenty-one, we have, I believe, a rather different problem. These people are usually already at work; many of them are settling down, getting married, and thinking about the future. They are voting citizens and already enrolled in some instances in political parties. They are members of unions, or may become so. They are entering upon mature life. And yet many of them do so with no outlook beyond their personal concerns, inert rather than anti-social, unawakened to the larger world. We have a great responsibility here, I think, not to direct social thinking but to awaken it, and to help people to find the way to function effectively at any point where their interests may lie.

There are as I have seen in three major devices helpful in this period—the provision of study classes that give consistent opportunity for enlarging knowledge, projects of all kinds that interest a larger number for shorter periods, and contacts and affiliations with various movements promoting causes of one kind or another.

Experience in the workers education schools and elsewhere suggest that serious study of social questions hardly ever can be expected much before twenty-one, but from there on a certain group, limited it is true, but significant, can be interested. For those few, classes, summer schools, etc., should be available. Because so few exist in any one agency, the Chicago experiment with a Social Problems Club drawn from all the agencies may be the best way to meet their need and to spread the stimulus to the less interested. An inter-settlement workers education committee of young people in Cleveland has had some success with similar inter-agency discussions and a week-end conference. Leaders' groups of old club members of all kinds are often also available for similar educational projects.

Although consistent study may be confined to a few, there is no reason why large numbers should not be drawn into various occasional projects. A bill in the legislature affecting them, a strike or an organizing campaign in which they are involved, a local political issue, all provide opportunities for active participation and analysis of that experience.

One of the most significant developments among youth today is the growth of organizations aiming at economic improvement. Dozens of these affiliated with political parties, churches, lodges, etc., have sprung up since the depression. Some, such as the American Youth Congress, aim to co-ordinate existing groups. The relation of groups inside the agencies to such movements is a crucial one. They have certain great advantages to offer our members. They provide wider acquaintance and the stimulus of a large movement. On the other hand, they open the way to the manipulation of the innocent. However, young adults today must learn to live in the midst of pressure groups, to understand their habits, to know how to use them and to control them democratically. As in everything, there is no way to learn without experiencing. It is not our function to try to keep young adults in a kind of sterilized social nursery uncontaminated from the polution of actual economic and political struggles, and fed only such social ideas as we or our boards may approve. It may be rather to provide a place where such experience can be discussed, its wider implications seen, and the learning from it clarified for use in renewed experimentation.

How do we gauge our success with this group? I should say for one thing we ought to scan our departments to see how many young adults we have whose interests have matured and widened to the place where they have any real concern on public questions. Where it has developed, we need to ask ourselves, how intelligent is it, how well founded in the needed knowledge, how adapted to reality not dogma, how implemented with satisfactory means to carry it out? It is only on some such basis that we can content ourselves that we have fulfilled our function as educators.

Administrative problems are likely to arise in connection with such programs. Those in executive positions are sometimes removed from the actual contact so that they do not always understand such activities. Boards are not always sympathetic and community chests not always enthusiastic. Time does not permit here the discussion of these problems. I should like, however, to say one thing only. I believe it is a part of our professional ethics as educators in a democracy to uphold the necessity for thought and discussion on controversial social issues among our membership, and more than that to see that such discussion can result in action when the group desires it. Anything short of this is not true education. It sounds harmless, perhaps, but all of us who have tried it know that to win the opportunity for such education requires the development of a new tradition of "academic freedom" in the field of informal education such as that which we have struggled to maintain in the colleges.

If that right can be maintained, the technical details of administration can be worked out. Upon that we, as group workers, must develop I believe an immovable conviction. Let us remember in these days the words of Justice Brandeis: "The greatest menace to freedom is an inert people."

7

Play as a Means of Social Adjustment

Neva Boyd pioneered in training programs in recreation, play theory, and social group work and was for a long time associated with Northwestern University. She died in 1963.

Neva L. Boyd

The prevalence of such forms of play as games, dancing, and sports throughout the world—in the most highly developed civilized social orders and in the lowest primitive cultural groups—provokes inquiry among those of us who are promoters of play. What does this prevalence of play mean, and what is its significance for us? We are aware that cultural groups—tribes and nations—have developed within themselves patterns of play common to all of them, some of which we label games. These games are essentially human *play-behavior* patterns, for traditional games are folkways or ways of behaving which tend, in a general way, to become patterned and set. In some of their simpler forms they are patterned by the functioning of the physical body in running, jumping, climbing, kicking, throwing, and so forth; but games are by no means confined to such elementary forms and obvious types of behavior. They range from the simple to the highly complex, and involve not only bodily functioning but the most subtle emotional and social behavior as well. The simpler forms arise independently in practically all cultural groups, and even though different cultures develop game patterns peculiarly their own, many of them are readily assimilated into other cultures.

Such dramatic events in everyday life as the capture of slaves, the going to market, and tribal combat may constitute the basis of board games similar in general pattern to backgammon and chess. The dramatic incident that gives rise to the game may fade out as the game passes from generation to generation or from one to another cultural group, but the pattern of the logical social process remains intact and stands out clearly, even as the patterns of cities seen from

Reprinted from *New Trends in Group Work*, edited by Joshua Lieberman. New York: Association Press, 1939, with permission from the *Journal of Health, Physical Education and Recreation*, where it was originally published.

an airplane become more vivid as the details disappear. Only through the perspective afforded by an extensive study of games, however, can these patterns be discovered.

Just as mathematics is a way or manner of thinking, so play is a way of social behaving. Thus, when games, used as educational nutriment, are well correlated with the growth and development of the players, they induce normal patterns of social play-behavior, characteristic of no other activity. Moreover, the players abstract or "learn," each according to his own growth, development, and sensitivity. Much of this "learning" is on the unverbalizable, or, as Korzybski terms it, the unspeakable level.

Do we realize when a player runs and catches a fly ball that he is behaving "intelligently" in a four-dimensional world but that it takes the physicist to make the theoretical abstraction? The player *experiences* on the unverbalizable level and the physicist talks about it on the intellectual level—a thing he could never do had he not himself had similar *experience* on the unverbalizable level. Much of learning and, in fact, much of living inevitably takes place on this level.

Games afford unique experience on the unverbalizable level, and, because the events of the game occur in such close sequence (are so restricted in time and space), cause-effect relations are more meaningful to the player; hence he abstracts more than he does in less meaningful situations. Both because play is meaningful and because in its more elementary forms it is essentially "primitive" behavior, it is easily invoked. This explains why all peoples, even the mentally deficient and the insane, play so readily.

A man released from the Chicago State Hospital for the insane related his experience with play as follows:

"I knew I was insane, but I couldn't pull myself out of it. Every day we were taken out to the play field where the attendant kept us sitting on the benches doing nothing. One day I looked up and saw a new attendant. He had a ball in his hand. I stood up and he threw the ball to me. The instant it struck my hands it was as if my spine was frozen. We threw the ball back and forth for a little while. I was perspiring and so exhausted I could hardly walk, but for the first time I knew I could be cured. It was the 'feel' of that ball in my hands that made me sure. It went all through my body the way it did when I played ball as a boy."

In response to this man's request, he was allowed to work in the occupational therapy department, which activity may be considered as manual play, and, within a year, was released from the hospital, cured.

More than twenty-five years ago, the principal of a public grade school employed a play leader in preference to a physical education teacher for the purpose of creating better social relations among the children. In the first grade was a little boy who had been there for two years. Although he had never been able to learn anything in the academic subjects, he was permitted to join the other first grade children in a twenty-minute, daily play period. He labored under two distinct handicaps—poor muscular development and co-ordination, and mental retardation. His behavior indicated utter frustration. The play leader took him by the hand and helped him through the games even though it was apparent they were meaningless for him. After about three months he began to "wake up," as the play leader expressed it, and to take initiative in the games. The primary teacher also observed his awakening interest in the classroom. Before the end of the school year the boy was playing games intelligently and running as fast as the other children, although he still showed some signs of poor co-ordination. In a period of three years (with no extra tutoring or special treatment of any kind) it was evident, by his activity on the playground and by the fact that he was doing better than average academic grade work of children of his own chronological age, that he had completely overcome his physical and mental handicaps.

These appear to be cases of blockage that one might expect would be released by play. No such prognosis is ordinarily made, however, for institutional cases of mental deficiency, and yet an experiment in the Lincoln (Illinois) State School and Colony (for mental defectives), in which active recreation is given to approximately two thousand patients, has resulted in phenomenal success.

Seventy boys who previously sat hour after hour in idleness later play good enough basketball to win their share of games in competition with teams from the local high schools; girls whose intelligence quotients range from forty to firty-nine mastered dances of the type taught to high-school girls of normal mentality, and a band of approximately sixty low-grade men, ranging in chronological age from eighteen to forty-six years, learned more than two hundred popular tunes, which they played on kazoos.

The work at the Lincoln State School reveals that the play program for the mentally deficient differs only slightly from that of normal children, the chief difference lying in the more limited ability of the mentally deficient and their total inability to play games having intellectual content.

There is no mystery about this when these activities are seen to be human play-behavior patterns produced by normal play-behavior and, in turn, inducing similar behavior. Games are chiefly group play-behavior; hence, they serve a unique purpose in development. They may be classified on the basis of various dominant factors, such as special types of bodily skills, social organization, co-operative interaction, team play, and intellectual content, and arranged in a scale on the basis of these factors. Such classification reveals the fact that a complex game may embody a great many different factors that coincide variously with the abilities of the players. Thus, individual equipment and potential capacity determine what the players put into and get out of the game.

Obviously, then, players may express simultaneously different levels of intelligence in the same game, just as persons differently equipped may deal on widely different levels of intelligence with the same data of another type. We know, for example, that the skilled mechanic and the trained engineer may deal with essentially the same problem but on different levels. The mechanic who has no theoretical knowledge of mathematics or physics may work successfully but necessarily on a lower level of intelligence or, more correctly, make abstractions of a lower order than does the engineer who knows the theory of physics. Both, however, deal with the same basic problem and, to some degree, with the same set of facts, although the engineer is aware of factors of which the mechanic knows nothing and can, therefore, deal with abstractions of a higher order.

The playing of an organized game parallels the experience of the mechanic and the engineer—the game admitting a range of play from a low level comparable to that of the mechanic to a higher level comparable to that of the engineer. The game of dominoes, for example, may be played on a low level by a child who plays without calculating more than the immediate result of his moves or it may be played on a higher level by one who determines his moves on the basis of all the exposed pieces and calculates both the immediate and remote results, and thus raises his play to a higher intellectual level without altering the fundamentals of the game pattern. Further, a playing group may include a range of intelligence comparable to that of the mechanic and the engineer, and yet the game may result in the social adjustment of all the players.

Another significant fact is that when the fundamentals of the game pattern are kept stable, even though there is considerable variation in the ability of the players, they are disciplined by being held to a pattern of behavior that has been created by generations of players. This discipline contributes to both the stabilization of the nervous system and to the social adjustment of the person.

So significant are the dominant factors in these play-behavior patterns in their effect upon persons socially, physiologically, and psychologically that a form which the dance represents should be included, for the dance is the same general type of behavioristic pattern as the game and, like the game, is essentially "primitive"; so primitive, indeed, that we make any type of event the occasion for its legitimate expression.

Dancing, then, must be included in this discussion even though I am incapable of analyzing its more profound aspects. When it is analyzed in terms of physiological and social behavior patterns, an immeasurable contribution will have been made to the theory of both education and psychiatry.

A type of dance closely related to the game and commonly called the folk dance—the dance of the people—is characterized by the spirit of play. Such dances have sprung up, like games, as forms of play and are danced for the pleasure they afford the dancers themselves rather than to influence fate, as do the ceremonial dances of primitive and many civilized peoples, or an audience, as do the artistic dances of the professional stage.

When we use these play-behavior patterns—games and dances—in education in the free style that characterizes their production, we bring this aspect of educational practice into line with organized and ordered group behavior by stimulating the functioning of the individual in his group relation. In other words, we create the conditions conducive to the functioning of the organism as a whole. Such educational procedure inevitably stimulates a healthy functioning of the nervous system and gives order and unity to group behavior. Therefore, a well-selected program that is co-ordinate with the growth and development of the person raises the behavior progressively to higher levels, for the game and the dance are patterns embodying not only "primitive" behavior but its higher social and psychological aspects as well.

Since one of the most subtle aspects of this play-behavior is the psychological, I shall attempt to analyze it. What is the psychological condition which makes games play instead of dull routine or boresome regimentation?

A play situation is a situation temporarily and imaginatively set up, and a game is such a play situation determined by rules and roles. Figuratively speaking, the act of playing is psychologically picking oneself up from a genuine situation and setting oneself down in an imaginative one and acting consistently within that situation; that is, not only complying with the rules and play the assigned roles of the game, but functioning co-operatively with other players in the process of doing so. As soon as the game is ended, the whole psychological structure of the game is dissolved.

Apparently this is what happens in a dramatic cast on the stage, but in this type of situation the audience vicariously enters into the situation and acts imaginatively with the actors until the curtain goes down.

We are all aware of the fact that the amateur actor must psychologically keep *in character* if he is to hold his audience. We are familiar with the phenomenon of the amateur losing his audience the moment he is psychologically diverted from the situation of the play and his role in relation to it; in other words, when he "gets out of character."

Playing a game is psychologically different in degree but not in kind from dramatic acting. The ability to create a situation imaginatively and to play a rôle in it is a tremendous experience, a sort of vacation from one's everyday self and the routine of everyday living. We observe that this psychological freedom creates a condition in which strain and conflict are dissolved and potentialities are released in the spontaneous effort *to meet the demands of the situation.*

If this psychological condition is present, it is sufficient inducement to make the players put into the game their sense of what it requires in effort, co-operation, and voluntary obedience to the rules. If it is not present, it makes necessary the injection of forms of stimulation extraneous to the game pattern in order to control the behavior of the players. One of the forms of such stimulation most commonly employed is an overemphasis on competition, which I contend is wholly unnecessary, provided the psychological condition, as I have described it, is present.

I want to make my point of view on competition clear. A study of games offers sufficient proof that competition is inherent in many of them. I accept competition, then, because it is a fact and, I think, of value not only in play but in life. A game may be conceived as a problem, and those who *play* it accept the challenge for its solution. Competition has no element of jealousy, envy, hatred, or unfairness; it is a process of abetting one another in progressively greater achievements in individual effort and in co-operative group interaction in which winning is not the chief source of enjoyment, but only one incident, even though an important one, in that it marks the final step in the solution of the problem. Thus, each repetition of a game, even when played with the same competitors, constitutes a new configuration, and hence it is a new problem and inevitably brings forth a new procedure or series of acts in its solution.

I contend that rewards of any kind, even an overemphasis on winning, with its concomitant publicity, cheering, flag waving, and the like, tend to divert interest from the solution of the problem itself and to make these extraneous factors the chief objectives of play. This would defeat largely all I have claimed for play.

Gambling is but an extreme example of this tendency. The gambler does not play the game for the enjoyment of pitting his wits against his opponent in solving the problem, but, on the contrary, he uses a game as a means of getting his opponent's money. In fact, the gambler is not interested in the game; he is interested in the stakes, a thing totally extraneous to the game itself. By substituting publicity, rewards, and points for the gambler's stakes, are we not tending to kill intrinsic interest in the game? When that interest is killed, players are like jaded gamblers, dead to everything but the extraneous rewards.

Competition, then, has its rightful place, because it is an inherent part of many games, but it has no place in many of them nor in such sports as swimming, skiing, and skating, which are not competitive in any sense and when they are made so they tend to lose their intrinsic value for the participants.

Play and sports are similar to, if not actually of, the arts. When the peasant woman, for instance, puts beautiful embroidery on her blouse, when her husband plays folk tunes on his concertina, or when the Indian woman shapes a bowl into a fine design, it is for their intrinsic value and because there is inherent in human nature a tendency to bring the object world into unity and harmony. Traditional games, many sports, and dances are structurally art designs, and one familiar with good design readily detects a poor one. To illustrate: I saw a Danish teacher give a class of Y.W.C.A. physical-education teachers what she called folk games. As I watched her, I noted that she had taken good *units of design*—that is, traditional dance figures—and combined them so that they did not make a good design. The combined elements did not express unity; the dancers did not move easily and naturally from one figure to another. I knew enough about folk games and dances to be sure these were "teacher" created and not "folk" created, and, upon inquiry, I found this to be true.

Just as we are disturbed by a bad design in our wall paper, whether we know anything about the theory of art or not, so we are disturbed by those poor designs in the game and the dance. Conversely, good designs give us a sense of harmony, because they are in harmony with what we might call organismal behavior.

One factor in the art aspect of play, then, is structure, or design, and another is that psychological point I have argued.

I anticipate a question: "How can a teacher create this psychological condition?" I answer: "By choosing such traditional play patterns as I have suggested and by herself getting psychologically into the situation and permitting the players to do so through freedom of action." When this psychological condition is present, the players are stimulated to action in a meaningful situation, which compels normal physiological functioning and ordered group action. When conditions prevent such functioning, the person is ill adjusted in relation to both his physical and social environment.

Because all these physiological, psychological, and social factors are dynamic and functional in human behavior, those of us whose work contributes largely to the determination of the behavior of children during the period of most rapid growth and impressionability may well be guided by the contributions of science in fields related to our own.

You no doubt recall that Pavlov created conditioned reflexes in the dogs with which he experimented by placing a plate of food before them simultaneously with the sounding of a buzzer. After several repetitions the buzzer was sounded without the food being present and the dogs salivated as if it were present. With repetitions of this latter performance—sounding the buzzer without the appearance of food—the dogs not only gradually ceased to salivate but manifested inertia, in some cases even going to sleep. To understand this inertia, it is necessary to understand Pavlov's explanation of the normal function of excitation and inhibition. When the excitation is such that it is carried on nerve fibers to more than one part of the brain, some must be inhibited while others function. When, in the case of the dog, all were inhibited, he manifested inertia; and when inhibition extended over the whole surface of the cortex, sleep resulted. When the dog refused to "respond" to the buzzer—that is, to salivate—after repeated omission of the food, Pavlov deduced the theory of partial "cortical sleep."

Are we not justified, then, in concluding that all frustration tends to create corresponding inertia and that normal functioning is thus interrupted? It is therefore apparent that the resolution of conflicting impulses is essential to a healthy functioning of the nervous system.

We know from experience that the play situation, so largely comprised of unverbalizable play-behavior patterns—the events of which occur in close sequence in time and space—and the psychological attitude of play constitute a unique condition for compelling meaningful action. And this action results in physiological and social adjustment.

8

Regulatory Principles

Prior to his death in 1972, Wilber Newstetter was a former Dean and Professor Emeritus, School of Social Work, University of Pittsburgh, Pennsylvania.

Wilber I. Newstetter

The selection and application of techniques and methods must be considered in the light of regulatory principles. Group work is in the early stages of defining regulatory principles. Any that are tentatively defined at this date are based, we realize, on what might be called a doubtful admixture of generalized knowledge gleaned from various disciplines including philosophy. They will need considerable revision in the light of better understanding in and of the social sciences, and the experience of a wider company of group workers than is represented by the Western Reserve group. It is therefore with these limitations in mind that we make so bold as to present below the embryonic tentative principles which we use at the School of Applied Social Sciences in courses on Principles of Group Work and Group Analysis. . . .

GROUP FORMATION AND ORGANIZATION

1. The deliberate formation of a new group should be encouraged only after the careful review of three considerations: a. the interests, abilities, experiences and needs of each prospective individual member; b. the agency's purposes; c. the availability of suitable facilities, leadership and supervision.

2. Organization within the group should be developed only in response to interest and need expressed by the group members; form of organization should be adapted to the purposes to be served by organization.

Reprinted from *Group Adjustment: A Study in Experimental Sociology*, by Wilber I. Newstetter, Marc J. Feldstein and Theodore M. Newcomb. Cleveland: School of Applied Social Sciences, Western Reserve University, 1938, with permission from Case Western Reserve University.

DISCOVERY OF INTERESTS, NEEDS, ETC.: DEVELOPMENT OF PROGRAM

3. The needs of individual group members and the germs of social purpose within the group comprise the basic material for which the worker searches; group activities should involve the relating of these basic factors to some framework of reference consisting of wider social needs and social purposes.

4. Interests of group members may be classified into three types: a. expressed interests, i.e., interests expressed by group members; b. inferred interests, i.e., interests inferred from expressed interests; c. assumed interests, i.e., interests assumed by the worker to be held by group members.

5. Interests of group members may be discovered by the worker through observation, through sharing experiences with the members, through exploratory periods of group activity, and through employing devices such as games, tests, exhibits, visits, reading, etc. Expressed interest frequently provides a clue to need.

6. As far as possible interests should be elicited from group members and developed through direct activity.

7. The so-called "laws of learning" should be employed by the worker.

8. The worker may initiate an activity which may interest the group and lead to associated interests. As far as possible present opportunities for a choice of activity.

9. As a general rule the workers' plans for activities should be easily abandoned in favor of those emanating from the group.

10. Activities should depend upon response to proposed activity; duration of activities upon response to activity itself. If possible, activities should last long enough to give satisfaction of accomplishment. "Kill an activity before it dies," that is, if you do not want to kill interest.

11. Activities should aim: a. to be as representative as possible of interests held in common by group members, b. to be as appropriate as possible for meeting common needs. But, in accordance with the general purpose of individualization, division of labor in connection with a multiple activity or project may afford opportunity to develop and the varied interests of different individuals simultaneously, and at the same time to meet specific yet different needs of particular group members.

12. Initial activities should be simpler and of shorter duration while individual interests and needs are being discovered, and while social objectives are being discovered and formulated; subsequent activities should increase demands upon individuals and the group

for: duration, creativeness, effort, skill, responsibility, concentration, cooperation, and social action, etc.

13. Avoid the emphasis on repression of undesirable modes of behavior except in extreme circumstances. Distract attention from less desirable patterns by emphasizing and approving more desirable patterns; as far as possible encourage those desirable patterns which occur spontaneously.

14. The activity or program is not *the* thing; it is only one *means* to be employed in providing the setting and environment for the growth and group acceptance of specific individuals, and for both passing on and evolving desirable cultural patterns.

DEVELOPMENT OF THE INDIVIDUAL AND ADJUSTMENT IN THE GROUP

15. The social adjustment of a given individual to a given group at a given time may be called the group adjustment of the individual. It is a function of time, a dynamic entity.

16. By group adjustment of an individual is meant the *quality or degree of his relationship with the other members of a particular group at a given time.*

17. The general concept of relationship may be described in terms of one entity taking position or status with reference to another or other entities. In the case of social relationship this means one person taking position or status with reference to another or other persons.

18. Accepting as a definition of group: "Two or more persons in a relationship of psychic interaction, whose relations with one another may be extracted and distinguished from all others so that they may be thought of as an entity," and applying it to the face-to-face primary group, we may define the three basic entities of group as: a. physical compresence; b. consciousness of kind or "we" feeling which may be called psychological bond; c. the manifestations of psychic interaction behaviors.

19. Applying the concept of social relationships to the basic entities of primary group, we have the basis for three possible measures of the quality or degree of primary group adjustment: a. compresence or physical proximity; b. bond or psychic proximity; c. interactions or behaviors *between* individuals, from and to individuals, bridging the gap or distance between them.

20. In order to distinguish group adjustment thus defined from other definitions of group adjustment, we may call it *group acceptance.*

21. This scheme of interpretation of group adjustment or accep-

tance should be distinguished from schemes of interpretation of individual behavior. Both are necessary.

22. Since there are two points of reference in the "distance" concept as here applied and interpreted, namely the individual and the other individual or individuals, group acceptance has two components: a. the acceptance of the individual by the group; b. the acceptance of the group by the individual. The evidences of acceptance according to the interpretation above, and in the light of the Wawokiye experimental evidence are: a. being found compresent in group; b. direct expressions of the individual wanting to be in the group and the expressions of the group wanting the individual; c. behaviors of group members toward the individual in terms of cordiality and conflict. All are indicative of the individual's status in the group at a given time.

23. This view of that part of social adjustment which we have termed group adjustment or acceptance, permits of its measurement independent of the social norm.

24. Physical compresence is to be observed in attendance, who comes or goes with whom, who is present or absent with whom, in sub-group formation, etc.

25. The verbal preferences taken as a whole which the members of a group express for a given individual, and taken under certain conditions and in a certain standardized way (Personal Preference Ballot), may be treated in such fashion as to measure group status at a given time. This measure of group status is a measure of bond.

26. The behaviors of the group members taken as a whole toward the individual in terms of cordiality and conflict are indicative of the individual's group status.

27. Explanations for changes, especially sudden changes in group status should be sought.

28. Sustained low group status in the face of sustained efforts on the part of the worker to assist in raising it may indicate the necessity for special personal guidance or removal from the group.

29. Depending on the nature of the problems involved the worker if qualified may offer the guidance or call in a person especially qualified.

30. The acceptance of the individual in relation to one or more sub-groups may be the important key to group acceptance as a whole.

31. Knowledge on the part of the worker of each individual's interests, needs, capacities, skills, degree of socialization, behavior environmental factors, attitudes, values is necessary for five reasons: a. so that individual expression may be integrated as far as possible into the group life thus affecting group status favorably; b. so that

individual expression and development apart from this particular group may be stimulated and if necessary guided; c. so that special or different group opportunities for a wider expression and development of talents and interests than is possible in the given group may be offered if necessary; d. so that a program of activities based on common interest may be projected; e. so that social purposes for the group may be discovered and developed.

32. The individual should be seen and dealt with in terms of his total social setting, not merely on the basis of the given group.

DEVELOPMENT OF SOCIAL PURPOSES

33. Expressed interests form the primary basis for determining values and goals held in common by group members. Those held by members of high group status are usually significant. These values and goals should be examined by the worker and the group in the light of socially desirable as well as socially acceptable values.

34. The worker when consistent with his own social philosophy should assist the group to articulate consciously and practice its values through activity, and should help stimulate and enrich the immediate environment of the group so that individual and group interests project to wider social interests and goals.

35. The worker whenever possible should help individuals and the group participate in the process of making social environment and social relationships in general coincide with ideals visualized.

36. Careful attention should be given to the development of financial responsibility and attitudes toward the value and use of money and material things from the point of view of social and educational implications.

CONFLICTS AND CONTROLS

37. Conflicts may be classified in three ways: a. conflicts of norms or standards; b. conflicts of objectives; c. personality conflicts. Conflict situations should be thoroughly scrutinized as to: a. issues involved; b. individual and groups involved. Controls should depend upon nature of conflict, the objectives, and the social situation.

38. Conflict situations may often afford opportunities for individual development and growth and for social action. In order to raise level of group experience, it is sometimes necessary for leader to introduce conflict.

39. In giving a choice to a group, leader must be prepared to accept the "wrong" decision. Groups should be led to understand and accept responsibility for their decisions.

40. The democratic, socially conscious control of group decisions and activities is the ultimate aim, but the democratic process may be tempered with authoritative (outside) control in order to insure equal opportunity for all, in order to protect personalities from undue encroachments, and in the interests of safety, health, etc.

41. Material awards should be sparingly used, if at all; and used only when their effect on each individual involved is carefully considered.

42. The controls exercised by the leader should, as a general rule, be exercised through the planning and stimulation of the physical and social environment, through control by means of the situation, rather than through personal authority.

43. Avoid breaking down the old securities abruptly and substituting entirely new ones. The new securities should be projected from the old.

SUMMARY

Throughout these detailed statements of "principles," five are basic:

44. Particularization, i.e., individualization of group members as to attitudes, backgrounds, capacities, needs, interests, group status, values held, not only on the basis of what is observed in the group itself, but also on the basis of all other information obtainable.

45. Self-direction, i.e., promotion of the assumption of maximum responsibility on the part of the group for determining and interpreting its own acts through practice.

46. Indirection, i.e., guidance and stimulation primarily through influence on the social and physical setting of the group rather than through the direct personal influence or authority of the worker.

47. Repetition, i.e., the promotion of habitual responses to a variety of life situations.

48. Integration. This has two aspects: a. guidance in the adjustive efforts of the group in its acceptance of each individual member, and the acceptance of the group by each individual member; b. guidance in the unifying of objectives of individual growth and adjustment with social result objectives.

Thus it may be seen in summary of these so-called principles*

*It should not be assumed that competence with respect to the use of these principles is all that is required of the professionally trained group worker. Other regulatory principles are embodied in his case work, community organization work and administrative work training and should also be required.

that five factors involving methods and techniques are of primary importance: (1) the means for discovering individual attributes; (2) the means for estimating the group status of each member; (3) the means for discovering the germs of social purpose in the group; (4) the means for helping develop a program of activities; (5) the means for dealing with individuals.

The program of activities is developed around these elements which are revealed in part through observation and interpretation of the social process in the group.

Why is it important to know individual interests, needs, capacities, etc.? Because of the known relations between learning and interest, between capacity and interest, between attitudes and learning, between backgrounds and attitudes, and between needs and expressed interest. All are related to learning. It is important to know these in order that some activity may be developed as a common interest through which the different individuals can express their discrete interests—let us say camping or dramatics. And the division of labor in the activity may thus be related to individual needs and therefore individual growth and development. For example, a child that has low status in the group, and therefore poor adjustment in that group at that time, may be encouraged to take some essential part in the dramatic production, for example building scenery, that may raise his status and therefore his adjustment in that group. At the same time this may provide him with the opportunity to grow in skill in carpentry, in understanding of history and art and mathematics. This is just as true of the adult.

And why is it important to know the germs of social purpose in the group, which means in the individual members of the group? Because there is no group without some fundamental social purpose. It may be very elemental—just a desire to cooperate to some common activity end. There is a germ of social purpose even in a group of gangsters. Now whatever these elemental social purposes may be, they need to be recognized and developed constructively. The leader of a children's group or of a group of adults can assist. Dramatics as an activity may be utilized to express to an audience and to the players the developing and creative ideas of the group. The group that produced Uncle Tom's Cabin rocked a nation. The group of twelve Disciples of the Nazarene helped to project a new cultural pattern. These examples are extreme, but are illustrative. It is from simple elemental social purposes that we ultimately achieve social action in society. And it is through social action that individuals achieve individual growth. There is no real social growth of an individual apart from it. Individual interest needs to be identified with social purpose.

Now the small stable group lends security to individuals. This is one reason the family persists. But the modern family does not provide the security that it once did. The industrial revolution is largely responsible for the fact that the small group is endowed with such considerable social importance today. There is no substitute for the small group. But if social horizons are not widened through it, it may become a liability to society, a narrow ingrown clique.

Hence experience in the larger group is a necessary compliment to experience in the small group. An agency that encourages nothing but small stable groups may be doing an unwise social thing unless some other agency provides also an opportunity of a mass educational or recreational nature.

And the small stable group of children and of adults exists whether we recognize it or not. And it is the group most vital to the individual. The group most vital to the individual is the one most powerful in determining cultural patterns for that individual.

Study Questions

1. As Lindeman points out, democracy is neither a "goal" nor a "gift," but an "exceedingly difficult mode of life that emerges as a result of certain kinds of experience and which places upon its participants an unusual form of responsibility." What role does group work play in this process today? Are many group services provided within the context of Lindeman's "front office psychology"? Or does the group work method consciously demand active participation of group members in formulating ends, goals, purposes, and values? Has the development of group work methods and techniques included efforts to find scientific methods to advance democratic processes? Do you think it is necessary today to develop specific methods aimed at preparing for citizen participation and responsibility?

2. Does social work's adherence to a democratic ethic mean that social group work methods are inappropriate in totalitarian societies? In coercive, correctional, or mandatory treatment settings? Strictly speaking, can the group work method be used to advance totalitarian causes?

3. If it is true, as Coyle and others (e.g., Sirls et al., Chapter 14, below) suggest, that group work requires that members be encouraged to bring about change in their social environment, how might this be translated into practical terms to address the appropriate levels of preschoolers, the profoundly retarded, antisocial gangs, or severely disturbed families? Can you expand on the list of activities and experiences that would qualify as "social action"?

4. Is Grace Coyle's definition of social action still viable today? Is it the same as or different from advocacy? To what degree is social action an end in itself, or a means to some other end? Is social action a prerequisite to social change? Can social action be "therapeutic" in and of itself? Is it the workers' responsibility to seek to bring about changes in their agencies as well as in the larger environment through public social action efforts in partnership with consumer groups and others? Or is social action primarily "training" for social participation that is better done under the guidance of social agencies and institutions?

5. How would Neva Boyd's concepts of play compare with today's views? How do they relate to Middleman's (1968; 1970, p. 89) concept of nonverbal content? What is the significance of play, fun activities, games, and recreation generally as a socializing experience? As a therapeutic experience? Although she used terms such as "conditioning" and "behavioral modification," Boyd didn't subscribe to behaviorism but insisted that play had its own intrinsic rewards based upon psychological involvement and spontaneous participation (Boyd, 1955). How does this differ from planned use of programs? Can you identify specific kinds of theories upon which the group worker's knowledge of programming is based?

6. How do Newstetter's regulatory principles stand up in light of today's formulations? What changes in emphasis have occurred through the years? For example, is the same kind of attention given to "activities" in current formulations? Which principles would you drop as outmoded, and what other modifications would you suggest to make the list more relevant today?

7. Earlier attempts to introduce group work into therapeutic settings were strongly influenced by the writings of Slavson (1943, ch. 1) and Redl (1944). How has group work as a therapeutic activity been changed and modified over the years?

Suggested Readings

BITENSKY, R., 1969. "Social Action—the Therapy of Poor Folk," *Mental Hygiene*, Vol. 53, No. 4.

BOYD, N., 1955. "Theories of Play," *Play and Game Theory in Group Work: A Collection of Papers*, P. Simon, ed. Chicago: Jane Addams Graduate School of Social Work.

GARVIN, C. D., and P. H. GLASSER, 1974. "The Bases of Social Treatment," in *Individual Change Through Small Groups*, P. Glasser, R. Sarri, and R. Vinter, eds. New York: Free Press.

GILBERT, N., and H. SPECHT, 1976. "Advocacy and Professional Ethics," *Social Work*, Vol. 21, No. 4.

JACOBS, J., 1964. "Social Action as Therapy in a Mental Hospital," *Social Work*, Vol. 9, No. 1.

MIDDLEMAN, R. R., 1968. "Non-Verbal Content and Professional Purpose," in *The Non-Verbal Method in Working with Groups*. New York: Association Press.

——, 1970. "Let There Be Games," *Social Service Review*, Vol. 44, No. 1.

REDL, F., 1944. "Diagnostic Group Work," *American Journal of Orthopsychiatry*, Vol. 14.

ROSS, A. L., and N. D. BERNSTEIN, 1976. "A Framework for the Therapeutic Use of Group Activities," *Child Welfare*, Vol. 55, No. 9.

SLAVSON, S. R., 1943. "Principles of Group Therapy," *An Introduction to Group Therapy*. New York: Commonwealth Fund.

SLOAN, M. B., 1953. "The Special Contribution of Therapeutic Group Work in a Psychiatric Setting," *The Group*, Vol. 15, No. 4.

Social Action Guide, 1965. Commission on Social Action Division of Social Policy and Action. New York: National Association of Social Workers.

THURZ, D., 1977. "Social Action," in *Encyclopedia of Social Work*, 1977, Vol. II. New York: National Association of Social Workers.

WHITTAKER, J. K., 1974. "Program Activities: Their Selection and Use in a Therapeutic Milieu," in *Individual Change Through Small Groups*, P. Glasser, R. Sarri, and R. Vinter, eds. New York: Free Press.

WILLIAMS, J., C. LEWIS, F. COPELAND, L. TUCKER, and L. FEAGAN, 1978. "A Model for Short-Term Group Therapy on a Children's In-patient Unit," *Clinical Social Work Journal*, Vol. 6, No. 1.

PART II
Current Perspectives

SECTION A
Contemporary Models

Although it should be clear that the many perspectives presented in this book are not easily classified and categorized, with the increased proliferation of formulations it was perhaps inevitable that attention would be turned to model-building. Some earlier groundwork had been laid, however, which contributed to the process of identifying and organizing practice themes into conceptual frameworks. Schwartz's analysis of the frame of reference papers, for instance, resulted in his identifying three models, labeled "medical," "scientific," and "organic." Vinter's historical analysis of practice, on the other hand, led him to identify three others: (1) democratic, (2) education and socialization, and (3) treatment and rehabilitation models.

The selections in this section touch on various aspects of contempory model-building in group work. Papell and Rothman's well-known paper, which identifies and outlines the basic features of the social goals, remedial, and reciprocal models, has perhaps had the greatest influence on current thinking. It seemed to stimulate interest in integrating and further refining models that were specific as well as general in scope. James Whittaker's chapter, for example, attempts to integrate existing formulations of small group development into one five-stage model and explores practice implications in terms of Papell and Rothman's overall models. Utilizing a systems perspective, the chapter by Tompkins and Gallo offers a comprehensive model for goal formulation which, the authors feel, allows for more blending and overlap of functions, client needs and purposes, and practice principles.

9

Social Group Work Models: Possession and Heritage

Catherine P. Papell is Professor and Director of the Practice Division, Adelphi University School of Social Work, Garden City, New York.

Beulah Rothman is Professor and Director of the Doctoral Program, Adelphi University School of Social Work, Garden City, New York.

Catherine P. Papell and *Beulah Rothman*

The social group work method, like all social work methods, has developed largely experientially. Yet it has done so within a framework of some kind of guiding consensus about its essential elements. Persistently, social group workers have sought to formulate a logical relationship between these elements and pragmatic solutions to the tasks that have confronted them in practice. The evolutionary efforts of group workers to describe repeated patterns of phenomena and to define practice, in the language of science, has resulted in the emergence of several different theoretical models of social group work method. We have arrived at that stage of theory construction that can now be identified as model building.

A theoretical model is described by Kogan as "a scheme or map for 'making sense' out of the portion of the real world" in relation to which the worker is seeking to act (Kogan, 1960, p. 90). A model is a conceptual design to solve a problem that exists in reality. A model orders those elements in a given universe that are relevant to solve the problem. Higher levels of generalization or theory can be formulated when relationships hypothesized from a model are found to apply to a multitude of problems involving similar elements.

In our opinion, three models for social group work method can now be identified. The sequence of emergence of these models is elusive. Rudiments of these models are found scattered historically throughout the development of group work. Each has had periods of ascendent or waning commitment as practitioners have responded to the social scene and innovative calls for our professional services.

Reprinted with permission of the Council on Social Work Education. From the *Journal of Education for Social Work*, Vol. 2 (Fall 1966), pp. 66–77.

A core problem to which each model is addressed is concerned in some way with the central search of all social work to identify its societal functions. One model tells us that our first priority is provision and prevention. A second model prefers restoration and rehabilitation. A third model attempts to encompass and reconcile these two historical streams. Thus our present state of theory building is but one of the several efforts within the broader arena of the professional struggle to establish a relationship between our methods and our service to society.

The question of function is intertwined with a second problem of major import. Historically in group work theory and in its practice there has existed the eternal triangle of the individual, the small group, and the larger society. These three have presented themselves as significant ingredients to be considered in any theoretical formulation, but the appropriate balance of each to the others has never been resolved. Thus, when one theoretical formulation tends to stress the individual, professional criticism is raised loudly from many quarters. When a formulation emerges that gives precendence to either of the other two factors, a similar reaction can be observed. The writers are not free of bias in regards to this triad. In our conjecture of the models that have emerged, a review of each will call attention to the gap or emphasis given these three integral parts.

It is perhaps the determination to resolve these two central problems, function and focus, that has deterred the development of a unified model for social group work, but has at the same time reaffirmed the common threads of our history. The three models that we describe and examine in this paper we shall henceforth identify by the following designations:

1. the social goals model
2. the remedial model
3. the reciprocal model

In order to grasp the attributes and characteristics distinguishing these three models, we shall address ourselves to the following three levels of inquiry:

First: How does the model define the function of social group work?
Who is the client to be served by the method?
How does the model view the group as the unit of service?
What is the image of the professional role?
What is the nature of the agency auspice through which the group work service is rendered?

Second: What are the knowledge sources that serve as theoretical foundations for the model?

Third: What practice principles are generated by the model? Since it is necessary to limit the scope of this paper, we shall be concerned primarily with practice principles that pertain to assessment and implementation.[1]

THE SOCIAL GOALS MODEL

Before proceeding with discussions of the social goals model, it must be understood that this model does not exist as a single formulation in our literature. It is not identified with a central theoretician who has systematically set forth all its elements. It is, in fact, a model that has its origins in the earliest traditions of professional group work practice. The central problems with which the social goals model attempts to deal are those related to the social order and the social value orientation in small groups. Historically, youth serving organizations, settlements, and Jewish community centers relied heavily on this model in developing and promoting group work services.

The early writings of such foremost thinkers as Coyle, Kaiser, Phillips, Konopka, Cohen, Miller, Ginsberg, Wilson, and Klein provide essential concepts and connecting propositions which, when combined, can be said to have produced this model. None of these writers would subscribe to this model in its entirety. In fact, several are clearly identified with the other two. However, each could find in the social goals model some piece that could be identified as his contribution and commitment.

The social goals model, although emerging from our past, has not been discarded. Interestingly, the model has been reaffirmed as critical strains have developed in the larger society. During the war era, the McCarthy era, and now during the period of struggle for integration, world peace and economic opportunity, this model has been presenting itself for use. Rooted as it is in the value system of our profession, every new effort at theoretical formulation of group work method either incorporates something of this model or is subjected to criticism in relation to it. Since 1962 a striking revival of interest in this model is evident. The University of Pittsburgh's recent position paper challenges the strains in the profession that seem to be abandoning this model (Sirls et al., 1964). Hyman J. Wiener's, work has produced a new level of theoretical sophistication in restatement of the model (Wiener, 1964).

Key concepts in the social goals model are "social consciousness" and "social responsibility." The function of social group work is to create a broader base of knowledgeable and skilled citizenry. "It is our role and function," state Ginsberg and Goldberg (1962, p. 30), to bring about "discussions of social issues . . . to help define action alternatives which in turn, hopefully result in informed political and social action."

The model assumes that there is a unity between social action and individual psychological health. Every individual is seen as potentially capable of some form of meaningful participation in the mainstream of society. Thus the social goals model regards the individual as being in need of opportunity and assistance in revitalizing his drive toward others in a common cause and in converting self-seeking into social contribution. The therapeutic implications of social participation makes the application of this model available to group work practice with groups of varying illness and health. In describing a social action project at Camarillo State Hospital, Joseph D. Jacobs (1964) illustrates the use of the social goals model in a treatment setting.

Consistent with its view of the individual, the social goals model approaches every group as possessing a potential for affecting social change. Program development moves toward uncovering this strength in the group, with social action as the desired outcome. This potential derives from the assumption that collective group action represents individual social competence.

The social goals model views the worker as an "influence" (Wiener, 1964, p. 109) person with responsibility, according to Wiener, for "the cultivation of social consciousness in groups . . . elevated to the same priority as . . . developing closer interpersonal relations" (p. 100). Wiener speaks of this as the "political man (p. 109)." He goes on to say, however, that the group worker "does not attempt to dictate a particular political view but does seek to inculcate a value system" (p. 109). The group worker personifies the values of social responsibility and serves as a role model for the client, stimulating and reinforcing modes of conduct appropriate to citizenship responsibility directed toward social change.

The social goals model primarily envisions group work services at a community level and agency as an integral part of the neighborhood. The setting is accessible and flexible in offering institutional auspices for a variety of collective efforts. It responds to the interests of various segments of the community and is willing to initiate and recruit for social action. The agency then becomes the vehicle through which members may acquire instrumental skills in social action and institutional support for communal change. The social goals model does not set up priorities for services but insists that such priorities develop out of the particular needs of the community at a given moment in time. Grappling with agency policies or agency limitations is not regarded as a deterrent to client strength. Rather it is the fabric from which practitioners and their clients learn to "test the limits of authority and sanction, demonstrating that sanction is the product of an ongoing process—constantly evolving and often susceptible to more influence than we think" (p. 109).

Furthermore, the agency conveys the value that increased leisure time shall be harnessed for the common good and not solely for individual enrichment.

Since the social goals model in the past has been reliant more on ideology than on science, its theoretical underpinnings have only recently become more apparent. It would appear that neo-Freudian personality theories have been utilized in attaching importance to cultural differences and to the significance of interpersonal relations. A significant degree of individual and group malfunctioning is attributable to the malfunctioning of the social system. From the newer body of sociological theory the model picks up on opportunity theory and on theories of powerlessness, cultural deprivation and inter-generational alienation. Current treatment theories of crisis and primary prevention are congenial to this model. The theories still to be seen exerting most influence on the model are theories of economic and political democracy and the educational philosophies of Dewey, Kilpatrick and Lindeman, particularly with regard to conceptions of leadership, communal responsibility and forms of group interaction.

To deal with the external environment of the group, the social goals model has generated a large body of principles designed to activate the group in relation to agency and community. Clarification of agency policy, positive use of limitations, identification with agency goals, determination of appropriate issues for collective action and the weighting of alternatives for action and their consequences, are all familiar principles heavily relied on in the social goals model. Furthermore, assessment and implementation with regard to the individual do not have to await intensive study of each member. The worker's assessment is first directed toward understanding normative behaviors manifested in the group as representative of the life style of the community and its sub-cultures. It is against this background that individual assessment can be formulated with respect to self-image, identity, social skill, knowledge of environmental resources and leadership potential. Principles related to the group emphasize participation, consensus and group task.

It is understandable that considerable explication of practice principles is to be found in recent writings pertaining to intergroup relations. We cite the work of Eleanor Ryder (1960) and Jack Wiener

(1960). In their papers they set forth principles which tell us how and when to make use of supraordinate goals to bring groups together, how to reduce the threat to individuals in heterogeneous groups, and how to engage members in inter-racial activities through a sequence of orderly and manageable steps. On a somewhat different level, but of major importance in this model, are those principles related to self-awareness and professional discipline particularly with regard to the value system and life style of the worker. It is interesting to note that the transfer of leadership from the professional to the indigenous leadership is implied in this model. Yet specific practice principles dealing with this aspect are noticeably absent in the literature.

A serious shortcoming of the social goals model is that it has not produced a theoretical design that is adequate to meet the problems facing practitioners in all areas of service. Its under-emphasis on individual dynamics and its lack of attention to a wide range of individual need leave the practitioner without guidelines for carrying out a social work function with client groups where individual problems take precedence over societal problems. It is difficult to see how this model would serve (except by distortion) to provide a basis for social group work practice with "admission" or "discharge" groups in a mental hospital.

Each of the models places the social group work method in some relationship to the other social work methods. The social goals model tends to move group work toward community organization method, but in so doing further obscures the boundaries between them. Ambiguity is particularly evident when group-serving agencies increasingly call upon grass roots membership to solve community problems sometimes in the name of the group work method and other times in the name of community organization method.

One last comment must be made about the social goals model. The principles of democratic group process that are fundamental to this model have become the hallmark of all social group work practice. Every practitioner, regardless of his theoretical loyalty, tends to work toward the adoption and institutionalization of democratic procedures in small groups.

In summary, the essence of the social goals model is embodied in the words of the late Grace Coyle:

> It is not enough . . . for man to seek enjoyment in isolation from others. Because of his essentially social nature his fullest growth comes only as he uses his expanding powers in conjunction with and for the benefit of others. For his own deepest growth he must be socialized . . . we . . . mean by this his ability to establish mutual relations with others and the capacity to identify himself with the good of the social whole

> however he conceives it, to use his capacities in part at least for social ends beyond himself. Each must find for himself his social objects of devotion, but to discover them is as essential to fulfillment as to find the objects of his more personal loves. To hope for such attainment in however small a measure is no doubt the common goal of all who sincerely wish to work in some capacity with people [1948].

THE REMEDIAL MODEL

Placed in historical context the remedial model further facilitated the integration of the group work method in the profession of social work. It offered a congenial base for the linkage of the social group work method with the method of social casework. As in casework, the remedial model established the treatment of individuals as the central function of group work. Through the remedial model the social group work method offered another means by which the profession could restore or rehabilitate individuals.

Early development of the remedial model was conspicuously influenced by the work of Redl in the institutional group treatment of children. Later the model was elaborated by social group workers such as Konopka, Sloan, Fisher and Ganter. A systematic formulation of the model has been presented in the writings of Robert Vinter, now identified as its major theoretician.

The problems of adjustment in personal and social relations that can be treated through the use of the group are considered within the special competence of the social group worker. Attention to such problems reaffirms "the profession's historic mission of service to those most in need" (Vinter, 1959a, p. 135). In this manner, the concept of priority is introduced in the remedial model. Criticism is directed towards the deployment of limited personnel to those services which are categorized as "socialization and consumption" services (p. 136). It follows logically, then, that the image of the client is that of an individual who is suffering from some form of social maladaptation or deficiency. In this sense, the remedial model is clearly a clinical model focused upon helping the malperforming individual to achieve a more desirable state of social functioning.

The group is viewed as a tool or context for treatment of the individual. Diagnostic goals for each individual as established by the worker, supersede group goals. " . . . changes in the group structure and the group process," states Arthur Blum, "are the means to the end goal of individual change . . ." (1964, p. 12). Group development is not conceived in the interest of collective growth that has meaning unto itself. There is no idealized image of a healthy group per se. A conception of group health transcends the particular needs of the therapeutic situation. Blum continues:

> A "good" group is the group which permits and fosters the growth of its members. This does not presuppose any fixed structure or level of function as being desirable except as it affects the members. . . . Evaluation of the desirability of its (the group's) structure and processes can only be made in relation to the desirability of its effects upon the members and the potential it provides for the worker's interventions [p. 12].

The treatment group primarily envisioned by the remedial model is the "formed" group, wherein membership is pre-determined and diagnostically selected by the worker (Sarri et al., 1964). Natural or friendship ties are not considered essential unless they meet the therapeutic prescription, or where there are no other bases of group formation open to the worker. Group composition is considered a significant factor in the potential of the group to serve as an effective treatment vehicle.

Processes within the group which help members to help each other are given recognition in this model but the limit of the self-help system is contained within the boundaries of the diagnostic plan. The remedial model deals only peripherally with a full range of collective associations such as are to be found in spontaneous groupings, informal lounges, and mass activities. Moreover, the preventive use of the group in relation to normal developmental needs is of secondary importance. The group program is primarily evaluated for its therapeutic potential rather than for its creative and expressive qualities.

The worker is viewed as a "change agent" rather than an "enabler" facilitating self-direction of the group. He uses a problem-solving approach, sequentially phasing his activities in the tradition of study, diagnosis and treatment. He is characteristically directive, and assumes a position of clinical preeminence and authority. He exercises this authority through such ways as the assigning of task and role, and the screening of activity against his own professional objectives. His authority derives from the mandate given to him by the profession and the agency. While his authority must be confirmed by the group, it is not fundamentally established by the group. From this position of authority his intervention may be designed to do *for* the client as well as *with* the client. The model does not require the worker to give priority to the establishment of group autonomy (Sirls et al., 1964, p. 6) nor to the perpetuation of the group as a self-help system.

With regard to setting, the remedial model seems to require a structured institutional context. It assumes clearly defined agency policy in support of treatment goals. When these are not available, it suggests professional efforts to develop them. The remedial model makes less provision for adapting service to the informal life style of the client. It appears to depart from the tradition that the group worker engages with people where he finds them as they go about the business of daily living.

From the earliest development of the remedial model it was necessary to draw upon individual psychological theories in support of its individualizing focus. The model relied heavily upon traditional sources of individual theory utilized by social casework. For example, psychoanalytic theory provided a set of concepts that sensitized the group worker to "resistance" and "transference" phenomena and the "symbolic" representation of the group as a family. More recently the utility of ego psychology to explain behavior in relation to internal and external forces is being recognized and explored.

Whereas social group work has had more difficulty operationalizing psychoanalytical concepts, social role theory has lent itself to a simpler and more direct application for understanding and treating the individual in the group. The significance of this theory lies in its power to provide conceptualizations that define and describe the "presenting" social problems more in harmony with the method of treatment to be used. Social role theory as an interactional theory, therefore, is congruent to the unit of service employed by the social group worker. It is this theory that has been employed prominently in the writings of Vinter and his colleagues at the University of Michigan School of Social Work (Glasser, 1962).

Since the remedial model assumes that "group development can be controlled and influenced by the worker's actions" (Sarri and Galinsky, 1964, p. 21), it must draw heavily from theories of small group dynamics. These theories help to account for changes in the group and suggest opportunities for professional interventions in carrying out the "change agent" role.

In the remedial model the central and most powerful concept is "treatment goal." Emphasis on this concept is intersticed throughout most of its practice principles. The influence of the "treatment goal" is to be noted in the following selected practice principles:

1. "Specific treatment goals must be established for each member of the client group" (Vinter, 1959b, p. 4).
2. The worker "attempts to define group purposes so that they are consistent with the several treatment goals established for the individual members" (Vinter, 1959b, p. 6).
3. The worker helps "the group to develop that system of norms and values which is in accord with the worker's treatment goals" (Vinter, 1959b, p. 12).
4. The worker prestructures "the content for group sessions based on the worker's knowledge of individuals expressed through

his treatment goals as well as his knowledge of structural characteristics and processes that take place within the group" (Glasser and Costabile, 1963 p. 4).

These principles state clearly that assessment begins with the needs of individual members. Knowledge of these needs is derived from information secured prior to the individual's participation in the group. It is assumed that with such knowledge the group worker can integrate individual needs into a needs-satisfying system through the formation of a group. Thus it is the group worker who diagnoses the needs and who formulates treatment goals *for the client.* The lesser emphasis on the concept *with the client* sharply differentiates the remedial model from the other two models.

The model places considerable import on possession of knowledge by the group worker as a key to diagnosis and treatment. The model assumes that (1) such knowledge is available, and (2) given the appropriate knowledge the group worker will know precisely how to act in relation to it. This is far removed from the realities of both theory and practice. Appropriate knowledge may not always be available. More often we know better from knowledge what *not* to do than what should be done. There is, in fact, a limit to prescriptiveness in the real world that is not taken into account in this model. There is a mechanistic quality about the remedial model which precludes the creative and dynamic aspects of human interaction.

A sense of unreality prevails in the demands that are made upon the group worker in the early contact with the group. In actual practice most of the group worker's initial efforts are directed toward problems of group management and maintenance in the external environment. Individual therapeutic goals are subject to the reality stress of group formation and may themselves be modified. Treatment goals during this phase provide less of an anchorage for professional activity than is implied in the model.

Further analysis of the remedial model reveals insufficient provision for a group to contribute to its environment. Actually the model constrains the group worker from viewing the group as a system to be sustained and utilized for the purpose of enhancing the milieu. "Obviously," says Vinter, "the aim of group work is not to help persons to become good members of successfully operating client groups" (Vinter, 1959b, p. 6). In the remedial model the human group has little claim to existence except for what it can give to the individual. In the light of this, it is difficult to determine from this model the specificity of the group work function in contrast to the general function of group therapy. Moreover, the model leaves unanswered what is the special contribution of group work in the full spectrum of social work with groups.

Within its circumscribed boundaries, the remedial model has made several theoretical advances. It has systematically set forth (1) guidelines for diagnostic considerations of individual functioning in the group, (2) criteria for group formation, (3) foundations for clinical team participation, and (4) diagnostic utilization of the group where other treatment modalities coexist. Thus the model has greatly facilitated the functioning of group work practitioners in clinical settings, and has drawn upon the learnings from these settings for incorporation in a general framework of social group work method.

THE RECIPROCAL MODEL

This model advances a helping process that is intended to serve both the individual and society. It proceeds on the assumption that social group work is a special case of a general social work method which is addressed to the human condition whether it be presented in a single or collective context. Whereas the reciprocal model has been specifically organized by one author, William Schwartz, it reflects the influence of many contributors. It opens the way for providing a larger theoretical umbrella to more adequately encompass the whole of the social group work method.

The duality of its focus suggests Kaiser's (1958) early conceptualization in this regard. The strong emphasis on process, enabling, and on quality of engagement is reminiscent of Phillips (1957). More recently the work of Emanuel Tropp (1965) illustrates possibilities of further developing several aspects of the model in greater theoretical depth.

The reciprocal model presupposes an organic, systemic relationship between the individual and society. The interdependence is described as "symbiotic," of basic urgency to both, and normally subject to crisis and stress. This interdependence is the "focus" for social work and the small group is the field in which individual and societal functioning can be nourished and mediated. The range of social work function can include prevention, provision, as well as restoration. Breakdown in the interdependence between systems may occur at any point on the continuum between health and pathology.

Within the logic of this model the group is in a position of preeminence. Since the group is accorded such central status in the model, it can be said that it is, in fact, the client of the group worker. It follows that key concepts in this model largely pertain to the group. The most striking concept of the reciprocal model is "mutual aid system."

Unlike the remedial model, the reciprocal model does not begin with a priori prescriptions or desired outcomes. However, it does conceive of an ideal group state, namely a system in mutual aid. Such a system is not dependent upon the specific problem to be resolved by the group but is a necessary condition for problem solving. To state it in still another way, the reciprocal model has no therapeutic ends, no political or social change programs, to which it is addressed. It is only from the encounter of individuals that compose a reciprocal group system that direction or problem is determined. Emphasis is placed on *engagement* in the process of interpersonal relations. It is from this state of involvement that members may call upon each other in their own or a common cause.

Group members, states Schwartz (1962, p. 274), "move to relate their own sense of need to the social demand implicit in the collective tasks of the group." Tropp takes this further by insisting that it is the "common goals group . . . with shared authority . . . pursuing common decisions" (Tropp, 1965, p. 234) that is the core group at the center of attention of the social group work method.

The concept of shared authority derives from the assumption "that people create many helping relationships in addition to and concurrent with the one formed with the worker" (Schwartz, 1962, p. 273).

The reciprocal model views the individual primarily in terms of his motivation and capacity for reciprocity. The model, therefore, focuses on the relational aspects of behavior as determined by the present reality of the group system. Understanding of the individual is bounded by the social context in which he, the group, and the worker interact. Diagnostic considerations or structural descriptions of the individual are not regarded as significant predictors of behavior in the group. Therefore they do not serve as a basis for selection of members for a group or assessment by the worker.

The image of the worker projected by this model is that of a mediator or enabler to the needs system converging in the group. The worker is viewed as a part of the worker-client system both influencing and being influenced by it. In the terminology of social work, he neither does *to* the client nor *for* him, but *with* him. The relationship between worker and client in this model involves deep investment and emotional commitment in which the worker reveals and makes available his aspirations, knowledge and effect within the boundaries of the "contract" between himself, the group, and the agency.

The reciprocal model makes no reference to a type of agency auspice, but it does assume that, whatever the agency, it will engage in the mutual establishment of a "contract." Thus the agency also accepts a place in a reciprocal system with inherent limitations. The authority of the agency is not emphasized in this model.

The knowledge base of the reciprocal model primarily originates in sociological systems theory and field theory. In analyzing group work and constructing a formulation of group work method, a structural-functional approach is employed. However, it is to be noted that while Schwartz posits the parts-whole concept, he chooses to focus on the relationship of parts to whole, paying scant attention to the specificity or autonomy of parts themselves.

A second theoretical source, although not directly acknowledged, is inferred by the reciprocal model. This theoretical source is known under the general rubric of social psychological theories of personality. Shades of Adler, Fromm, and Sullivan are to be found in the assumptions that underlie the individual's motivation and capacity for reaching out to collectivities.

In turning to the practice principles generated by the reciprocal model, they are found to be first developed as generic methodology for social work as a whole and subsequently transformed for utilization in a worker-group system.

Schwartz has conceptualized five major tasks to be carried out by the social work practitioner. In every brief form they are as follows:

> 1. The task of searching out the common ground between the client's perception of his own need and the aspects of social demand with which he is faced.
> 2. The task of detecting and challenging the obstacles which obscure the common ground. . . .
> 3. The task of contributing data—ideas, facts, value concepts—which are not available to the client. . . .
> 4. The task of "lending a vision." . . .
> 5. The task of defining the requirements and the limits of the situation in which the client-worker system is set [Schwartz, 1961, p. 17].

Each of these generic tasks has been operationalized through a series of principles that specifically guides social group workers.

To illustrate, we will take task #1, that of "searching out common ground." The model suggests three primary principles as follows: (1) The worker helps the group to strengthen its goals through a consideration of what it is in common that the members are seeking. (2) the worker interprets his role through clarifying with the group what it is they wish from him that he has available to give from which a clear "contractual" agreement can be drawn. (3) The worker acts to protect the focus of work against attempts to evade or subvert it.

Pervading this model is a series of practice principles that are devoted to worker honesty and directness and the avoidance of withholding knowledge and effect. These principles seem to reflect as much the author's determination to dispel a "mystique of professionalism" as to relate to the functional tasks.

The contribution of the reciprocal model lies in its unifying abstractions. Intensive individualizing and social focusing within the small group are rendered in a conceptual balance, providing a coherent footing for further theoretical development.

The limitation of Schwartz's formulation lies more in theoretical *gaps* than in inconsistencies. Middle range supporting theories are insufficiently developed in several areas. For example, interest in the individual system is strikingly sparse. Schwartz does not make allowance for the latitude of human personality which may be necessary to explain the manner in which the individual coheres in any system in aid of others. There is a sense of unreality in the notion that the motivation toward collectivity is always productive of individual and/or social good. Without guidelines in relation to individual dynamics and normative expectations. there is no basis for assessing the impact of change upon individuals. There is produced a tendency toward permissiveness and abdication of worker's authority. Process itself is elevated to an unreal superordinance.

It is to be noted that ego-psychological concepts increasingly being utilized by social group workers may fill the gap regarding individual dynamics without violating the central logic of the reciprocal model (Levine, 1965).

Group system theory is likewise underdeveloped. Schwartz does not sufficiently take into account similarities or differences in a variety of group systems. Moreover, while his conceptualization is useful in beginning with a group, it does not offer a framework for dealing with changes that may occur in the group over time. Thus the model ignores what has been observed experientially by group workers and is known from scientific study of small groups. Group development is perceived simplistically, without conceptually accounting for new levels realizable as a result of group experience and achievement.

Schwartz's formulation is distressingly lacking in any clarification of group program. One might deduce that discussion as a channel for communication overshadows all others.

It seems appropriate now to recall Irving Miller's comments on an earlier form of this paper. He addressed himself to the level of abstraction of a theoretical model. He raised the possibility that "the concrete solutions and specific applications which may be eventually deduced from a broad and generalized model may be so attenuated as to suggest that the specific applications do not necessarily flow from or require the original abstraction."[2]

Despite limitations of the reciprocal model, its outstanding contribution is the construct of a mutual aid system with professional interventions flowing from it. What has been vaguely referred to in the past as "helping members to help themselves" has acquired a higher level of theoretical statement. It is possible now to systematically consider the attributes and culture of such a specialized system and to transmit the skills necessary to support its realization. This is probably the single most important contribution that group work method can make to the social work profession at large.

In conclusion, we submit that the significant movement of social group work in theory building lies in the production of models systematic designs by which the elements of social group work practice have begun to be ordered and problems in practice rendered more solvable. We have found three models to be clearly in existence. Each independently pursues lines of inquiry relating historical tradition to present societal requirements. The foremost contribution of each is not made by the other two. Each falls short in encompassing the totality of social group work method. This suggests that new models will emerge either parallel or in a subsuming relationship to those that presently exist.

Even as the kinship of all social group workers to each of these models insists itself upon us, so also the continued authorship of our theory lies with each of us. Regardless of the particular bias of practice or educational institution, it is essential that all new practitioners enter the profession with a knowledge of the state of its theoretical development and with ability to relate their thinking to the models that exist.

Furthermore, all practitioners and educators writing today about social group work practice should in some manner take into account where their work falls in relation to these patternings that have developed. Thus each of these models will be moved ahead in order, fullness and complexity or will be replaced by more useful theoretical structures. The possession of models provides a baseline for further elaborating the utility of the social group work method in the profession's service to mankind.

NOTES

1. The formulation of this analytical frame borrows heavily from Robert D. Vinter (1960).
2. The original form of this paper was presented at Columbia University School of Social Work Alumni Conference, April, 1962. Irving Miller served as a discussant.

REFERENCES

BLUM, A., 1964. "The Social Group Work Method: One View," *A Conceptual Framework for the Teaching of the Social Group Work Method in the Classroom.* New York: Council on Social Work Education.

COYLE, G. L., 1948. *Group Work with American Youth.* New York: Harper & Brothers.

GINSBERG, M. I., and J. R. GOLDBERG, 1962. "The Impact of the Current Science on Group Work Policy and Practice," *Summary Presentations: Group Work Section Meetings.*

GLASSER, P. H., 1962. "Social Role, Personality, and Group Work Practice," *Social Work Practice.* New York: Columbia University Press.

GLASSER, P. H. and J. COSTABILE, 1963. "Social Group Work Practice in a Public Welfare Setting." Ann Arbor: University of Michigan School of Social Work (mimeographed).

JACOBS, J. D., 1964. "Social Action as Therapy in a Mental Hospital," *Social Work,* Vol. 9, No. 1.

KAISER, C., 1958. "The Social Group Work Process," *Journal of Social Work,* Vol. 3, No. 2.

KOGAN, L. S., 1960. "Principles of Measurement," in *Social Work Research.* Chicago: University of Chicago Press.

LEVINE, B., 1965. "Principles for Developing an Ego Supportive Group Treatment Service," *Social Service Review,* Vol. 34, No. 4.

PHILLIPS, H., 1957. *Essentials of Social Group Work Skill.* New York: Association Press.

RYDER, E. L., 1960. "Some Principles of Intergroup Relations as Applied to Group Work," *Social Work with Groups, 1960.* New York: National Association of Social Workers.

SARRI, R. C. and M. J. GALINSKY, 1964. "A Conceptual Framework for Teaching Group Development in Social Group Work," *A Conceptual Framework for the Teaching of Social Group Work Method in the Classroom.* New York: Council on Social Work Education.

SARRI, R., et al., 1964. *Diagnosis in Social Group Work.* Ann Arbor: University of Michigan School of Social Work (mimeographed).

SCHWARTZ, W., 1961. "The Social Worker in the Group," *New Perspectives on Services to Groups.* New York: National Association of Social Workers.

——, 1962. "Toward a Strategy of Group Work Practice," *Social Service Review,* Vol. 36, No. 3.

SIRLS, M., et al., 1964. *Social Group Practice Elaborated: A Statement of Position.* Pittsburgh: University of Pittsburgh Graduate School of Social Work (mimeographed).

TROPP, E., 1965. "Group Intent and Group Structure: Essential Criteria for Group Work Practice," *Journal of Jewish Communal Service,* Vol. 41, No. 3.

VINTER, R. D., 1959a. "Group Work: Perspectives and Prospects," *Social Work with Groups, 1959.* New York: National Association of Social Workers.

——, 1959b. "The Essential Component of Social Group Work Practice." Ann Arbor: University of Michigan School of Social Work (mimeographed).

——, 1960. "Problems and Processes in Developing Group Work Practice Principles," *Theory Building in Social Work,* Workshop Report, CSWE 1960 Annual Program Meeting. New York: Council on Social Work Education.

WIENER, H. J., 1960. "Reducing Racial and Religious Discrimination," *Social Work with Groups, 1960.* New York: National Association of Social Workers.

——, 1964. "Social Change and Social Group Work Practice," *Social Work*, Vol. 9, No. 3.

10

Models of Group Development: Implications for Social Group Work Practice

James Whittaker is Professor of Social Work, University of Washington School of Social Work, Seattle.

James K. Whittaker

In 1960, Robert Vinter said of the then nascent state of group work practice principles:

> Despite the profession's intense interest in methods and techniques of practice, and the large literature on practice, there has been very little analysis of the processes of formulating practice principles. Anyone undertaking this task enters relatively uncharted territory and can be expected to do little more than identify the major peaks and valleys [Vinter, 1960, p. 4].

In ten years, the body of group work practice principles has grown so much that, at least in some areas, the group work practitioner is faced with an abundance, rather than with a scarity, of guidelines for practice. One such well-developed area is that of small-group development, in which a number of different models have been proposed, each with its accompanying implications for practice. The result has been that the group work practitioner often finds himself as disillusioned with the "affluence" of too many practice models—often with overlapping categories and different terminology for the same phenomena—as he was with the "poverty" of too few.

It is the thesis of this paper that the five-stage model for group development proposed by Garland, Jones, and Kolodny represents the most complete statement to date on the subject and contains within its stages the basic elements of the models proposed by the other major contributors to the social work literature in this area (Garland et al., 1965. See also Kindelsperger, 1957; Maier, 1961-62; Sarri and Galinsky, 1967; and Trecker, 1955). The purpose of this paper, then, will be twofold: (*a*) to integrate the other major practice

Reprinted from *Social Service Review*, Vol. 44, No. 3, © 1970, with permission of The University of Chicago Press and the author.

formulations of group development into the model suggested by Garland, Jones, and Kolodny, and (*b*) to develop implications for practice for each of the stages of development, on the basis of the three overall models of social group work practice: the social-goals model, the remedial model, and the reciprocal model (Papell and Rothman, 1966).

CURRENT MODELS OF GROUP DEVELOPMENTS

The knowledge base for group development draws from small-group sociology, social psychology, group psychotherapy, human relations, and social work.[1] Researchers in these areas have provided many studies that illustrate the general cycles and phases through which groups seem to progress. In general, most theorists look upon group development as a series of phases through which all small groups progress, or at least as some sort of recurring cycle of member attraction based on different factors.[2] For example, Bales and Strodtbeck have suggested three phases of development in problem-solving groups: orientation, evaluation, and control, with each of these assuming prominence at any one given point in time (Bales and Strodtbeck, 1951; Cartwright and Zander, 1960).

In the literature of social group work, we find a number of studies of group development. Only the more fully developed of these models—those of Maier, Kindelsperger, Trecker, and Sarri and Galinsky—will be considered in terms of how they may be integrated with the Garland, Jones, and Kolodny formulation.[3]

Henry Maier has proposed four phases through which small groups progress: locating commonness, creating exchange, developing mutual identification, and developing group identification. Maier chooses not to look upon termination as a phase of group development, but otherwise his scheme most closely resembles the Garland, Jones, and Kolodny model in its essential components.

Kindelsperger has suggested a six-stage model of group development consisting of the following phases: approach or orientation, relationship negotiation or conflict, group role emergence, vacillating group role dominance, group role dominance, and institutionalized group roles. This formulation, while helpful in some respects, appears to be too inadequately developed to be of any substantial benefit to the practitioner. For example, we are told: "No group ever fits exactly into these categories and all groups do not go through all of the stages," without being told why this is so. Similarly, the author says little about the character of worker intervention at each stage of development and leaves us only with the rather tenuous statement that "it is risky to bypass the stages and to force movement ahead." It is not made clear why this is necessarily so.

Trecker has also proposed a six-stage model for group development that is more behaviorally descriptive than the others. It consists of the following stages: beginning stage; emergence of some group feeling, organization, program; development of bond, purpose, and cohesiveness; strong group feeling—goal attainment; decline in interest—less group feeling; and ending stage, or decision to discontinue the group. Like Bernstein, Tecker suggests a number of key indices which the worker can use in determining the group's stage of development.

One of the best theoretically developed and well-articulated statements of group development has been offered by Rosemary Sarri and Maeda Galinsky. Unlike the other formulations, theirs derives from an analysis of small-group research, primarily in sociology and group psychotherapy. This model of development is congruent with Vinter's conception of the group as both the means and the context for treatment (Vinter, 1967). The Sarri and Galinsky model, which rests upon four basic assumptions,[4] consists of seven distinct phases:

1. *Origin phase.* This phase refers to the composition of the group and is distinguished primarily for analytic purposes, since it is at least a precondition for later development.

2. *Formative phase.* The initial activity of the group members in seeking similarity and mutuality of interests is the outstanding characteristic of this phase. Initial commitments to group purpose, emergent personal ties, and a quasi-group structure are also observable.

3. *Intermediate phase I.* This phase is characterized by a moderate level of group cohesion, clarification of purposes, and observable involvement of members in goal-directed activities.

4. *Revision phase.* This phase is characterized by challenges to the existing group structure and an accompanying modification of group purposes and operating procedures.

5. *Intermediate phase II.* Following the revision phase, while many groups progress toward maturation, the characteristics outlined in Intermediate phase I may again appear, though the group generally manifests a higher level of integration and stability than in the earlier phase.

6. *Maturation phase.* This phase is characterized by stabilization of group structure, group purpose, operating and governing procedures, expansion of the culture of the group, and the existence of effective responses to internal and external stress.

7. *Termination phase.* The dissolution of the group may result

from goal attainment, maladaptation, lack of integration, or previously made plans about the duration of the group.

The writers go on to develop a series of strategies for each of the phases. Despite the theoretical sophistication of the model, it appears to fall short in its description of what is happening to the members in each of the phases, as contrasted to the richly descriptive material offered by Garland, Jones, and Kolodny. In fairness to the authors, it should be noted that their main reason for omitting descriptions of individual member reactions was that several writers in the past had failed to distinguish worker intervention and individual client reaction from the group developmental processes. One wishes that the authors had made such a distinction and then gone on to describe both the group developmental processes and the reactions of individual members, as well as the strategies of worker intervention. In addition, the Sarri and Galinsky model contains no "real life" group-process examples, in sharp contrast to the highly illustrative examples integrated into the Garland formulation.

Finally, the names of the different stages in the Sarri and Galinsky model, while certainly in keeping with the research studies from which they were derived, sound somewhat as if they were contrived strictly for taxonomic purposes. The Garland model, on the other hand, employs, in describing its stages, a rich "central theme" approach which seems to have more overall benefit for the practitioner. Despite these few shortcomings, the Sarri and Galinsky model constitutes a distinct and significant contribution to the group work literature, particularly in terms of its scientifically based descriptions of group structure and processes.

GARLAND, JONES, AND KOLODNY: FIVE STAGES OF GROUP DEVELOPMENT

This five-stage model of group development was derived from an analysis of group-process records at a children's agency over a three-year period. It is solid in its theoretical underpinnings, well articulated, and richly exampled with group-process materials. It offers the most advanced statement in the literature concerning worker focus at each of the various stages. The authors have identified the five stages in terms of the central theme characteristic of each. They are as follows.[5]

1. *Pre-affiliation.* "Closeness" of the members is the central theme in this stage, with "approach-avoidance" as the major early struggle in relation to it. Ambivalence toward involvement is reflected in the members' vacillating responses to program activities and events. Relationships are usually nonintimate, and a good deal of

use may be made of rather stereotypic activity as a means of getting acquainted.

2. *Power and control.* After making the decision that the group is potentially rewarding, members move to a stage during which issues of power, control, status, skill, and decision-making are the focal points. There is likely to be a testing of the group worker and the members, as well as an attempt to define and formalize relationships and to define a status hierarchy. Three basic issues are suggested by the power-struggle phenomena: rebellion and autonomy, permission and the normative crisis, and protection and support.

3. *Intimacy.* This stage is characterized by intensification of personal involvement, more willingness to bring into the open feelings about club members and group leader, and a striving for satisfaction of dependency needs. Siblinglike rivalry tends to appear, as well as overt comparison of the group to family life. There is a growing ability to plan and carry out group projects and a growing awareness and mutual recognition of the significance of the group experience in terms of personality growth and change.

4. *Differentiation.* In this stage, members begin to accept one another as distinct individuals and to see the social worker as a unique person and the group as providing a unique experience. Relationships and needs are more reality based, communication is good, and there is strong cohesion. As clarification of power relationships gave freedom for autonomy and intimacy, so clarification of and coming to terms with intimacy and mutual acceptance of personal needs brings freedom and ability to differentiate and to evaluate relationships and events in the group on a reality basis. The group experience achieves a functionally autonomous character in this fourth stage. In freeing perceptions of the situation from distortions of extraneous experience and in creating its unique institutions and mores, the group becomes, in a sense, its own frame of reference.

5. *Separation.* The group experience has been completed, and the members may begin to move apart and find new resources for meeting social, recreational, and vocational needs. The following reactions have been observed repeatedly in groups in the process of termination: denial, regression, recapitulation of past experiences, evaluation, flight, and pleas from the members who say, "We still need the group."

The way in which these different models of group development may be integrated is best represented in tabular form (Table 10-1). It should be noted that a relationship of exact equality between the various stages is not being proposed. It is simply suggested that the stages of development in the other models most nearly approximate those offered by Garland, Jones, and Kolodny in the manner indi-

TABLE 10-1. **Integrated Stage Model of Group Development**

	Parallel Stages of Group Development			
Garland, Jones and Kolodny	Maier	Sarri and Galinsky	Kindelsperger	Trecker
I. Pre-affiliation	1. Locating commonness	1. Origin 2. Formative	1. Approach-orientation	1. Beginning
II. Power and control	2. Creating exchange	3. Intermediate I 4. Revision	2. Relationship negotiation or conflict	....
III. Intimacy	3. Developing mutual identification	5. Intermediate II	3. Group role emergence 4. Vacillating group role dominance	2. Emergence of some group "feeling," organization
IV. Differentiation	4. Developing group identification	6. Maturation	5. Group role dominance 6. Institutionalized group roles	3. Development of bond, purpose, cohesiveness 4. Strong group feeling — goal attainment
V. Separation	....	7. Termination	....	5. Decline in interest, less group feeling 6. Ending stage; decision to discontinue the group

cated. For example, Sarri and Galinsky's "Intermediate I" and "Revision" phases can rather easily be subsumed under the heading of "Power and control." In fact, they add greatly to the description of what is happening to group structure at this particular stage. Similarly, Maier's phase of "Locating commonness" appears to be closest to the "Pre-affiliation" stage in the Garland model. Generally speaking, the stages in the other models continue to run in their normal sequence when placed alongside the Garland model, with some stages collapsed for purposes of clarity.

What is suggested here should in no sense be taken as a complete synthesis of the various models. It is this writer's belief that such a synthesis would create more problems for the practitioner than it would solve, for it would create new stages of group development, which would require, among other things, a new set of terms to describe the various phases. To an area of practice theory already burdened with too much ambiguous terminology, the addition of another set of stages would run counter to fundamental canons of parsimony. What is suggested here is that the other models of group development may be used selectively to complement the Garland model. It can be argued that in specific areas—for example, in descriptions of group structure and processes—the Garland model can be significantly enhanced by some of the other formulations—in this case, by the model offered by Sarri and Galinsky. Overall, however, it must be noted that the five-stage model offers the most complete statement in the social work literature, and, far from being contradicted, it is actually supported to a large extent by the other models of group development.

MODELS OF SOCIAL GROUP WORK PRACTICE

It is evident that the implications for practice of the five stages of group development will vary according to the overall model for practice utilized by the worker. The author will attempt to show how implications for practice will differ in relation to the three models of group work practice proposed by Papell and Rothman: the social-goals model, the remedial model, and the reciprocal model (Papell and Rothman, 1966). Only a brief description of each will be outlined here, and the reader is directed to Papell and Rothman for a more complete development.[6]

1. *The social-goals model.* This model of social group work does not exist as a single formulation in the literature, nor does it owe its existence to a central theoretician who has systematically set forth all of its elements. It is, as Papell and Rothman state, a model that has its origins in the earliest traditions of social group work practice.

The social-goals model envisages social change brought about by responsible members of groups within society. The principle of democratic group process that is fundamental to this model has become a cornerstone of all social group work practice. Perhaps the leading current exponent of the social-goals model is Hyman Wiener, who states that social responsibility and social identity can be achieved only through scientific projects that must be chosen according to the location of the group worker in the agency, the distribution of power within the agency and community, and the time dimension. Wiener's approach utilizes social-systems theory, and he borrows strategies from Chin and Lippitt in seeking points within society vulnerable to change (Wiener, 1964).[7]

2. *The remedial model.* The remedial, or treatment, model of social group work is primarily concerned with the remediation of problems of psychological, social, and cultural adjustment through the use of a selected group experience. The group is viewed as both the "means and the context" for treatment by Vinter, who has outlined five phases in the treatment sequence: intake, diagnosis and treatment planning, group composition and formation, group development and treatment, and evaluation and termination (Vinter, 1967).

The remedial model was influenced early by the clinical work of Fritz Redl and David Wineman and by the writings of Gisela Konopka, whose *Therapeutic Group Work with Children* (Konopka, 1949) did much to establish group work as a full-fledged clinical modality (See Blum, 1964; Glasser, 1962; Kolodny, 1961; Kolodny and Burns, 1958; Konopka, 1967, 1954; Maier, 1965; and Vinter, 1959).

3. *The reciprocal model.* Unlike the other models of social group work, the reciprocal model has been most closely associated with a single theoretician, William Schwartz. The theoretical base for the reciprocal model derives largely from systems theory and and from field theory. Indeed, Schwartz seems to make the point that the system within which the method is practiced should be considered first and that one cannot properly speak of the "group work" method as such. "It seems more accurate," he writes, "to speak of a social work method practiced in the various systems in which the social work finds himself, or which are established for the purpose of giving service: the family, the small friendship group, the representative body, the one-to-one interview, the hospital ward, the committee, etc." (Schwartz, 1961).

Since goal-setting is an intrinsic part of the client-worker relationship, it is meaningless, in the view of the reciprocal theorist, to speak about the worker's goals for the client as if they were autonomous, independent entities. Since there are initially no specific social or therapeutic goals, emphasis is placed on engagement in interpersonal relationships. The worker carries out his function if he focuses on the symbiotic interdependence of the client and society and attempts to mediate between the two.[8]

IMPLICATIONS FOR PRACTICE

To summarize, this paper has attempted to integrate several models of small-group development from the social group work literature with the five-stage model suggested by Garland, Jones, and Kolodny. In addition, a brief outline of the three overall models of social group work practice, as developed by Papell and Rothman, has been provided. The final section of the paper is an attempt to develop strategies of intervention for each of the five stages of group development in relation to the three overall models of group work practice. These strategies of intervention will be consonant with the major requirements for the development of practice principles in social work, as outlined by Vinter (1960).

Vinter has identified four major requirements for the development of practice principles in social work:

1. Practice principles must specify or refer to the desired ends of action, the changed states of being in which it is intended that effective action will result.
2. Practice principles must incorporate the ethical principles, commitments, and values which prescribe and circumscribe professional activity.
3. Practice principles should incorporate valid knowledge about the most important phenomena or events with which professional workers are concerned.
4. Practice principles should direct the professional worker toward certain types of action, which, if engaged in, are likely to achieve the desired ends or goals (Vinter, 1960).

Vinter's criticism of the group work literature is that it tends to be valuative and ideological, rather than instrumental. That is, it stresses the larger ends toward which practice should be directed, while it seems relatively uncertain about specific means toward particular objectives. The following implications for practice will, in the main, adhere to the criteria advanced by Vinter, with some slight alteration of the second criterion concerning the identification and incorporation of values.

Jones has analyzed the three models of social group work practice in terms of group purposes, type of service, role of worker, image of group member, activities, requisite worker skills, and theory base (Table 10-2). It is the view of this writer that the overall values

TABLE 10-2. Models of Social Group Work Practice*

	Social-Goals Model	Remedial Model	Reciprocal Model
Purpose of group	Social consciousness and social responsibility	To remedy social dysfunctioning by specific behavioral change	To achieve a mutual aid system; initially, no specific goals
Type of service	Socialization and consumptive services	Integration and adaptive services	Adaptive, socialization, integrative and consumptive services
Role of worker	Enabler	Change agent	Mediator or resource person
Image of group member	Participating citizens and indigenous leaders	Deviants, to at least some degree	Ego vis-à-vis alter
Types of activity	Wide range of activities and tasks, including those of community organization	Use of direct and indirect means of influence, including extra-group means	Engagement of group members of process of interpersonal relations
Requisite worker skills	In programming	In intervention in group process to achieve specified goals	In definition and dialogue
Theory base	Eclectic theory base	Social role theory, socio-behavioral theory, ego psychology, group dynamics	Systems theory and field theory

*See Jones (1967).

are implied in the group purposes for each of the three models. Beyond these general statements, the practice implications, or action principles, contain, at least implicitly, value components of their own. Put even more simply, what the worker does defines the value orientation and ethical structure he is operating within in relation to his clients.[9] In effect, then, if the social work theoretician has specified the desired ends of the action, as well as the means for achieving those ends, he has, in the very process, made a statement of value preference. Therefore, outside of a statement of the general goals of the group or individual client, and in addition to the set of ethics which the profession holds in common, any further statement of values is superfluous and may even be misleading. In short, one may judge the value component of any practice principle by what it says to do, rather than by why it says to do it.

Action strategies will be suggested for each of the five stages of group development under each of the three overall models of group work practice.

STAGE I: PRE-AFFILIATION

Social-Goals Model

The worker makes a special attempt to identify and involve indigenous community leaders in the group and uses program for the purpose of acquainting group members with and involving them in the process of democratic participation. This is achieved, for example, in the worker's approach toward resolving decision issues, such as when the group should meet, and where.

Remedial Model

The worker provides an orientation to the group, outlines its purposes, and establishes a treatment "contract" with the members. A well-structured—and a worker-controlled—program allows for distance among the members, while it provides opportunities for exploration and invites trust. Activities that require a high degre of facilitative interdependence are passed over in favor of those that allow for parallel participation of the members.

Reciprocal Model

The worker begins to explore with the group the common elements that bind the members together, as well as those that separate them. The worker may suggest, but not insist upon, various program activities that will help to lay the basis for a mutual-aid system in the group. Through clarification, he helps the group to articulate common needs and explore possible group actions to meet those needs. He is not nearly as directive or controlling as the worker in the remedial model, but he may mediate between the demands of a larger social system (for example, the agency) and the needs of the individual group members.

STAGE II: POWER AND CONTROL

Social-Goals Model

The worker encourages all members of the client group to participate in decision-making but, essentially, he must go along with the group's decision about the leadership structure and work with those leaders who seem to have the support of the majority of the group members. Ideally, if he has been successful in laying the groundwork for democratic participation (in Stage I), then the leaders chosen will most likely be representative of the total group.

Functioning as an enabler, he makes his expertise in social action techniques and strategies available to the group members, but does not attempt to formulate objectives for the group. He may, at times, suggest specific action strategies, which will test the ability of the leadership to muster the support of the members in attempting to secure a specific objective. The task of policy-making, however, clearly rests with the members.

Remedial Model

While allowing for a certain amount of member rebellion and power struggle, the worker acts in his capacity of group executive and controller of membership roles to forestall the crystallization of any power takeover by a particular clique or subgroup. Sarri and Galinsky speak of maintaining the group through the revision stage and, in a similar vein, Garland, Jones, and Kolodny speak of the importance of protecting the safety of the individual members and their physical property. For example, the worker may wish to assign the various roles in activities, choose sides in games, promote low-status members through task assignments, and, generally, exert his influence as group leader to maintain an "open" group structure.

Reciprocal Model

The worker strives to clarify the power struggle and to focus again on the function of the group: to provide a mutual-aid system. In addition, he makes clear that worker, agency, and members are related to each other by certain rules and requirements imposed upon them by the terms of their agreement to come together. Schwartz stresses that any rules for the group should emerge from the function of the group and the necessities of the work, rather than from the personal authority of the helping agent (Schwartz, 1961). Thus, in terms of his manipulations of the group influence structure at this stage—through direct, personal intervention—the worker's function is considerably less directive than it would be in the remedial model and slightly more directive than it would be in the social-goals model.

STAGE III: INTIMACY

Social-Goals Model

As the leadership crisis is resolved and the members are more solidly linked together, they will likely raise questions about the worker's role and function within the group. He amplifies his function as consultant on strategy, while disavowing a policy-making role. He also clarifies the growing interdependence among the members and relates this to the ability of the group to attain its stated objectives: "If we stay united, we can achieve success." Finally, he encourages group activities that will reinforce the belief that working together brings results.

Remedial Model

The worker supports the group through the emotional turmoil of increased interdependency; he helps the members to sort out and discuss the positive and negative aspects of increased closeness and works with them to clarify how this group is different from the others (family group, peer group) in which they participate. He is constantly on the lookout for opportunities to entrust the members with responsibility, which in the earlier stages he has reserved for himself. Program is becoming more flexible and is now largely determined by the members themselves. Finally, the worker takes care to allow the group only the amount of program responsibility which it can reasonably handle; specifically, he has some structured activities ready to fall back on if the group seems unable to plan adequately for itself.

Reciprocal Model

In this stage, more than any other, the worker strives to "detect and challenge the obstacles which obscure the common ground between the members." Using clarification and confrontation, he may explore with the members those things that are keeping them from accomplishing their present tasks. While the causes of these obstacles may be fantastically complex, the focus of the worker is on dealing with the specific problems they are presently causing for the group. Through the contribution of ideas, facts, and value concepts, the worker helps the members to "see" what is keeping them from their stated objectives. This process may range all the way from having the members voice very specific complaints: "We don't like the way Joe always butts in when somebody else is talking," to discussions of more intricate and detailed misperceptions, or value conflicts: "If we go with you to the community center, then the rest of the kids on the block will think we're 'goodies.' "

STAGE IV: DIFFERENTIATION

Social-Goals Model

In this stage, the group has resolved most of its power problems and has high mutual support among the members, as well as good communication. The worker helps the group to formulate new objectives (as the original social-action goals may have already been attained) and continues to identify areas of need that might provide a basis for future social action. In carrying out these tasks, the worker takes care not to jeopardize his non-policy-making role. Even in this next-to-the-last stage of the group's development, the worker begins the process of extricating himself from the group, while doing all he can to insure its continued effectiveness by encouraging new members to join and participate.

Remedial Model

The worker helps the group to run itself by encouraging individual members to take responsibility for the planning and execution of program activities. With the increased cohesiveness and the heightened sense of the group's special identity as a separate, meaningful influence system, the worker can begin to direct the group toward projects which involve other groups and agencies in the larger community. He is constantly re-evaluating goals for the individual members and seeing how they may be related to the activities of the group at this particular stage. He gets the members to begin evaluation of their group experience in preparation for the group's termination. Typically, this may involve discussion of how the members had worked out some of the problems that they had brought with them to the group in the beginning.

Reciprocal Model

With the establishment of a mutual-aid system within the group, the worker helps the members to focus on changes they may wish to make in other systems outside the group. For example, a cottage group in an institution may focus on strategies of intervention designed to get the administration to change its policy on off-campus recreation. The worker uses his skill in definition to make clear when he is operating in his role as group member and when he is functioning primarily as agency representative. The worker aids the group in relating—while not necessarily adjusting—to its environment and helps the group in its effort to provide satisfaction for its members.

STAGE V: SEPARATION

Social-Goals Model

In this final stage, the worker aids the group in establishing linkages with other community structures and agencies in order to insure its continued effectiveness after his departure. In short, he tried to prepare the group for the fact of his absence and encourages members to think about new objectives when the original goals of the group have been realized. He may arrange for periodic consultation with the group, but the real test of his success will be made evident when he, literally, has "worked himself out of a job."[10]

Remedial Model

The worker helps the group through the process of termination by encouraging evaluation, recapitulation, and review. He is prepared to deal with nihilistic flight, denial, "separation anxiety," repression, and anger of the members that they are losing the group. Using extragroup means of influence, he helps the individual members plan for the meeting of their needs through other resources after the group has disbanded (Vinter and Galinsky, 1967). Program is highly mobile and community-oriented and designed to utilize the skills that the members have learned in the group.

Reciprocal Model

The worker helps the members to evaluate the process by which they develop the mutual-aid system and encourages them to think about ways in which they can achieve similar need satisfaction in the other systems in which they function. In addition, he works with the members to define the limits of the external situation in which the client-worker system is set and helps the members to determine how they will continue to operate within those limits (or modify them), once the group has been disbanded.

DISCUSSION

In 1962, Paul Glasser called for group work to broaden its theory base and make use of more concepts from the social and psychological sciences (Glasser, 1963). Unfortunately, a recent review of group work literature reveals just how little this suggestion has been implemented (Silverman, 1966). While it is undeniably true that group work is both art and science, it is equally true that the literature to date has focused much more on the art than on the science. Though some progress has been made, there are still far too few attempts to integrate knowledge from the behavioral sciences in models of practice and still fewer attempts to validate these practice models through empirical research. [11] The net result is that practitioners are too often left without clear guidelines for practice and are forced instead to rely upon their own intuition in decision-making. Without denying the value of intuition in practice, one can legitimately raise the question: "If intuition becomes the only basis for practice, then doesn't practice itself become so idiosyncratic as to preclude even speaking of any group work method?"

It is suggested that research in social group work should proceed in at least two directions: First, there should be an attempt to integrate existing practice models (as this paper has tried to do in the area of group development) and to develop implications for practice in terms of some overall conception of group work practice. The Papell and Rothman model, despite its limitations, seems best suited for this purpose, especially as it makes the distinction between remediation and social action. The time is past when group work theoreticians can afford themselves the luxury of developing models for practice without taking into consideration what has taken place before.

Second, a concerted attempt should be made to utilize knowledge from the social and behavioral sciences to inform group work practice theory. This process should involve not merely the transposition of theoretical models from the social sciences, but their empirical testing as well. While social group workers once viewed themselves as the arbiters of all that happened in groups, it is now sad to note that many group modes currently popular in social work (sensitivity training, family group therapy, and guided group interaction) have developed outside the pale of social group work. Unless, it seems to this writer, group work can look beyond its boundaries and at least attempt to incorporate appropriate strategies and techniques from other group modes, group workers will be in the unseemly position of having convinced only themselves of the efficacy of their work.

The practice implications suggested in this paper are clearly not exhaustive, and it is the intention of the author that they be expanded, modified, or discarded according to their utility. Current formulations of how small groups develop raise more questions than they answer. What, for example, is the relationship between the worker's intervention and the manner in which the group proceeds through the stages of development? Similarly, to what extent should we think of the various stages as mutually exclusive phases, or as elements which are always present in group life to some degree, but achieve prominence only at certain times? These and other questions remain to be answered. Social group work needs not fixed but flexible theoretical models that can incorporate new practice formulations as they are developed. If this brief paper serves as a first step in that direction, then its purpose will have been well served.

Finally, the ever increasing "haziness" between the traditional methods of casework, group work, and community organization makes it all the more urgent to define and develop a scientifically grounded theory for practice—not to rekindle the old arguments over "what" constitutes casework, or "what" is the role of group work, but in order to develop a unified theory of social work practice, which will include the best elements of each.

NOTES

1. For an introduction to the subject, see Cartwright and Zander (1960); Hare (1965); Hare, Borgatta, and Bales (1961); Homans (1950); Lewin (1951); Lippitt et al. (1958); Mann (1955); Martin and Hill (1957); Psathas (1960); Redl (1961); Scheidlinger (1957); and Theodorson (1953).
2. Homans (1950), for example, posits such recurring and reciprocal cycles, with activity, interaction, and sentiment being the essential basis for formation.
3. The author is well aware of the important contributions of Austin (1957), Bernstein (1949), Northen (1958), Paradise (1968), Shalinsky (1969), and Thomas and Fink (1963) to our knowledge of group development, but these materials will not be considered here.
4. The group is a potent influence system and can be used as an efficient vehicle for individual change. The group is not an end in itself. Group development can be controlled and influenced by the worker's actions. There is no optimal way in which groups develop.
5. This necessarily brief description of the five stages does not do justice to the full and intricate job done by the authors (Garland, Jones, and Kolodny, 1965).

6. For an insightful view of the historical development of the three models see Jones (1967).
7. See also Ginsberg and Goldberg (1961-62) Wiener (1961), and the early writings of Cohen, Coyle, Ginsberg, Kaiser, Klein, Miller, Phillips, and Wilson. For an excellent view of the values underlying the social-goals model see Konopka (1958).
8. See also Polsky (1962, 1968), Schwartz (1964, 1962), Shulman (1968) and Tropp (1965). For an introduction to systems theory see Bennis, Benne, and Chin (1961), Lippitt et al. (1958), and Parsons (1951).
9. For a further statement of how theoretical orientation influences philosophical outlook see Maier (1967).
10. As one group leader recently stated, "I'll know when I have achieved success, when the community group demands my resignation."
11. One recent empirical study in group work was executed by Feldman (1969). See also Trieschman, Whittaker, and Brendtro (1969) for an attempt to blend psychoanalytic ego psychology, social learning theory, and Redl's life-space theory into a unified model for milieu treatment.

REFERENCES

AUSTIN, D. M., 1957. "Goals for Gang Workers," *Social Work*, Vol. 2, No. 4.

BALES, R. F., and F. L. STRODTBECK, 1951. "Phases in Group Problem-Solving," *Journal of Abnormal and Social Psychology*, Vol. 46.

BENNIS, W., K. BENNE, and R. CHIN, 1961. *The Planning of Change.* New York: Holt, Rinehard & Winston.

BERNSTEIN, S., 1949. *Charting Group Progress.* New York: Association Press.

BLUM, A., 1964. "The Social Group Work Method: One View," *Conceptual Framework for Teaching the Social Group Work Method in the Classroom.* New York: Council on Social Work Education.

CARTWRIGHT, D., and A. ZANDER, 1960. *Group Dynamics.* New York: Harper & Row.

FELDMAN, R. A., 1969. "Group Integration, Intense Interpersonal Dislike, and Social Group Work Intervention," *Social Work*, Vol. 14, No. 3.

GARLAND, J., H. JONES, and R. KOLODNY, 1965. "A Model for Stages of Development in Social Work Groups," *Explorations in Group Work*, S. Bernstein, ed. Boston: Boston University School of Social Work.

GINSBERG, M., and J. GOLDBERG, 1961-62. "The Impact of the Current Scene on Group Work Policy and Practice," *Summary Presentation: Group Work Section Meetings.* New York: National Association of Social Workers.

GLASSER, P., 1963. "Group Methods in Child Welfare: Review and Preview," *Group Method and Services in Child Welfare.* New York: Child Welfare League of America.

——, 1962. "Social Role, Personality, and Group Work Practice," *Social Work Practice, 1962: Selected Papers from the 89th Annual Forum, National Conference on Social Welfare.* New York: Columbia University Press.

HARE, P. A., 1965. *Handbook of Social Group Research.* New York: Free Press.

——, E. F. BORGATTA, and R. F. BALES, eds., 1961. *Small Groups.* New York: Knopf.

HOMANS, G., 1950. *The Human Group.* New York: Harcourt, Brace.

JONES, J. F., 1967. "Social Group Work Method." Minneapolis, Minnesota (mimeographed).

KINDELSPERGER, W. L., 1957. "Stages in Group Development," *The Use of the Group in Welfare Settings.* New Orleans: Tulane University Press.

KOLODNY, R., 1961. "A Group Work Approach to the Isolated Child," *Social Work*, Vol. 6, No. 3.

——, and V. M. BURNS, 1958. "Group Work with Physically and Emotionally Handicapped Children in a Summer Camp," *Social Work with Groups, 1958.* New York: National Association of Social Workers.

KONOPKA, G., 1967. *The Adolescent Girl in Conflict.* Englewood Cliffs, N.J.: Prentice-Hall.

——, 1958. *Edward C. Lindeman and Social Work Philosophy.* Minneapolis: University of Minnesota.

——, 1954. *Group Work in the Institution.* New York: Association Press.

——, 1949. *Therapeutic Group Work with Children*, Minneapolis: University of Minnesota Press.

LEWIN, K., 1951. *Field Theory in Social Science.* New York: Harper & Brothers.

LIPPITT, R., et al., 1958. *The Dynamics of Planned Change.* New York: Harcourt, Brace.

MAIER, H. W., 1967. "Application of Psychological and Sociological Theory to Teaching Social Work With the Group,"*Journal of Education for Social Work*, Vol. 3.

——, 1961-62. "Research Project on Group Development." Seattle: University of Washington School of Social Work (mimeographed).

——, ed., 1965. *Group Work as Part of Residential Treatment.* New York: National Association of Social Workers.

MANN, J., 1955. "Some Theoretical Concepts of the Group Process," *International Journal of Group Psychotherapy*, Vol. 5.

MARTIN, E. A., and W. HILL, 1957. "Toward a Theory of Group Development: Six Phases of Therapy Group Development," *International Journal of Group Psychotherapy*, Vol. 7, No. 1.

NORTHEN, H., 1958. "Social Group Work: A Tool for Changing Behavior of Disturbed Acting-Out Adolescents," *Social Work With Groups, 1958.* New York: National Association of Social Workers.

PAPELL, C. B., and B. ROTHMAN, 1966. "Social Group Work Models: Possession and Heritage,," *Journal of Education for Social Work*, Vol. 2., No. 2.

PARADISE, R., 1968. "The Factor of Timing in the Addition of New Members to Established Groups," *Child Welfare*, Vol. 47 No. 9.

PARSONS, T., 1951. *The Social System.* Glencoe, Ill.: Free Press.

POLSKY, H. W., 1962. *Cottage Six.* New York: Russell Sage Foundation.

——, 1968. *The Dynamics of Residential Treatment: A Social System Approach.* Chapel Hill: University of North Carolina Press.

PSATHAS, G., 1960. "Phase Movement and Equilibrium Tendencies in Interaction Process in Psychotherapy Group," *Sociometry*, Vol. 23.

REDL, F., 1961. "Group Emotion and Leadership." *Small Groups*, A. P. Hare, E. F. Borgatta, and R. F. Bales, eds. New York: Knopf.

SARRI, R., and M. GALINSKY, 1967. *Readings in Group Work Practice*, R. D. Vinter, ed. Ann Arbor, Mich.: Campus Publishers.

SCHEIDLINGER, S., 1953. "The Concept of Social Group Work and Group Psychotherapy," *Social Casework*, Vol. 34.

SCHWARTZ, W., 1964. "The Classroom Teaching of Social Work with Groups," *A Conceptual Framework for the Teaching of the Social Group Work Method in the Classroom.* New York: Council on Social Work Education.

——, 1961. "The Social Work in the Group," *New Perspectives on Services to Groups: Theory, Organization and Practice.* New York: National Association of Social Workers.

——, 1962. "Toward a Strategy of Group Work Practice," *Social Service Review*, Vol. 36, No. 3.

SHALINSKY, W., 1969. "Group Composition as an Element of Social Group Work Practice," *Social Service Review*, Vol. 43; No. 1.

SHULMAN, L., 1968. *A Casebook of Social Work with Groups: The Mediating Model.* New York: Council on Social Work Education.

SILVERMAN, M., 1966. "Knowledge in Social Group Work: A Review of the Literature," *Social Work*, Vol. 11, No. 3.

THEODORSON, G. A., 1953. "Elements in the Progressive Development of Small Groups," *Social Forces*, Vol. 31. No. 4.

THOMAS, E. J., and C. F. FINK, 1963. "Effects of Group Size," *Psychological Bulletin*, Vol. 60.

TRECKER, H. B., 1955. *Social Group Work: Principles and Practices.* New York: Association Press.

TRIESCHMAN, A. E., J. K. WHITTAKER, and L. K. BRENDTRO, 1969. *The Other 23 Hours: Child Care Work in a Therapeutic Milieu.* Chicago: Aldine.

TROPP, E., 1965. "Group Intent and Group Work Practice," *Journal of Jewish Communal Service*, Vol. 41.

VINTER, R. D., 1967. "The Essential Components of Social Group Work Practice," *Readings in Group Work Practice*, R. D. Vinter, ed. Ann Arbor, Mich.: Campus Publishers.

——, 1959. "Group Work: Perspectives and Prospects," *Social Work with Groups, 1959.* New York: National Association of Social Workers.

——, 1960. "Problems and Processes in Developing Group Work Practice Principles," *Theory Building in Social Group Work.* New York: Council on Social Work Education.

—— and M. GALINSKY, 1967. "Extra-Group Relations and Approaches," *Readings in Group Work Practice*, R. D. Vinter, ed. Ann Arbor, Mich.: Campus Publishers.

WIENER, H. J., 1964. "Social Change and Social Group Work Practice," *Social Work*, Vol. 9., No. 3.

——, 1961. "Toward Techniques for Social Change," *Social Work*, Vol. 6. No. 2.

11

Social Group Work: A Model for Goal Formulation

Rosamond P. Tompkins is Service Coordinator, Prince William County Community Mental Health and Mental Retardation Services Board, Manassas, Virginia.

Frank T. Gallo is Director of Social Service at Lowell General Hospital, Lowell, Massachusetts.

Rosamond P. Tompkins and *Frank T. Gallo*

In devising a conceptual model for goal formulation in social groupwork one must draw from existing models for ideas on structure and content. The intent here is to combine the elements of existing models, as well as to add new elements, to develop a more comprehensive and useful model of social groupwork than presently exists.

Any model for social work practice should be viewed as a tool that can be used by the worker in evaluation and goal setting. The implication in this paper is not that our model should be rigidly adhered to as the only way to understand social work groups, rather, it is one way, and it is hoped that as its secondary purpose it can serve as the basis for future models.

One distinction to be made at the outset is that between a conceptual model and a developmental model. For our working definition, a conceptual model for groupwork is one that portrays the purposes, functions, and methods of social work groups. Understanding that different social work groups have different purposes, functions, and methods, the conceptual model must be broad enough to allow universal application. Developmental models are built on the theory that groups go through various stages. They attempt to describe these stages through which groups progress, and sometimes regress, during their existence. Conceptual and developmental models complement one another but in no way substitute for one another.

The original version of this article appeared under the title "Social Groupwork: A Model for Goal Formulation," by Rosamond P. Tompkins and Frank T. Gallo, published in *Small Group Behavior*, Vol. 9, No. 3, August 1978, pp. 307-317, and is reprinted herewith by permission of the Publisher, Sage Publications, Inc.

The models discussed in this paper are conceptual models. For examples of developmental models, see Garland et al. (1973), Yalom (1970), Northen (1969). For an excellent illustration of the complementarity between developmental and conceptual models, see Whittaker (1970).

Both developmental and conceptual models have implications for practice. The former gives clues to the worker for a group diagnosis and treatment depending on *where* the group is dynamically. The latter aids the worker to make practice decisions based on *what* the group is and *how* it works.

Implicit in all discussions of social work practice is the question of goals and goal formulation. Lowy (1973, p. 116) discusses the goal formulating process in the various stages of the developmental model but states that "eventually, practice theory will have to relate goal setting to the other models as well." It is from this context that our conceptual model for goal formulation in social groupwork developed. A discussion of some of the existing models and their limitations will show the genesis of our attempt to formulate an encompassing groupwork model that facilitates goal formulation.

EXISTING MODEL

Several conceptual models for groupwork have been presented in social work literature. Papell and Rothman (1966) discussed three of these which they termed the social goals model, the remedial model, and the reciprocal model. A fourth model which includes elements of the other three is described by Lang (1972). Although there are others, these are representative of the spectrum of models available. The first three describe specific ways of conceptualizing a group. The Lang model places elements of these three into one comprehensive model and is more in line with the model we envision.

The social goals model, as described by Papell and Rothman (1966; p. 68), has as its key concepts "social consciousness and social responsibility. The function of social group work is to create a broader base of knowledgeable and skilled citizenry." The implication is "that there is a unity between social action and individual psychological health. Every individual is seen as potentially capable of some form of meaningful participation in the mainstream of society" (Papell and Rothman, 1966, p. 68). The worker is an influencing person who personifies social responsibility and serves as a role model for the group. The worker's goals are directed toward the group's realization of group goals.

The remedial model is the traditional "clinical" model. Individual clients are identified in terms of their problems and how these can be remedied. The worker takes an active role and is seen as "change agent rather than enabler" (Papell and Rothman, 1966, p. 68).

Slavson (1964, p. 130) claims that the "general aim of all psychotherapies . . . is to improve or cure the patient." He sees individual diagnosis as the fundamental key to this improvement or cure.

> Experience with several thousand patients has impressed upon us the importance of an exhaustive understanding of each patient; his background, his early formative relations, his medical history, psychic structure and dynamics, his organic and psychic pathology and ego functioning in interpersonal relations [Slavson, 1964, p. 130].

In essence, the individual member's growth has ascendancy over the group in the remedial model.

The third model presented by Papell and Rothman, the reciprocal model, can be seen as a combination of the first two. Much of the thinking on this type of model came from Schwartz (1961). The focus is on the interdependence of the individual and the society. Group interaction through personal encounter among members is the goal of these groups. The worker becomes a mediator.

Each of these models addresses only a portion of the total continuum, i.e., from individual change as represented by the remedial model on one end, to societal change as expressed in the social goals model on the other. The reciprocal model seems to combine the two extreme views. In focusing on only one part of this continuum, none of the three models can be considered an encompassing social groupwork model.

These models are limited further in their views of the worker's role. When we see a social groupworker as primarily any one thing, e.g., influence person, enabler, broker, advocate, or agent, we are contradicting the inherently necessary flexibility of social workers. Different groups and different situations within each group will require that the insightful professional worker recognize when one role is more appropriate and beneficial to the group's members.

In 1972 Lang (p. 77) submitted a "new model" that essentially combined the three previous models into one model. She labels groups as "allonomous," "autonomous," and "allon-autonomous," referring, respectively, to groups that are controlled by external stimuli, are self-controlled, or are a blend of external and internal control. Her allonomous group corresponds to the remedial model, her autonomous group is the equivalent of the social goals, and her allon-autonomous or transitional group resembles the reciprocal. What is unique about the Lang model is that it incorporates a consideration of individual, group, and/or societal change by means of the group process into one model.

What would make the Lang model more realistic and useable for social workers would be the application of social systems theory with its implications of permeable boundaries. That is, within this comprehensive model, we need to allow for more blending and overlap of functions, client needs and purposes, and practice principles. It is upon this systems foundation and within this comprehensive framework that our model is based.

ELEMENTS OF THE GOAL FORMULATION MODEL

A social work group has the purpose of meeting the needs of its members or the members should not and indeed will not want to be there. The needs may be social, psychological, or a combination of both. (Certain other specific needs centering around spiritual, educational, athletic, or entertainment activities can indeed be met by groupwork but are not usually the main focus of social work groups and thus are not intended to fit into this model. A social work model focuses on the psychosocial milieu.) The method of groupwork employed to meet these members' needs may be task-oriented, activity-oriented, or specifically treatment-oriented, or a combination of these orientations. Any one or any combination of these will fit into the model.

The social work group provides the arena for people to work together on common needs. It is too limiting for a social worker to think in terms of a social work group as *only* a place for individual members' therapy or *only* a place for social consciousness raising. Social workers must recognize that people's individual and social needs vary from time to time in proportion and in relative intensity to one another. If we are going to have a model for groupwork practice that includes this recognition, then it must also be one that allows variation.

The worker can be an enabler, influence person, mediator, broker, advocate, or direct change agent. He selects his major role after assessment of group needs but recognizes that from time to time he will be required to move to another role temporarily or even for extended periods.

Thus, the social groupworker needs a broad base of knowledge to perform properly in the various groupwork situations that he will find himself. This consists of information in social work theory, sociology, psychology, social systems theory, psychiatry, and economics. In addition, he must familiarize himself with the specific knowledge base pertinent to the agency and the field of practice. Thus, the person trained exclusively in psychology, for example, will probably not be adequately trained to do social groupwork.

Clients are viewed from various perspectives although the focus is usually on one particular system. The Client is seen as an individual, as a member of a small group, as a member of a family system, or as a member of a community. We focus on one of these systems depending on the needs of the client. What is most important in terms of our model, however, is that although groupworkers must focus on one particular system in which the client belongs, we must also recognize that they are members of other systems and all of these affect the system we are focusing on.

A criticism of models that attempts to be comprehensive is that the cost of comprehensiveness is lost specificity. This model, however, allows the worker to focus as specifically as necessary on client group, function, or professional role. The model is not a compromising effort to combine the elements of a few other models. Rather, it is an attempt to conceptualize the entire spectrum of social groupwork so that the worker will have a design to aid him in applying theory to practice in any social groupwork situation.

THE MODEL

With a comprehensive knowledge source and a systems view, the worker is equipped to evaluate the quality of relationships among the individual, the group, and society to formulate group goals.

Papell and Rothman point out that groupwork theory has never resolved the appropriate balance between the individual, the small group, and society. We have seen how the remedial, reciprocal, and social goals models emphasize one aspect of this triad, jeopardizing the effect of the interrelationship of the other two. The Lang model gives equal emphasis to each part of the triad but, again, fails to recognize the interrelatedness of the systems. Our model intends to give equal consideration to the three systems, and the various subsystems that come together to make each system what it is. While the "appropriate balance" of individual to group to society is perpetually changing, the model enables the worker to conceptualize this triadic relationship more clearly than previous models.

In assessing a group for goal formulation, the worker examines what each system brings with it (subsystems) to interact with the other systems, and what the quality of this interaction will be, given the character of each system. The quality of interaction refers to the degree of stress and strain, e.g., patterns of communication, producing tension between or among systems. This interaction (represented in Figure 11-1 by lines of the triangle) will determine what part of the change continuum (represented by the goals circle) must be addressed and according to what priorities. Goals change as the quality of interactions changes; goals may be remedial, reciprocal, or social in nature, or a combination thereof.

In considering each system, we have selected factors, i.e., subsystems, that specifically contribute to the social functioning of each system. The things that most significantly affect society's relationship to people, be they in groups or as individuals, are its economic and political conditions, philosophical values, and cultural norms and stereotypes. What society—be it government, community, or social environment—thinks of its citizens will be manifest in activities and behavior that society does and/or does not sanction.

An individual's style of relating to people in groups or to society

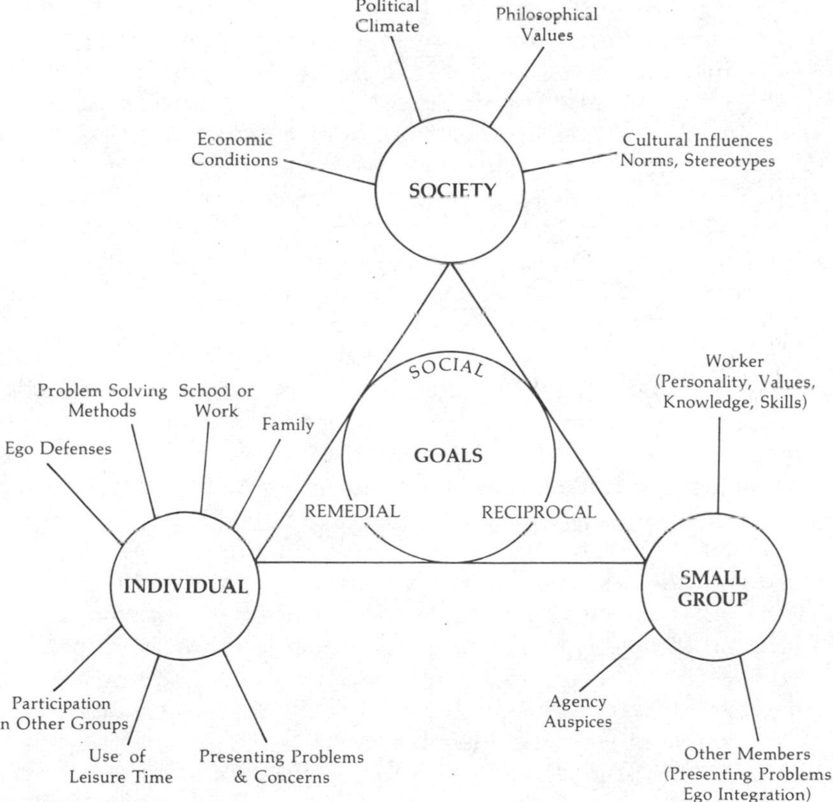

NOTE: Lines between systems represent the "quality of interaction" between systems. They may be solid, as here, depicting smooth relationships, broken, -----, depicting poor communication, or jagged,/\/\/\/\, depicting extreme tension between systems.

Figure 11.1

at large will be determined by the nature or quality of his present and past relationships, with his family, at work or school, and in other groups. From these experiences, the individual develops a perception of himself and a repertoire of "ego defenses" and problem-solving behavior, which will be labeled adaptive or maladaptive by society. Tension develops between systems when those things that each expects and/or needs from the other are not forthcoming. For example, an individual expects society to either provide job opportunities or money for sustenance. The society demands that people work to be valued, but economic conditions eliminate people from the work force. Conflict ensues. The individual's presenting problems may range from these large societal conflicts, i.e., cannot secure employment, to more personal psychodynamic concerns, i.e., the effect of unemployment on self-esteem, and will help determine the goals and point of intervention.

The relationship of the social group to the other two systems is probably most affected by the personalities and presenting problems of the other members, the worker's personality, knowledge, values, and skills, and the auspices of the setting, be it institution, agency, or elsewhere. What makes up the group in turn makes up the quality of interaction with the individual member and the society in which the group finds itself. Again, tension occurs when what the group expects of the individual and/or society is not forthcoming or vice versa. The relationships among the various systems are presented in the diagram.

The worker's task, in assessing a situation using this model, is to determine wherein lies harmony and disharmony among the three systems and why. A goal formulation follows from such an appraisal. The goals circle is to be viewed as a continuum from individual to societal change. Once it is determined which systems' relationships are most tension ridden, it becomes clearer where to address efforts at change. If an individual's experiences in relation to others have been so destructive that his problems are primarily psychodynamic in nature and are the main source of conflict between the individual and the other systems, then the goals must be of a remedial quality, focused on the individual's self-enhancement. If, however, the group is composed of integrated, well-functioning individuals who are trying to come to terms with some societal injustice, e.g., racial discrimination in housing, then the social goals perspective will be utilized. Which goals are selected will depend upon the proportion of change desired among the systems. That is, if change in both the individual and change in the group is warranted, then the goals will neither be entirely remedial nor reciprocal, but instead, will incorporate elements of both. Likewise if psychodynamic issues and task issues arise simultaneously, goals will be formulated around both. We adhere to the notion commonly expressed in the literature that psychodynamic issues usually should be addressed before the task.

Illustrations of the model put to use will demonstrate its applicability. Consider, for example, a welfare mother seeking day care for her three-year-old so that she can look for a job. Having just moved into the housing project, she feels isolated and alone in tackling her problem. The settlement house groupworker puts her in touch with an ongoing group of mothers who are attempting to deal with this and other issues common to their experience. There is tension between the individual and society and the group and society. In an effort to alleviate this tension, the individual and the group, not in conflict with each other, come together for the achievement of goals not entirely "remedial" in nature nor "reciprocal" either. Concerned with both the individual member's functioning and with what the group can do for itself, the mothers begin to talk of organizing a volunteer day care center from among the project's mothers and older children. Concerns and goals have moved along the continuum from remedial issues of a person's functioning to more reciprocal self-help goals. Eventually these mothers approach the settlement house to secure funding for a day care center. Their goals become more congruent with the social goals model. If the groupworker were a subscriber to only one of the other three models mentioned, he would fail to perceive change goals capable of accomplishment by this group over time.

Consider another example. A juvenile offender has been taken to court for possession of drugs and referred to a youth detention center (tension between individual and society's expectations.) The fifteen-year-old boy has a history of conflicts with his mother (his father is out of the home since parents' divorce when he was five); low achievement in school, acting out disruptive behavior, and generally antagonistic social relationships; his self-image is poor. (Individual's presenting problem is low self-image, unsuccessful problem-solving methods, disintegrated family life, poor peer relationships.)

The detention center is currently running a wilderness group which is developing survival skills in nature, e.g., learning to white-water canoe and rock climb. The group has met only twice. The center's experience has been that boys who have participated in such endeavors have substantially enhanced self-images and capacity for working together as a group. In view of the boy's background and presenting problems, the worker speaks to the group about his participation. Though they agree, his arrival causes discord and tension between the individual and the group. The goals will fall somewhere on the bottom third of the goals continuum, depending on the quality of their interaction and how it changes over time. While at times the goals may focus on his successful integration into the group, the activity they are engaged in will demand that they work cooperatively. The goals are neither totally remedial in nature, nor reciprocal, but fluctuate somewhere in between.

It is possible that, if the group becomes invested enough in the wilderness activity and sport and sees a threat to the conservation of their wildlife area, they could redirect some of their "antisocial" energy into social goals concerns with regard to the wilderness environment. A worker subscribing purely to the remedial model would never consider this as a possibility.

SOME IMPLICATIONS FOR PRACTICE

If utilized in practice, the comprehensive model for social groupwork we have outlined could have a number of ramifications for agencies and workers, some of which have already been mentioned.

Groupworkers could no longer claim to be "therapists" or "organizers" alone, but indeed must be flexible enough to address themselves to the potential for change on a variety of levels, individual to societal. In like manner, agencies offering a specific, narrow range of groupwork services might find such a model useless, given the narrow definition of their service. A frequent criticism of social services is, in fact, that a client's problems are identified according to the service the agency provides. Agencies subscribing to this model could no longer do this because, clearly, a client's problems are determined by systems external to the agency.

Although it may appear that the worker has substantial authority and control in the goal formulation process, we subscribe to the concept of the group's self-determination. While the model is useful to the worker in fulfilling his part of the contract process, it does not negate the importance of the group's role in the process. Both are necessary for goal formulation. There is no contract until both worker and members agree upon stated goals.

Certainly there are other practice implications that apply, and it is hoped that after either studying or using our model, other workers will elaborate on these. It is further hoped that this model will be viewed as an attempt to supplement existing groupwork theory and to provide one link in a continuous chain of groupwork research.

REFERENCES

GARLAND, J. A., H. E. JONES, and R. L. KOLODNY, 1973. "A Model for Stages of Development in Social Work Groups," in *Explorations in Group Work*, S. Bernstein, ed. Boston: Milford House.

LANG, N. C., 1972. "A Broad-Range Model of Practice in the Social Work Group," *Social Service Review*, Vol. 46, No. 1.

LOWY, L., 1973. "Goal Formulation in Social Work with Groups," in *Further Explorations in Group Work*, S. Bernstein, ed. Boston: Milford House.

NORTHEN, H., *1969. Social Work with Groups.* New York: Columbia University Press.

PAPELL, C. P., and B. ROTHMAN, 1966. "Social Group Work Models: Possession and Heritage," *Journal of Education for Social Work*, Vol. 2, No. 2.

SCHWARTZ, W., 1961. "The Social Worker in the Group," *Social Welfare Forum* New York: Columbia University Press.

SLAVSON, S. R., *1964. A Textbook in Analytic Group Psychotherapy.* New York: International Universities Press.

WHITTAKER, J. K., 1970. "Models of Group Development: Implications for Social Group Work Practice," *Social Service Review*, Vol. 44, No. 3.

YALOM, I. D., 1970. *The Theory and Practice of Group Psychotherapy.* New York: Basic Books.

Study Questions

1. How would you define such terms as: model, perspective, frame-of-reference, theory, approach, formulations, etc.? Clearly, these terms are used interchangeably in the literature. Is it essential that there be precision and agreement in the way such terms are used? Why or why not?

2. What are the benefits to be derived from the model-building activity as found in literature on group work? How has it helped to rationalize the increasingly complex functions that characterize practice? How has it contributed to our theoretical understanding?

3. Do you agree with Papell and Rothman's assessment of the strengths and weaknesses of the various models? For example, does the tendency of the social goals model to negate individual dynamics limit its utility, as they suggest? Has the emphasis on democratic group processes become the hallmark of *all* social group work practice? How, specifically, has the remedial model facilitated the functioning of group work practices in clinical settings? How has it failed to allow for the potential contributions of the group to the larger environment? Do you agree with the theoretical issues raised concerning Schwartz's position?

4. Do the various models equally reflect a common social work frame of reference? Can clear distinctions be made between these models and group methods in such other disciplines as medicine, counseling, and psychology? (See Alissi, Chapter 24 below.)

5. Lang (1972) indicates that the models are not easily compared because they have been formulated in different conceptual terms. Whereas the reciprocal model is based on process, the social goals and remedial models are conceptualized in terms of goals. How might the categorization be modified to eliminate this divergence? "Models," Lang says, "are made to be dismantled." Better models can always be built which more accurately reflect the reality of practice. How would you go about modifying and changing current models to approximate more closely the reality of practice?

6. In discussing the inherent dangers and limitations of model-building, Papell and Rothman (1978) also note the discrepancy that exists between "logical systems of thought" and actual practices. They suggest certain uncharted areas that could be explored. Contemporary models do not, for example, deal with the multiple impact of worker interventions to show how the focus of intervention can have multiple consequences throughout the group. Moreover, the models offer little help in dealing with issues regarding intimacy, privacy, openness, and autonomy in relations between the worker and group and among the members themselves. What kinds of issues do you see that should be explored?

7. Whereas Whittaker was able to integrate various practice formulations regarding group development within a single five-stage model, developed by Garland and his associates, the models described by Papell and Rothman were not similarly integrated but were accepted as distinctive strategies guiding worker interventions. Can Papell and Rothman's framework be taken as an overall conception of group work practice without integrating the models? If

you are given to eclecticism, how would you go about combining the best elements of each into a unified framework?

8. What is the significance of differentiating between conceptual and developmental models? Are there other types of models as well? Can you think of specific examples to show how Tompkins and Gallo's model for goal formulation may be applied in practice? Does the existing service system allow for the kind of worker flexibility required? What kinds of skills would workers need to develop further? Does the model deal with incompatible approaches? How, for example, does it allow for integrating the medical model with Tropp's humanistic developmental orientation? (See Tropp, Chapter 15 below.)

Suggested Readings

ALISSI, A. S., 1970. "Establishing Patterns of Intervention in Group Work," *Journal of Jewish Communal Service*, Vol. 46, No. 4.

CHURCHILL, S. R., 1974. "A Comparison of Two Models of Social Group Work: The Treatment Model and the Reciprocal Model," in *Individual Change Through Small Groups.* P. Glasser, R. Sarri, and R. Vinter, eds. New York: Free Press.

LANG, N. C., 1972. "A Broad Range Model of Practice in the Social Work Group," *Social Service Review*, Vol. 46, No. 1.

MOORE, E. E., 1978. "The Implication of System Network for Social Work with Groups: Literature and Experience," *Social Work with Groups*, Vol. 1, No. 2.

NORTHEN, H., and R. W. ROBERTS, 1976. "The Status of Theory," in *Theories of Social Work with Groups*, R. W. Roberts and H. Northen, eds. New York: Columbia University Press.

PAPELL, C. P., and B. ROTHMAN, 1978. "Editorial," *Social Work with Groups*, Vol. 1, No. 3.

SCHWARTZ, W., 1964. "Analysis of Papers," in *Working Papers Toward a Frame of Reference for Social Group Work*, M. Hartford, ed. New York: National Association of Social Workers.

VINTER, R., 1965. "Social Group Work," *Encyclopedia of Social Work*. New York: National Association of Social Workers.

SECTION B

Personal Growth and Social Change: "Social Goals" Perspectives

The readings contained in this and the following two sections represent the major perspectives on social group work today. These can, of course, be classified in any number of ways, depending upon the organizing principles used. Although the sections seemingly reflect the prevalent tripolar view (social goals, remedial, and reciprocal), the aim here is not to highlight or reinforce any particular categorization scheme but simply to offer a representative picture of the various conceptions as they are found in the group work literature.

It is only partially true that the chapters in this section represent the social goals model. Unfortunately, the use of the term "social goals," while helpful in differentiating between approaches, tends at times to be narrowed in conception to an extent where social consciousness and responsibility are assumed to outweigh individual needs. Yet it is clear from the readings that concern for advancing social purposes was never intended to supplant or overshadow concern for the individual. Perhaps Newstetter put it most succinctly when he wrote, "It is only when we find the combined and consistent and balanced pursuit of both these objectives—meeting personal needs of particular individuals and specific community needs—that we have what I call social group work." This dual concern characterizes all the perspectives, whether the emphasis is on individual growth or remedial change or whether the focus on society changes from reform and progress to social control. And again, all, in one way or another, share a belief in the interactive influences of the individual, group, and society.

The dual emphasis on helping people to enhance their own personal well-being and to participate in changing social conditions for the common good is clearly reflected in the chapters in this section. Thus in Wilson and Ryland's definition and description of the "what," "who," and "how" of social group work, excerpted from their influential textbook, both purposes grow out of the growth and development of the group. Similarly, Helen Phillips, reflecting a functional point of view, stresses both personal development and responsible social participation in her classic discussion of group work skills. The social goals perspective is perhaps best illustrated in the "Pittsburgh" position, which states flatly that group work cannot be considered group work unless members are in some way encouraged to bring about change in their environment. But even where it is acknowledged that the uniqueness of group work stems from its combined interest in the individual and the group as well as in social goals. And finally, the chapter by Emanuel Tropp puts forth a humanistic orientation that holds strongly to the view that the most effective means for achieving social growth is through participation in self-directing groups where members are able to achieve common group goals and objectives.

12

The Social Group Work Method

At the time this was written, both authors were on the faculty of the School of Social Work, University of Pittsburgh. Gertrude Wilson is now Professor Emeritus, University of California, Berkeley.

Gladys Ryland is a former professor at Tulane University School of Social Work, New Orleans.

Gertrude Wilson and *Gladys Ryland*

One cannot examine the life of any group without realizing its potentialities for affecting the attitudes and consequently the values of the members. Group interaction is the social force through which individual growth and development take place. It is also the means through which societal growth and change are accomplished. While group life makes growth possible, it does not necessarily mean that *any* group life develops a happy, well-balanced individual or a democratic society. Achievement of these ends depends upon the set of values which are the dominant ideals of the members and of the society of which they are a part. A worker is assigned to a group in order that he may influence it for some social purpose which is of value to the sponsor of the group. That social purpose may be totalitarian or it may be democratic (Lewin, 1947). . . .

Most social agencies serving groups have two purposes in common: (1) to help individuals use groups to further their development into emotionally balanced, intellectually free, and physically fit persons; (2) to help groups achieve ends desirable in an economic, political, and social democracy. Social group work, as developed in this book, is a method of affecting group life with reference to these purposes which are the lifeblood of the social welfare movement. We therefore see social group work as a process and a method through which group life is affected by a worker who consciously directs the interacting process toward the accomplishment of goals which in our country are conceived in a democratic frame of reference. . . .

Both of the purposes—that is, (1) to help individuals personally and (2) to help the group achieve socially acceptable corporate ends—for which the social group work method is used are dependent upon the growth and development of the *group*. Since the group is the vehicle through which the members are served, the survival and achievements of the group are essential to the first purpose. The importance of the survival of the group to the attainment of the second purpose is self-evident. Thus it is seen that the two purposes merge; for service to individuals is predicated upon service to the group-as-a-whole, and service to the group-as-a-whole is possible only through helping individuals. Through this process individuals and groups contribute to society, whose development is dependent upon the changes which emerge from socially significant groups.

We shall discuss social group work, then, as a method through which the worker uses his knowledge and understanding of the members of groups as he affects the social processes involved in personal and group situations. We pose three questions summarized as what? who? and how?

THE "WHAT" OF SOCIAL GROUP WORK

The Group Situation

The situation in which members and worker find themselves includes the values and norms of the member, and the attitudes of the members toward one another, toward the worker and the agency; the agency's values and norms as revealed in its purposes, policies, and programs; and the values, norms, and attitudes of the worker as revealed in his professional behavior.

Members join groups for a variety of reasons. Sometimes they come to agencies in groups; and sometimes they come or are sent or even brought as individuals. Sometimes they come because they know that they have problems which may be rooted in family relations or personality conflicts, or in the need to make new friends and have new experiences. Many times they come simply because they are looking for a good time or because they have nothing else to do.

The motivation in a hospital, clinic, or health institution may be voluntary or prescribed. Groups are established in these institutions in order to provide diversion and treatment. Membership in a diversional group may be motivated either by a desire to escape the boredom of the institutional routine or by a real interest in companionship or in the activities carried on within the group. Membership in treatment groups is accepted as part of the program of the institution and may or may not be in line with the patients' personal desires.

Groups in custodial institutions have even greater significance than those offered as a general community service. They are substitutes for home and community group life. This is particularly true in children's homes, reformatories, institutions for the chronically ill, and homes for the aged. In these settings, individuals have a great need for something to which they can belong and through which they can exercise their capacities for decision-making. Individuals in these settings usually are eager for the opportunity to participate in the semi-autonomous group serviced by social group workers.

The purposes of agencies in providing group service may be quite different from the expressed purposes of the participating members; they are often more closely related to the unexpressed, often unconscious, desires of the membership. This is particularly true of the agencies whose primary purpose is related (1) to the development of personality and of socially significant groups and (2) to the use of the group work method for therapeutic ends. When the objectives of an agency are related to a specific frame of reference of values and norms, there may be a hiatus between its primary purpose and the purposes of many of the members whose motivations, interests, and needs may be quite different from those presupposed by the auspice. In this case, the program of the agency will take on some of the aspects of propaganda, conversion, or reform, and the method of working with groups will take on many aspects of manipulation rather than of enabling, unless the members clearly understand and accept the purposes of the agency and have a well-defined area in which they are free to make decisions related to their own activities.

Since the decision-making process is the central core of the social group work method, it is essential that the structure be such that the members have the privileges and responsibilities of the management of their own corporate affairs. A collection of individuals will not develop the characteristics of a social group unless they have the right and the ability to make decisions significant to their own group life. Nor will they grow and develop unless they experience the discipline which comes from the adjustment of personal claims to the claims of the group-as-a-whole.

All individuals are not physically, intellectually, or emotionally equipped to participate in the decision-making process and are either lost in the group or not enrolled in the agency's program. They are, however, in the community or institution and they need the special attention which they can receive in a protected group situation. Some agencies provide special groups for such individuals; it is acknowledged from the start that there will be very little decision-making until the personalities of the members have developed considerably. In such groups, the social group worker participates very actively in planning the program. In fact, he may have to do all the program planning until the members become less aggressive or more expressive of their individual and collective interests and needs. The latter situation is particularly true of groups sponsored by hospitals, clinics, and institutions.

The worker's aim is to help the members of groups develop the capacity to carry on their own group life; make their plans and decisions and carry them out. Groups vary in their capacity to function on this level, either because of the developmental period of the members, their state of emotional health, or their social knowledge and experience. Accordingly, the extent of the worker's activity varies greatly. When the members are unable to cope with the demands of group life, he must act in a controlling capacity. At the other extreme, where the members are eager and competent to participate in group life, to accept its responsibilities and enjoy its satisfactions, the worker is an enabling observer. . . .

It is not the function of the agency to provide a program for the group. The agency has an overall objective which it accomplishes through the provision of facilities and services to groups whose purposes are related to its objectives. The social group worker helps the members to carry out these purposes through the development of their own program. It should be apparent, therefore, that whatever is defined as the purpose of the agency has a direct bearing on the decision-making process within the agency's constituent groups. . . .

THE "WHO" OF SOCIAL GROUP WORK

People of all ages, of all ethnic, occupational, religious, economic and social class groupings, in sickness and in health, constitute the who of social group work. While the basic principles of social group work remain constant in working with all groups, their form of application is affected by the factors of difference in the behavior of individuals and in the social processes these factors create. Most groups, as we have seen, can be classified by the age-range of their members as preschool, school age, adolescent, young adult, adult, and the aged. Norms of physical, emotional, and intellectual development of people within these age classifications have been established by the research of the social, biological and psychological scientists. These findings are of prime importance to the social group worker, who must not only be familiar with the norms of each age grouping but also be sensitive to the many deviations from them. Similarly, from this study of the researches of the social scientists, particularly the anthropologists, the worker is able to incorporate within himself an understanding of the customs and habits of different ethnic, occupational, religious, and class groupings. The members of groups are understood against the norms of all these studies, but always with an eye to the exceptions and differences inevitable with any generalization that involves human beings.

It is essential that the social group worker identify the generalized characteristics of the stratum of society of which the group-as-a-whole is representative. It is also essential that he learn the specific identification of each member within the group. He should know the age, educational background, religious and ethnic identifications, occupation, and living conditions of each member. He should have information which will provide him with some understanding of the experience of each member in other groups—information about the family constellation is of particular significance. A knowledge of the number of persons in the family of each group member, and his ordinal position therein, will aid the worker in his attempts to understand the member's *present* use of the group, whether the member be a child or an adult. Information about the program content, including interpersonal relationships and corporate achievements, of other groups to which the member belongs or has belonged gives the worker further understanding of the member's use of the group in question.

The worker seeks to understand the group-as-a-whole by asking himself: What do these facts about the members mean in regard to program media? structure of the group? homogenity or heterogeneity of the group? *esprit de corps?* What is the group's corporate capacity for decision-making? What clues do these facts give to the role of the social group worker?

When the worker has gathered these data about the members, analyzed their meaning and studied them against his sensitive observation of the members' behavior, he is able to answer the question: Who are the members of the group?

THE "HOW" OF SOCIAL GROUP WORK

One of the most disappointing experiences faced by students engaged in professional education for the practice of social group work is the realization that there is no set of rules to follow in achieving the purposes for which the social group work method is used. The social group method is a process based on the relationship which is established between the worker and the members of the group he serves. It is through his professional use of this relationship that the members and the group-as-a-whole are helped to achieve their personal and corporate purposes. The success of the social group work method depends upon the worker's wisdom and discretion in developing the interpersonal relationships within the group and with other groups. The how of social group work is therefore discussed in terms of the attitudes and relations of the worker to the members and the group. We quote and use as a frame of reference for this section the first line of a jingle composed by a group of students engaged in this process: "Love them and limit them and help them to achieve."

"Loving" the Members

In Chapter 1, we pointed out that it is humanly impossible for a worker to like, personally, each individual with whom he comes in contact. In fact, there is no more reason for a social worker to like all the people with whom he works than for a doctor personally to like all his patients, a lawyer his clients, a teacher his pupils, and so on throughout all the service professions. In each of these professions, however, it is essential that the practitioners have a love of human beings which transcends their dislike of the behavior patterns of specific individuals. The desire to serve human beings should motivate each person who undertakes the obligations of any of the service professions. The love of human beings is the core of the profession of social work; without love there is no intrinsic value in any service of any social service agency. We have previously termed the attitude of social workers to those whom they serve as that of "professionally regarding." We are now using the word *love* in this sense.

The members feel loved and accepted by the worker because his tested reactions to them have proved that he does not stop loving them when he disapproves of their behavior. This is the essence of the attitude of the professional worker. Not only must he be able intellectually to regard behavior as symptomatic of the individual's adjustment to the tensions caused by conflicting drives of hostility and friendliness, but also he must have this concept emotionally. His acceptance of it must be so thoroughgoing that his behavior toward the members leaves no doubt in their minds that they are regarded by him as persons worthy of respect and consideration.

The members feel loved and accepted because the worker's tested reactions to them have proved that they do not have to "be good" to be loved by him. The worker puts no premium upon his attitude toward them. They can neither buy his affection by "being very good" nor lose it by "being very bad." The worker is frank in his approval or disapproval of their behavior and he is just as clear in his recognition of the naturalness of the feeling which lies back of the behavior. His recognition of the cause of the behavior, however, is seldom if ever expressed in words. It is, rather, conveyed indirectly by the tone of his voice, the position of his body, and the quality of his response in words or actions. In these ways he lets the members know that it is natural to feel cross or angry; that when one has something to be angry about and recognizes the causes of that anger, it is natural to express one's feeling in some way; and further, that everyone feels angry at times without apparent cause and without really knowing why. The worker does not blame the members for feeling angry or hostile, and his attitude assures them that their behavior has not changed his love or regard for them.

The members feel loved and accepted by the worker because he helps them to handle their aggressive hostile feelings in a socially acceptable way through the medium of satisfactory group experience. He helps them to accept the angry feelings as natural and to find ways for expressing these feelings without harm to themselves, to their companions, or to property. Let us affirm here that the handling of interpersonal relationships is not so much dependent upon words as upon attitudes, reactions, and the skillful introduction of appropriate program media at the needed moment.

The members feel loved and accepted by the worker because they feel in him the strength of a stable person on whom they can depend. This of course means that the worker must be a reasonably well adjusted adult who is able to be the bearer of values in areas where the members need support. But the worker must handle with care this matter of dependency. There are times when it is helpful to a member or to the group-as-a-whole to depend upon the worker for support or even for decisions. In groups of very young children, or in groups composed of emotionally immature or ill adults, the members may need to be very dependent upon the worker. There are also occasions when the stress within a group is so great that, for the sake of the group's life, the worker undertakes the making of decisions; but in the normal group this is a rare occasion, and the function is one which usually should be avoided by the worker. However, the worker should be a constant source of strength both to the group as it carries out the decision-making process and to the members as they learn to participate in the give and take of organized group life. . . .

Limiting the Members

We have not been able to discuss the social group worker's role of loving and accepting without also discussing his role of limiting (Smith, 1942). The two functions go hand in hand. The worker who loves is able to limit without being judgmental or punishing, but he who does not love is incapable of setting constructive limitations. Hate or indifference takes precedence over love, leaving the worker impotent rather than strong when the members need his strength to help them in their struggle between the positive and negative forces within them. The handling of the feelings of hostility and friendliness within an individual, whether these are expressed in a group meeting or in a personal interview, is the test of the social worker's skill in practice. Handling the expression of these feelings in a group is a delicate operation because of the many complicating factors in the interacting processes of the group. The worker must be aware of not only the meaning of the expressed behavior to the member but also the meaning of the reaction of the other members to that behavior. In order to understand the chain reaction of members in groups, the worker must be emotionally free to concentrate upon the members; he will not be thus free unless he is able to love and accept them as persons needing his help, and unless he has little concern over their reaction to him as a person, or over their behavior as a reflection upon his competence. In other words, the worker must be free to regard behavior only as symptomatic of the members' interests and needs. Any other concern about behavior will blind his eyes, stop his ears, and dull his feelings to the real meaning of the behavior he is seeking to understand. If the worker permits his personal feelings to enter into his relations with members of groups, he will be unable to handle their feelings of hostility professionally and will read personal attachment into their friendly feelings rather than the regard of members for their workers. When the worker interprets the behavior of the members in terms of their reactions to him as a person, he will be angry when their behavior displeases him and flattered when it pleases him. Neither reaction is conducive to the development of wholesome personal growth or healthy group morale. There is no place in the practice of social group work for the narcissistic worker; and when the indigenous leaders of the group are "prima donnas," they must be helped to become democratic leaders and followers.

The social group worker consciously affects the interacting processes within the group to further the personal development of the members through the achievement of satisfactory activity. He is continuously using his wisdom and discretion to determine what types of expression will meet the needs of members and those of the group-as-a-whole. He is now permissive, now limiting, in response to his evaluation of the needs of the moment. Limitations are not to be regarded as arbitrary restrictions imposed by the worker; they are rather the support given by the worker to the member in exercising self-control. The worker, through his support, strengthens the ego of the member in order to enable him, whenever possible, to meet the conflict situation. Most limitations are inherent in the situation itself. As society imposes limitations upon the conduct of its members, so the group's customs and laws, the agency's policies, rules, and regulations are all seen as limitations coming from society. The worker helps the members to live within these limitations or to take socially acceptable measures to change the limitations to meet their needs. The program content sets some of the limits within which the members must abide if they are to feel a sense of accomplishment in their activity. Playing a game according to the rules, following a recipe for cooking, preparing materials for arts and crafts, showing consideration to others in a discussion group, sharing in a week-end camping trip—all these and other activites impose limitations on the members' freedom to do just as they please when they please. The worker helps the members to accept these limitations and to use them for personal growth and the good of the whole.

Some members need protection from their own hostility, which may be expressed through very aggressive behavior disruptive to the group and destructive to the status of the individual in the group. Maladjustment to the group may be expressed by "being very good" and becoming the drudge of the group; or it may be expressed by clowning, gift-giving, treating and other forms of bribery, stealing, telling "dirty" stories, tattling, or other behavior indicative of need for help. The worker helps members with such needs through using the limitations in the situation: those set by society and those set by the program. There are, however, members for whom these are insufficient, and when this is the case the worker himself is responsible for supplying additional limitations.

The worker, then, supplies additional limitations when the hostility of one or more of the members is too drastically expressed, when the repressed hostility of one or more of the members ought to be expressed, when the expressed hostility of some of the members will destroy the group, when the hostility of the group-as-a-whole endangers its continuance as a group. He also supplies limitations when the program content is insufficiently defined and when the program content is beyond the capacity of the members; young children and immature adults are likely to have "big" ideas about programs, and the worker is responsible for helping them to plan in the realm of reality.

Some groups choose ends which are contrary to the philosophy and purpose of the agency and to the values and norms of the society which sponsors it. The social group worker is the bearer of values for the agency and for society, and in such a situation he helps the members to clarify the issues and to use the channels between the club and the policy-making committees in the agency for the discussion of differences. It is then the worker's responsibility to help the agency's staff, board, committees, and general membership to understand the values and norms of the group in question and the meaning of the suggested activity. These differences may arise in the area of manners and customs (type of dress, language used, issues like smoking, drinking, or kissing games); of law (use of agency truck without a carrier's license, money-raising events involving the sale of chances, use of rooms which have been condemned for group dancing, and other matters covered by legal codes); of morals (limitation of activity of group in area of boy-girl relationships, use of stolen goods in money-making projects, lying, cheating, gambling games and other activities regarded as contrary to the accepted moral code of the agency); and of social and economic philosophy (programs leading to political or social action). Whenever a conflict occurs between the members' plans and the policy of the agency, the worker helps the members to work with the appropriate committees of the agency toward a possible change of agency policies in light of their needs; and at the same time he helps the members to understand and accept, if need be, the limitations imposed by the agency. It is self-evident that the frequency of such conflicts is closely related to the degree of autonomy which the group enjoys and to the skill of the social group worker in helping the members choose socially desirable forms of behavior. Many controversial issues arise out of the variety of social norms represented in agency memberships. For instance, while raffles are illegal in most states and hence contrary to the policy of social agencies in those states, the members will often be able to cite churches and other institutions highly esteemed in their community which use this device for raising money. In other words, raffles are accepted as a norm in the community. The social group worker, as the representative of the agency, therefore finds it very difficult to help the members to accept the agency ruling on the basis of legality; yet it is seldom, if ever, that an agency changes its attitude on the validity of raffling as a money-raising device.

Social action on the part of so-called autonomous groups under agency auspices also leads to perplexing conflicts. The agency is here brought face to face with the meaning of its objective: to provide social group work service for the purpose of helping the individual to develop his personality and the group-as-a-whole to achieve socially desirable ends. Socially desirable to whom? The members of the group itself? The members of the board and committees of the agency? Unless the administration provides for the democratic process to be operative throughout the entire agency, groups will not have the opportunity to learn effectively the skill of demoractic participation in society; they will be denied the opportunity of feeling the full satisfaction of group achievement. The answer of many individuals and groups to situations of this kind is to withdraw from the agency auspice. This might well be one of the reasons why the membership of so many recreational and informal educational agencies reflects such a large proportion of children up through early adolescence and such a sharp dropping off in late adolescence and early maturity.

Helping Individuals and Groups to Achieve

The worker loves and limits the members in order to help them achieve, for it is in *action* that useful learning takes place.[1] The sense of achievement, however, is based on something more than just "doing"; the action must be purposeful. The common decision which precedes the activity and the evaluation which follows it are essential factors in the process by which group members, individually, develop this sense. It is the achievement of the group-as-a-whole which gives meaning and significance to the individual achievements, yet there would be no achievement of the group-as-a-whole if there were no individual achievements; thus we see the circular nature of the process.

The social group worker is concerned with the quality and meaning of the *ends* (achievements) as well as with the means through which the ends are achieved. The ends or achievements of a group in which the means have been determined by the use of the social group work method are different from the *ends in view*. It is in this difference between the ostensible objective (the end in view) and the accomplished result (the achievement) that most of the value of the group experience lies; there is also of course the value inherent in satisfaction with the end itself. End and means are interdependent; the end will have little significance if the means have failed to engage the interest and satisfy the needs of each member, and the means will have little sustained value if the end is disappointing. Within the process through which objectives are achieved, members learn to accept new ideas, expand or discard old ones, acquire new skills and improve old ones, develop new attitudes and change old ones. The process of achievement, in short, is a process of change. The social forces of the community, the agency, and the group itself are at work influencing the members as they establish the new frame of reference required for the accomplishment of their group's objectives.

The most important contribution which the group makes to the individual is the opportunity to learn how to function within the structure of group organization. Malinowski says, " . . . everywhere and in every effective performance the individual can satisfy his interests or needs and carry out any and every effective action only within organized groups and through the organization of activities" (Malinowski, 1944, p. 46). The satisfaction of both basic and derived needs is dependent upon the individual's ability to function with his fellow men in organized groups; hence the mere fact of participation in the group process is an achievement of no mean consideration. The concomitant gains accruing to the individual are increased knowledge and skill, and hence increased opportunities for satisfactory living.

The values to individuals of group experiences are directly related to the achievements of the group-as-a-whole. For the member, the significance of his individual achievement is rooted in the status of the group within the agency and the community. And the group-as-a-whole has a status in the agency and the community because of the behavior of its members and their collective achievements as a group. In the last analysis, individual achievement and group achievement are so interrelated that it is practically impossible to discuss them separately. An illustration of this point is provided by the Roaring Aces, a club of young veterans who came to the agency with the wish to form a basketball team. The members had had no experience in organized groups where the management of their group was their own responsibility. They met frequently but seemed unable to undertake the necessary organization which their request necessitated; instead they played aimlessly with the ball, were unwilling to learn the rules of the game, and spent the greater part of their time in arguing and wrestling. They complained to the worker about the equipment in the gymnasium and the poor ball which they had been given. The worker suggested that they hold a club meeting and discuss what they could do about the situation. Following this advice, the members got together, expressed their dissatisfaction, drew up a petition, and appointed a committee to take their requests to the executive of the agency. The executive received the committee as the *representative* of the Roaring Aces, not just as a collection of individuals, and through this experience these members became aware of themselves as part of a group which was *theirs.* They were successful in communicating this idea to the other club members. Because of the achievement of the group-as-a-whole in securing a place in the agency sun, they were able to organize themselves so that they could carry on co-operative activities. In this case, lack of self-esteem and of social experience blocked the members from becoming effective within their own group. The executive's respect for the group-as-a-whole encouraged them to move ahead to a group achievement in which each was able to share, and by which they were enabled to develop new personal skills both in basketball (their conscious objective) and in the use of the group to accomplish a social objective. Through working together they made some progress in learning to respect one another's opinions and in using group discussion in the decision-making process upon which corporate action is dependent. The worker helped the members to achieve these results through accepting them in their retarded state of social development, limiting them in their attempt to disregard the orderly procedures through which they could attain their objectives, and finally supplying the structure through which they could work when it became evident that they could not develop it themselves.

Individuals need to have satisfactory experiences in many groups. When they have learned to function in small primary groups, they are ready to move on to larger groups and intergroup situations. Participation in intergroup organization, such as interclub councils, demands the ability to think of the needs and interests of a community of groups; here the member learns the responsibility of representing his group-as-a-whole, in contrast to the role he fulfills in the primary group. It is through relations with interclub councils and other intergroup situations that the individual becomes aware of his own group's achievements or lack of them.

The social group worker helps members to achieve through helping their groups to become part of the social forces within the community in areas of their interests. Many of the same problems which beset a particular group are also perplexing other groups in the community and in the country at large. The social group worker helps the members to become aware of the relationship between their areas of concern and those of others, and to join with other groups in common study and action.

Finally, the social group worker helps the members to achieve through helping them to develop and strengthen their philosophy of life as an integrating force in their personal life and as a directive in their social concerns. This the individual achieves through the process of adjustment which he experiences within every group of which he is a part. The social group worker is only one of many factors in the member's growth and development, but he is in a strategic position because he can affect the social processes within the primary group in such a way that personal integration takes place, and can help those whom he serves to use all the resources of the community toward this end.

NOTE

1. ". . . the psychology we are considering teaches us that the ideas of people are not formed in their 'minds' as conceptual pictures, but depend on their

activities. . . . Concepts can never be presented to me merely, they must be knitted into the structure of my being, and this can be done only through my own activity" (Follett, 1930).

REFERENCES

FOLLETT, M. P., 1930. *Creative Experience.* New York: Longmans, Green.

LEWIN, H. S., 1947. "A Comparison of the Aims of the Hitler Youth and the Boy Scouts of America," *Human Relations,* Vol. 1, No. 2.

MALINOWSKI, B., 1944. *A Scientific Theory of Culture and Other Essays.* Chapel Hill: University of North Carolina Press.

SMITH, T. V., 1942. *Discipline for Democracy.* Chapel Hill: University of North Carolina Press.

13

What Is Group Work Skill?

Helen Phillips is Professor Emeritus, School of Social Work, University of Pennsylvania, Philadelphia.

Helen U. Phillips

In this brief article I have not attempted to describe group work skill comprehensively. As a matter of fact, one of the reasons that our particular field of practice is so dynamic and exciting to be engaged in, is that its practitioners are constantly in the process of testing and refining the group work method of helping people. This has been going on for approximately the last twenty-five years, ever since group workers started to give attention to their methodology—building on their past tested experience, and seeking new ways of making their work more effective. I believe this constant examination of practice to be an important function of our professional association of group workers and certainly of every worker in a group work agency, as well as of the educational centers for professional training in group work.

The intent of this paper is to state and examine some of the fundamental principles or concepts that I believe to be essential to social group work skill. But we will have to start a little behind the skill to consider briefly what has brought about the need for its development and, therefore, our concern with it. Group workers are committed to a professional purpose. Our group work literature is full of definitions of the professional group work purpose including the provocative statements of national committees of our own professional association. In essence, all of these definitions affirm the dual aim of the development of individuals and development of the group as a whole toward social usefulness. In more specific terms, the professional purpose of group work is:

1. to help the members of a group to become and to value their real selves and to discover, use and develop their strengths through their group associations so that they may find a more

Reprinted with permission of the National Association of Social Workers, Inc. From *The Group*, Vol. 16, No. 5 (June 1954), pp. 3-10. Copyright 1954, American Association of Group Workers.

responsible and satisfying relation to other group members, the worker, agency and community

2. to help the group as a whole to develop social interests and activities that will contribute to movement toward a more democratic society

Most group work agencies subscribe in general to the professional purpose of group work and, in addition, have formulated unique objectives for which the agencies are organized. Specific purposes grow out of the particular community and clientele which the agency serves, combined with the aims of the national agencies with which it may be affiliated and the unique interests of the original or present leadership of the agency.

Every worker in every group work agency must focus his efforts on contributing to the fulfillment of the professional and agency purpose. In the last analysis, the effectiveness of the help given by group work agencies to people of the community rests on the skill of the workers who meet directly with groups or who supervise those who carry the direct responsibility of group leadership. This is our reason for considering what is meant by group work skill and for examining concepts that underlie helpful group work practice.

One word on the relation of professional skill to dedication—the professional commitment, implicit in professional purpose, that demands more of the worker's concern for the people whom he serves than for himself: dedication exclusive of skill results in questionable service; but skill without dedication is practically useless. Indeed, I would go as far as to say that professional commitment to the service of others is a basic quality, essential to the group work skill I will be describing.

THE AGENCY FUNCTION

Let us start out with the group work agency itself since it is the agency that gives the worker his reason for being. The very fact that the worker is part of an agency means that he has a professional rather than a personal relationship to offer to his group members. Quite naturally, I think, groups will often try to separate their worker from the agency—especially when he is holding them to some requirement that they do not like. Older teen-agers will say, for example, "But why do we have to report the *full* amount of money we made at our dance? Nobody except you will know about it!"

Or, in the usual turnover of leadership, the group will test out each new worker to find out if he is really part of the agency or if he will just "be a good fellow." When the worker is clear about an agency policy and can interpret it in reasonable terms, he removes the issue from the area of personal battle and puts it into the agency frame-work. Certainly this is supporting for the worker but, more important, it provides something stable for the group members in that they know what they can count on, along with the sense that the agency is there for other groups as well as themselves. Those of you who meet with groups outside of an agency building—in homes, schools or on street-corners—have to be especially conscious of the agency connection since there is no visible reminder in the form of a physical building, of the auspices under which the group is meeting. You approach your groups, not just as the friendly, interested person that you are, but as the representative of your agency which provides services to community groups.

The function of the group work agency is to give help to people through group experiences. If one can be clear about that, he finds direction for his answer to the somewhat controversial question of what kind of help to individuals is a legitimate part of the group worker's responsibility. (I am aware that some agencies that offer group work services do not call themselves group work agencies. A recent statement from the National Federation of Settlements made it quite clear that most social settlements and neighborhood houses are multi-functional and include group work as only one of their important functions. This may be true of other agencies as well as settlements but I am addressing myself here to the group work part of the agency function and to you as group workers.)

If a worker knows that his focus is to be on helping people to use their group experiences as fully as possible, he will find that every contact that he has with individual members of the group will be related to that end. Individual interviews or just informal conversations with group members are a familiar part of every group worker's activity. Many of the individual problems that group members feel free enough to discuss with their worker may be directed back to possible program development in the group. Vocational questions, impending draft for the young men, relations with the opposite sex—these are examples of this. Problems that have to do with relationships with other group members or with the worker, stem directly from the group situation and clearly must be dealt with by the group worker to help the member to participate in the group with more satisfaction to himself and with greater benefit to the group. But when the group member brings problems of personal relationships, with members of his family, for example, the worker is faced with a question: what is my responsibility here? Can I help this person with something that is very important to him but that has nothing to do directly with the group experience that I share with him? One unsatisfactory answer to these questions is that the group worker does not have time for intensive, individualized work; another, that he is not trained in giving individualized help. Either of these answers would leave the worker filled with guilt for what he cannot do—and, furthermore, begs the question. Doesn't the answer lie in the function of the agency? If the function of the group work agency or of the group worker's part of the agency service is to help people to use group experience, the worker has his direction for the kinds of problems on which he can truly help his group members. This does not exclude the necessity of helping members to move toward casework services in the process of referrals. But, I believe that it is very supporting to the group member to discover that his group worker will be there every minute for him as his *group* worker to help him on every conceivable aspect of his group experience but that he will not try to be all things to him.

The point of view I have been expressing could be stated as the following concept: *The worker who clearly represents his agency and holds to its function in all of his relationships with his group members provides stability for them.*

THE DYNAMIC OF PRESENT REALITY

Lest this principle of holding to the agency function appear to be too limiting or to cut off the worker from the group members' needs, I hasten to state a second group work concept, namely, that *there are dynamic possibilities for helping through the group work process.* When the group worker believes this to be so, he does not feel guilty or frustrated for what he *cannot* do, because he knows the rich potentialities of group participation to which he contributes—not confining in nature, but expansive and positive, with unknown depths of experience and development there to be plumbed. He knows that he can help and he considers the *reality* of the group meeting as the framework where his help can be effective.

Perhaps a word is pertinent here as to what the worker needs to know about his group members if he is to help them. It is my conviction, as I have often said publicly, that it is not necessary for a worker to know about his members' family, work or school relationships in order to be able to help them; that indeed, possession of such information may block the worker's freedom to feel and know what the members are like right in the current group situation. Certainly, the worker's richest source of understanding of members' needs is the group meeting itself where he not only sees each member in relation to the others and to himself but is in direct interaction with him. The worker's real connection with the group member, as well as his competence, is in the group experience which he shares. The engagement between group members and worker, right in the present group situation can have profound significance for the members in bringing about change in their way of relating to others. The worker attempts to meet the needs as he senses them, as he actively relates to the members in the ever-changing facets of their use of program activities, their relations with each other, with him, and with the agency.

Every one of you from your rich experience in leading groups could readily give illustrations of what I am asserting—where you have seen clear indication that group members have changed in their attitudes and in their relations to others in the course of a group meeting. Here is one such example, recorded by the worker with a gang of older teen-agers who had sought the leadership services of a settlement house although they lived too far from the agency building to avail themselves of its facilities. They were looking for a meeting-place in their local neighborhood since the police were objecting to their habitual use of street-corners.

> . . . Angelo said, "Man, we can't stand here any more! It's getting too hot around here. We can't even have our old corner." Vic asked how we were doing about places to meet. I said that neither the boys who were working on it nor I had any success to date but that we had applied to Humboldt School. This brought up a whole flurry of feeling—"Man, if we go over there, we sure are going to fight with those niggers!" I questioned this and said that they seemed to do a whole lot of talking about fighting everybody. I couldn't help thinking that guys who fought absolutely everybody must be pretty much in the wrong themselves and I was getting a little tired of hearing them down everybody else and say they were going to fight wherever they went. There really wasn't much sense in our trying to find a meeting-place because wherever they went, they would find somebody to fight. This sobered them down. . . .
>
> Chris said, Look, you guys, how about going up to St. Vincent's? They have a gym there and everything. Man, that would be a terrific place if we could get in. Rocky said, We sure are going to tangle with those guys up there! I turned to the group and said, there you go again! Before you even get to a building you're getting into a fight. You'll never get a place to meet if you figure on fighting. If we go up there figuring we're going to mind our own business and have our own fun, then we won't have any trouble. If we go there the way you are talking now, we'll be out of there in a week—out in the cold again. Stan and Ted told Rocky to shut up and Chris said, Look, you guys, if we get our own place and time, we can get along with those guys up there. They're not so bad anyway. They never bothered me too much. The boys began to simmer down and talk in a more positive way about the opportunities at the church. . . .

Now here was a real problem these boys were facing—one very important to them. They wanted and needed a place to meet but they wouldn't be able to find one until they began to take some responsibility for their behavior. And what did the worker do in this meeting? He helped them to face one of the reasons for their dilemma and the boys seemed to take in what he was saying and to move a little, in response to him. It would be ridiculous to assume that with this slight beginning, this club of boys would never get into another fight! But the worker did start them looking at their own responsibility. After all, it does take two to start a fight! He knew that they had chosen to be belligerent and he knew that there was another choice they could make that no one else could make for them. I am convinced that in such an incident that lasts for only a few minutes of time, right in the reality of the present, a group can be helped to discover something new and useful in themselves.

DEVELOPING STRENGTHS

We have been looking briefly at the concept that there are dynamic possibilities for individual and group growth in the group work process. The very word "process" connotes in the world of nature, movement between two or more substances in which organic change can occur in reaction to an external force. In the area of human society, the word denotes dynamic movement or interaction between one or more persons or groups. In group work terms, process requires that both worker and group are actively involved in reaction to each other—each in a different way since the worker carries the professional responsibility of the helping person—and the group members, as individual participants in the group. I believe that the strongest factor that keeps the group worker from being controlling and manipulative is his conviction that *all people have strengths.* This I submit as a third concept essential to group work skill although, if I were pressed to say which concept of the several we are examining today I hold to be the most significant, I would put this one *first* at the head of my list.

Some of the clearest statements and elaborations of this concept of belief in the strength of the person who comes to the social agency for service are to be found in the writings of Kenneth L. M. Pray. The final paper of Mr. Pray's productive life was "A Restatement of the Generic Principles of Social Casework Practice." In describing functional casework, he wrote: "This approach clings steadily to the conception that the client, whatever his strengths and weaknesses, carries responsibility for his own life as a whole and must continue to carry it. At least he has not asked us and we cannot consent, to take that responsibility from him. He has asked us, rather, to help him to carry that responsibility by helping him to overcome some obstacle he has faced in carrying it, and in the very act of seeking this help he has disclosed at least some elements of strength for dealing with this responsibility. The worker's task is to enable him to build on this latent strength, to face whatever realities are decisive in determining his own use of himself and of available resources in relation to the problem he faces and upon which he wants to work. The problem remains his own; the responsibility for dealing with it remains with him. Furthermore, this approach . . . also starts with the assumption—indeed, the profound conviction—that the helping dynamic, the source of healing power, is also in the client himself as he reaches out for help. It is not primarily in the worker" (Pray, 1949, p. 249).

Mr. Pray was addressing himself to social casework but he was expressing a philosophy, universal in its meaning and fully applicable to social group work.

In the excerpted record of the meeting with teen-age boys previously referred to, it would seem that the worker was acting from this principle. He could help them with external arrangements such as finding a meeting place but the deeper problem of their behavior was their responsibility alone and his greatest help to them lay in enabling them to face their attitudes and the reality of the consequences of their behavior, with the *expectation*, not expressed in words, that they were quite capable of responsible behavior if they chose it for themselves.

THE SIGNIFICANCE OF FEELINGS

If the group worker is to be engaged in a process with his group members, it is essential that he be sensitive to their feelings. I find it difficult to describe this important area of group work skill in the limited words of a concept. It might be expressed in this way: *The acknowledgement of one's own feeling is important to inner movement, and the expression of it produces something real for another person to respond to.* This applies both to worker and to group members. Sensitivity to feelings is not enough but the feelings must be responded to if the worker is to have relatedness to his group members—and relatedness is the essence of group work skill.

Could we look first at the worker's own feelings? Perhaps one of the most difficult things for a beginning social worker to get hold of is the willingness and freedom to face his own feelings—both sides of them, the negative as well as the positive—and then, as well as acknowledging them to himself, to be willing to share them with someone else. And yet, I am convinced that not until a group worker has claimed and shared his real feelings, can he be sensitive to and respond to the feelings of his group members. Think of what happens, for example, when a worker realizes and admits to himself that what he had fondly thought was his deep desire to help his group to have a good experience was actually his own need to have a "successful" group, stemming from his own feeling of insecurity. With that sudden revelation, he is free to permit and to help the group members take their rightful part of the responsibility for their group life. Or, the worker who has always felt hostile toward a particular economic class of society—and this could be upper, middle or lower economic group—who has to examine his feelings before he can let himself know, accept and welcome the feelings of his group comprised of that class and begin to help them.

I have mentioned the matter of sharing feelings with another and this applies to letting the group members know how one feels. The members have the right to know the worker as *real*—a person with both positive and negative feelings but in this, the worker has the responsibility of disciplining his feelings so that they do not damage the group members. And how is feeling communicated? Not only by spoken words but by facial expressions and gestures and an intangible sort of air. The workers' concern with his own feeling, acknowledgement and expression of it, is legitimate and indeed, essential, only as it frees the worker to "take in" the feelings of his group members, to let them have their feelings and to hear what they really are saying.

Much of the worker's effort must be directed to sensing and meeting the positive and negative feelings of his group members and helping them to claim, break up into parts and express their feelings as they move into new relationships—but more important, to take responsibility for their feelings and the expression of them. There is so much concern over helping members to express their negative feelings—perhaps because when unexpressed they produce hostile behavior that is disruptive to the group—that it is necessary to emphasize the need for help in acknowledging and expressing positive feelings as well. These may emerge as identification with the group, worker or agency or positive acceptance of one's self or just a general sense of well-being. At any rate, whether the feelings are positive or negative, the worker must be free to be sensitive to them and actively respond to them.

A recorded incident in a club of eleven- and twelve-year-old boys will serve to illuminate the concept we are discussing. The group had been driven by the worker in the agency's stationwagon to a playground for a game of baseball. The worker records:

> After the ball-game, as they piled into the station-wagon, Earl accidentally stepped on Sam and Sam shoved him. At that, Earl completely lost his temper and started after Sam with a rock that he picked up from the road, shouting, "I'll kill that guy!" I got between them and Earl hollered, "Get out of the road, Mr. Mac! I'm going to split his head open." I said that was exactly why I wouldn't get out of the way. I wasn't protecting Sam so much as I was protecting him. Cliff said, "Cut it out, Earl. You do that and you'll end up in jail sure. Mr. Mac's only seeing you take care of yourself." Earl said, "I ain't fighting Mr. Mac. I want that Sam!" I said that as long as he wanted to kill somebody, I guessed he'd be fighting me because I certainly wouldn't let him do that if I could help it. When Earl began to quiet down. I told Sam to get out of the station-wagon and re-arranged the seating. I told Earl to get in and cool off and that we could talk about this after the meeting.
>
> When we got back to the agency and the other boys had left, Earl and I talked about what had happened out on the road by the playground. Earl said: "Mr. Mac, I get so mad I can't see straight." I said I knew that and could understand that sometimes he had a right to get mad but I was worried about what would happen to him. Earl leaned over and sort of put his arms around me and said, "We're friends, aren't we, Mr. Mac?" I replied, "You know we are, Earl. Even when you do something I don't like, you know I'm still your friend." He smiled a little wistfully and said, "You just tell that Sam to stay away from me, that's all!" I said I couldn't tell everybody in the world that he got mad at to stay away from him. Maybe he just had to learn to be with people and maybe be angry without getting so angry that he would let himself go and mess up his own life. . . .

This conversation was centered right on the boy's feeling—the angry, mad hostile feeling that must have felt "bad" to the boy. At the same time this boy could express the warm, scared, little-boy side of himself that reached out for the security of the worker's acceptance of him. And the worker responded to both sides of the feeling, assuring him that he was his friend and letting him know his understanding of the "mad" feelings and his concern for the boy's welfare if he let his feelings control him. But he was putting the responsibility on to the boy and he helped him to move toward that responsibility by responding to the feelings that he was encouraging the boy to express. There was relatedness between these two that encompassed the reality of both the positive and negative kinds of feeling, with no pretense between them. And relatedness comes only when the worker has separated his own feelings sufficiently that he can let himself know what feeling the other person is conveying to him.

I have touched briefly on four of the major concepts whose use is essential to group work skill: the use of the agency function; the dynamic possibilities for helping in the reality of a present group situation; the strength in people; the significance of feelings in relationships. The use of one of these concepts without the others does not result in group work skill. To hold to the agency function, for example, without taking in the feelings of the members, would be more damaging than helpful. It is the use of these concepts *combined* that creates skill in group work.

I have had a real problem of selection as I faced the limits of a short paper and I have omitted several concepts that carry significance equal to those I have discussed. Some may be puzzled by my failure to include the concepts that relate to the constructive use of limits; the worker's responsibility for introducing and sustaining a focus; the dynamic of difference. There may be other concepts that many have found give direction to their work. It will be noticed, too, that I have not been using the word "techniques." It is many years since I have thought that techniques as such were essential to group work practice. I am a little fearful that a technique may be like something in a bag of tricks that a worker opens up now and then to select from and use *on* a group. I believe that a worker's sureness in his work with people comes from a steady base of underlying principles—or concepts as we have been calling them today—and that when a worker has made those principles his own by his use of them, he finds a way to help people use the services of his agency.

Knowledge about group work principles is not enough to produce skillful group work. Anyone who has the interest can become familiar with these concepts if he takes the time to do so—but skill comes from using them in practice. In the early forties, Virginia Robinson discussed the meaning of skill in a volume called, *Training For Skill in Social Casework.* She wrote, "Skill implies first of all an activity, an ability to perform, and while it rests on knowledge it is clearly distinguishable from knowledge. . . . The skillful way of working . . . develops out of some relationship between the workman and the material in which he works. . . . His understanding of his material and his capacity to work *with* it, instead of *against* it, to utilize and not do violence to its essential nature, determine his ability to develop skill in his handling of the process. Skill might be defined, then, as the capacity to set in motion and control a process of change in specific material in such a way that the change that takes place in the material is effected with the greatest degree of consideration for and utilization of the quality and capacity of the material" (Robinson, 1942, pp. 11-12).

Translating this general definition of skill into social work—specifically group work—terms, I would say that group work skill rests on the worker's sensitive relatedness to group members, his firm connection with the agency and its function, his clarity of focus—all of which enable him to develop a process with his groups which he consciously accelerates, trusting them to take their part in it and helping them to do so.

Skill is developed only as one turns concepts to convictions as he tests them in his work with people, integrating his knowledge with real, living experience. As a group worker gets hold of these basic concepts—has them "in his muscles," as Gertrude Wilson would say—he finds a steady and sure way to help the members of his groups and thereby to make his contribution to the fulfillment of the professional purpose of social group work.

REFERENCES

PRAY, K. L. M., 1949. "A Restatement of the Generic Principles of Social Casework," *Social Work in a Revolutionary Age.* Philadelphia: University of Pennsylvania Press

ROBINSON, V. P., 1942. "The Meaning of Skill," *Training for Skill in Social Casework.* Philadelphia: University of Pennsylvania Press.

14

Group Work Revisited: A Statement of Position

At the time this article was written, the authors represented the Group Work Faculty of the School of Social Work, University of Pittsburgh.

Mildred Sirls, Jack Rubenstein, Erma Myerson, and *Alan Klein*

Historically, social group work is rooted in the social settlement, in recreation, and in secular and religious education. As it grew from those roots it drew nurture from the social and psychological sciences which, in combination with its ethical commitment, formed a base which was compatible with the socially sanctioned mission of social work. This common base included, as it does now, concern for the individual in helping him to strive for personal fulfillment, and concern for the social conditions within which the individual acted out his striving.

The uniqueness of the group worker, his particular contribution to the profession of social work, has been in his promotion of client involvement through group life as a means for reaching these agreed-upon ends. Thus, while the group worker formulated goals for each individual, he also formulated goals for the development of the group; in developing goals for the individual and the group, he also formulated goals for constructive and meaningful action toward desirable social goals (Wilson and Ryland, 1949).

This tripartite view of client participation has been echoed throughout the development of social group work down to the present day. Definitions of social group work by the American Association of Group Workers (Trecker, 1955), formulated in 1947, and the definition of group work in the Social Work Year Book of 1957 (Luck, 1957) both contain the same three elements in a similar relation. The writings of Dr. Grace Coyle (1948), of Gertrude Wilson, of Gisela Konopka (1963) and others supported this thesis.

This view of group work which places it squarely within the ethical and philosophical framework of social work, also provides for a particularly broad definition of practice, permitting broad application across the range of expression which the client's problem takes.

Reprinted from *Jewish Social Work Forum,* Vol. 4, No. 2, with permission.

The uniqueness of group work, the contribution it makes to social work practice, lies in this very breadth. Rather than restricting practice to a conceptual segment of the client's behavior, its potency lies precisely in its ability to deal with the relevant expressions of dysfunction along the full experiential range, individual-to-individual, individual-in- and individual-to-group, and individual and group in their social milieu.

Previous definitions of social group work have, as well, been clear as to the breadth of application to a variety of client groups. That is, one distinguished social group work based on the methods of the worker, not on the structure of the group (NASW Questionnaire). An important mark of group work is its flexibility, its application to a variety of problems which lie within the purview of social work.

Present day social group work theory and practice strongly reflect the multifarious influences of the past. We confirm that our inherited commitment to social action is an equal partner today with our commitment to work toward individual self-fulfillment and toward group development; we confirm that the skill, training and ethical commitment of the practitioner define him as a group worker no matter what the nature of the client group.

SOCIAL ACTION IN SOCIAL GROUP WORK PRACTICE

Social group work, in practice, cannot be considered social group work unless the members of the group have the opportunity and are encouraged to work to bring about change in their social environment. For the individual or the particular group, social action may mean effecting change in the group or in the agency. This is equally important with broader social change in the community or society at large. Social action has traditionally been regarded as inherent in group work practice for many reasons. Most important were (1) values which regarded service and social betterment as interdependent, (2) the belief in a democratic political process based on citizen participation and self-determination, and (3) the premise that there is a concomitant relationship between positive health supports in the environment and the positive health of the individual.

These suggest the following goals for social group work practice: (1) enhancement of the individual's social functioning through group experience, (2) development of mature functioning groups, and (3) participation of such groups in actions directed toward social betterment.

Social group work practice must relate to these three dimensions of the human life experience for they constantly interact and are by their very nature inseparable. A change in any one affects the others as well as the totality of life experience. A healthy individual does not exist in a social vacuum. To maintain and further his own social and emotional well-being he must strive, in community with others, to create and maintain a healthy environment. Thus an opportunity for experiences in social action on the part of the group becomes a desirable goal. Without it social group work practice denies the meaning of social experience in a democratic society.

The group worker who ignores the social milieu in which the individual functions and its interdependence with the individual and the group fragmentizes his efforts. His diagnosis will be piecemeal, his planning isolated, and his outcomes unpredictable. To have lasting value social group work practice must be directed toward effecting change which encompasses more than individual functioning.

In citing history it is not our intent to turn back the clock. We cannot maintain that because social group work was thus-and-so it must remain so forevermore. To state what we have been is not a valid argument against change. However, to endorse change for its own sake or to equate it with progress is equally unjustified. Most professions legitimately refine their practice with time, experience, and the acquisition of new knowledge. This process involves discarding old methods as better ways are discovered for achieving professional goals.

In our view, many of the current changes in social group work do not derive from this sort of process. Many changes have not resulted in better ways to achieve our goals. On the contrary, these changes suggest abandoning our social goals and making a fetish of method. One may, indeed, practice group work with reference solely to method, serving any cause with a collection of techniques. However, this only remotely relates to professional social work practice. Group work so defined is empty, does not properly belong within the province of professional social work (Greenwood, 1957).

We hold that the present trend away from social action in social group work is movement in the wrong direction; it represents change but not progress. Unless we revitalize our commitment to clearly stated social ends as well as to means the consequences of our present activity will be self-destructive.

ROLE OF THE WORKER

Another marked trend today is the emphasis placed upon the worker as the central person in the group. This makes the professionally-led group a worker-centered, rather than a member-centered group. What the group worker does is termed an *intervention* and his approach is called a *strategy of intervention*, one which is based upon his diagnosis and treatment plan. Such thinking opposes a professional role which focusses upon helping the group move toward goal formation, self-determination and eventual group autonomy. This violates the integrity of the group and its members. By its nature it creates dependency. The worker becomes sole arbitor of what shall happen, why it happens, and how. The group worker diagnoses, prescribes, and intervenes to his predetermined ends. Under these conditions the group and the group members are influenced by an autocratic decision-making process and may be rendered impotent by the strong central figure, the group worker.

By contrast, the concept *enabling*, views members as the actionists and the group as capable of movement and growth. The word *enabling* has all but disappeared in more recent writings. We hold no brief for the term itself. At times its use was vague and weak, but the underlying principle is sound. It implies that group action is the province of the group members, that these members have potential for self direction.

If we abandon this principle we substitute the notion that it is the worker who effects change; he is referred to in this context as the *change agent*. The connotation of that term, as Lippitt used it in early writings in group dynamics, is legitimate, but in social work literature it has come to mean worker-centered control. In this modification of approach, or at least in the statements of theory, the group process is no longer at the center of the group work process. In fact, one cannot assert that member behavior is influenced by *group process* while advocating that the worker's role is to direct the process toward *his* goals. In the latter instance the group process is no longer determined by the group members. One would be more accurate in stating such a formulation if he were to say that the worker takes over control of the group process and uses it as a tool to accomplish his ends. However, it is rarely possible to reach socially desirable ends with these socially inappropriate means.

We do not hold that a group process cannot be democratic should the social group worker intervene. Intervention in its purest sense merely describes the worker's action. The group worker may, and appropriately should work toward effecting a more democratic process on the part of the group. Our concern is not that the worker participate in the group process; that is the core of group work practice. We are concerned, however, that his actions be guided by clearly defined goals for helping the group to function more effectively. We are concerned, too, that he function primarily *within* the group process.

There are times, of course, when one strategy is preferable to another, when it is suitable for the worker to offer more direction and control. However, when the worker's direction and control are seen as central to the method, it becomes suspect. Such intervention cannot be supported by the democratic ideal.

SOME CONSEQUENCES OF A NARROW CONCEPTUALIZATION ON PRACTICE

We have described the change of focus in social group work from concern with the individual, the group, and the social milieu to a single emphasis upon individual social functioning. This change to a singular focus has affected both the nature of practice and the settings in which practice was traditionally carried out.

One evidence of this is seen in the adoption of new nomenclature. *Group Service agency* is deemed to be a more fitting title for what was formerly the *Group Work agency*. This newer term is seen as encompassing a wide variety of agencies giving service to groups. The change in terminology has sanctioned the discontinuance of social group work in many such agencies. The effect, in agency practice, has been to highlight a dichotomy between social group work and work with groups. By implication, all group serving agencies work with groups but considerably fewer practice social group work. The costs of this has been a retrenching. Agencies that once worked to incorporate social group work principles into all their work with groups now give less support to such efforts.

Such agencies have been led by this recasting of practice to confuse method with practice. They have rationalized lower levels of practice by accepting the false assumption that social group workers work only to enhance individual functioning. A distinction has been drawn between "work-with-groups" and social group work. This distinction seems valid only if it is based on the methodology of the worker and not on the characteristics of the group. We must be careful not to confuse a definition of method with a definition of practice, nor to characterize practice by any one method utilized within it.

Evidence of such thinking may be found in two recent documents: the Frame of Reference Statement developed by the NASW Commission on Practice (Hartford, 1964) and the Working Definition of Social Work Practice (Wilson, 1956). The former document leads one to assume that social workers have all but renounced social action as a part of social group work practice and theory. While the latter document does not suggest the abandonment of social betterment as a goal, it nevertheless does not state it explicitly as a goal. The profession recognizes that any effort dedicated to improvement of the human condition within our kind of society cannot ignore the necessity to involve people in constructive action. It was in this area that social group work should provide leadership, for it was through the medium of the groups with which it worked that responsible citizenship participation was encouraged.

In abdicating this role, social group workers create a void in the social work field. It is to the credit of the profession that others have attempted to meet this need. Community Work has embraced many of the social action functions which were formerly a strong component in social group work practice. Social action is not the exclusive prerogative of social group work nor is it realistically a social work monopoly. However, we maintain that by virtue of its inherent nature, social group work provides a direct and effective channel for stimulating such action. By relinquishing this opportunity as part of social group work, we weaken our total effort and diminish our practice.

The over-all results of the current trends in social group work have been deleterious. The group worker's goal in working with the group toward responsible self-direction and social participation has been placed in opposition to goals for the enhancement of individual functioning. Emphasis on the latter has gradually focussed on problems of the individual to the exclusion of other necessary goals. Much of what is now described as social group work practice is treatment, or therapeutically based.

The value of employing the social group work method as a treatment approach cannot be denied nor can the restoration of adequate individual functioning be excluded from an enunciation of social group work practice goals. However, individually focussed treatment goals must be seen in perspective, for they are but one segment in the total range of goals of social group work practice in any professional setting.

Restoration of individual social functioning is social in nature. The health of individuals is interdependent and interrelated with the environment. The responsible participation of the individual in the improvement of his treatment environment is an appropriate goal in social group work practice. It has been said, "First, total institutions disrupt or defile precisely those actions that in civil society have the role of attesting to the actor and those in his presence that he has some command over his world—that he is a person with 'adult' self-determination, autonomy, and freedom of action" (Goffman, 1961). It is precisely here that group work can play its special role.

The question of treatment, task fulfillment, and social action is not an either/or, nor are these functions mutually exclusive. These ends are inseparable in practice. One's professional practice with treatment groups is not at variance with what one does in developmental groups.

We agree that it is appropriate at this stage of development for our profession to delineate method carefully and precisely. However, we cannot agree that method dictates practice nor that social group workers are specialists in only one dimension of practice. This would relegate the professional's job to one small segment of social work practice with groups, excluding him from use of his expertise in groups of all kinds within the purview of social work. Social group work, we hold, is social work with groups.

Within our framework, an important aim of social group work practice should be the provision of services which promote individual and group development and work to prevent breakdown. Formulations limited to treatment goals are therefore unsuited to the agencies whose purposes are educational, developmental, and community service centered. Without a broader framework group work practice is in danger of becoming devoted solely to helping sick people adapt to a sick society—a limited, and unacceptable goal.

The events resulting from the newer definition precipitate a strong inconsistency. A majority of the groups in therapeutic settings are not being led by social group workers and the method in use is not social group work. Social group workers in group service agencies are not in any significant numbers leading groups nor practicing social group work by the latest definitions (Main and MacDonald, 1962).

Community Organization workers are engaged in work with groups and in social action in the community. Persons trained in Community Organization are being hired by neighborhood centers, settlements, YWCA's and the like to fill jobs formerly thought to require social group workers. Practically, we have so narrowed our practice that it is now offered to a very limited clientele in only a few settings and cities.

There are some who argue that social group work no longer has a place in the group services agencies. The proponents of a more narrowly focussed group work practice charge that group service agencies have been unable to define the value, skills and personality attributes necessary for personal and social well being. Thus we are told that there is an "indeterminancy of needs [that] contributes to the vagueness in formulation of service objectives and confusion in designing service programs" (Vinter, 1961).

It is argued since we have difficulty in determining socialization needs, we have no guidelines for the allocation of scarce resources. Undoubtedly group service agencies have been lax in stating their objectives in operational terms. Too often they have not designed programs to meet specific needs. However, this state of affairs does not justify the assumption that there is no available knowledge of developmental and social needs. The behavioral sciences provide an extensive body of factual material in this area much of which may be of help in delineating the needs of agency clientele (Havighurst, 1953; Sorenson and Dimock, 1955; Erikson, 1950; Duvall, 1967; Kearney, n.d.; French, 1957; Hummel and Smith, n.d.). Concrete agency goals for socialization, development, and prevention can be stated in behavioral terms. Programs can be planned to meet these stated needs. This is a task to which group service agencies must apply themselves as quickly as possible.

The argument of indeterminancy of needs falls by its own logic. The concept of deviance presumes norms and treatment goals that envision a more desirable state of social functioning. The very notion of dysfunction and correction assumes a norm of social functioning which some claim, when they argue indeterminacy of needs, cannot be explicit. Yet they must be explicit to be treatment goals!

It should be apparent that there is need for social group work in treatment and correctional settings, as well as in developmental and preventative programs. This calls for creative ingenuity in the provision of supports for positive health as well in corrective and treatment services. Social work has only just begun to think of prevention as a priority in structuring services. A preventative approach opens almost unlimited possibilities for tapping the so-called "scarce resources." If by "scarce resources" we mean the financial support needed to develop and promote our programs, scarcity of funds is not our problem. Vast sums of money are available, though not always allocated wisely. There is, to be sure, the Chest dilemma and funds are scarce from that source. The argument that scarcity of resources exists merely because most group services are financed by Chest funds is not valid. Our sights must be broadened to more than the local and the immediate. Current legislation at the federal level has allocated considerable funds for a wide range of community mental health efforts. Well designed group service programs are a logical part of any community mental health effort. Social group work must relate itself to these as well as more narrowly drawn treatment programs. When we redesign and expand some of our services we will be able better to meet the problem of necessary resources.

While the social work profession is moving forward to a belated consideration of provision and prevention, it is ill advised for social group work, which has always had strong commitment to this point of view, to change its course and move solely to a treatment focus.

We believe that social group work is an appropriate method for assisting individuals and groups to achieve developmental tasks. Moreover, we believe that the concept of positive health is a "high-level wellness" where functioning of the individual is oriented toward maximizing his potential or of achieving the greatest potential of which he is capable within his environment (Dunn, 1959).

We believe, as stated by the Commission on Practice of the NASW, "Prevention in Social Work is defined as activities which have merit in averting or discouraging the development of specific problems, or in delaying or controlling the growth of such problems . . ." We subscribe to Dr. Alfred J. Kahn's statement that "while social work has a major preventive task on all levels, in the public health sense of the term, the profession should also address itself to developmental provision. The distinction between preventive activity and provision may have significant consequences for the public at large, for 'clients,' and for social work" (Kahn, 1962).

There is a distinction between prevention of specific dysfunction and helping to achieve developmental tasks. The latter include broad categories of socialization such as learning appropriate role behavior, achievement of ego integration, and the provision of experiences in a democratic living. The former focuses on specified probable areas of behavioral dysfunction. While the prevention of specific dysfunction is highly desirable, the developmental tasks are appropriately in the domain of social group work.

We believe that developmental provision is not only possible and desirable, but an imperative. Group serving agencies can and should state their objectives in behavioral (social functioning) terms; program can and should be designed specifically to reach these objectives; social group work offers vast potential for achieving these ends through guided group experiences; provision and prevention are ethically more attractive in a world beset by permanent social change than the alternatives of correction and treatment alone.

Social group work practice must be defined irrespective of setting—individual enhancement, group development, and environmental change are components of all social group work practice! We, at the University of Pittsburgh, believe that a definition of social group work practice must transcend the demands of current experience; we believe that a definition of social group work must subsume all of group work practice under one roof.

Definitions of group work practice which are in current vogue act to obscure rather than clarify the role and function of the group work practitioner. They suggest that his tradition makes him too diffuse to be effective, that his hope of professional future lies in parochialism. Such definition binds group work practice to transitory assumptions of social need, rather than to the skill, training and ethical commitment of the worker. It results in an inflexibly institutionalized form of practice which limits the practitioner's ability to meet needs where they may exist rather than where practice is. We therefore, offer the following position statement:

1. A major function of social group work is to act in self-fulfillment.

2. The individual and his social environment are inseparable. The social group worker works toward enhancement of the social functioning of the individual, of the group and of the society.

3. The mature, socially well functioning individual in our culture is one who is most adequately socialized into a democratic society with democratic values. The democratic tradition in social group work is, therefore, therapeutically as well as ethically, sound.

4. A personal sense of efficacy is an important component of each individual's well-being. The client's involvement in a group which works to effect socially desirable environmental change provides this sense of efficacy while effecting change which is meaningful to the client. Social action, in a form and with content suitable to the client and the setting, is for this reason, inherent in definitions of social group work practice.

5. The interrelation of the individual and his social environment suggests an extension of practice beyond the small group. Considering its appropriateness in the particular situation, the practitioner may consciously use the total agency milieu, may work with small socio-groups and small psyche-groups, may work with large groups of various kinds, may use the two-person interview and other forms of practice which provide appropriate access to change.

6. The group process lies at the center of social group work practice. The group work practitioner works toward facilitating this process toward freeing members and the group process itself to bring about change.

7. The worker may be more or less active in the group process at a particular time as a specific technique in reaching his goals. However, the model of practice which places the group worker at the center of the group is not appropriate for all of group work practice and does not, per se, define the social group work method. Group goals are the product of a collaborative effort by both worker and group members. The functioning of both individual and the group is enhanced by the process of goal formulation as well as by the goals themselves.

8. The goals of the agency, the worker and the group must be made explicit. Neither practitioner, agency, nor group members can easily attain unknown goals. The more specific and better understood, and more easily and directly can goals be attained.

9. The social worker is a part of the agency for which he works. He can practice social work only insofar as agency purposes further social work ends. Agency setting is a vehicle through which social workers carry out their professional ethical and moral responsibilities.

10. We believe that specific techniques from among the many available may be employed differentially by the social group worker to deal with particular situations and problems. However, the essential elements of social group work practice remain the same, regardless of setting.

The Group Work Section Practice Committee of the NASW recently re-issued a statement which postulates a frame of reference for social group work practice (Hartford, 1964). The document delineates a "range of purposes of the groups in social group work." Examination of the manner in which these purposes are detailed shows that they emphasize method rather than goals. Thus the reader concludes that the group worker's purpose in helping members to "learn to participate actively in group life" is so that he may "learn to lead and to follow, to delegate, to assume responsibility" etc., etc.

But to what end?? Apparently the group worker focuses exclusively on *how* members function with no regard for the *why* beyond individual needs. And so means become ends. The fact that a group meets under the sanction of an agency which has a formulated philosophy and articulated purposes, with a worker having professional commitments and within a community with its ethical, moral and philosophical norms seems unrelated to the group worker's task. What is group work practice by this definition? The obvious deduction is that social group work practice, in its sum total, is a method. Practice has been confused and confounded with method. The statement gives cursory acknowledgement to democratic action in its value statement but neglects to use this concept in its description of practice. Note the working of the Practice Statement. "*To help group members learn to participate actively in group life as experience in developing a sense of responsibility for active citizenship, and for improving the nature of participation in social action . . .*" The statement, while placing focus on training and experience that will lead to action, avoids the action itself. Thus the group is reduced in status to a mechanism employed by the worker with no purpose beyond enhancement of the individual member.

In stating our position, we wish to make particular note of our disagreement with the definition of practice of the Group Work Section Practice Committee. We hold that it has supported the narrow definition of social group work practice. We consider it time for a review and a recasting of the statement to represent all of group work practice, in order to retain the breadth and flexibility which will permit the group worker to meet needs where they are rather than where he is.

REFERENCES

COYLE, G. L., 1948. *Group Work with American Youth.* New York: Harper & Brothers.

DUNN, H. I., 1959. "High Level Wellness," *American Journal of Public Health,* Vol. 49.

DUVALL, E. R., 1967. *Family Development.* Philadelphia: Lippincott.

ERIKSON, E. H., 1950. *Childhood and Society.* New York: Norton.

FRENCH, W., 1957. *Behavioral Goals of General Education in High School.* New York: Russell Sage Foundation.

GOFFMAN, E., 1961. *Asylums: Essays on the Social Situation of Mental Patients and Other Inmates.* New York: Doubleday.

GREENWOOD, E., 1957. "Attributes of a Profession," *Social Work,* Vol. 2, No. 3.

HARTFORD, M., ed., 1964. *Working Papers Toward a Frame of Reference for Social Group Work.* New York: National Association of Social Workers.

HAVIGHURST, R. J., 1953. *Human Development and Education.* New York: Longmans, Green.

HUMMEL, and SMITH, n.d. *The Task Method of Program.* Omaha: YMCA.

KAHN, A., 1962. "Therapy, Prevention and Developmental Provision: A Social Work Strategy," *Public Health Concepts in Social Work Education Proceedings.* New York: Council on Social Work Education.

KEARNEY, n.d. *Elementary School Objectives.* N.p.

KONOPKA, G., 1963. *Social Group Work: A Helping Process.* Englewood Cliffs, N.J.: Prentice Hall.

LUCK, J. M., 1957. "Social Group Work," *Social Work Yearbook.* New York: National Association of Social Workers.

MAIN, M. W., and M. E. MACDONALD, 1962. "Professional Functions and Opinions of Social Group Workers," *Social Service Review,* Vol. 36, No. 4.

NASW Questionnaire, Gertrude Wilson, n.d.

SORENSON, R., and H. S. DIMOCK, 1955. *Designing Education in Values.* New York: Association Press.

TRECKER, H., ed., 1955. "AAGW. Definition of Group Work," *Group Work Foundations and Frontiers.* New York: Whiteside Press.

VINTER, R., 1961. "Restructuring Group Services," *Social Work with Groups.* New York: National Association of Social Workers.

WILSON, G., 1956. "The Practice of Social Group Work," *Summary of the Report, The Committee on Practice, Group Work Section.* New York: National Association of Social Workers.

WILSON, G., and G. RYLAND, 1949. *Social Group Work.* New York: Houghton Mifflin.

15

A Humanistic View of Social Group Work: Worker and Member on a Common Human Level

Emanuel Tropp is Professor of Social Work, School of Social Work, Virginia Commonwealth University, Richmond.

Emanuel Tropp

At the Tenth Anniversary Symposium of NASW in 1965, Helen Harris Perlman (1965) offered the following proposition: "It would be a service to all social work methods if group work did not too immediately and too slavishly imitate the casework model; if, rather, it asked and answered some questions of its own" (p. 171). In the few years that have elapsed since then, it would appear that not too many people were listening to this message. It is a real pity, because history will apparently have to go through the same tortuous process that the same writer described at the end of the very same paper: "When in 1952, I urged that we 'put the social back in social work' I thought it was a lost cause. Today there is a ground swell toward this goal in every part of our practice" (p. 178). It appears today that the time is long past due to urge that we *put the group back in group work.*

If we look carefully at the current straws in the wind in social casework theory and practice, it may be possible to predict that—in the ironic way that cultural lags often have of catching up with us—just as group work reaches the full crest of its discovery of individual study, diagnosis, and treatment, casework theorists will be re-examining and eventually relinquishing these ideas as outmoded remnants of the past.

But, regardless of whether present trends in casework move so clearly or quickly in this direction, it can nonetheless be established that the use of the study-diagnosis-treatment model (hereinafter referred to as SDT for reasons of brevity) in group work practice was

Reprinted from *A Humanistic Foundation for Group Work Practice: A Collection of Writings by Emanuel Tropp*, New York: Selected Academic Readings, 1969, with permission from the author.

a distinct historical error, a kind of transplant that was out of place in the medium. This position will be developed in this paper along the following lines:

1. that the use of SDT in group work is patently based on a false assumption that, oddly, has never been seriously questioned—having to do with the justification of group work as a social work method through the process called "individualization";
2. that the use of SDT runs counter to the most important contemporary revolution in the human relations disciplines;
3. that the use of SDT in group work represents a nullification of the medium, and that it is antithetical to and disabling of what that medium can accomplish.

In 1956, in one of the first issues of *Social Work*, a memorable article was presented by Jacob Hurwitz (1956), dealing with the need to systematize group work practice. Those engaged in this practice knew full well the seriousness of this call and the enormous work that remained to be done.

Among the first formulators of a systematic approach in group work was Robert Vinter, who said in 1959:

> An adequate group work theory should provide goals and ends toward which it directs action. It should present a set of means that can be employed to attain the desired ends, a system for action. . . . [P]articular states of problematic social functioning are always individual and must be specifically determined. . . . Location of the individual in a diagnostic category also involves determination of treatment or change goals. . . . That is, treatment goals must be specific to individuals [1960, pp. 125-26].

This position became the prototype for the stance adopted in many schools of social work in their training for group work practice. It gained strength in group work practice at the very time when group work was seeking to firm up its sense of identification with the totality of social work, and was rapidly moving into the restorative settings, side by side with casework practitioners. At a time like this, it was understandable for group workers to become painfully self-conscious in the face of Vinter's further structure, an ironic statement that "implicit in such [existing] conceptions is the notion that an aim of group work practice is to help persons become good members of successful client groups" (Vinter, 1960, p. 126). If this aim was truly representative of group work, then, compared with the sophisticated depth-manipulations of the group psychotherapists, it sounded so primitive as to be unworthy of a place in the social work profession.

Thus, the response of group work to the simultaneous demands of both systematization and legitimization within the profession was to become "more like the other" by demonstrating the capacity to "individualize." But, since group workers had always individualized, this needed to be offered anew with sufficient clarity and force—and, for this, there appeared to be only one road: study, diagnosis, and treatment.

THE FALSE ASSUMPTION

When the charge was made that group work was not sufficiently specific, planful, or scientific, it seemed at the time that the only logical conclusion to be derived from this proposition was that such standards required differentiated individual treatment goals. Now this is about as non sequitur as one can get; and, as a conclusion, it truly strikes at the heart of the total social work enterprise.

For what does it really mean to individualize? For example, does it mean to *care for* human beings affected by some planned social work action? Then surely the social action roles of the profession in obtaining improvements in social welfare legislation would imply a most effective caring for many, many individuals—without the benefit of particularized or differentiated knowledge of each individual affected. *What must be known to be effective in their behalf is what problems or needs they have in common.* Yet the end results of such caring for people do enormously contribute to the welfare of great numbers of individuals.

To take this one step further, does "individualizing" mean to have special information about each individual who is to be affected by some act of social work intervention, plus a special assessment of each one's problem, plus a special plan of action for each and every one? If so, then to what limbo do we consign both traditional community organization and modern community action? If, for these methods to be considered "legitimate" within social work practice, they need to apply SDT to each member of the communities they serve, then we have truly created the ultimate absurdity.

Since it is obviously not necessary for the established community organization branch of the profession to have differentiated individual goals, what, then, do we do about group work? To say that group work is really more like casework (hence requiring the same techniques) while community organization is somehow different, clearly begs the question, out of a blocked capacity to see the true richness and variety that each of the social work methods has to offer in its own right, For, just as it is unnecessary to have an SDT approach in community organization, because the unit of work is the community (and that unit is what needs to be identified, evaluated and consulted with), so it is with group work, where *the unit of work is the group.*

If it is established as the foundation aim of social work that the various methods are practiced for the purpose of helping human beings in the enhancement of their social functioning, then it will be understood that this is exactly why some social workers work with groups and some with communities. And then it need not be added as an article of faith that the only way a social worker can possibly help human beings in a social situation is by having individualized them.

In this light, it is worth returning to the earlier derision of *group-oriented* group work as merely helping persons to become "good members of successful client groups," and to see it for what it is: a profound oversimplification of vital group work practice wisdom. The question that has really been blocked is: What is it that requires the scientific understanding of the social worker in order for his practice to be considered truly professional? It is posed here that the *focal point* in casework is the individual, in group work the group, and in community work the community. These are the unique contributions that each makes to social work and to society, and they can enrich each other most by not succumbing to the ever present push to homogenization (Tropp, 1966).

THE REVOLUTION IN PROFESSIONAL—"CLIENT" RELATIONSHIPS

A sense of deep concern is beginning to pervade the entire social work profession about how social workers view and deal with the people they serve. The question keeps coming up with ever increasing urgency: Do we see the users of our services in a subject-object perspective or in an I-Thou relation? The latter terminology is, of course, derived from the rapidly growing existential movement in all the helping professions, more so in psychiatry and psychology than in social work, which strangely should be finding this conception of human relations especially congenial to its cornerstone value, namely, respect for the dignity of the human being.

In its most essential form, it has been stated by the existential analyst Binswanger, who sees the analyst and patient as two human beings "on a common plane of human existence", engaged in a common human enterprise, although with different roles to perform (Matson, 1964, p. 238). On a much larger canvas, this respectful view of man has been definitively set forth by Floyd Matson (1964).

In social work, it is not necessary to look for something with an existential tag to find the same trends. Not long ago, Carol Meyer, speaking about casework in our time, said that

> . . . it seems that people will not stand still and wait for us; nor will they accommodate themselves to translating their discontent and malaise into clinical entities. . . . Will we continue to see clients as cases rather than as citizens and members of the community? [This] practice mode will have to change . . . earlier derived from structured office visits and formal relationships conceived from the therapist–patient or worker–client roles [Meyer, 1966, pp. 12–18].

Still more recently, Lydia Rapoport (1967) addressed herself to some "fallacies and myths" in casework, saying that one such myth is "that in order to bring about a cure one must at least know and get at the causative factors. The relationship of cause and cure comes from medicine, with its doctrine of specific etiology" (p. 33).

It is now generally recognized that social work (originally casework, and now group work too) drew heavily from the medical model, with special emphasis on the psychoanalytical derivative. The client was essentially seen as a kind of patient who needed some form of treatment. In order to treat, one had to (as the doctor did) first diagnose, and in order to diagnose, one therefore needed to study.

Now, where there is a psychiatric illness, the need may be for psychiatric treatment. But, at this time in history, it would verge on the nonsensical to maintain that the predominant modes of social dysfunctioning, falling within the normal range of life situations, that come to the attention of social workers are to be seen as illness in the psychiatric sense. By far, most of the situations social workers are called upon to handle are either based on the stresses of the developmental tasks at various life junctures or are the by-products of stresses created by having to cope with some unusual circumstance (Falck, 1967). Looked at in this way, do these human needs and problems equate with "illness," which then requires treatment? And if the individual is for this reason regarded as being ill, how responsible can he feel for handling his own situation? The concept of diagnosis flows from that of treatment. It tends to imply that the person is "figured-out" or "decided-upon." It further implies a subject–object relation.

Is it not more appropriate, and more respectful of those who use our services, to say that we work together with them, as openly as possible, to *identify* their problems or needs, to *examine* the components of their situation, to *assess* the possible resolutions and to *come to some common understanding* of what is needed to be done (Gottlieb and Stanley, 1967)? Is this not a much more apt contemporary substitute for the old, tired, borrowed concepts of SDT, which no longer fit the increasingly humanistic view of man in the helping professions? In this view, the helper looks at the seeker as a fellow human and attempts to offer a relationship as authentic on both sides as possible, which includes a real humility on the part of the "expert," a recognition that the seeker may have surprising strengths, and a basically phenomenological approach, in which both parties seek together: What is really happening?

THE INHERENT QUALITIES OF THE GROUP WORK MEDIUM

While it may be argued in another context as to the changing merits of the SDT approach in casework, it is posed here that this model of work with individuals is in direct contradiction with the nature of the medium that is inherent in the group work process. It is important to state clearly that reference is being made here not to *any* group medium, but to the group work medium. As recognized recently in a collaborative writing of medical caseworkers and group workers, there are many kinds of social work with groups, of which *one* is social group work (Frey, 1966). A definition of social group work that would clarify this distinction is: The social group work method aims (1) to help people in the enhancement of their social functioning through group experiences in which the members are involved in common engagement with common interests or concerns, and (2) to help such groups to function effectively and responsibly in the fulfillment of those purposes, in consonance with the society around them. This definition is thus concerned with groups that are engaged in the group-goal-achieving process or, in other words, are taking hold of their collective lives as groups.

Further, in the words of the publication last quoted,

> If the director of a social work department continues to see the prime objective of service as the helping of *individual* patients, then group work is only an extension of the individual service. . . . This is the state of affairs which generally exists today, But there is another way. The other way starts with the premise that in the last analysis it is the health of the population being served at any given time that is the key target. This population may be a large urban community, a local neighborhood, a hospital or a ward [Frey, 1966, p. 16].

Essentially, then, the underlying question in group work is: What is the target of service? The answer is inherent in the medium, which tells us in many ways that the group is the target in group work, as the community is in community work. Then it is toward the group target that the group worker must address his planning questions, in such terms as: identification of the common concerns and needs and purposes of the group, evaluation of the capacities and limitations of the group in carrying out these purposes, and the preparation of a variety of proposals and options to be presented to the group for mutual consideration with the worker, along with whatever proposals the group makes itself.

To turn away from these basic considerations and to insist on an atomistic, particularistic, individualistic approach is, in effect, to waste the medium of service. The human gain in a group-focused approach is greater than in an individualized style because of the inherently respectful stance of the worker toward the common humanity of the members as they face their common life situation together.

A number of major distinctive characteristics of the group work process that define the qualities of the medium and contraindicate an atomistic approach are described as follows:

I. The Medium Has a Kaleidoscopic Effect

The group work process is such a fast-moving, kaleidoscopic interchange among so many individual and group variables that its prime demand upon the worker is, first and foremost, in the area of phenomenology. Simply to be able to observe *what* is happening—to the group as a whole and to *some* of its individual members at any given time (and how much one must inevitably miss because of human limitations)—is the first order of business. A worker who gets too busy interpreting, on any level, before he has seen and heard what is really going on, will be getting in his own way. With refinement of skill, certain levels of understanding can take place, sometimes instantaneously, sometimes slowly, sometimes long after the group session. These levels are related to: the group-as-a-whole, group to worker, group to member, member to member, member to group, subgroup to group, member to worker—and many variants thereof. The kinds of understanding may be: What does this action mean to the group-as-a-whole, to the particular member, to various segments of the group, and to the worker? The worker's level may be in terms of how, if at all, his understanding of meaning is different from the members' and what this understanding can do to enable him to help the group or help a member in relation to the group's purpose.

But, much as this entire process can be logically ordered as a system, for purposes of analysis, it does not flow that the worker can simultaneously *observe, comprehend, evaluate, and act* in relation to all of these variables. This would not only require a computerized leader, but would leave very little for the group. It is, in other words, both impossible and undesirable. If a single caseworker, facing a single client, must mobilize such a skilled combination of science and art to perceive, comprehend, evaluate, and act on one set of individual variables, it is simple common sense that something has to give when dealing with six to twelve such complexities and their infinite interconnections.

If caseworkers are beginning to question today how much "baggage" they need to take along on a journey with a single client (by way of study and diagnosis and planning), then certainly there never could have been a time when group workers could take with them more than a very small load—otherwise they might never get off the ground. The questions that the group worker must ask himself about his individual members are:

a. How much do I need to know about each one of them, except what life situation they have in common, and possibly in what ways some members show important variations from this commonness? How much can I and will I use? Which knowledge is essential and which expendable?

b. How much of this knowledge is simply brief factual identification and how much need is there for "causal" computations?

c. How much evaluation and planning data for each member can realistically be put to work, and how much will get in the way of my efforts to deal with all the members' common concerns?

II. The Message of the Medium Is That the Group Is the Helping Agent

As the group worker continues to work with his group, he discovers that, if he is counting on *his* prior knowledge of individuals and *his* handling of them, he is losing his grasp of the essence of the process, which is *what the group can do to help its own members.* As he redirects his attention away from group-centered needs and problems, he loses his central function as a helping agent in this medium—he will eventually find himself either with a very weak group or else doing casework in the group. His function will be most effectively discharged as he maintains a clarity of focus and concentration on the group phenomena, and this is a task of major proportions.

Throughout social work today, groups are found adrift, "at sea," with very little sense of direction and weak motivation, or engaging in "games" of cooperative talk or activity to accommodate the worker, but signifying very little. Those workers struggling with these problems know the intensity with which they must prepare for the group session, the complexity of skill they must be ready to muster in order to motivate and involve the group, in order to help make the experience meaningful and productive for the group, to know how to stay on group focus, when to yield and change, and so much more—all for the sake of the best interests of the group-as-a-whole and therefore for its members. The refinement and organization of this central body of group work knowledge is of so many dimensions and of such real depth of human meaning that little time, energy, and effort are left to expend on individual strategies. But the worker need not be concerned about not "individualizing," because he is making the unique contribution of creating the conditions whereby the group work medium does its main job: to help the members to help each other (Tropp, 1968).

The very fact of the group's existence and task-at-hand creates *expectations for coping.* The member is in the group because it is expected that he can deal with the common task and, in the course of it, engage in productive social relations. (In this sense, the role of *member* is significantly different from the role of individual *client.*) This expectation of coping is a built-in dynamic that calls forth the strengths in the members—strengths that continually surprise both members and worker. As these strengths are drawn out by the common undertaking, they produce behaviors that are likely to be the very ones desired by the worker and appreciated by the member, but without benefit of SDT planning.

In this medium, which expects and produces strengths and coping, the member becomes truly the source of his own growth, as he takes his life in his own hands, gaining strength from others, who also share a portion of his life challenge. He need not wait for the worker to "arrange" his personal changes. In fact, it is even likely that he and his peers will move to help the worker to do his job. He cannot wait for the worker, for too much is happening. While the worker may sometimes support him or stimulate him, he will more often be the initiator of his own increased self-direction, as he responds to stimuli coming from the group.

III. The Medium Places the Individual in a Communal Perspective

What is seen in the group is the *common human condition.* The uniqueness of the group lies in the fact of its common humanity, which implies a shared experience, in which the members are like each other in some important respect: a common concern or common interest or common life situation. It is *likeness rather than difference* that is brought into bold relief in this experience. It is at least as respectful to see the common human ties as to see the individual variations. The individual is respected as a fellow human being in a community of humans who have something important in common.

What, then, is the meaning of "individualization" in group work? It means seeing the individual members in the group as they engage with the demands of the group, seeing them as they come to life in the drama of this engagement. In this drama, each person is seen both as a *member*, who has certain needs, concerns, interests, and tasks in common with all the other members, and as a unique *individual*, who performs these tasks and deals with these concerns in his own special way. The members then respond to each other in both similar and uniquely different ways, as each solicits these responses by his expressions of *role* and *person.* All the members learn to respect the right to be different but also to share the job of how much they are the same. In other words, *the individual's uniqueness is seen within the context of his commonality with others* (Frankl, 1962).

Yet the act of individualizing in group work does not mean that the worker need have studied each individual's life history, come to some diagnosis of the unique causes of his current situation, and determined a special treatment plan for each member based on this pregroup knowledge. These very steps will be more likely to impede the worker's efforts truly to see the *individual-in-the-group*, which is a much more reliable basis for evaluating whatever is different in any particular individual's need as compared with those needs of all the members that brought them together. If there are significant differences, and if these can be handled by the worker while keeping his focus on the group-as-a-whole, then they can be dealt with in the living milieu of the group situation within the sense of meaning that takes shape as they present themselves.

As the worker relates to the members of the group, they individualize themselves before his very eyes by their unique behavior. As a result, he inevitably relates to each one in response to their differential action and reaction patterns in the group. He will also be affected by the previous behavior of individuals *in the group* as he tries to evaluate current behavior, to the extent that memory, clarity, and time will allow. But his knowledge of each member's background *prior* to the group experience is not only a very tall order to both retain and use but, even more important, may turn out to be grossly misleading and more harmful than helpful. *The person-in-the-group is not the same as the person-pregroup.* Rather than "knowing all about" and having "figured out" and "planned for" an individual member, it is far more respectful to see him as he is in the group, to allow him to be whatever the group brings out in him, to allow him to be different from what he was. *To work with an individual essentially on the basis of the expectations called forth by the group tasks is the ego-strengthening nature of the group work medium.*

To see the individual in the group on the basis of prior knowledge may, in fact, tend to guarantee that he will act in the way he acted outside the group and will thus produce a self-fulfilling prophecy to confirm the diagnosis. Is it not better for the worker to humanize his view of all the members of the group because of his respect for what they have in common rather than merely individualize his prior knowledge and determination of each member's differential problem, which tend to push him strongly in the direction of a subject-object attitude?

The very fact of knowing so much about the individual, rather than being helpful, will be very likely to interfere with the relationship by creating a constant strain on the possibilities for a real and spontaneous relationship. When the worker brings with him considerable data, this tends to add up to *an awareness of problem or inadequacy*. The member then becomes *aware of the worker's awareness*. This dual awareness proves to be quite debilitating, for, instead of structuring for strength, for capacity, for expectation, the stage is set for weakness.

It might be asked whether the entire SDT culture is not, in fact, a highly professionalized defense of the worker's need to be stronger than the user of service, since this relation of prior knowledge of weakness places the worker in a kind of "one-upmanship" relation. This relation, in ways both subtle and overt, fosters further weakness and dependency and creates a sense of worker power. It contaminates the relationship of mutual trust and respect that is so vital. Could the worker afford not to be one-up? Would the relation then be too equal and leave the worker defenseless? What kind of power over people does this whole outlook entail?

And so, it is not too difficult to say that what has come to be called the process of individualization in group work may very well be the process of dehumanization. It has always been implied that seeing each person separately in the group was somehow more human, but the ways in which it has been done have resulted in making the individual less than human—and that is not a very good bargain!

IV. The Medium Places the Worker in a Common Human Perspective

In this context of the living community of the group, the worker must find the common human bond that *links him to the members*. It is this bond that creates the climate for a humanistic approach to group work practice. Basically the roots of the humanistic stance in group work go back to Grace Coyle, with a line of continuous development by Wilson, Ryland, Phillips, and Schwartz. This mainstream has been subjected to a serious diversion and, in effect, obliteration by the diagnostic-treatment orientations of both the psychoanalytic and behavioral conditioning varieties. Since the very word "humanistic" is subject to many uses and much vagueness of intent, it is important to state it in a more definite manner.

The humanistic thesis in group work can be developed as follows:

a. The worker shares one overriding characteristic with the members of the group—the common human condition. No matter how great the differences between them might be, their common humanity creates links of life progressions, experiences, and crises that form the basis for the worker's "feeling with" the group.

b. In effect, therefore, this stance is *the view of one human being by another.* It says: "I see in him what I am too—mortal, fallible, subject to pain, misfortune and crisis, strong and weak, sometimes assured and sometimes fearful, sometimes at ease with the world and sometimes torn with agony, having the same human needs to love and be loved, to do something of value, to have a place that counts, to be needed, to find meaning in life. Today, he (dare I call him 'client'?) is ridden by things that are in the saddle—tomorrow it may be me. How, then, can I play a god, if I am as one human being to another? How can I rather learn from him and respect him? I can only help, as sometimes I too may need help from a fellow human, whether professional or otherwise. I help because I have dedicated myself to helping, to learning how I may be most useful in giving that help to my fellow humans sharing the same human condition."

c. In this spirit, making contact with the common humanity of the group and joining the members on a common plane of human existence is the necessary prerequisite for a meaningful and useful relationship. *The member is not a client,* for his key relations are with the other members rather than with the worker. *The members of this community are not guests to the worker's host, but they become the hosts and he the guest.* Then, despite the difference in function, the worker must accept his relative position of one among many, involved in *their* common undertaking.

d. To be able to *feel with* and *be with* a part of the member's experience as it connects with something within the worker's own humanity—*this is the humanization of the worker.*

e. To be able to show reverence for the member, compounded of compassion and expectation and respect—*this is the humanization of the member.*

f. To be able to make the really important gift, the gift of self, the act of human love, by caring and giving—*this is the humanization of the helping process.*

For some, these indicators of a humanistic stance might appear to be an offering of the heart and an elimination of the mind. To be on a common human level might seem to excuse the need to have any professional knowledge or skill. Yet the demand is actually more challenging than what passes for skill in the SDT culture, because it asks for a combination of *both* professional skill *and* human involvement. It is really much easier to be removed and to be one-up than to be involved, while still retaining a crucial professional difference. Yes, there is a need for science in the humanistic approach, but scientific knowledge does not automatically imply technological programming of people or groups, based on predictable behavior.

Further, the humanistic view has often been associated with a Gestalt orientation, and scientific minds are realistically alert to the possibility that the Gestalt can become a mystique, a hiding in the wholeness of things to escape the difficulties of analysis. As a mystique, the Gestalt can turn into a denial of knowledge, intimating that we dare not tamper with the whole person and that therefore we can never know anything. This can lead to nonthinking and ultimately to the abdication of the worker principle, i.e., nonperformance. But tampering is not the issue in the humanistic way. The reverential role of the worker in dealing with the whole person calls for him to be a person himself, to make contact, to make a contribution, to create a confrontation, to create expectations, in short, to make a difference. And the individual whole, as well as the group whole, does not defy understanding, which is both intellectual and empathetical, but defies a *totalness* of understanding and requires that considerable room be left for the unpredictable, even that it be expected and considered a norm in itself. It is, in the last analysis, the unpredictable that makes the group work medium (*as compared with more controlled group media*) so useful as a reality experience, full of the stuff of life (Matson, 1964; Sypher, 1967–68; Chomsky, 1968).

Finally, then, what is the function of the group worker as he humanizes his view of the group and its members?

First, he starts from the fact of the group as a living community, gathered around a common life situation. It is the common concern which brought it together that is his prime focus of attention, because it is, by its very nature, the prime mover for whatever gains may be forthcoming for its members.

Second, he sees the group as the medium within which, and in relation to which, the individual members are involved in action and interaction; it is the medium for both the action and the worker's perceptions of and responses to the action.

Third, he therefore sees that his most critically productive efforts, for the gain of all the members, are those which are engaged with this focal point of common concern and with the group-as-a-whole.

Fourth, as each member brings individual difference to the group's engagement with its purpose, the worker uses his efforts to enable these differences to contribute to the common good, thereby strengthening both the group and the individual.

Fifth, to the extent that his concentrated attention to the common needs of all the members will allow, he may selectively utilize the group interaction in specific and differentiated ways for some members at some times, as their needs may indicate; but the stress of the overall group efforts must limit the extent of this selective handling to a supplementary role.

Sixth, as he engages with the entire group around its common purpose, he shows that he deeply cares about that purpose, that he is moved by the common needs, that he has a clear expectation that the group can achieve what it has set out to do, and that he shares its joys and frustrations.

Seventh, as he relates to the members, he is open in manner (not devious), real as a person (not just a role), and with the group in its efforts (not above it, observing and manipulating). His attitude is: "Help me to understand your needs and aspirations, so that I can better help you to find the way to meet them" (not "I know all about you and I already have plans for you"). He not only hears and sees what is being said and felt and done, but he believes it for what it is intended to be. He is not so busy "interpreting" that he fails to make human contact with what is being expressed (for what the member means on *his* "surface" may be more important than what the worker interprets "underneath").

Eighth, he helps the group to deal with its tasks in the most satisfying, effective, and responsible manner. Through the common engagement of the members with these tasks, all individuals will gain, in varying degrees and in uniquely individual ways, self-esteem through expression, achievement, and recognition; release of pent-up feelings; stronger grasp of their own uniqueness through contending with others' differences; and self-reappraisal through increased perspective, objectivity, judgment, and control in relation with others.

CONCLUSIONS

This chapter has attempted (1) to identify the fallacy that all social work objectives require differentiated individual goals; (2) to describe the changing attitudes in the helping professions around worker-user relationships; (3) to demonstrate that the study-diagnosis-treatment model of practice is in fundamental conflict with the group work medium, which lives most naturally with a humanistic view of professional function.

From these positions, it flows that it is time to reinstate the place of the group in group work. It is so startingly simple to find that casework, group work, and community work can all share the same values, aspirations, and objectives for the people served without serving them in the same way. It is perfectly sensible for a caseworker to see the individual as his unit of service, for the group worker to see the group as his, and for the community worker to deal with the community. And so it should not be so strange to find that, within the same broad purposes, the function and structure of service will be significantly different. Thus, there need be no apologies for the group worker to see the *group* as the unit requiring assessment, planning and, evaluation—and not the individual.

At the same time, there is nothing that has been said that would deny that a humanistic view of worker function might be applicable to methods other than group work. It was simply the intention here to develop the case that this view is what is most congenial to the group work process, and that it has been in many ways the path through which group work got started and which may be just now becoming clear as its main gift to social work as a whole.

If one does accept the humanistic thesis, then there is little room left for the medical, analytical, or behavioral conditioning models, based on study, diagnosis, and treatment. These modes do not live with each other at all; there is a deep-rooted clash of values. In effect, the humanistic call today is for a rediscovery of that vital core of social work that inspired so many to enter this profession—respect for the dignity, the integrity, and the value of the human being. Here is a challenge for our time, worthy of the best, the most giving, the most knowledgeable, and the most human in social work, enough to inspire the profession to pick up once more the unfinished business of man's ever present need to find meaning and fulfillment in his relations with his fellow man.

REFERENCES

CHOMSKY, N., 1968. "Language and the Mind I," *The Columbia University Forum*, Vol. 9, No. 1.

FALCK, H. S., 1967. "Crisis Theory and Social Group Work." Topeka, Kans.: NASW Mid-Continent Regional Institute (mimeo).

FRANKL, V. E., 1962. *The Doctor and the Soul.* New York: Alfred A. Knopf.

FREY, L. A., ed., 1966. *Use of Groups in the Health Field.* New York: National Association of Social Workers.

GOTTLIEB, W., and J. H. STANLEY, *1967. "Mutual Goals and Goal-setting in* Casework," *Social Casework*, Vol. 48, No. 8.

HURWITZ, J., 1956. "Systematizing Social Group Work Practice," *Social Work*, Vol. 1, No. 3.

MATSON, F. W., 1964. *The Broken Image*. New York: George Braziller.

MEYER, C. H., 1966. "Casework in a Changing Society," *Social Work Practice 1966*. New York: Columbia University Press.

PERLMAN, H. H., 1965. "Social Work Method: A Review of a Decade," *Social Work*, Vol. 10, No. 4 (Supplement).

RAPOPORT, L., 1967. "Crisis-oriented Short Term Casework," *Social Service Review*, Vol. 41, No. 1.

SYPHER, W., 1967-68. "The Poem as Defense," *The American Scholar*, Vol. 37, No. 1.

TROPP, E., 1966. "The Further Development of Group Work as a Separate Method," *Social Work Practice 1966*. New York: Columbia University Press.

——, 1968. "The Group: In Life and in Social Work," *Social Casework*, Vol. 49, No. 5.

VINTER, R. D., 1960. "Small Group Theory and Research: Implications for Group Work Theory and Research," *Social Science Theory and Social Work Research*, L. S. Kogan, ed. New York: National Association of Social Workers.

Study Questions

1. Wilson and Ryland noted that group members feel loved and accepted by the social worker to the degree that they have been helped to "handle their aggressive hostile feelings in a socially acceptable way through the medium of satisfactory group experiences." Can you give some examples to show specifically what this means? What do these authors mean when they say that most limitations are inherent in the situation itself? How does the group worker as "bearer of values" of the agency and society help group members work within the agency structure to deal with their problems while at the same time helping them to understand and accept the limitations imposed by the agency? How is individual achievement related to the achievement of the group-as-a-whole?

2. Wilson and Ryland speak of some individual hostile behavior that can be "devastating" to a group. At such times, they argue, the social purpose—that is, the good of the group—"must take precedence over individual interests and needs of some of the parts." Do you agree? How would a group worker go about adjusting personal claims to the claims of the group-as-a-whole? Is this likely to occur naturally?

3. What is meant by the "functional" approach to social work with groups? What are its basic ideas and premises? How is it currently viewed?

4. What is the relationship between group work purposes and social work skills? According to Phillips, how do the specific group work skills contribute to group work purposes? To what extent does Phillips's view of social group work skills focus attention on helping individuals and groups to take responsibility for their own development for societal change and improvement?

5. Do you agree with the statement by Sirls et al. that social group work in practice "cannot be considered social group work unless the members of the group have the opportunity and are encouraged to work to bring change in their social environment"? Would you agree that the move away from social action is a move in the wrong direction? Can you give specific examples of changes which abandon social goals and make a "fetish of method"? Do you feel that there is an overemphasis on individual social functioning to the exclusion of the group and social milieu in some of the current formulations? To what extent do you think agency structures facilitate or impede social action purposes?

6. What is the "developmental" approach to group work? What is the nature of its underlying conceptions: developmental, phenomenological, and humanistic? Is the approach limited to groups that seek to promote the social growth of members? How do Tropp's perceptions of human behavior differ from the problem-oriented approaches? What differences exist regarding the functions of group work, the role of the worker, the use of specific skills and techniques, the place of research in practice, and the relation of group work to social work generally?

7. Is Tropp's humanistic thesis the same as or different from Wilson and Ryland's concept of the worker's "Love"? Where do you think the agency fits into Tropp's orientation? Do professional values take precedence over the agency?

8. What does Tropp mean by the statement that it's time to put the group

back into group work? Do you agree that the establishment of the study-diagnosis-treatment model in group work practice was a distinct historical error? If so, what have been the undesirable consequences?

9. What is meant by "individualization" in group work? How is it different from working with individuals? In what sense can it be said that all of the social work methods individualize? Do you agree that the SDT model of work with individuals is in direct contradiction to the medium of the group work process? Can these orientations be combined? If the group is the target of service, then is the success of the group work also to be measured in terms of group changes? Does the group take priority over the individual? How is the role of the "member" different from the role of the individual "client"?

Suggested Readings

KLEIN, A., 1972. *Effective Groupwork.* New York: Association Press.

NEWSTETTER, W. I., 1948. "The Social Intergroup Work Process," *Proceedings of National Conference on Social Work, Selected Papers, 1947.* New York: Columbia University Press.

NORTHEN, H., 1955. "The Place of Agency Structure, Philosophy, and Policy in Supporting Group Programs of Social Action," in *Group Work: Foundations and Frontiers*, H. Trecker, ed. New York: Whiteside, William Morrow.

——, and R. W. ROBERTS, eds., 1976. "The Status of Theory," in *Theories of Social Work with Groups.* New York: Columbia University Press.

PHILLIPS, H. V., 1957a. *Essentials of Social Group Work Skill.* New York: Association Press.

——, 1957b. "Social Values and Social Group Work," in *Group Work Papers, 1957.* New York: National Association of Social Workers.

RYDER, E. L., 1976. "A Functional Approach," in *Theories of Social Work With Groups*, R. W. Roberts and H. Northen, eds. New York: Columbia University Press.

TROPP, E., 1966a. "The Further Development of Group Work as a Separate Method," *Social Work Practice, 1966.* National Conference on Social Welfare. New York: Columbia University Press.

——, 1966b. "Maturity in Social Functioning: The Developmental Goal of Group Work," *Journal of Jewish Communal Service*, Vol. 43, No. 2.

——, 1976. "A Developmental Theory," in *Theories of Social Work with Groups*, R. W. Roberts and H. Northen, eds. New York: Columbia University Press.

——, 1977. "Social Group Work: The Developmental Approach," in *Encyclopedia of Social Work*, 17th ed., Vol. II. New York: National Association of Social Workers.

SECTION C

Personal Change and Social Adjustment: Remedial Perspectives

The chapters in this section move us farther along the continuum from attention to the use of the group as a medium for personal growth and self-actualization to its use as a vehicle for changing behavior and alleviating personal maladjustments. At the same time, the emphasis on using social processes to accommodate individual needs is accompanied by a reduced interest in pursuing social goals or bringing about social change.

Konopka makes it clear in her chapter that social group work's greatest contribution to social work was its refusal to separate the individual from his physical and human environment. The application of group work in psychiatric settings, in her view, is not inconsistent with the generic thrust of group work but simply calls into play certain specifics of group work practice that are appropriate to meet the demands of the therapeutic situation. Although society is conceived to be "changeable," the specifics of treatment require that the individual be seen as the target for change. In advancing what has been described as a problem-oriented approach, Vinter presents his views regarding the core competencies of group work practice. The focus is primarily on bringing about individual change in and through the small group experience. The worker, who is seen as an agent of legitimate societal norms and values, serves to inculcate the essential values of the larger society in the treatment process.

16

The Generic and the Specific in Group Work Practice in the Psychiatric Setting

Gisela Konopka is Professor Emeritus and Consultant, Center for Youth Development and Research, University of Minnesota, St. Paul.

Gisela Konopka

WORKING WITH GROUPS

Work with groups in a helping capacity is as old as humanity. It is the conscious use of the method transmitted in a concentrated and systematic way which we now call social group work and which we are reexamining today.

We have by tradition, and often by teaching, identified group work with the informal recreational and educational agencies. Historically it is much broader than this. As long as social work was a broad endeavor it related itself to many different societal institutions. The bond which united the profession was its concern for suffering human beings and the protection and care of all those who could not care for themselves. These included children and young people, those who were poor and those who were sick, and those who were disadvantaged for economic reasons as well as those who were handicapped because of ignorance and prejudice.

At the time of the great social reforms of the nineteenth century, at the "watershed" of American history as Henry Steele Commager calls it, the social worker stood for child labor laws, for family services, for care of the unmarried mother, as well as for decent playgrounds in overcrowded city streets. He stood for work with the foreign born in settlement houses, for constructive and creative youth activities—as in the emerging youth organizations—and concern for and help to the lonely young men and women who moved into the industrial areas—as exemplified by the YMCA's and YWCA's. We must not forget that at this same time social workers made an earnest effort to use every available knowledge to be as effective as possible. While Mary Richmond, through her close contact with the beginnings of medical education, began to develop the details of the casework method, the early pioneers did not overlook the importance of group relations. Mary Richmond herself, with her keen sense of the essential, presented the following thoughts to the National Conference of Social Work in 1920:

> This brings me to the only point upon which I can attempt to dwell at all, to a tendency in modern case work which I seem to have noted and noted with great pleasure. It is one which is full of promises, I believe, for the future of social treatment. I refer to the new tendency to view our clients from the angle of what might be termed small group psychology. . . .
>
> Halfway between the minute analysis of the individual situation with which we are all familiar in case work, and the kind of sixth sense of neighborhood standards and backgrounds which is developed in a good social settlement, there is a field as yet almost unexplored [Richmond, 1930, pp. 487-88].

Five years before this paper was given, Zilpha Smith (1915) had pointed out that field work should always be in a family agency as well as in a neighborhood agency: "The kinds of social work which do not in the long run require both the family and the group work method as approach are few" (p. 624).

It was only with the increased interest in method and technique in social work that group work and casework separated sharply. Some of us may regret this. Some of us may think that it was healthy, because it forced the development of tools. However we may view it from the 1955 vantage point, we must accept the fact that the two methods developed somewhat differently. It is important, though, to state that we have returned in recent years to a clearer focus on underlying philosophy and services and we are at a point where we can better define our concepts and principles. In this way we may develop *generic social work thinking*, and move away from the heavy emphasis on method alone.

Much of what I present here as generic group work obviously belongs also to other methods in social work.

VALUES

Method in social work is by necessity related to *values*. Since we deal with relationships among human beings, ethical values permeate the whole fabric of our work. We have sometimes tried to imitate "scientific attitudes" by trying to avoid value judgments or by trying to avoid value judgments or by trying to create an "impersonal atmosphere." I do not need to argue against this here. It was demonstrated not only that this did not work but also that it was harmful to the person in need, to the social worker, and to the reputation of the profession. Since the roots of social work lie in religion and in humanism, the values it represents are those common to societies based on those philosophies:

The belief in the dignity and worth of each individual
The right of each individual to full development of his capacities
The responsibility of each individual not to harm or misuse others
The responsibility of each individual to contribute to the common welfare—within the limits of his capacities.

These values are incorporated in the most recent definition of social group work:

> The group worker enables various types of groups to function in such a way that both group interaction and program activity contribute to the growth of the individual and the achievement of desirable social goals. The objectives of the group worker include provision for personal growth according to the individual's capacity and need, the adjustment of the individual to other persons, to groups and to society, and the motivations of the individual toward the improvement of society, the recognition by the individual of his own rights, limitations and abilities as well as his acceptance of the rights, abilities, and differences of others [Coyle, 1954, p. 480].

These values coincide with values expressed in mental hygiene as seen in the last White House Conference Report which defines healthy personality as being happy and responsible. We sometimes present the development of group work as if in the beginning it was all activity, and as if only later did we add the understanding of the emotional forces of interaction and relationship to the worker.

This is a misconception, and we see it if we follow the literature back into the past. Perhaps theories were expressed in different ways (they usually are) but there was early sensitivity to the emotional impact of group relations. For instance, Jane Addams, in 1909, wrote about a group of young people who were drug addicts and how the settlement house worked with them: "It is doubtful whether these boys could ever have been pulled through unless they had been allowed to keep together through the hospital and convalescing period, unless we had been able to utilize the gang spirit and to turn its collective force towards overcoming the desires for the drug" (Addams, 1909, p. 66).

Miss Addams' thinking is not different from what we are finding today in our discussion of therapy groups or in work with street gangs.

In the early years of the twentieth century we find Hull House experimenting with housing groups of mentally sick patients released from the hospitals. This was the result of Julia Lathrop's trip to Europe during which she had observed the placement of mentally sick people in the community and produced her ardent plea for such an experiment: "If familiarity taught the peasants of Gheel not contempt, but fearless sympathy and skill a thousand years ago, why should we learn less readily now?" (Lathrop, 1909, p. 197.)

Our group work theory and principles have grown out of well-observed practice and knowledge acquired in sciences dealing with human behavior: psychiatry, psychology, sociology, anthropology, and related disciplines, namely, education and our sister method, casework.

Our developing concepts related the individual to group process and to society. It is perhaps social group work's greatest contribution to present-day social work that it never, even in theory, isolated the individual from his physical and human environment. While the group worker learned, from psychiatry and casework, a growing awareness of individual differences and dynamics, he constantly kept alive his awareness of the individual's relatedness to others. It is interesting to observe that psychiatry itself now is struggling to return to this insight. This is exemplified in Nathan Ackerman's writing, in the recent interest in more family-centered psychiatric treatment, and in the small group approach to the family. These will give increased impetus for a united endeavor of the different professions.

GENERIC GROUP WORK CONCEPTS

What are some of the generic concepts and theories of social group work? I shall try to summarize them in three parts: (a) in relation to the individual, (b) in relation to the group, and (c) in relation to society. All three parts are interrelated and only presented separately for greater clarification.

In relation to the individual. We consider the human being as a whole: physical, mental, emotional, and spiritual. As social workers we are dealing with all of this and not only with a part. We see the human being as a social being who is in need of interdependence all through his life. There is always a struggle between dependence and independence according to the different stages of development. The human being has a capacity to grow and change (there can be disruptions, blocks, regressions). Human behavior is influenced by values which are strongly formed by the primary group, the family, but secondary groups also have a great influence, and it grows with increase in age. We recognize that each human being has his own self-image which is largely formed by his relationships to others. The role an individual plays varies in different situations. We ought to be aware of this, since most of the time we deal only with a part of a person's life and in a specific relationship.

Most of our personality theory is based on knowledge derived from psychoanalysis but there have been modifications in recent years. For example, in schools of social work we have taught the stages of development according to the teachings of Freud. We are beginning to rethink them together with such writers as Erik Erikson and Ian Suttie, the latter an English psychiatrist whom I consider especially interesting. Suttie puts greater stress on early affectionate feelings and sees human development not as a constant struggle with frustration of instincts, but more as a development of this early interdependence. I cannot take a stand at this moment as to the soundness of this theory. I do not think that we in social group work have taken a stand, or should. We have accepted the thinking of dynamic emotional development and recognized that behavior is always purposeful (conscious or unconscious) and that there is ambivalence in every human being. It will be our task as well as that of other professions to continue our search for better understanding.

In relation to the group process. Our thinking has been based mainly on sociology and our own observations. We consider the group to be two or more people in interaction who can be regarded as a separate whole from other such formations. This concept separates it clearly from the concept of "mass." It also separates it from an accidental and loose gathering of several people. The degree of interaction may be varied and will depend greatly on the maturity, health, and purpose of the group and of the individuals composing it. We consider *bond*, the feeling of belonging, as one of the most important parts of a group. The measurement of its degree is a very valuable diagnostic tool for the social group worker. It is not always based on friendship feelings but sometimes on life interests, on aspirations, or needs. As part of the group process we must be aware of *group goal* not only in its content but also in its origin. We must distinguish between conscious and unconscious group goals.

We have to see the acceptance-rejection pattern in the group and recognize it again as dynamic. Part of this is the understanding of subgroups and what they mean to individuals, of isolation and leadership, and of scapegoating. The latter is a group equivalent to projection in the individual.

We see the group as a power to give support, to reject, to express hostility, to develop the phenomenon of contagion. We see it developing conflicts and solving conflicts through withdrawal of one part of the group, subjugation, majority rule and minority consent, compromise, and integration. Finally, we consider decision-making in a group to be one of the achievements in the life of individuals and communities.

In relation to society. We see culture as a value determinant in individual and group behavior, yet we must recognize that it is not a mechanical one and that we never can stereotype individuals in a particular culture.

We recognize social and economic environment as an important factor in influencing behavior as well as personality structure. The status of the individual or the group to which he belongs or feels he belongs has a great meaning to him.

We know that most societies, including our own, are stratified and that it helps us in our understanding to know the specific stratum from which the individual emerges, which he accepts or rejects. This includes not only the economic situation but the social, his professional or vocational affiliations, and his religion.

We see functions of social institutions as determined by historical development, popular consent, and law. We consider them changeable.

PRINCIPLES AND METHODS

If those, summarized, are our concepts and theories, our principles and methods grow out of them, and our value system. Some of the principles we all can agree upon are:

The right of the individual and the group to self-determination as long as this right is not misused by limiting that of others

The right of individuals and groups for participation in decision making

The ethical use of confidential material by the social worker

The use of the group work method only when competent judgment calls for its value to the group

The use of consultation, when need arises.

A *method* is a "special form of procedure, in any branch of mental capacity." Its main characteristic is that it gives only general directions but *never* allows the practitioner to simply follow the same rules. He must always adapt it according to his diagnostic understanding of the individual or the group. A good practitioner must be able to modify the basic guidelines according to the needs of the given situation.

Such guidelines and essential parts of the generic group work methods are:

The function of the social group worker is a helping or enabling function. This means that his goal is to help the members of the group and the group as a whole to move toward greater independence and capacity for self-help.

In determining his way of helping, the group worker uses the scientific method: fact finding (observation), analyzing, and diagnosis in relation to the individual, the group, and the social environment.

The group work method includes the worker forming purposeful relationships to group members and the group. This includes a conscious focusing on the needs of the members, on the purpose of the group as expressed by the members, as expected by the sponsoring agency, and as implied in the members' behavior. It is differentiated from a casual unfocused realtionship.

One of the main tools in achieving such a relationship is the conscious use of self. This includes self-knowledge and discipline in relationships without the loss of warmth and spontaneity.

There should be acceptance of people without accepting all their behavior. This involves the capacity for empathy as well as the incorporation of societal demands. It is the part of the method that is most closely intertwined with a high flexibility and abundance of warmth in the social group worker, as well as identification with values and knowledge.

Starting where the group is: the capacity to let groups develop from their own point of departure, of capacity, without immediately imposing outside demands.

The constructive use of limitations: limitations must be used judiciously in relation to individual and group needs and agency function. The forms will vary greatly. The group worker will mainly see here himself, program materials, interaction of the group, and awakening of insight in the group members.

Individualization. It is one of the specifics of the group work method that the individual is not lost in the whole, but that he is helped to feel himself to be a unique person who can contribute to the whole.

Use of the interacting process. The capacity to help balance the group, to allow for conflict when necessary and to prevent it when harmful. The help given to the isolate, not only through individual attention by the group worker alone but also by relating him to other members.

The understanding and conscious use of non-verbal as well as verbal material: I put non-verbal material first, since the group worker deals a great deal with this, especially in work with children.

His capacity to use program materials, which do not demand verbal expression and yet are helpful, should be very wide.

Specific group work tools[1] are:

The use of program media
The use of group interaction
The use of discussion method
The use of individual interviews (outside the group)
The use of individual contacts (inside the group)
The use of consultation
The use of referral
The writing and use of case and group records
Observation.

SPECIFICS IN PSYCHIATRIC SETTINGS

If what I have presented are generic group work principles, then what are the specifics in the psychiatric settings?

After much struggle, psychiatric casework evolved a definition of its work as "case work practiced in a psychiatric setting in collaboration with a psychiatrist." This clarified the focus of generic casework as nothing "special" in method, but special in the profession with which it collaborates.

It would be simple to parallel this in group work and state that group work in psychiatric settings is "group work in psychiatric settings in collaboration with psychiatrists."

Yet (perhaps because of our historical development) we do see in practice some specifics and we must at least investigate them.

I repeat—basically all group work is related to the purpose of its agency, and method must be used judiciously. The practitioner confronted with a YWCA teenage group will start at another point, move at a different speed, and help with different program content than the group worker dealing with a street gang. The main professional skill lies in *diagnosis* and in the capacity to use one's tools with flexibility.

The people we work with in psychiatric settings are sick, and our focus is on helping them to recover or improve. The specifics of our methods, therefore, are:

Intensified individualization and less emphasis on group goal. (I am not saying "*no* consideration.")

An especially high skill in and focus on formation of groups. Most, though not all, such groups are formed groups.

Skill in dealing with emotionally charged verbal material in discussion groups, especially with adults

More intensive acquaintance with medical and psychiatric knowledge than is needed in some other aspects of group work practice

Capacity to accept other professions, yet to keep one's own identity and be able to interpret it to others

Capacity to accept mental and emotional illness and work with it.

I hope that we may have some discussion regarding these specifics. In some degree they will appear in other aspects of practice, but I consider them especially necessary in this area.

GROUP WORK AND GROUP THERAPY

At this point I cannot avoid getting into the question of group work and group therapy, since I included the need for the skill in discussion method. Actually there is little sense in quarreling about definitions. At the meeting of the American Orthopsychiatric Association in 1948, some forty definitions of psychotherapy were collected. And if we accept Harry Stack Sullivan's definition of psychiatry as "the field of interpersonal relations, under any and all circumstances in which these relations exist" (Sullivan, 1947, p. 485) all of us would be practicing psychiatry. I am afraid that I cannot quite accept this wide definition. In a very important attempt at clarifying the concepts of the group in education, group work, and psychotherapy, Clara Kaiser gave the official definition mentioned in the beginning of this paper while Saul Scheidlinger defined group psychotherapy as representing "the planful harnessing of the motivational forces inherent in face-to-face groups for purposes of treating emotionally disturbed individuals" (Scheidlinger, 1953).

This parallels Fritz Redl's early definition given in a letter to me in 1947, calling our work with groups "therapy" if a "repair job" is involved. I personally can agree with both of those definitions and would not mind saying that the group worker in those settings and in several others is therefore doing group therapy.

We have hesitated in social group work to say that we do therapy because we wanted to avoid the idea that group work in psychiatric settings is qualitatively different and perhaps of a higher status than other group work, and the temptation to become little psychiatrists and lose our own identity as social workers.

I think that this was wise, but it has its shortcomings because we left the field open to too many others who actually are less well qualified than the social group worker to work with patients in groups. And therefore I am repeating what I said to another group recently:

> *We did not avoid the word therapy because we did not think we worked and could work with disturbed and unhappy people or because we thought that the group worker can only work with activities and not with verbal material.* I want to make my point as clear as possible: a social group worker is a social worker and he should know individual dynamics and the impact of environment on the human being. He should know community resources. His skill should consist of dealing with the individual in the context of the group and in aiding the group process. He should be able to do this through the media of the spoken word and different program activities. It seems almost amusing to me that in some agencies the group worker is called upon to conduct groups even with disturbed people as long as the group uses *activities.* The moment those same people begin to *talk* in a group, it is assumed that the group worker's usefulness has reached its limits. In my opinion, it is not a question of whether there is talking or not, but what one talks about. I hold no brief for the social worker, either case worker or group worker, who wants to be a little psychoanalyst and gets himself involved in dealing with many unconscious, repressed feelings. This area belongs to the medically trained psychiatrist. As social workers, we have a specific and important contribution to make. It lies in our capacity to work with feelings directly related to the actual people, around the client, the father, mother, playmates, teachers, etc. As social group workers we not only have the skill of observing a group but also the skill of diagnosing it quickly [Konopka, 1955].

I should like to add that our specific skill as social group workers also lies in our focus on and our skill in helping patients toward some reality achievement and the resulting self-confidence. Our responsibility also lies in changing the environment, if it is necessary, through legislation or other action beyond the direct help given to the patient.

To return to the definition: I would prefer to say that we are always doing social group work when in psychiatric settings, but that we are not afraid of the word therapy if that is the goal of our work. I cannot help but agree with Annette Garrett (1949) when she calls this whole question "a two-cent semantic one" or Gordon W. Allport who says, "We quarrel . . . over the hairlike boundary between case work and psychotherapy, while most of the world has never heard of either. . . . Specialism is a peculiar hazard in any profession devoted to helping people in distress . . . distress defies job-analysis" (Allport, 1954).

There is no question that if we can agree on the general and specific of social group work as it was presented, or if we make some changes, they will have implications in our teaching of students entering the psychiatric field.

I have refrained in this paper from presenting case material. It is there where the theories, the concepts, and the principles come alive. Yet, if we want to teach we must work out theories without becoming dogmatic. Beyond the capacities and skills that I presented in this paper, the basis of all social work skills remains the deep concern for anybody who suffers, and the real capacity for empathy.

I borrow from Erik Erikson:

> Only in so far as our clinical way of work becomes part of a judicious way of life can we help to counteract and reintegrate the destructive forces which are being let loose by the split in modern man's archaic conscience. Judiciousness in its widest sense is a frame of mind which is tolerant of differences cautious and methodical in evaluation, just in judgment, circumspect in action, and—in spite of all this apparent relativism—capable of faith and indignation [Erikson, 1950, p. 371].

NOTE

1. I prefer the use of the word "tool" to the use of the word "technique," because to me technique implies the possibility of mechanical handling, which is never permitted in group work.

REFERENCES

ADDAMS, J., 1909. *The Spirit of Youth and the City Streets.* New York: Macmillan.

ALLPORT, G. W., 1954. "The Limits of Social Service." New York: Columbia University Bicentennial Celebration (mimeographed).

COYLE, G. L., 1954. "Social Group Work," *Social Work Year Book 1954.* New York: American Association of Social Workers.

ERIKSON, E. H., 1950. *Childhood and Society.* New York: Norton.

GARRETT, A., 1949. "Historical Survey of the Evolution of Casework," *Journal of Social Casework,* Vol. 30, No. 6.

KONOPKA, G., 1955. "Social Group Work in Relation to Treatment," paper given at the Alumni Conference at the School of Social Work, University of Michigan.

LATHROP, J., 1909. Proceedings, National Conference of Charities and Correction, 1909.

RICHMOND, M., 1930. "Some Next Steps in Social Treatment," *The Long View.* New York: Russell Sage Foundation.

SCHEIDLINGER, S., 1953. "Group Psychotherapy," Round Table given at the American Orthopsychiatric Association Annual Conference.

SMITH, Z. P., 1915. "Field Work," *Proceedings of Conference of Charities and Corrections 1915.*, p. 624.

SULLIVAN, H. S., 1947. "Conceptions of Modern Psychiatry," *The William Alanson White Psychiatric Foundation.* Washington, D.C.: The Foundation.

17

The Essential Components of Social Group Work Practice

Robert D. Vinter is Arthur Dunham Professor of Social Work, University of Michigan, Ann Arbor.

Robert D. Vinter

INTRODUCTION

This chapter presents the essential elements of social group work practice and aims to develop the understanding necessary to help individuals through small, face-to-face groups. As staff members of social agencies, group workers must engage in many activities: they must participate in staff meetings, make referrals, prepare reports, and interpret their functions to the public. But these endeavors, however important, are not immediately necessary to serve people in groups, and the skill and knowledge they require is not distinctive to group workers. The core competencies of group work practice—the methods and techniques which are directly involved in serving clients in groups—are addressed here.

Concern for brevity requires that there be no discussion of variations in practice that occur within different agencies or in work with different types of clientele. Similarly, in focusing on the essentials of group work, comparisons with other professional treatment approaches that involve group methods are ignored.

THE TREATMENT SEQUENCE

Group work service begins when the practitioner first meets the client, continues through the diagnostic and treatment stages, and ends with evaluation and termination of contact. This entire process is referred to as the *treatment sequence.* This sequence consists of several distinct processes and actions; it includes each client's experiences, the group's development as affected by the worker, and the worker's decisions and overt activities. Since the treatment sequence proceeds through time, the identification of significant events, by locating them along this continuum, will be helpful. For this purpose, the several major stages of the treatment sequence can be defined, along with the events and the practitioners' decisions and activities typical of each stage. The recurrent nature of events and activities, more or less distinctive to each period, permits the identification of the segments of the treatment sequence. However, this presentation should not mislead one into supposing that the events and activities are invariant or that one stage is always neatly completed before the next begins.

These stages can be identified only by looking for similarities in a wide variety of actual treatment sequences and by noting the patterns that emerge. Analysis permits a useful, but somewhat arbitrary, codification of the treatment sequence. The practitioner deliberately intervenes in an extended social process which would develop in quite different directions (or not at all) if he acted differently. Helping people requires that practitioners *do* something; therefore, attention will be given to what it is that workers do as they intervene.

The first stage, the process by which a potential client achieves client status, is customarily termed *intake.* For the client this often involves some kind of presentation of himself and his problem or "need," as he experiences it. On the worker's part, this typically involves some assessment of the client and his problem—a preliminary diagnosis—and of the adequacy of resources available to resolve this problem. The intake stage ends in one of two ways: either the worker or the client decides not to proceed, for whatever reasons; or the client commits himself to client status (however tentatively or reluctantly) and the worker commits himself and his agency to provide service (however limited).

The second stage, identified as that of *diagnosis* and *treatment planning* (Sundel, Radin and Churchill, 1974), marks a more comprehensive and exacting assessment by the worker of the client's problem(s), his capacities for helping and change, and of the various resources that might be useful. This stage involves a preliminary statement of the treatment goal, that is, of the desired changes which can result if the intervention effort is successful. The diagnosis also involves a preliminary plan of the ways the helping process will be undertaken and the direction in which it will be guided. This stage often requires the collection of additional information about the client and his situation and the use of consultation or other resources provided by the agency. At the culmination of the treatment planning stage, a concrete statement should be prepared by the worker to crystallize his assessment of the client and to make explicit the objectives he will pursue and the ways he will seek to implement these objectives.

The third stage is *group composition* and *formation*. During this period, the worker assigns clients to groups, gathering the persons who he believes can be served together. Under some circumstances—as in work with delinquent street groups—the practitioner may exercise relatively little control over this stage. He also sets the purposes for the group, at least within broad limits, in accordance with his treatment goals for its individual members. He begins the establishment of relationships with the group members and helps the group to commence its program. The way he initiates the group's process and the roles he plays initially with the various members have considerable significance for subsequent phases.

The fourth stage is that of *group development* and *treatment*. The worker seeks the emergence of group goals, activities, and relationships which can render this group effective for the treatment of its members (Sarri and Galinsky, 1974). The worker guides the group's interaction and structures its experience, to achieve the specific treatment goals he holds for each of its members. The particular nature and degree of group cohesion, client self-determination, and governing procedures, as well as the type of program, are defined by the individual treatment goals, not by any uniform standards workers have about "successful" or "well-organized" groups. His main concern is that each group become the most potent possible to attain the ends he seeks for its members. The worker should not regard the treatment groups as ends in themselves, apart from their contribution to the client members. Since practitioners do not hold the same goals for all groups and because of differences among the members who compose them, no two groups ever appear to have the same experiences or advance along the same developmental path.

The final stage is *evaluation and termination* (Johnson, 1974). The treatment sequence may last for short or long periods of time, depending on a variety of circumstances. Obviously, services to clients in groups may be terminated when it is apparent that treatment goals have been substantially achieved. Group services may also be terminated when it appears that maximum benefits for the member clients have been attained or when any anticipated additional gains are insufficient to merit continuation. Groups may also terminate because clients drop out, because pressing commitments arise elsewhere in the agency, or for a variety of other reasons. In any event, the decision to terminate should be made with a view toward the achievement of treatment goals. This decision necessitates a review of the progress made by each of the client members and an estimation of whether continuation of this group would be worthwhile. The worker is compelled, therefore, to return to his original diagnostic statements and treatment goals, to evaluate the progress made in terms of them.

The presence of several clients requires a more complex termination decision than with a single case since, as expected, group members will show different degrees of achievement. A single termination decision is often inappropriate for all members of the group. Accordingly, the worker may reconstitute the group, keeping those who have not yet shown satisfactory progress (but who may be expected to do so), terminating those for whom maximum benefits have been achieved, and adding new members. Persons also may be transferred to different groups or to other services.

It must be kept in mind that these five stages represent general patterns, not ideal periods that ought to be accomplished neatly. Reality often makes it difficult to determine the end of one stage and the beginning of another. Events and activities, identified in a specific period, also are likely to be evident in others. The worker does not follow a timetable and he must engage in activities that are responsive to the group's process and which advance his treatment goals. Activities that may occur during any stage include the continuing search for diagnostic information to enhance understanding of clients, inclusion of a new group member long after the others have been admitted, and evaluation of change at earlier points in the treatment sequence.

Two crucial distinctions must be made in referring to the treatment sequence. As initially stated, this sequence is inclusive of *all* events that occur during the group work process. The first distinction is between the worker's decisions or mental activities, on the one hand, and his overt behavior or social interactions with clients, on the other. Thus, in the foregoing review reference was made to decisions like diagnosis, evaluation of progress, etc.; workers also talk with clients, participate in group programs, and do many other visible things. Practitioners not only participate in significant interactions with clients, but also they engage in important activities that are not visible to or even in the presence of clients. This leads to the second distinction between the reality of the group's structure and process and the worker's interpretation of and response to its reality.

Although the focus throughout this analysis is on the practitioner, his thinking and his actions, the individuals' subjective experiences, the unfolding of the group process, and the emergence of group structure must each be seen as independent reality. These events are affected by the presence and activity of the worker, but they should not be regarded entirely, or merely, as consequences of practitioner effort. There are other influences on individual and group behavior, only some of which can be known and affected by the worker. Furthermore, the practitioner can neither observe nor assess objectively all the events which occur, even within the group. It is the worker's dual aim to comprehend sensitively and accurately the group's experience and the experiences of its individual members, and to guide these experiences in accordance with treatment goals. But these distinctions can serve as reminders of the complexities of group process and of the constraints on practitioners' perceptions and actions.

TREATMENT GOALS AND GROUP PURPOSES

As stated, specific treatment goals must be established for each member of the client group (Schopler and Galinsky, 1974), since individuals never enter the treatment sequence with identical problems and capabilities. Clients are often discussed in terms of certain broad categories (e.g., delinquents) but this tends to obscure the very great differences characterizing individuals within each category. *Treatment goals* are those specific ends the practitioner pursues in the interests of particular clients within particular groups. This emphasis on the unique and idiosyncratic is referred to as *individualization* in social work literature.

A treatment goal is a specification of the state or condition in which the worker would like *this* client to be at the end of a successful treatment sequence. The concept of social dysfunction is sometimes used to denote all the problematic states of social work clientele. Treatment goals, then, embody more desirable states of social functioning. Several considerations must be introduced at this point. *First*, treatment goals must realistically reflect probable outcomes of group work service. It is impractical to think of ideal but unattainable states of well-being. For example, how to "cure" mental deficiency or brain damage through group work is not known. When working with clients having such problems, therefore, the worker should not suggest their resolution in treatment goals. Group work may, however, seek to ameliorate undesirable secondary effects or to achieve optimum functioning within the limits set by these conditions. Given the present development of the helping professions, workers are obligated to think in terms of limited goals. *Second*, treatment goals must relate directly to the presenting problems expressed by individual clients. While diagnosis is discussed in a later chapter (Sundel, Radin and Churchill, 1974), it is necessary to assert here that a treatment goal must anticipate improvement in the client's social functioning as defined by individual assessment and diagnosis. The distinct advantages to defining treatment goals in specific, concrete behavioral terms are that the goals can be more readily derived from clearly stated diagnoses and movement toward them can be assessed more definitely. *Third*, the treatment goal must be linked to diagnosis in still another way; it should seek reduction of the stress or difficulty *as experienced by the client.* Treatment goals also must bear a relationship to the capacities of the clients, and to their readiness or motivation to change; in this sense, they include prognoses about the likelihood that clients can and will change.

If two clients manifest identical problems, yet differ in their personality attributes, attitudes, or social circumstances, these differences would have important consequences for treatment outcomes; some would facilitate treatment (e.g., a high level of discomfort); others would hinder this process (e.g., peer support of problematic behavior). Since treatment goals must be realistic, they should reflect such relevant differences.

Fourth, the treatment goal should refer to improved client functioning outside the treatment group itself. Problematic behavior or conditions exist prior to service and pervade major spheres of the clients' lives. Service, therefore, should improve these *other* spheres of life. This is referred to as the requirement of *transferability:* gains achieved by clients within the treatment process must be transferable beyond this process. Further, the degree and quality of improvement should be assessed according to conventional standards of the world inhabited by the client. Professional criteria should not subordinate community standards of conduct, achievement, and role performance.

Groups are typically composed of from four to twelve clients and, if unique treatment goals are established for each client, a complex and multiple set of aims must be formulated for every group. The practitioner must seek a composite of treatment goals that can be served simultaneously through a given group's process. Defining and harmonizing goals that serve several clients through the same group's process is obviously no simple task. There are at least two ways that practitioners handle this problem. The worker often has significant leverage in his control over the group's initial composition. He can attempt to compose a group so that the particular treatment goals are compatible and can be balanced. Although group composition involves more than the compatibility of treatment goals, this is one criterion for selecting persons for a given group. The practitioner, also, defines the *purposes* for the group; i.e., the particular collective ends it will pursue. Since the worker often has considerable control over the concrete purposes the group exists for and the activities it will engage in, he can attempt to define group purposes that are consistent with and instrumental to the several treatment goals he has established for the individual members.

Some aims, goals, and purposes pertain to all groups. The agency and the practitioner have certain ends in mind for each group; in most general terms, they seek to develop groups with strong enough influences to change or move clients toward improved social functioning as defined by specific treatment goals. For the worker, then, the group is intended to serve as the best possible means for achieving the composite of treatment goals. For each particular group, the worker must translate these objectives into more concrete purposes, which in turn lead to variations among group programs, plans, experiences, and processes.

Individual client members also have desired aims or objectives even if they are to "have a good time," to accomplish some task, or to achieve something which lies outside the group itself (e.g., prestige in the eyes of nonmembers). Some of these objectives are crystallized in members' thinking and aspirations, while some are only latent. In addition, each group tends to develop its own concrete purposes, which can be thought of as a composite of the members' expectations and motives to be fulfilled by the group. Customarily, these purposes are shared and stated, in various ways, and tend to shift over time.

Thus, four different types of ends can be distinguished analytically: (1) the worker's treatment goals for the group members, (2) the worker's functional purposes for the group, (3) the individual members' goals and objectives for themselves through the group, and (4) the shared purposes of the group. These various ends interpenetrate and are interrelated, as we have indicated. Figure 17-1 shows typical relations between such aims and expectations:

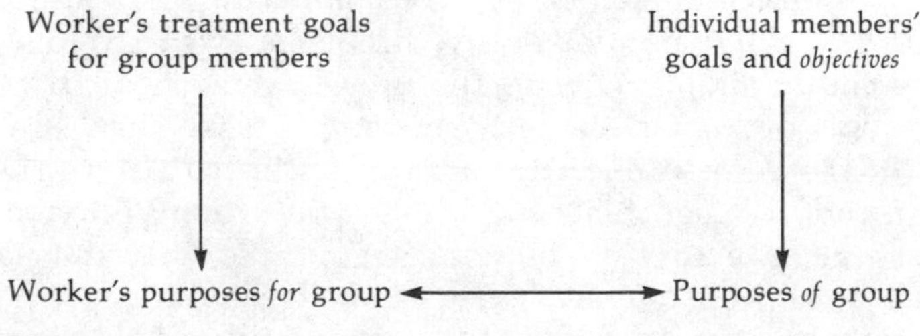

Figure 17.1

The degree of compatibility between these ends always differs among groups and varies through time for the same group. For example, the worker's purposes for a group may differ greatly from the initial expectations and preferences of its individual members. Unless the worker can change these orientations, he may have to make his purposes more congruent with client preferences, in order to achieve greater member involvement and motivation. Practitioners are confronted with increasing difficulties as the degree of compatibility among these end decreases. The plausible solution of, "Let's do what the members want," is seldom effective.

THE STRATEGY OF INTERVENTION

In addition to the assertions that significant help can be given individuals through experience in groups, and that groups provide both the context and means for treatment, the treatment group can be thought of as a deliberately structured influence system to effect change through social interaction. The kinds of changes sought, as defined by treatment goals, range from acquiring new relationship skills, to changes in self-images and attitudes toward others, to behavioral modifications or integration into conventional social structures. Some tendency exists to regard worker-member interactions not only as having special import, but as being the essential means by which individuals are helped. This view regards the group merely as the context for treatment, as a process carried on primarily and directly between the worker and each client. This limits the concept of the group's potential. Although practitioners do interact directly with clients to implement specific treatment goals, potent influences are also exercised through interactions between members, through the group's activities or program, and through its structure. The skilled practitioner uses all of these to implement his treatment objectives. Frequently, the group implements treatment by directly influencing the individual.

The worker must possess a strategy of intervention to make use of these potential resources. Not only must he know where he wants to go (treatment outcomes) but also he must formulate approaches and techniques, taking maximum advantage of every legitimate way to achieve these ends. Besides his concern for the group's composition, the worker is concerned also with the group's purposes and major activities. Getting groups "off to a good start," assuming that a well-initiated group can move along successfully with occasional assistance, is not enough. The worker must be concerned with every point in the group's movement and must participate actively to guide it in desired directions. Similarly, he is concerned with the group's organization and the governing procedures it develops, as well as the quality of interpersonal relations among all the members.

All of these concerns and the way they are made instrumental is the practitioner's *strategy of intervention.* The formal requirements of this strategy are that the worker act (or not act) to "treat" at any given moment throughout the treatment sequence, and to facilitate the long-term development of the group's structure and process to different treatment effects for the client members. As a corollary, the group can be evaluated at any given moment in terms of its immediate treatment effects *and* its long-run potential for mediating treatment outcomes.

Practitioners may employ several modes of intervention or *means of influence,* to serve these dual objectives.[1] The worker should direct each action at immediate "treating," setting the conditions for treatment via the group, or both. These are viewed as essentially compatible and mutually instrumental, and the approaches are categorized by whether the practitioner is directly or indirectly influencing an individual member. *Direct means of influence* are interventions to effect change through immediate interaction with a group member. *Indirect means of influence* are interventions that modify group conditions which subsequently affect one or more members. In the former, worker and client join in face-to-face contact (in or apart from the presence of other clients). In the latter, the group mediates the relationship between the worker and the member(s) affected by the intervention. The distinction between direct and indirect provides an analytical reference for the variety of practitioner interventions, and emphasizes the immediate context and effects of interaction, i.e., whether or not a specific client member is directly interacting with the worker, who is being influenced, when and how. While these means of influence refer to actions engaged in by practitioners, they cannot achieve immediate, full treatment outcomes; instead, they are steps toward outcomes, however minute.

Examples are offered to clarify the distinction between the direct and indirect means. When the worker praises a group member while talking with him, perhaps thereby raising his self-esteem, he directly influences the client (i.e., using direct means). Similarly, when he suggests a new solution to a client's dilemma, conducts a marginal interview with him, or visits him at home, he is directly interacting with the client. The effects from any of these actions may not have great consequence, but that is beside the point. The distinction between direct and indirect means of influence does not refer to how potent the worker's actions are, or how subtle his approach is, or even how active he is. Such variations must be characterized in other terms.

In contrast, indirect means are employed to influence the group so that it in turn influences the members. The worker may modify group governing procedures to encourage more voice in affairs for all participants; this may result in greater satisfaction and acceptance for one or two dissident members. Or the worker may introduce new program activities which gratify most members, perhaps raising the status of one who can succeed now but could not in former activities. All members may be influenced by such worker interventions, some more than others.

A third major means of influence is employed by practitioners when they attempt to affect clients apart from both the group and personal contact. *Extragroup means of influence* include activities conducted on behalf of clients outside the group (Vinter and Galinsky, 1974; Glasser, et al., 1974). Targets of these interventions are nongroup persons whose behaviors affect clients and nongroup situations involving clients (i.e., classroom, family). Workers may seek to increase opportunities for their clients in these other situations, to alter attitudes and behaviors of other persons toward their clients, and to restructure elements of clients' social experiences. Parents, employers, classroom teachers, friends, cottage parents (in residential programs), and other agency staff members may be individuals with whom the practitioner interacts on behalf of his clients. Whereas, through the indirect means of influence, the treatment group mediates the relation between worker and client, through the extragroup means these *other* persons and situations mediate the relation. Both working through the group and through "significant others" could be considered indirect approaches, but the distinction between indirect and extragroup is preferred.

These terms largely constitute a codification of what group workers seem to do frequently in actual practice. One advantage of this analysis is to order and categorize what otherwise seem to be a confusing welter of worker activities; however, these categories do not encompass all activities employed by practitioners in groups. Only the direct and indirect means are discussed fully here; additional kinds of actions can be employed to exercise influence.

DIRECT MEANS OF INFLUENCE

The four types of direct means of influence presented all involve direct confrontation and contact between worker and client, in or outside the group session. The specific methods, the areas of client behavior affected, and the techniques employed are stated in each case.

Worker As Central Person—Object of Identifications and Drives

Under most circumstances the worker is preeminent in the treatment group, both with respect to his position in the structure and in terms of his psychological effect on the members. The several sources of this preeminence typically combine and reinforce each other: the worker's activity in initiating the group and in beginning its process; the authority vested in the worker by agency and community, which he can exercise by controlling resources and facilities available to the group and which enhance his prestige; and the personal resources (competencies, skills, and personality attributes) possessed by the worker. The worker's preeminence is particularly marked in newly formed groups; as he may be the only person who knows all the others, he is "mobilized" at the outset and free to participate actively without being cautiously passive, and, typically, he has personal qualities that are valued by the members. These characteristics, coupled with the clients' knowledge that the worker possesses considerable control over the destiny of the group, render the worker highly significant.

For these reasons the worker serves as a "central person," a focal point for group emotions (Redl, 1955; French and Raven, 1959). Emotional responses of members to the worker constitute ties to him; the worker becomes the object of member identifications and drives. The worker serves as the object of identifications when the members want or try to be like him. He serves as the object of drives when the members are emotionally invested in him. Because of the worker's position and his attributes, the potentiality of these psychological relationships with client members might be enhanced for two reasons. First, such worker-client relationships provide the basis for continuing service to individuals, for whom the worker has special psychological meaning. The relationships thus formed are crucial conditions for subsequent interpersonal influence, but the difference between actual relationships and those which are desired or intended by practitioners must be distinguished. Second, such relationships also serve to strengthen member-to-member ties; clients may identify with each other as they experience the similarity of their relationships with the worker. The unity of the group can thus emerge, as common psychological responses among members lead to shared and reciprocated responses between members.

This means of influence focuses on the psychological relationships that are established between the worker and the members.

Psychological responses of the members may be manifested in overt behavior (e.g., evidences of liking, affection, compliance with worker requests, or modeling of the worker's behavior), or they may remain at the covert level (changed attitudes toward oneself or others, a shift in values, or resolution of some internal conflict). Covert responses are less readily apparent but may be as significant or real as more obvious behavioral changes.

The specific techniques or actions used by practitioners to exercise this influence are especially difficult to identify. Some of the members' psychological responses are associated with the social or structural position of the worker. Structural sources, that might contribute to the technique, are the worker's status in the agency and his mobilization (i.e., his initiative and freedom of action); however, these represent *potentialities* for influencing members through exercise of power and through active participation in group interaction, respectively. They remain potentialities unless deliberately exercised by the worker; that is, the worker may serve as an insufficient "central person" by abdicating his position vis-à-vis the group or by remaining a passive participant in its processes. As indicated above, the worker's personality attributes, competencies, and skills also generate emotional responses from client members. Such attributes may be either instrumental or socioemotional: an instrumental one is useful in achieving some objective or completing some task (e.g., tutoring or teaching a skill), a socioemotional attribute is one for psychological gratification (e.g., friendly responses to another). Who the worker is as a person, and how he interacts with clients, however minutely or subtly, has consequences for his becoming an object of identification and drives. A wide range of worker attributes and behavior becomes highly relevant in these terms: cordial and interested responses to others, suggestion of good ideas, capacity for responding to nuances of client feeling and interest, ability to do things clients enjoy, and even personal appearance.

Since groups differ in many respects and clients possess different personalities, obviously specific worker characteristics and behavior will have different psychological consequences for different people. A worker's prowess in swimming will be of little salience in a street gang, and his "cool" will not be prized among aged clients. Similarly, a worker's tendency toward repressiveness will have quite different psychological meanings among clients in the same group. The principle of "conscious use of self" directs practitioners to be sensitive to these differences between groups and individuals, and to vary appropriately their presentations of themselves and their specific behaviors. As the worker becomes more skilled, he can achieve these variations to become the kind of "central person" who will advance treatment for a particular group and client. In general, positive identifications are likely to be increased when workers are friendly, manifest warm and cordial relations, and show sensitivity to the needs and interests of individual members. The issue of negative identification is important but will not be developed here.

Worker As Symbol and Spokesman—Agent of Legitimate Norms and Values

Many clients served through social group work manifest difficulties with the values and behavioral norms they have internalized. Indeed, for some clients, these difficulties may be the essence of their social functioning problems. Client diagnoses may indicate no psychological malfunctioning, but an internalization of socially unacceptable values, perhaps through membership in deviant or antilegal groups. Inducing change in these areas is generally termed resocialization. One function of group work service can be socialization, or the acquisition of values and behavioral standards defined by the larger society. Thus, children, immigrants from other societies, or persons moving into new sociocultural situations and strata typically need help to acquire conventional orientations and behaviors. Avoiding the extremes of abject conformity and destructive rebellion, the individual must develop a viable interdependence with others by acquiring the basic values essential to community life, and minimal adherence to the norms of conduct required for effective social functioning.

Without imposing his personal value system and standards or those of any particular stratum on clients, the worker must inculcate the essential values of the larger society. He is obligated not only by his agency but by the community and by his profession to represent both society and the long-run interests of the client. And he must mediate the clients and certain values and norms created informally within the treatment group itself. Thus, values and standards are derived from the larger society environing the group (community, agency, etc.) and are developed within the group. Some are specified as laws, rules, or role prescriptions; others appear less tangibly as orientations, patterns of conduct, and generalized attitudes. The worker's task is to determine which of these are crucial, as treatment goals, to individual clients and to the group. Crucial values and norms are then emphasized in practice.

Values and norms may be transferred by the worker in several ways. They may be *personified* by the worker as they pervade his total behavior and outlook. What the worker does and does not do, the events to which he responds, and his views and attitudes toward persons and issues, all convey to clients basic values and norms. Thus, as the worker continuously responds to client interests and feelings, he "cues" group members to the value of individual dignity and worth and to positive interpersonal norms, without having to state explicitly that he accepts them. Through member-worker identification and modeling, commitments are inculated or strengthened among members and become the bases for desirable behavior.

The worker may also be a *spokesman* for values and norms; that is, he must frequently give utterance to both. Even when a large degree of permissiveness is necessary in worker-client relations the worker must still set limits and voice expectations. What is important is that practitioners act and speak to exemplify a particular set of values and norms which can become operative for clients, rather than interacting in ways which offer few, ambiguous guides (although a "do what he wants" attitude should be avoided).

Values and norms within the group may also be informally *created* by workers, especially when the group is newly formed. The creation of such norms and values, whether explicit or implicit, may be facilitated by the worker as personifier or spokesman. Worker hesitation or inactivity in the creation of group standards can handicap group development and curtail movement toward treatment goals.

As indicated previously, the behavior of the worker itself serves as a model for clients and the worker may define or strengthen norms by setting limits on the behavior of members, by requesting, requiring, or forbidding certain behaviors. The worker may state precepts and rules of conduct. Or the worker may apply various positive and negative sanctions against members, that is, encourage, reward, or chastise group members for their behavior. Rewards and deprivations may be material or social (e.g., praise). Finally, the worker sometimes must use his power of coercion and physically prevent a client from engaging in certain behavior (e.g., assaulting another person) or must eject him from the group. Generally, positive techniques are more effective than negative techniques, and inducements or rewards more helpful than deprivations. The worker must state precepts to define clearly his expectations for clients, but by itself this has little utility for enduring change.

Although some workers may be hesitant to act in the area of values and norms, in actual practice they often seem to devote considerable energy to this area. The critical problems are determining which values and norms are crucial and what the effective ways are to implement them. Since the group customarily develops its own values and normative system which the members then participate in enforcing, the worker has a potent resource at hand. He can help the group develop a system of norms and values in accord with treatment goals. Since the primary concern here is with direct means of influence, worker-client interactions should modify an individual client's norms and values in accordance with the specific treatment goals for him.

Worker As Motivator and Stimulator—Definer of Individual Goals and Tasks

Throughout the treatment sequence many opportunities occur for practitioners to motivate and stimulate individual members toward specific ends or activities. These opportunities may take the form of encouragment for certain objectives or expectations for individuals, such as undertaking a specific project or acquiring certain skills; or they may enable the stimulation of a member to engage in different behaviors or to act differently in familiar activities or to direct him toward new interests. The worker perceives such opportunities within the developing experience of the group and its larger activities, with reference to the immediate social and material environment of the individual and group or with reference to the larger community and society.

For example, a creative adult may see potentialities in the pebbles and sand of a beach or in the repair of an old car; and the alert practitioner may see many more significant possibilities in the urban community than the adolescent does. Making the most of such opportunities—whether immediately discerned by the client or beyond his horizon—requires that the worker be aware of the potentialities inherent in the social and physical context. Maximizing such opportunities requires that the worker be guided by specific treatment goals.

This means is primarily directed toward individual interests, aims, activities and skills. Essential is the worker's use of his relationship and interaction with members to orient them toward experiences that they might not otherwise engage in and that will facilitate treatment. Regardless of age or problem, clients tend to restrict themselves to conventional and familiar activities, to have limited perspectives, and to be less aware of the full potentialities offered by their social and physical environment. Stimulating clients to use material objects in more creative and satisfying ways is perhaps the most obvious manifestation of this means of influence. But one may also think of motivating clients toward opportunities for the development and different use of their capabilities in social situations (e.g., getting a different job, discovering unknown talents and abilities).

The worker's control over resources permits him to use them as "props" or objects to stimulate clients. Introducing or sharing new and unfamiliar materials or using familiar ones in novel ways are customary approaches. Thus, a worker can show clients new games that can be played with old objects (e.g., cards, dice, boxes), or the worker may call the client's attention to things and events he overlooks in everyday life (e.g., interesting insects or items in the newspaper). Incentives, inducements, and rewards can be employed by the worker to motivate clients. Thus, encouraging, suggesting, proposing, and expressing enthusiasm or excitement are effective interaction techniques. The worker's own interests and responses to objects and situations convey meanings to clients for whom the worker's behavior is especially salient, and the worker may direct or instruct clients in these terms.

Worker As Executive—Controller of Members' Roles

In addition to the discrete and relatively concrete tasks and purposes discussed above, the practitioner is also concerned about clients' more general orientations and roles. These may be thought of as configurations or sets of specific behaviors. Each group develops its own structure of roles, responsibilities, and positions (Sarri and Galinsky, 1974). Within the group each member may be characterized as having distinct positions in these structures which may be deliberately modified by the worker with regard to his treatment aims. For example, tasks or projects undertaken by the entire group require some division of responsibilities among the members (Vinter 1974; and Whittaker, 1974). Assignment of these responsibilities may refer to the larger task objective, the abilities of members, and the needs of the individual members. The worker must be concerned not only with what is good for the group, but also with what is desired for individual clients in terms of the treatment goals.

When the worker develops or modifies these group structures (as when he proposes a set of positions or division of labor), he is using indirect means of influence. However, when he directly interacts to modify an individual's particular role or position within these structures, he is using direct means of influence. To continue with the example of task assignments suggested above: when a client is given a specific responsibility, the worker can help him directly in discharging his part of the total task. Such intervention by the worker may have several effects, all different from the effects of allowing the client to "go it alone." Undertaking the task in the way proposed by the worker exposes the client to expectations and experiences he might not have had otherwise. The standards and values implicit in this event may have carry-over effects for the client in subsequent situations; and the response of the group to the client's performance may be quite different than if he had not been helped by the worker (e.g., praise for accomplishment rather than criticism). The worker himself may make the individual assignments, determining the pattern of member tasks as well as helping clients undertake them. The worker may interact directly with clients to affect more general behavior than the mere performance of a specific task. Thus, a worker may assist an individual who holds a particular position in the group's formal structure to perform more effectively or differently in this position. Whether in terms of these positions or of more general roles, the worker can seek to modify the member's behavior with reference to his treatment goals.

As viewed so far, the worker's effort in assigning or modifying membership roles has focused on the behavior and experience of an individual client. Through direct interaction the worker attempts to develop or change a client's personal attributes, thus modifying his role performance. The worker may attempt to increase a member's sensitivity to group norms so that he becomes a less deviant member, perhaps by clarifying the relevant norms for the client or by informing him more precisely of other members' expectations as they apply to him. Or the worker may attempt to change the client member's role behavior by raising his self-esteem, giving him support, or setting limits on his behavior.

The worker can serve as an "executive" by defining new or modified roles for members and by helping the clients to perform differently in their present roles. The emphasis is on interaction with individual clients, in terms of their role behavior, not on the entire role system of the group, which will be discussed later. In the previously discussed means of influence emphasis was on concrete interests and goals. This means of influence can be differentiated by the focus on general patterns of behavior (roles) rather than on specific interests and objectives, and by focus on patterns of client behavior which have particular relevance to other members and to the entire group. All of the techniques previously referred to may also be employed with this means.

These four direct means of influence tend to overlap, particularly with respect to the specific practitioner activities or techniques that may be employed. Distinctions between them mainly have to do with the worker's aims and the consequences for individuals that follow. The range of client experience and behavior which group workers can seek to modify includes attitudes, values, gratifications, tasks, identifications, roles, and so forth. A wide variety of worker-client interactions can be utilized to implement desired change. The similarity of techniques (e.g., praising, encouraging, or setting limits) should not, however, obscure the marked differences in effects for clients when the worker directs activities toward different ends, under varying conditions.

INDIRECT MEANS OF INFLUENCE

Indirect means of influence are those practitioner interventions used to effect modifications in group conditions which, in turn, affect the members. The worker acts on and through the group, its processes, and its program. Some of these approaches closely parallel the direct means of influence, and, conversely, certain direct means might implicate changes in the group.

Group Purposes

Groups that persist over extended periods of time develop distinctive aims. And, for all groups that they serve, social workers have purposes in mind which they make more or less explicit to the client members and which have significance for the nature and development of each group and for the experiences of the members. The kinds of purposes held by a group and the extent to which they are achieved are important determinants of member motivation to belong to the group, and of the satisfactions gained through participation in it. Similarly, the purposes set for the group by the worker are determinant of his own actions and these, in turn, vitally affect the group and its members. Diverse group goals and purposes characterize those served by social group workers: planning groups; groups focused on resolution of members' personal problems; activity groups; groups to orient or prepare members for some event (e.g., new clients entering an institution or patients about to be released); diagnostic groups; socioeducation groups for professionals, paraprofessionals, other socialization agents, and adults in role transition; and so on.

The relations between a worker's treatment goals, his purposes for the group, member objectives, and purposes of the group have been discussed above. Here consideration is given only to the worker's purposes *for* the group and the purposes *of* the group. Practitioners have considerable control over definition of purposes and goals, although there are wide variations in actual practice. In some instances, the worker and agency may set the purposes of the group in advance and select group members with avowed reference to these. Adherence to these purposes may then be a condition for continued participation in the group. At the other extreme, the group may have much autonomy in determining its own purposes (but this does not imply that the worker lacks treatment goals). In still other situations, after very broad purposes are set for the group it determines its own specific plans within these limits. Regardless of the source of initial purpose determination, the worker has many opportunities during the treatment sequence to modify group purposes and to alter members' objectives. Thus, even when serving a delinquent street gang which sets its own purposes, the worker can gradually influence the group toward different aims.

Two specific influences on clients that can be indirectly mediated through group purposes and aims have already been mentioned: selection of clients for the group can be made explicitly with reference to its established purposes, and a client's attraction to and satisfaction with the group is partially dependent on its purposes (Cartwright and Zander, 1960). The purposes of the group also determine the distribution of leadership functions and member rôles within it, thereby significantly affecting the experience of each client member. Similarly, group purposes shape the program and the activities developed in pursuit of these aims. And finally, group purposes will have some implication for the particular kind of decision-making and governing procedures to be employed. In these terms a group of adoptive parents contrasts with a play group of young children. The former may be directed toward consideration of common problems that couples face in adopting children, while the latter is directed toward pleasurable learning experiences, "having fun" in the youngsters' terms. Each will involve quite different activities, group processes, and member roles and will lead to markedly different effects for their members.

Finally, a word about the relation between purposes of the group and worker's purposes for the group. Group purposes have been defined as the composite of members' objectives and motives encompassed in some definite expression of collective purpose. Worker's purposes for the group, written in a specific statement, are the aims which a group ought to pursue to achieve treatment goals set for the individual clients. Obviously the worker seeks compatibility between his and the clients' aims, so that he is not oriented in one direction while the group is heading in another. Although both sets of aims tend to change over time and there cannot be perfect identity between them, the worker customarily seeks acceptance of his purposes as those of the group. Thus, in an institutional context a worker may attempt to gain members' acceptance of his treatment goals, and to orient them accordingly. Or, with a street gang, the worker may gradually seek acceptance of his prolegal purposes in working with the group. In a very real sense, therefore, client objectives and group purposes are targets, not determinants of worker interventions. However, the distinction between worker purposes and group aims should be kept in mind so that the *intentions* of the practitioner are never confused with the *reality* of member interests and motivations.

Selection of Group Members

Selection of group members and size of group (discussed next) are aspects of group composition. As a basic step in group composition, selection of members is one of the most problematic aspects of group practice. Practitioners cannot always select those who join a particular group; sometimes agency circumstances affect group composition, as when a treatment group consists of all the youngsters in the same orthopedic ward or all the inmates about to be released from an institution. Or the group's membership may be set by a decision to serve as existing or "natural group": friends living in the same housing project or all the members of a street gang. By and large, the greater an agency's general control over the clients, the more probable will be its determination of group membership (e.g., residential settings as contrasted with other community services).

Before considering the various criteria useful in determining membership, some of the consequences of this indirect means of influence will be examined. The experiences of the members, the interpersonal relations and even the particular nature of the activities will differ depending on who and how many others there are in a particular group. Thus, the capacity of the group to meet the desires and objectives of its members, as well as the goals of the worker, is partially dependent on its composition.

The worker's goals and purposes for the group provide a general guide for group composition: the reason the group is established and served, and what it is expected to accomplish, serve as determinants of membership selection. For example, if a group were designed to serve children who manifest serious school conduct problems, it would require the identification of such pupils and their inclusion in the group. Obviously, a group would have different characteristics if its purpose was to serve parents experiencing difficulties in childrearing or home management practices. The statement that purposes for the group should govern selection of its members may seem to be a truism, but in actual practice this is often ignored, usually because the agency and worker's purposes are too general or too unclear to serve as guides. However, group goals and purposes only point to a category of potential clients, and do not indicate specifically which persons within the general category should be selected. Referring to the illustrations cited above, which school children or which parents should be selected for treatment group membership? Or, to state it differently, what particular attributes or characteristics should the clients possess in addition to their belonging to a general category?

More concrete specification of the type of treatment group and its purposes can point toward particular persons within the general categories of potential clients. Regarding the group to serve pupils manifesting conduct problems, the worker might make two other decisions in advance: (1) that the group will include children manifesting classroom conduct problems and will exclude those who exhibit only academic difficulties; and (2) that the group program will include behavioral retraining as well as discussion of members' problems. These two decisions would provide some concrete direction for the worker in selecting clients from among all the pupils belonging to the general category as described.

The conception of the group as the *means* of treatment suggests another set of criteria. Practitioners would seek groups that have maximum impact or change effects for their client members. To accomplish this, treatment groups must be potentially capable of developing appropriate levels of cohesiveness, solidarity and mutuality, viable internal structures, and so forth. These requirements, in turn, direct the selection of members with a view to their similarity of interests, their potentiality of attraction for each other, their adequacy to participate in the general type of activity and group structure planned by the worker, and their capacity to form certain relationships with each other and with the worker. Knowing that the treatment sequence is more likely to be effective if these conditions are met within the group, the worker can attempt to select particular individuals who possess the attributes *with reference to each other* which promise to meet these conditions. Similarity or complementarity is desired with respect to the more important characteristics, however dissimilar the clients may be in other respects (Bertcher and Maple, 1974).

Great incompatibilities in age, interest, problems, interaction style, maturation level, and so forth, make it very difficult for group members to form cohesive groups. Reference here is to compatibility or complementarity, and not identity. Persons may form effective treatment groups because of the compatibility of their attributes even though they vary in terms of the similarity of attributes. For example, under certain circumstances, age and sex differences among group members may be essentially compatible. Thus, adolescent boys and girls might be placed in the same group on an orthopedic ward, but might not be selected for membership in certain sports activity groups.

A number of guidelines can be summarized. First, the types of primary client attributes for which compatibility and complementarity are desired depend on the nature of the group and its program. Second, complementarity is sought with reference to other members of the same group and not with reference to any absolute standards of personality attributes. Third, clients need not be identical with respect to their characteristics, but should be potentially compatible. Practitioners find that it is impossible to attain homogeneity with respect to many attributes, and must attempt to "match" individuals in terms of primary criteria while expecting considerable difference with respect to secondary criteria.

Size of Group

The size of a group tends to affect members. The worker must determine the appropriate group size for the desired effects for clients as defined by their treatment goals. First, some of the effects associated with differences in size will be examined. *Large* groups (e.g., ten or over) tend toward anonymity of membership, less consensus among the members, lower rates of participation, and higher demands for leadership abilities. Larger groups are able to undertake certain tasks beyond the capacities of smaller groups or to engage in certain types of program (e.g., tasks requiring a complex division of effort). Any of these effects may be desired for individual clients under specific circumstances. More mature and more capable clients are better able to cope with the participation requirements of large groups. Older adolescents and adults are probably more able to participate in larger decision-making units than are younger children.

Small groups, in contrast, tend toward high rates of member participation, greater individual involvement, greater consensus, and increased restraint upon members. Relations among persons in smaller groups tend to be more intensive. Effects such as these are often desired by practitioners for treatment groups. It is also easier for workers to cope with serious problems or acting-out behavior in small groups, when clients present these patterns.

In some agencies clients may participate concurrently in several different groups; this is especially true for most residential programs—camps, institutions, hospitals, etc. Under these conditions it is often desirable to vary the kinds of groups in which clients participate so that they can experience the different effects associated with size, type of program, and so forth. Practitioners must guard against a bias toward small groups so that they are not always established, even when clients might benefit from the anonymity or reduced intensivity provided by larger groups. Although workers are not always able to set the initial size of the group, as members drop out or others are added, there are opportunities to influence the size of the continuing group. Workers may find it desirable to vary the size of the treatment group during the treatment sequence.

Small group effects may be achieved *within* larger groups in many ways. In all larger groups, individuals tend to form smaller subgroups, thereby achieving informally many of the effects of small group participation. Practitioners may deliberately design such opportunities and influence the formation and structure of these subgroupings. Ways of doing this include facilitating interpersonal ties among clusters of members, introducing program activities that provide for smaller participation units, or developing a structure of subgroups (e.g., committees) for task and governing purposes.

Group Operating and Governing Procedures

Group workers have been strongly oriented toward democratic leadership and governing procedures because of their high valuation of client self-determination. Permissiveness in guiding the group, and helpfulness and friendliness in contacts with members, have probably characterized most group workers in actual practice. The very strength of this orientation becomes its weakness, however, as permissiveness by the practitioner and high automony for the group are widely sought regardless of differences in treatment goals and group member characteristics. Treatment goals and other specific group characteristics warrant deliberate variations in the degree of autonomy granted each group, in its procedures and formal organization, and in worker control practices. Each of these will be discussed briefly.

The degree of autonomy should vary with the type of group and its purpose, the treatment goals of the worker, and the member's characteristics. With younger, less capable, or more disturbed clients the worker may greatly limit the autonomy of the group, at least initially. The location and situation in which the group exists also affect its autonomy—delinquent groups in their own neighborhoods usually retain high autonomy, while institutional groups composed of clients with similar problems often have limited autonomy. High control by the worker tends to induce dependence upon him, reduces the members' assertiveness, and limits the satisfactions which they may achieve within the group. The practitioner may vary the *areas* within which groups have autonomy, as well as the degree of self-determination. Thus, a group may be granted high autonomy in its program of activities, but little choice in its size and composition.

Democratic relations, generally sought within treatment groups, are associated not only with the quality of worker-member interactions and relationships, but also with the nature of procedures that are used in governing the group. Governing procedures evolved spontaneously within client groups often reflect and enforce inequalities of power, prestige, and gratification. They can also introduce constraints due to members' unquestioned adherence to tradition or sentiment. In contrast, democratic procedures tend to be more rational, permit more flexible change as circumstances dictate, and provide certain guarantees of channels for individual participation. Unfortunately, workers sometimes equate democratic decision-making practices with parliamentary procedures, and often introduce an array of "businesslike" patterns. Parliamentary procedures are essentially formalistic and can easily be subverted, and the same positive effects may be achieved by simple norms as "everyone gets a chance to talk," "the majority rules," and "taking turns." The important concern is to increase group-centered decision making and wide distribution of member gratifications. Group-centered (as contrasted with worker-centered, or clique-controlled) decision-making results in greater member participation, greater consensus, and greater pressures toward uniformity, thus maximizing the impact of the group. The formal organization of a group affects its operating and governing procedures. Along with a predisposition toward parliamentary procedures, practitioners are sometimes inclined to introduce formal systems of officerships within groups. The intent is often to provide members with definite roles within groups and to insure democratic self-determination. Both aims may be achieved by less arbitrary approaches, however, and a system of officerships often achieves neither. The degree and type of formal structure appropriate for groups varies and the worker must sensitively create (or circumscribe) patterns within particular groups according to his treatment goals and client characteristics.

Much that has been stated with respect to group autonomy and governing procedures applies directly to worker control practices. In general, group workers attempt to be friendly, responsive, and permissive to the appropriate degree. They can exercise controls and make crucial decisions without being authoritarian or undemocratic. Particularly with newly formed groups and with less capable clientele, workers must be very active in setting group directions, guiding processes, and exercising controls. The degree and method of worker control should vary among different types of groups and over time within the same group.

Group Development

Group workers typically serve groups that exist for extended periods of time. They are concerned with the entire periods as much as with particular sessions. Their intent is to help the group develop through time as an effective treatment or service vehicle, with cumulative impact on its participants. Groups that maintain themselves through time, whether or not they are served by practitioners, develop definite structures and deal with similar problems. They pass through roughly comparable stages and may develop roughly comparable patterns of organization. The worker's task is to influence the course of a group's development so that it permits maximum attainment of the treatment goals set for clients. Therefore, the worker must act continuously to *effect treatment at any given moment* and to *facilitate the long-run development of a cohesive and viable group.* This dual task requires attention to the immediate events and their treatment potential, and also knowledge of the stages of group development and of the strategic foci for worker intervention. . . .

NOTE

1. Appreciation is expressed to Edwin J. Thomas for his contributions to the initial formulation of these conceptions.

REFERENCES

BERTCHER, H., and F. MAPLE, 1974. "Elements and Issues in Group Composition" in *Individual Change Through Small Groups*, P. Glasser, R. Sarri, and R. Vinter, Eds. New York: Free Press.

CARTWRIGHT, D., and A. ZANDER, 1960. "Individual Motives and Group Goals," in *Group Dynamics: Research and Theory*, D. P. Cartwright and A. Zander, eds. Evanston, Ill.: Row, Peterson.

FRENCH, J. R., III, and B. H. RAVEN, 1959. "The Bases of Social Power," in *Studies of Social Power*, D. P. Cartwright, ed. Ann Arbor: Institute for Social Research.

GLASSER, P., B. CARTER, R. ENGLISH, C. GARVIN, and C. WOLFSON, 1974. "Group Work Intervention in the Social Environment," in *Individual Change Through Small Groups*, P. Glasser, R. Sarri, and R. Vinter, Eds. New York: Free Press.

JOHNSON, C., 1974. "Planning for Termination of the Group," in *Individual Change Through Small Groups*, P. Glasser, R. Sarri, and R. Vinter, eds. New York: Free Press.

REDL, F., 1955. "Group Emotion and Leadership," in *Small Groups: Studies in Social Interaction*, P. Hare, E. Borgatta, and R. Bates, eds. New York: Knopf.

SARRI, R., and M. GALINSKY, 1974. "A Conceptual Framework for Group Development," in *Individual Change Through Small Groups*, P. Glasser, R. Sarri, and R. Vinter, eds. New York: Free Press.

SCHOPLER, J., and M. GALINSKY, 1974. "Goals in Social Group Work Practice: Foundation, Implementation and Evaluation," in *Individual Change Through Small Groups*, P. Glasser, R. Sarri, and R. Vinter, eds. New York: Free Press.

SUNDEL, M., N. RADIN, and S. CHURCHILL, 1974. "Diagnosis in Group Work," in *Individual Change Through Small Groups*, P. Glasser, R. Sarri, and R. Vinter, eds. New York: Free Press.

VINTER, R., 1974. "Program Activities: An Analysis of Their Effects on Participant Behavior," in *Individual Change Through Small Groups*, P. Glasser, R. Sarri, and R. Vinter, Eds. New York: Free Press.

—— and M. GALINSKY, 1974. "Extragroup Relations and Approaches," in *Individual Change Through Small Groups*, P. Glasser, R. Sarri, and R. Vinter, eds. New York: Free Press.

WHITTAKER, J., 1974. "Program Activities: Their Selection and Use in a Therapeutic Milieu," in *Individual Change Through Small Groups*, P. Glasser, R. Sarri, and R. Vinter, eds. New York: Free Press.

Study Questions

1. Do the "specifics" of social group work in psychiatric settings as outlined by Konopka suggest parallel distinctions for social group work in other settings? Can you develop "specifics" for school settings, medical treatment in hospitals, social justice in criminal justice settings? After having done this, has your conception of what is generic changed?

2. Konopka points out that efforts to divorce values from practice in order to be "scientific" did not work and were harmful. Can you think of some examples of how value-neutral scientific attitudes harmed people, social workers, and/or the profession?

3. What response would you make to the charge that social workers let their own values enter into their judgments? Can you distinguish between personal and professional commitment? What assurance do we have that our values have not been confounded with our "body of knowledge"—especially where practice wisdom is concerned and where there is a lack of research?

4. Vinter's description of the core competencies of group work practice are quite explicit. To what degree do you feel we have the body of knowledge at hand to carry forth the treatment sequence and devise intervention strategies as described? For example, have we been able sufficiently to explicate worker interventions at varying stages of group development? (see Whittaker, Chapter 10 above). What do we know about compatibility in grouping? How skillful are we in blending group goals with individual goals? What is the state of knowledge regarding termination? What do we know about diagnosis in the group context?

5. Vinter points out that defining and harmonizing goals that serve several clients through the same group process is no easy task. What kinds of knowledge and experience are used to guide workers in this? How much of what is known is verified and tested? How much is based on theory, beliefs, practice wisdom, folklore? What if any is based on action research? What, for example, is the predictive power of our knowledge of intervention into group processes? Are these in the form of tested cause-effect propositions? To what degree is it appropriate to introduce new treatment methods where there is little verified knowledge?

6. Vinter says that at the point of intake a client assumes a "client status." What is implied in this concept? How would you outline the roles attendant to such a status? Who determines these? Can they be consciously guided? Should they be? Does Vinter's description of the intake process allow for a "group" intake? How would natural groups such as the family, street gangs, or work group be approached? Is the diagnostic activity aimed at assessing groups as well as individuals?

7. If the worker defines and sets the purposes for the group, placing treatment goals at the center of concern, then how is the concept of self-determination defined by treatment goals? Do you agree with Vinter that letting the members do what they want is seldom effective?

8. If treatment goals are the specific ends practitioners pursue in the interest of particular clients in particular groups, how then does the individual develop his or her own inner capacities for change in future group associations? Is this learned naturally through experiencing the treatment process?

9. Are the larger social cultural influences adequately addressed in the remedial model? Does Vinter's concept of extra-group intervention help? How is it different from the enabling, mediating, and advocacy roles in other formulations? Building on the remedial model, Glasser and Garvin (1977) have described an organizational and environmental approach that addresses the social environment as a source of influence in maintaining or altering individual behavior patterns. How might the individual be viewed in the context of the larger social environment as well as in the context of the group? What specific interventions might be applied?

Suggested Readings

BERTCHER, H. J., and F. MAPLE, 1974. "Elements and Issues in Group Composition," in *Individual Change Through Small Groups*, P. Glasser, R. Sarri, and R. Vinter, eds. New York: Free Press.

CHURCHILL, S. R., 1965. "Social Group Work: A Diagnostic Tool in Child Guidance," *American Journal of Orthropsychiatry*, Vol. 35, No. 3.

FOX, E. F., M. A. NELSON, and W. M. BOLMAN, 1969. "The Termination Process: A Neglected Dimension in Social Work," *Social Work*, Vol. 14, No. 4.

FRANKEL, A. S., and P. H. GLASSER, 1974. "Behavioral Approaches to Group Work," *Social Work*, Vol. 19, No. 2.

GLASSER, P. H., and C. D. GARVIN, 1977. "Social Group Work: The Organizational and Environmental Approach," *Encyclopedia of Social Work*, 17th Issue, Vol. II. New York: National Association of Social Workers.

KLEIN, A., 1970. "Schema for Diagnosing Group Functioning," Chap. 5 of *Social Work Through Group Process.* Albany: School of Social Welfare, State University of New York at Albany.

LOWY, L., 1970. "Goal Formulation in Social Work with Groups," *Further Explorations in Group Work*, S. Bernstein, ed. Boston: Boston University School of Social Work.

PARADISE, R., and R. DANIELS, 1970. "Group Composition as a Treatment Tool with Children," *Further Explorations in Group Work*, S. Bernstein, ed. Boston: Boston University School of Social Work.

SCHOPLER, J. H., and M. J. GALINSKY, 1974. "Goals In Social Group Work Practice: Formulation, Implementation and Evaluation," in *Individual Change Through Small Groups*, P. Glasser and R. Vinter, eds. New York: Free Press.

SHALINSKY, W., 1969. "Group Composition as an Element of Social Group Work," *Social Service Review*, Vol. 43, No. 1.

SUGARMAN, R. S., 1974. "Termination of Treatment: An Examination of Selected Literature from Social Group Work, Casework, and Psychoanalysis and Psychotherapy," masters thesis, University of Connecticut School of Social Work.

SUNDEL, M., N. RADIN, and S. R. CHURCHILL, 1974. "Diagnosis in Group Work," in *Individual Change Through Small Groups*, P. Glasser, R. Sarri, and R. Vinter, eds. New York: Free Press.

SECTION D

Personal and Social Interaction: Mediative Approaches

The chapters in this section share the belief that group work can play a significant role in people's lives and that societal benefits may be derived therefrom. The emphasis, however, is not placed on achieving variously defined individual and social goals and purposes. Instead, the focus is on how needs emerge and are met through the mutual influences of the individual, group, and society interacting on one another.

Schwartz's mediating approach advances no particular individual goals, other than perhaps to help people negotiate difficult environments, nor does it have any political or social change program to encourage. The crucial idea is that the encounter of individuals composes a reciprocal group system, a kind of "mutual aid society" in which the direction for action is jointly determined and worked upon. The focus of practice is on dealing with the interdependence of individual and societal functioning as it can be nourished and mediated through group association. Similarly, the excerpt from Klein's model reflects a basic thesis that both social and psychological frames of reference are essential, not as separate determinants of behavior but rather as interacting phenomena. If there is a goal, it is to "free" the members and help them to "be" and to "become." Techniques are unimportant and unreliable, for the medium of change is not the worker but the group. Goroff's "intersystemic" perspective also stresses the interactional aspects of group work and maintains that the essence of group work practice requires that simultaneous attention be paid to three components: (1) relationships that exist among individuals, their subgroups, and the group as a whole; (2) the dynamics pertaining to the group itself; and (3) the relationships among the individual, the group, and their environing social and cultural systems. Collectively, these selections highlight an interactional perspective characterized by an interest not so much in advancing individual or social goals as in realizing the full potential that can emerge from reciprocal relationships.

18

On the Use of Groups in Social Work Practice

William Schwartz is Distinguished Visiting Professor, Fordham University Graduate School of Social Service, New York.

William Schwartz

In the introduction to his book on social behavior, George Homans describes his subject as a "familiar chaos." By this he means that we "have been at home with the evidence since childhood," but our knowledge remains unsystematic and poorly organized, and generalizations consist mainly of proverbs, maxims, and other half-truths (Homans, 1961, p. 1).

Many social workers think of their small group experiences in just this way; they have been in groups all their lives and they have developed maxims to express their understanding of those experiences. But they feel vaguely inexpert when asked to consider this area of work from a professional's point of view. Nevertheless, it is important to remember that the familiarity is as vital as the chaos. Any theorizing about the group experience should have a familiar ring as one measures the ideas against his own sensations and recollections. This requirement has important implications for both professionals and their clients.

SOME BACKGROUND ISSUES

It is helpful to recall some of the institutional and professional events that have led up to the present situation in which workers trained in the traditional settings of "social group work" talk to audiences composed largely of "social caseworkers" for whom the subject of groups is fast becoming highly relevant to their professional tasks and to the service of their agencies.

We should understand, for example, that this is not a new tradition but a tradition reclaimed. Group work historians are now

From W. Schwartz and S. R. Zalba, *The Practice of Group Work*, New York: Columbia University Press, 1971, by permission of the publisher.

fond of quoting Mary Richmond on the importance of groups; and she did, in fact, comment "with great pleasure" in 1920 on "the new tendency to view our clients from the angle of what might be termed *small group psychology*" (Richmond, 1920, p. 256, emphasis in original). But the paths of individual and small group preoccupation soon diverged and went their separate ways—to the point where Eduard Lindeman complained, in 1939, that "I cannot see why . . . groups and group experiences do not stand at the very center of social work's concern" (Lindeman, 1939, p. 344). Now, more than 40 years after Mary Richmond's observation, the group experience has indeed begun to move closer to the center of social work's concern, and caseworkers are again coming to view their clients from the vantage point of small group psychology. What is it about today's world that has compelled social workers to look again to the forces of mutual aid and peer group association—not only in the group work and community organization settings where you might expect it, but in the family agency, the hospital, the school, the child welfare setting, and others that have from the outset identified themselves as the "casework agencies"?

The rebirth of interest seems due more to the necessity in clinical settings for professionals to utilize techniques that help meet the needs of their clients than to any particular influence exerted by the traditional group workers; the latter have indeed complained of the paucity of classical group work references—the Coyles, Treckers, Wilsons, *et al.*—in the developing literature of group services in the casework and clinical settings. One might, in fact, say that the lines of influence have been reversed; as the small group has become a more general instrument of social work practice, group workers in the traditional leisure-time agencies have had to re-examine some of their historic confusions and ambiguities. The portion of their work that is related to creating people in their own image—good Americans, good Christians, group-identified Jews, middle-class prototypes—seems less and less useful, and the part that is connected with the traditional social work function of helping people negotiate difficult environments assumes new significance. So, as we move into this new era of group work, we must think not of an old service teaching a new but of both services striving together to redefine and clarify the function of the social work profession. And this presents another theoretical problem undergirding the problems of group service—namely, how to define social work function in a way that will explain the operations of all social workers.

When professionals grow tired of a difficult problem it is a familiar gambit to sneer at the problem itself. So it is with the current fashion to belittle efforts at defining social work function in generic terms. But no amount of indifference or disdain will change the fact that the various parts of social work have been drawn together from the most diverse sources of experience, and that there is a strong need to examine their relationships to each other to find out what they have in common. It is no accident that we are developing into a single, unified profession, integrating the widest differences in practice, philosophy, and social origins—no accident, but something of a mystery. Over the years we have made many efforts to probe the mystery, but from rather safe ground. We have said, for example, that we are held together by a common body of knowledge, common values, common aspirations; but we have hesitated to explore what it is we *do* that identifies us as social workers, and by what professional *skills* we want to be recognized. It is this formulation of a common methodology—a commonly characterized way of working—that provides the context in which any contemporary definition of group practice must be embedded.

In actual fact, the requirements of practice are forcing most workers into the role of expert in the generic enterprise. The work itself is beginning to persuade us that the idea of a common method is neither utopian nor premature. On the contrary, practitioners will inevitably fashion their group skills out of those they learned in their work with individuals; and they will learn, in the process, the integral connections between the two. Casework students comment repeatedly that the group work courses help them understand their casework more deeply; and I have no doubt that a good casework course is similarly significant for group work students. And so it is that as we build our understanding of social work in groups, we are both drawing from and adding to a general theory of social work practice.

It would be possible, in a longer exposition, to describe in detail how the face-to-face group is a special case of the encounter between the one and the many—between the individual and his social surroundings. What are the ways in which people try to negotiate the various systems of demands and relationships with which they must come to terms in their daily lives? And what are the ways in which collectives—people working together—integrate their individuals into a working whole, producing things, dividing the work, and making decisions? How we view this encounter between a human being and his society will fashion our view of work, our conception of function, and our theories about how to have an impact on this children's club, that patients' group, this group of mothers on welfare, and others.

Finally, there are issues related to the problem of coming to terms with the tremendous upsurge of knowledge and hypotheses emerging from the small group research of recent years. How does one develop work strategies incorporating this overwhelming accumulation of new knowledge about group behavior?

Having thus outlined all the themes that *could* be developed, let me now try to move into the middle of my subject by citing a few connected propositions about the nature of group experience, the settings in which groups are embedded, and the operational skills of group work practice. I would also like to make a few points about the problems faced by agencies moving anew into the area of group services.

THE "CLIENT" DESCRIBED

In considering the nature of the client group, what we have before us is *a collection of people who need each other in order to work on certain common tasks, in an agency that is hospitable to those tasks.* This simple definition carries within it all of the necessary ingredients for a strategy of practice. The following are some of the propositions it yields.

Need. The group members' need for each other constitutes the basic rationale for their being together. If people do not need to use each other, there is no reason for them to be together—which may seem like a truism until we recall all the experiences in which the mutual need was not apparent and the members struggled to understand what brought them together and why someone thought they had to interact with each other.

Tasks. This need for each other is specifically embodied in certain common tasks to be pursued. Defining "tasks" as *a set of needs converted into work*, we may say that these common tasks will constitute the purpose of the group and the frame of reference from which the members will choose their responses. It follows, then, that unless there is some fair degree of consensus about what these underlying tasks are, the members will find it difficult to find responses, judge the appropriateness of their responses, and plan their impact on the culture of their group. The number and complexity of these common tasks will, of course, vary with the nature of the group—ranging, in a broad spectrum, from the multipurpose adolescent gang, to the six-session group of foster parents discussing child-rearing problems, to the single-meeting group of prospective adoptive parents, and others.

Agency. The group purpose is further clarified and bounded by the agency service in which it is embedded. In society's division of labor the agency has been designated to apply itself to some human problems and not to others. Thus, the agency has a stake in the proceedings; it is not simply a meeting place, or a place of refuge. Its own social tasks are involved and become an integral part of the group experience.

Contract. The convergence of these two sets of tasks—those of the clients and those of the agency—creates the terms of the *contract* that is made between the client group and the agency. This contract, openly reflecting both stakes, provides the frame of reference for the work that follows, and for understanding when the work is in process, when it is being evaded, and when it is finished.

Work. The moving dynamic in the group experience is *work.* Let me define the term "work" as I am using it: (a) each member is trying to harness the others to his own sense of need; (b) the interaction between members thus reflects both the centripetal force of the common tasks and the centrifugal force of those tasks that are unique to each member; and (c) there is a flow of affect among the members—negative and positive in varying degrees—generated by their investment in each other, their sense of common cause, and the demands of the *quid pro quo.* This emphasis on the importance of work, on an output of energy directed to certain specific tasks, is also a comment on the common fallacy that the group process, in itself and in some mysterious way, solves problems. This naive belief that the sheer interaction of people with problems is somehow productive is often reflected in the records of workers who describe the group process in great detail yet all but obliterate their own movements. Indeed, the function of the worker emerges from the fact that the group process is not a panacea: the members must work for everything they get; they must invest heart and mind in the process; and they need all the help they can get in doing so.

Self-Consciousness. At any given moment the group members may be working on their *contract,* or they may be occupied with their *ways of working.* As in any problem-centered enterprise—casework, research, education, psychotherapy—obstacles to the pursuit of the group's basic work will require diverting energy to the task of finding ways through and around them. When a group is frustrated by such obstacles it will need to work collaboratively on them; and when the obstacles are, for the moment, cleared away, the members are then free to put their strengths together to work on what they came together for. The important point here is that group self-consciousness—attention to its own processes—is not an end in itself, however, attractive this might be to the worker; it is a way of wrestling with the obstacles that impede the group's work.

Authority and Intimacy.[1] In the culture of the group two main themes come to characterize the member's ways of working together: one, quite familiar to the caseworker, is the theme of *authority*, in which the members are occupied with their relationship to the helping person and the ways in which this relationship is instrumental to their purpose; the other, more strange and threatening to the caseworker, is the theme of *intimacy*, in which the members are concerned with their internal relationships and the problems of mutual aid. It is the interplay of these factors—external authority and mutual interdependence—that provides much of the driving force of the group experience.

THE TASKS OF THE WORKER

Having described some of the essential features of the client group system, let us turn now to the job of placing the worker inside it. What is his part in the internal division of labor? What is his function within the system? I have written elsewhere about the movements of the worker in the group (Schwartz, 1961) and will not repeat the details of the scheme here. For present purposes, let me simply present some general propositions about the worker's major tasks.

Parallel Processes. Most important is the fact that the tasks of the worker and those of the clients are different and must be clearly distinguished from each other. Where one takes over the tasks of the other—as workers are often asked to do by supervisors who demand that they state their "goals for the client"—the result is a typical confusion. The worker, trying hard to understand the nature of his helping acts and their impact on the client's process of taking help, is, in effect, asked to obliterate the differences between the two sets of movements rather than to sharpen and clarify them. I have tried to clarify the differences by positing the principle of the *parallel processes*, by which I mean that the worker has his tasks and the client has his, that these processes are interdependent but different, and that any violation of this division of labor renders the work dysfunctional and the encounter itself manipulative, sentimental, and generally frustrating for both parties.

Mediation. The worker's central function is to mediate the engagement of client need and agency service. For a long time we have been ruled by two major fallacies about how needs are met in social welfare: one is that we meet a need when we have learned to identify it; the other is that needs are met when we have established the appropriate structure of service. Granted that both of these achievements are necessary, the sad fact is that the landscape is littered with identified but unmet needs within elaborate but impotent agency structures. The encounter between client and agency is not in itself productive; it can, and too often does, misfire. What is needed is a catalytic agent to activate both client and service. That catalyst is the skill of the worker, which helps the client reach out actively for what he needs and helps the agency reach out for the clients whom it seeks to serve.

Demand for Work. In general terms, the worker carries out the mediating function by clarifying and calling for adherence to the terms of the contract that keeps client and agency together. This means that the worker, of all the participants in the system, must see most clearly into the symbiotic relationship between the client and the agency—must see the specific ways in which they need each other to carry out their own purpose. Furthermore, the worker also represents what might be called the *demand for work*, in which role he tries to enforce not only the substantive aspects of the contract—what we are here for—but the conditions of work as well. This demand is, in fact, the only one the worker makes—not for certain preconceived results, or approved attitudes, or learned behaviors, but for the work itself. That is, he is continually challenging the client to address himself resolutely and with energy to what he came to do; and he is also, at the same time, trying to mobilize his agency to clarify what it has to offer and to offer it wholeheartedly.

Authority. In the group, as in the interview, the authority theme remains; there is the familiar struggle to resolve the relationship with a nurturing and demanding figure who is both a personal symbol and a representative of a powerful institution. But the theme is modified by the addition of numerical reinforcements to the dependent member of the relationship. The caseworker first experiences this as "there are so many of them and only one of me." From both sides of the relationship interesting things begin to happen: the worker moves—a little reluctantly at first—to share his authority and to learn to live with a "diluted" control over the events of the helping process; and the client's battle with authority is markedly affected as he learns that his feelings about dependency and strength are part of the human condition and not necessarily a unique and personal flaw. The "all-in-the-same boat" dynamic has a strong impact on the nature of the transference phenomena.

Intimacy. Complementing the work with the authority theme, the social worker in the group helps his clients exploit the theme of intimacy, mobilizing the healing powers of human association and mutual aid. The group members' investment in each other constitutes the new dimension to which professional skill must be addressed. Not only must the worker be able to help people talk but he must help them talk to each other; the talk must be purposeful, related to the contract that holds them together; it must have feeling in it, for without affect there is no investment; and it must be about real things, not a charade, or a false consensus, or a game designed to produce the illusion of work without risking anything in the process. We might say that much of the client's "internal dialogue" should be out in the open, with the internalized parts represented by real people, and the worker's movements directed more clearly and openly to the actions and reactions among them.

The Power of Specific Purpose. Finally, it should be pointed out that just as the member's role is limited by time and purpose, so is the worker's. This is a limitation that adds to the power of the worker because it directs his energies to what he and his clients are working on *together*, what they are doing together, rather than what the clients *are*, how he can make them different, or how he can change their characters, their personalities, their morals, their manners, or their habits. As a practitioner I am strengthened by the idea that I do not have to change anybody's basic state of being; but there is work to be done and my skills can help the work. And, in order for the professional to accept this idea, he must accept another—namely, that the life processes into which he enters and makes his limited impact have been going on for a long time before he arrived and will continue for a long time after he is gone. The process by which the client reconstructs his experience is not one that the worker creates; he simply enters, and leaves. Another way of saying this is that he is an incident in the lives of his clients. Thus the worker should ask himself: What kind of an incident will I represent? What kind of impact will I make? More specifically, how do I enter the process, do what I have to do, and then leave?

THE PHASES OF WORK

The above questions serve to introduce another dimension that may be helpful in describing this way of analyzing work with groups—the dimension of time. I believe the tasks of the worker can be understood more precisely if we watch him move through four separate phases of work in sequence. The first is a preparatory "*tuning-in*" phase, in which the worker readies himself to enter the process, to move into the group experience as a professional helping person. The second phase is that in which the worker helps the group make its *beginnings* together. The next is the period of *work*, encompassing the essential business of the enterprise. And the final period of *transitions and endings* concerns itself with the problems of leaving, of separation and termination.

As I discuss each of these phases, I am suggesting that they apply not only to the total group experience but to each of the separate meetings that comprise it. Each encounter has its own tuning-in, beginning, middle, and end-transitions; the same logic and the same necessities of work make the terms of the analysis equally applicable, although considerable work remains to be done in testing out the details of this conception in action.

The process of preparation, described here as the "tuning-in" period, is one in which the worker readies himself to receive cues that are minimal, subtle, devious, and hard to detect except by a very sensitive and discerning instrument. It is important to note that the tuning-in idea is different from certain current conceptions about the preparation of workers, where the main emphasis is on the formulation of "goals" and the construction of "diagnostic" pictures—that is, on developing a structural and cross-sectional version of what the client *is* (and what he ought to be) rather than of what he might *do* in a given situation. If you say that a person tends to do what he is, and is what he does, that proposition needs more detailed examination. The fact is that we have not been very successful in predicting behavior from personality assessment; people tend to do different things in different situations, and they may thus be said to "be" different under different conditions. In any event, the tuning-in process tries to use prior knowledge to anticipate clues that will be thrown away so quickly, and in such disguised forms, that the worker will miss them unless he is somehow "tuned" to the client's frequency. We may, if we like, call this a kind of "preliminary empathy," as the worker prepares to enter the life-process of his clients. A young person properly attuned to a group of aged clients may instantly perceive and address himself to the possibility that the comment "What a nice young man!" may be a suspicious rather than an approving judgment—that is, "What could you know about our troubles?" In this phase the worker tries to unearth both the themes that may emerge in the worker-group engagement and the ways in which these themes may be expressed. For example, a group of adoptive parents in the supervision period may be expected to express in various ways the themes of the "bad seed," the problem of whether, how, and when to tell the child that he is adopted, the tyranny of the agency, and the ambivalence toward the supervising social worker. Thus, the tuning-in phase is devoted to making oneself receptive to veiled communications, making use of our knowledge about the issues that tend to be of concern to any particular type of client—to the aging, the adoptive parents, adolescents under stress, and others—and our knowledge about these clients in particular. It is an attempt to relate knowledge to action as the worker prepares himself for this action.

The second phase is that in which the worker tries to help the group make its beginnings under clear conditions of work. He asks them to understand the terms of the "contract" under which they have established themselves within the agency context. In effect, he is asking the members to understand the connection between their needs as they feel them and the agency's reasons for offering help and hospitality; the contract embodies the stake of each party. This beginning phase is particularly important; if its tasks are not properly and directly addressed at the outset, they will plague both group and worker for a long time—in the prolonged testing, in the endless repetition of the what-are-we-doing-here theme, and in the fits and starts with which the group approaches its business. Record analysis discloses many ways in which group members can raise and re-raise the questions of who the worker is, what he is supposed to do, what the group is for, what the agency *really* expects, what the hidden rewards and punishments are, how much latitude they *really* have, and what the talking is supposed to be about.

Simply put, the worker's tasks in this phase are: (a) to make a clear and uncomplicated (unjargonized) statement of why he thinks they are there, of their stake in coming together and the agency's stake in serving them; (b) to describe his own part in the proceedings as clearly and simply as he can; (c) to reach for feedback, for their reactions to his formulation and how his formulation squares with theirs; and (d) to help them do whatever work is needed to develop together a working consensus on the terms of the contract and their frame of reference for being together.

It is not assumed that this settles everything; nor is it true that contract work is limited to the opening stage of the group experience. Negotiation and renegotiation take place periodically, as they do in any relationship. But this does not negate the need to develop an initial working agreement, a frame of reference from which to choose one's first responses. The only alternative is ambiguity of purpose, which results in a prolonged period of subtle dickering about the terms of the engagement.

The third phase is related to the main body of the work together and is directed to the primary tasks of the helping process. Assuming that the worker has sensitized himself, that he has helped establish a fairly clear sense of purpose, and that the members have begun to address themselves to the job ahead, the worker's skills can now be employed freely in carrying out his part in the process. His central questions now become: Are we working? What are we working on? At this point there is a high premium on the worker's ability to make accurate judgments in identifying when work is going on, what it is about, when it is being avoided, where it runs into obstacles, and when the group is remobilizing itself.

I have written elsewhere about what I believe to be the five major tasks to which the worker addresses himself in the group situation

(Schwartz, 1961). I have suggested that these consist of: (a) finding, through negotiation, the common ground between the requirements of the group members and those of the systems they need to negotiate; (b) detecting and challenging the obstacles to work as these obstacles arise; (c) contributing ideas, facts, and values from his own perspective when he thinks that such data may be useful to the members in dealing with the problems under consideration; (d) lending his own vision and projecting his own feelings about the struggles in which they are engaged; and (e) defining the requirements and limits of the situation in which the client-worker system is set. For present purposes let me simply identify some of the skills required to carry out these tasks. I have mentioned the ability to perceive when work is going on and when it is being avoided; further, there is the ability to reach for opposites, for ambiguities, for what is happening under the good feelings or the bad; there is the skill of reinforcing the different ways in which people help each other; of partializing large problems into smaller, more manageable pieces; of generalizing and finding connections between small segments of experience; of calling not only for talk but talk that is purposeful and invested with feeling; of being able to handle not only the first offerings but the second and third stages of elaboration; and, throughout, of being able constantly to make the demand for work inherent in the worker's helping function.

Most of these skills are familiar to those working with individual clients; what is less familiar is the set of adaptations required in the small-group situation where, as I have said, "there are so many of them and only one of me." What is crucial here is that there is a *multiplicity of helping relationships* rather than just one, and this is disconcerting to many who have not realized how much professional control they are accustomed to using in the one-to-one interview. The role of the authority factor comes home with renewed force to the caseworker who begins to work in the spontaneous, interactive, mutually-reinforcing, rather unpredictable climate of the small group. Workers begin to question how much control they have really been using and how comfortable it has been to be able to regulate the flow of the interview, to turn themes off and on, and to take a new tack when the present one is too confusing to them.

However, the disease is not incurable; when such an evaluation takes place it often has significant effects on the worker's practice—not only in the learning of group skills but in deepening the casework skills as well. The group process has the power to move the worker as well as the members.

In the final phase of work—that which I have called "transitions and endings"—the worker's skills are needed to help the members use him and each other to deal with the problem of moving from one experience to another. For the worker it means moving *off* the track of the members' experience and life-process, as he has, in the beginning, moved *onto* it. There is a great deal to be said about how people join and separate, what beginnings and endings mean to them, and the kinds of help they need in the process. For example, one of the most interesting of the separation phenomena is what has come to be called "doorknob therapy." Within the life of any particular group we have found that the last few minutes of every meeting yields us the most significant material; that is, people will raise their most deeply-felt concerns as a "by-the-way," almost with a hand on the doorknob. We find, further, that these themes do not lend themselves to easy reintroduction at the beginning of the next meeting. The intention to "start with that at our next meeting" is more often subverted, and the theme re-enters only at the next doorknob period. The point is that beginnings and endings are hard for people to manage; they often call out deep feeling in both worker and members; and much skill is needed to help people help each other through these times.

THE MOVE TO GROUP SERVICES

What happens when the "casework" agency begins to serve some of its clients in groups? The first point that needs to be made is that those involved should not be trapped into making invidious comparisons between the one-to-one situation and the small group as contexts of treatment. There is a kind of tempting chauvinism in this "battle of methods," but it is a useless enterprise that blocks the development of agency service. The fact is that the authority theme creates certain kinds of demands for professional skill, and the intimacy theme calls for others, with different possibilities and limitations. There are things clients can do in a group that they will find more difficult to do in an interview; and there are things they feel free to share with a worker alone that they will not part with in the peer group. We need to learn more about what these differences are, and we are learning all the time. But we are learning from the work itself, not from the arguments of those who, by a strange historic arrangement, first learned to specialize by numbers.

The workers in one agency, evaluating their first group experiences to determine which phenomena seemed to offer the most interesting new dimensions for service, described the following factors (Schwartz, 1966). A worker reported on the "amazing rapidity" with which her group members moved into intensive consideration of their problems. She felt there was something about the small group climate that stimulated an early sharing of important ideas and feelings. Another worker talked about the ways in which her members found "echoes" in each other of wishes and feelings that were hard to express; this seemed to create an atmosphere in which there was "less emphasis on denial." One commented on the release of anxiety that seemed to accrue from "the knowledge that such feelings are shared by all."

There was emerging awareness among the workers that the group created a considerable degree of peer pressure to face reality and work on it. A dramatic example was given of a father who produced heart symptoms while the group was on a difficult subject; he was reminded forcefully by the members that this was his familiar reaction to tough problems, and he promptly returned to what he was struggling with. This was offered as an illustration of how the members regulated and supported each other in their reactions to pain and shock. In several connections the point was made that the group seemed to make more demands for tolerating negatives than the professionals themselves dared to make, and that it supplied, in addition, both the support and the incentives for the members to reach for difficult themes, explore self-doubts, endure painful feelings, and search into tabooed areas.

The group process seemed to lend itself particularly well to the way problems need to be broken down and elaborated in order to work on them. The members called for more information, swapped examples, asked for details on this or that aspect, contributed ideas, and shared their interpretations from different perspectives.

These points are all related, of course. The thread that ties them together is the theme of *mutual aid*, and the helping process is tangibly affected by the ways in which people challenge and support each other in the common work. I have already mentioned some of the effects upon the worker—the problem of giving up some controls, the need to adjust to a situation in which there are not one but a multiplicity of helping relationships, the feeling of "so many of them and only one of me." In addition, there is at the outset a considerable uneasiness about what is experienced by caseworkers as a "lack of privacy" in the group situation. Reared in the rigorous and respected tradition of confidentiality, many workers have begun by promising their group members that material emerging in the group would not be shared with other workers and stipulating that they should observe the same rules of confidentiality. To their surprise, they have subsequently found that their clients wanted more communication between their different professionals rather than less. A worker with a group of adolescent boys in foster care found himself repeatedly charged with messages to take back to the caseworkers, to be sure they understood what had happened in the group. Another found it impossible to prevent communication between her girls and their parents about what was happening in both the daughter and the parent groups. Furthermore, the sharing of information, far from creating the problems she expected, actually seemed to contribute greatly to the process in both groups. She concluded that in this context "confidentiality is a myth." It takes time for the caseworker to learn that the group has its own regulatory powers, and that people will make their own decisions as to what they will and will not share with workers, with peers, and with those outside the system.

However, the practice similarities far outweigh the differences; it has become a familiar event to hear caseworkers exclaim, as they discover a group work principle, that this is just what they have always done in the one-to-one relationship. It is true. The group work problems of developing a clearcut contract, helping the members talk to each other with feeling, breaking big problems into smaller, more manageable parts, putting small clues together into generalized learnings, setting the tone of tolerance for ambiguity and struggle, helping the group deal with the various parts of its environment, and helping the members use the resources of this and other agencies are familiar to the caseworker and are part of his stock-in-trade.

What is most important is that, in moving into work with groups, the object of the enterprise should not be to develop a new esoteric terminology to take its place alongside the old; the language of group dynamics can be as seductive and as mystical as that of psychoanalysis. Workers should be prepared not to write articles about the group process but to learn how to *move* in the group situation, how to develop the skills and perform the operations needed to help people in groups. And I do not believe it is possible to teach these skills to social workers by placing them in groups as observers, or even by making them co-leaders with members of other disciplines. I am not saying that these may not be interesting experiences, or that workers cannot learn from them. What I do question is whether they can learn what needs to be taught—namely, the skills of practice. I believe that what we know of pedagogy will bear out the idea that the student can learn how to do something only by taking the responsibility for doing what he is trying to learn to do.

There is a related problem here about which I would like to state another bias; it concerns the question of who should supervise the work with groups—whether this function should go to specialized personnel in group work "departments" or to existing casework staff making itself expert in the new form of service. I believe the latter is the only feasible alternative if the new service is to be securely incorporated as a basic requirement, and if the conditions created are to be the most effective for education of social workers. The unnecessary specializing and the dual supervision that often accompanies it (the group practice supervised by group workers and the casework by caseworkers) create both administrative and technical confusion without any sound professional reasons to justify the arrangement. My position implies that casework supervisors will need to work with groups of their own, at least in the first stages of the enterprise. They can then begin to teach from their own practice, from first-hand experience with the problems their workers are being called upon to face.

It is most important—returning to the note on which I began—that the subject of groups be kept close to the professional experience, uncluttered by any new mystique. To the professional, good practice in any context should have the same moving quality and the same ring of simplicity. Here is a caseworker in one of her first group assignments:

> My opening was brief—after a warm greeting I mentioned that this was the first foster parents group meeting we have held in the community. . . . I continued by stating that we are coming to them, as we recognize that travel can be difficult for them. Several mothers shook their heads vigorously in agreement. I added that being a foster mother is a tough job; but they have it even rougher because the area in which they live lacks so many essential services. We want to know their concerns; and what they think and feel will enable us to learn from and help each other.
>
> I then asked if someone would like to start off. . . .

Later in the meeting:

> From this point, the discussion, which revolved around a foster child's search for identity, became more and more animated. For example, a member felt that it is too painful for a foster child to learn the truth as to why he is different. After a long discussion as to a child's uncomfortable feelings around using a name that is different from that of his foster parent, I asked if we could always protect a child from learning parts of the truth in the outside world. Mrs. W. felt that even though she had told her youngster about his natural mother, the child thinks of her as his "real" mother. This statement brought forth many contributions by the group that were in a similar vein. I added that they seemed to be saying that in many senses of the word they are the real mothers. A group member said this was really so; but she thought that a child should be helped to understand that he also had a different biological mother. I said that perhaps if they thought they were the true mothers it might be hard for them to talk to their youngsters about their biological mothers. . . .

> Mr. F., a foster father, then spoke. He announced that he guessed he was the first man to speak this morning, and I gave him brief and good humored recognition for this. Mr. F.'s voice was calm and very earnest when he started; but as he finished his comment, his voice broke with emotion. He told the group that he was a stepchild, but that he was never told the truth. He regarded his stepmother as his real mother until he was thirteen years of age, when a distant relative informed him of his true identity. His real mother was not only living, but residing in the community. He described the pain of this sudden discovery, and said he would never want this to happen to his foster children.
>
> There was a hushed silence in the room; but the expressions on the faces of the foster mothers showed that Mr. F. had their sympathetic understanding. I supported Mr. F. by telling him that his sharing of his childhood experience with us certainly helped us understand a great deal.

And here is a group worker talking to an individual member of her group:

> At Coney Island Judy and I were standing alone while the others were on a ride. Judy asked if we were going to the beach, and I said I thought so if they all wanted to go. Judy said she couldn't understand why some people wanted to get tans. She looked up at me pointing to her skin. "You know, most colored people would like to take their color away," and she laughed as if it were the funniest joke. I didn't laugh or say anything, and she added, "It really isn't so pretty." I replied, "On you it looks good, Judy." "No," she answered, "black don't look good on nobody." She didn't move away as I had expected but just stood beside me, now with a perfectly serious face. She seemed to have expressed so directly and with such feeling the essence of this whole issue and struggle. I felt very moved by her words and said, "I guess it is easy for me to say that, just standing here looking at you. But the hard part is to know what you are really feeling like inside your skin." We were interrupted by everyone rushing back, screaming from the ride, and with them I began gathering up things to move to another place. As we started walking along, Judy slipped her arm through mine.

NOTE

1. For further inquiry into the group themes of *authority* and *intimacy*, see Bennis and Shepard's (1962) discussion of the T-group experience.

REFERENCES

BENNIS, W. G., and H. A. SHEPARD, 1962. "A Theory of Group Development," in *The Planning of Change*, W. G. Bennis, K. D. Benne, and R. Chin, eds. New York: Holt, Rinehart & Winston.

HOMANS, G. C., 1961. *Social Behavior: Its Elementary Forms.* New York: Harcourt, Brace & World.

LINDEMAN, E. C., 1939. "Group Work and Education for Democracy," *Proceedings of the National Conference of Social Work.* New York: Columbia University Press.

RICHMOND, M., 1920. "Some Next Steps in Social Treatment," *Proceedings of the National Conference of Social Work.* Chicago: University of Chicago Press.

SCHWARTZ, W., 1961. "The Social Worker in the Group," *The Social Welfare Forum, 1961.* New York: Columbia University Press.

——, 1966. "Discussion" (of three papers on the use of the group in providing child welfare services), *Child Welfare,* Vol. 45, No. 10.

19

The Mechanics of the Model

Alan Klein is currently Professor Emeritus, School of Social Welfare, State University of New York at Albany. He was formerly on the Faculty of the School of Social Work, University of Pittsburgh.

Alan F. Klein

Techniques are not important and cannot be relied upon in working with groups for social work objectives. There are only a few techniques in social work and these have been stated and restated in the literature by each writer as though he had found something new. They can be worded to sound like discoveries or reworked into many formats, but essentially, they are similar in all of the helping professions. They fall into three main categories; support, awareness, and learning. They may be important to learn from the point of view of study and theory, but there is no bag of tricks or kit for working with a group. The worker is unable to control all of the inputs in the group's operation because the members, the environment, and the culture are feeding into the interactions and transactions at all times. The intra- and intersystem action is much too complicated and rapid for the worker to be able to analyze immediately all the data so as to make conscious and specific professional interventions into the group process with considered, immediate goals in mind. When the worker is engaged with a group, each member is feeding in stimuli along with the group entity, the setting, the events just past, the impinging neighborhood environment, invisible committees, and so on ad infinitum. Each member as well as the group are responding. The worker would have to be like a computer doing complex factor analysis to be able to react in a split second with a calculated intervention supposedly chosen to effect a particular result.

In a real sense, the worker is a computer and he is making rapid-fire decisions in response to the data that is being fed into him (and from within him), but he is not able nor is it feasible for him to make interventions, act by act, to effect specified results. The worker is not the change agent; the group is the medium for change.

Reprinted with permission from Alan F. Klein *Social Work Through Group Process*, Albany, N.Y., School of Social Welfare, State University of New York at Albany, 1970.

However, the worker is part of the system and his behavior is an influence depending upon the many factors of structure, group stage, psychological predispositions, and the like.

The worker operates from a stance. He cannot hope to be effective on the basis of specific interventions or acts per se. The worker must be clear in his own mind about his stance as well as comfortable with it. He must know his own function, his goals, what he believes, and who he is. To the extent possible, he should also know about his own predispositions and modes of adaptation. Moreover, the worker ought to be aware of his feelings and be able to express them appropriately. The worker is a poor example if he is unable or unwilling to express anger, hostility, anxiety, fear as well as love and concern. Why should the members be expected to express their feelings if the worker cannot or will not express his? How can the members experience an appropriate handling of feelings if the worker is unable or unwilling to handle his own human feelings?

This point of view is different from that help by many competent authorities. Nonetheless, I am proposing that it is useful for the worker to be able to say, for example, "I am feeling quite anxious because of your attack on me" or "Such disregard for others makes me angry at you." Many children and adults are emotionally upset because they have learned (been taught) that it is unsafe to express feelings and, therefore, they have no outlet for them. If the worker cannot express or accept feelings he is reinforcing the prohibition. If the members are restrained from expressing feelings, they are not having an experience in learning how to handle them.

When a worker in a group meeting is intent upon analyzing the process so as to make conscious interventions, the chances are excellent that he is not hearing what is going on and that he is oblivious to the feelings of the group, the members, and to their concerns. It is of the greatest importance that the worker be responsive to the entreaties of the members. To do this he must be free to listen and to hear the messages that are imbedded in their communications. The more the worker is engaged in an intellectual analysis of the events and persons, the less he listens and hears the group process.

The worker must be comfortable about his stance; that is, he must agree with it philosophically, he must believe in it and have confidence in his ability to help the members achieve their goals. A variety of studies seem to confirm these factors as being indispensable in the helping endeavor (Truax, 1964). It seems clear that the worker must know who and what he is and what he believes so that his behavior will flow naturally therefrom and, also, so that he will be free from conflict.

There is no question about it, the worker reveals himself to the members through his para- and metacommunication and no matter what he says or how he says it, the message comes through. If he feels punitive his statements will be punishing, if he thinks domination he will be dominating, if he feels superior he will convey superiority. If the worker uses the model proposed here but does not believe in it, the model will be ineffective in his practice.

On the other hand, if he is committed to meeting the needs of others, if he believes in the equality of members and worker, if he is convinced about self-determination, and if he is comfortable with freedom for himself and others, his stance will elicit responses commensurate with it. If he likes the members, they will know it but if he thinks of them as little monsters they will know this too, be they children or board members.

It is because of the messages in the communication as well as the noise that techniques are unimportant. If the worker sees himself as a helping person and respects the members' right to their goals, his acts will flow from his stance and he will be responsive. Consequently, he must see his function as enabling the group process, as helping the members accomplish what they can within the limits of the well-being of each and all, and of freeing the group. He must view himself as a partner in the group enterprise.

In the past, it was believed that the worker should not meet his own needs in the group. This is patently nonsense. Let us say that he should not meet his needs at the expense of the members and the group. Little has been written about the meaning of the therapeutic experience for the therapist or of the group experience for the social worker. The experience must affect the worker if there is any validity to the thesis of this book. The worker can and should grow as a direct result of his involvement with the members. He is part of the system and he is a partner in the enterprise. If the group is engaged in mutual aid, the worker is included.

The worker is environmental to each member as well as being within the boundary of the group. The worker in this model does not handle situations, make people do things, or manipulate factors. The worker handles himself, that is the only thing he can handle; he is the only person he can make do anything because the decision to act always lies within the actor. By handling himself, he can affect some aspects of the environment of others and by being responsive he can provide resources that might be needed or used by others. The worker and his behavior are part of the reality.

He is not a mediator between systems unless the members are unable to mediate. Preferably, he helps the members and the group to mediate. He is not a negotiator for them either unless they are unable to negotiate. He helps the group and the members to negotiate. He is not an advocate for the members but he helps the members to advocate on their own behalf. He may advocate with them, but not for them. However, and this is the important point in these last paragraphs, he is *their* man. His function is unequivocally to help them achieve their goals within the context of matching. This was not the purpose in *Girls at Vocational High*, nor is it in most agencies. Trecker's old concept that the worker is a representative of the agency is no longer a viable concept (Trecker, 1955). This is a new era, and there is a different conception of helping. We are helping the members to be and become, not helping the agency to mold them.

This concept creates many problems with some agencies and administrations. Some have always given lip service to self-determination and democracy but really have not believed in it. Some of the problems are obvious, such as the worker is paid by the agency and the agency calls the tune; the board makes the policy and the worker must execute it; and the agency represents the organized community and it wants to socialize its members (social control). It creates problems for the ideological agency which has a purpose and the right to fulfill its purpose. The most vexing problem comes when the members aim to change the agency or community which is paying the worker. It has been said before that social agencies should be committed to change and have built-in mechanisms to facilitate change in function, procedures, and policies so as to keep in tune with the needs of the members and the times. Organizations tend to stabilize and to resist change. However, the social worker should be dedicated to change. The entire system for the delivery of social work services is in need of an overhaul. However, this book is not about policy or social work institutions; it is about method.

There is also a hidden factor which is that professional workers often are not comfortable in that function and do not accept it. If we are in agreement on the freedom proposition in this model, then the worker can be the servant only of the group and its members. The contract contains the proviso that what is maximizing for the members must also match the maximization for others; the entire premise is within the context of self-realization and growth. This enjoins us from securing firearms and eliminating anyone we do not like. Also, it has been pointed out that within the group experience there is learning about the relationship of goals, actions, and consequences.

The worker is not a mediator or negotiator for the members or the group unless they are unable to perform these functions for themselves. He can be and often is a liaison and in that function he can explain and interpret the extrasystem, he can act as a communication bridge, or in some instances he can act as a linkage as, for example, when he is the only point at which the two systems can transact in order to attempt to match.

He is, of course, a role model but so are the members models for each other, depending upon position, status, power, norms, and the ability to meet the needs of others. Should the worker become significant in the lives of the members, they may emulate him and should he become a "fink" in their eyes, they may reject his values. If he demonstrates that he is genuine and is their man, the probability is that some or all will learn about interpersonal relations and appropriate behavior from him. Then they may learn the meaning of closeness from experiencing it and also find that many of their fears are unconfirmed; they may experience honesty, learn how to express and deal with feelings, and learn about respect. If the worker is to be such a role model, one concludes that he has learned to trust others as well as himself, he has successfully negotiated autonomy so that he can be independent and allow independence with no need to control others; he must have achieved purpose through initiative and be secure in his identity. Having hope within himself, he can hope that the members will grow and gain confidence through sensing his vision of what is possible.

Strupp and Bergin have become convinced, they say, that the therapy of the future will consist of a set of specific techniques which can be differentially applied under specifiable conditions to specific problems, symptoms, and cases (Strupp and Bergin, 1969). This may be so, but our knowledge up to now does not make this possible and, until it does, the approach that is suggested here seems to be the most effective one we have. The socio-behavioral, learning theory, operant approaches do seem to change behavior but to the best of my knowledge we have no evidence that they promote self-realization or the birth of the real self.

Strupp and Bergin are correct, no doubt, insofar as one can assume the importance of a differential approach, that is, some groups sometimes need more structure than others, or more demand made upon them to get to work. The characteristics of the worker may be an important variable and some groups at certain times may need more authority or control than others. The developmental stages in a group's life require different worker stances. We may at some later date know more about the kind of worker that is most effective with a particular group having a specified set of tasks. As of now, when I speak of being responsive, I mean that the worker is flexible enough to respond to the needs of the members and the group within a range of acceptability. It is axiomatic that the worker responds differentially to each member depending upon the member's need. This is natural and normal for a social worker.

The word "enable" in groupwork came into disrepute a few years ago because some authors thought it was mealymouthed, weak, and lacking in goal. These writers, like Strupp and Bergin, are looking for techniques that can be specific to particular behaviors and can make it possible to designate which buttons to push, levers to pull, and which identifiable target areas to hit. The word enable can connote a lack of goal but it need not. If I can find out what you want to achieve, help you to recognize why you are not succeeding in achieving it, help you to eliminate the blocks and to develop skills, then I am enabling you to move toward your goals. The strength and the power lies within you. The model in this book is predicated on the belief that strength lies in the members and in the group, and that social work builds upon the strength of the members.

I am aware that analogies are imperfect and illustrations often misfire, but in the interest of clarity I will try to define and refine the concept of enabling. When the engineers built the tunnels at Niagara and diverted the water so that it dropped hundreds of feet and hit the fins of the turbines, they harnessed the power of the river and directed it. Some schools of thought in groupwork use this approach; this is not our model. When physicists found a way to unlock the energy of the atom, they freed its power and then they could direct it. In our model we free the power and let the group direct it.

It is my assumption that much of the power in the members and in the group is locked up and inhibited and that other forces may be misdirected. The members and group are enabled through unlocking this power.

The major function of the worker and the main concept in this model is to free the members. One could say "free them up." This means such things as free them from inhibitions, free them from old conflicts and the residues of old conflicts (mistrust, shame, guilt, doubt, anxiety, fear, and so forth), free them from the effects of previous domination (fighting against father and mother figures, transferences, rebellion) and from current domination, so that they can be themselves. It means to provide an opportunity for a freedom of choice among reasonable options with support and encouragement to risk making choices. It means the explication of and clarification of goals, the examination of the assumptions underlying these goals, the beliefs they hold, and the contradictions that have been compartmentalized.

This requirement of the model is the most difficult for the worker and the members. For them, freedom of choice is frightening and risky, and they find it difficult to believe that they have that freedom or that they can trust the worker or themselves. Why should they believe it when each time it has been promised they have been deceived by parents, teachers, friends, and employers? "Feasible citizen participation" was promised by the anti-poverty program but was soon withdrawn when citizens' groups began to exercise choice. Up until recently, students have been given the impression that they could make choices affecting their lives and were admitted to the conference table only to find that faculties did not intend to negotiate in good faith. It turned out to be a procedure used by them only to convince the students that the faculty decisions were right. Organizations, government, universities, institutions, student councils, and social agencies have used the trappings of democratic structure to give the illusion of free choice and, therefore, people do not trust the agency or the worker when he professes to give them their right to decide for themselves.

It is difficult also for the worker because he is beset by anxiety lest the choices they make turn out to be "wrong." Unless they can make some wrong choices they will never learn the consequences of certain acts. Such learning occurs only through experience. The problem in the American culture is, partially, that adults do not trust their children and professionals do not really trust clients. Due to our schooling and the way our political institutions operate, Americans do not really learn to believe in and trust democracy. The potential for education for democratic living lies in social work through group process, especially in the group services agency, and it also needs to be freed.

REFERENCES

STRUPP, H. H. and A. E. BERGIN, 1969. "Some Empirical and Conceptual Bases for Coordinated Research in Psychotherapy, etc.," *International Journal of Psychiatry*, Vol. 7, No. 2.

TRECKER H., 1955. *Social Group Work*. New York: Whiteside.

TRUAX, C. B., 1964. "Significant Developments in Psychotherapy Research," in *Progress in Clinical Psychology*, L. E. Abt and B. F. Riess, eds. New York: Grune & Stratton.

20

Social Group Work: An Intersystemic Frame of Reference

Norman N. Goroff is Professor of Social Work, School of Social Work, University of Connecticut, West Hartford.

Norman N. Goroff

INTRODUCTION

The increasing proliferation of the use of the group by a variety of professions in their attempts to help human beings is resulting in considerable confusion as to what differentiates these various group approaches. Evidence of this confusion may be culled from the variety of names given to the group approach by practitioners. A major factor in contributing to the confused state is that the names given do not clearly define what happens in the group nor what the professional does in them.

It is possible to examine the most recent professional journals and find the following in the titles of the articles: "Social Group Work, Group Therapy, Group Counselling, Group Psychotherapy, Group Education, Supportive Group Therapy, Group Guidance, Family Group Work, Family Group Therapy, Cognitive Group Therapy, T-Group, Group Activity, Group-Analytical Play Therapy, Therapeutic Discussion Group, Group Case Work, Casework Oriented Group Treatment, Group Psychoanalytical Therapy, Group Social Therapy, Group Treatment, Group Intake, Group Orientations."

If this is not sufficiently confusing, we can come back to social group work and find increasing proliferation of settings in which social group workers are asked to practice. One of the problems resulting from the diffusion of social group workers has been that the practice of social group work has been adapted to the settings and inappropriate "models" for the practice of social group work were "integrated." It then became necessary to legitimatize these changes and the development of "models" of social group work practice has

Reprinted with the permission of the *Journal of Jewish Communal Service*, where it appeared in Vol. XLVII, No. 3.

ensued. Thus we now talk about a "remedial" or "restorative model," a "social goals model," a "reciprocal model" with the attendant rise of adherents to each "model" which begins to border on the "cult phenomena."

The "model" building phase takes on the form of post-factum explanations. As Merton (1957, p. 94) points out, the logical fallacy underlying such explanations "rests in the fact that there are available a variety of crude hypotheses, each with some measure of confirmation but designed to account for quite contradictory sets of affairs."

It is recognized that a science can make use of models and model building in the development of its knowledge. The utility of models in the practice professions is questionable. Models are abstractions from reality whereas practice is reality. The danger inherent in model building in practice is that the practice may reflect the model rather than the reality of the needs of the people in the situation. This is particularly true if the criteria for differentiating the models are based on the "population" served, the "specific purpose" the group is intended to have, or the particular activity of the worker.

Social group work in essence must always consider the three basic components; (1) the relationship which exists among individuals, their sub-groups and the group as a whole, (2) the dynamics pertaining to the group itself and (3) the relationship between the individuals and the group and their environing social and cultural systems. Unless there is this simultaneous concern over the links between individual and group, interactions within the groups and the links between the group and significant others we would be hard pressed to recognize the efforts as social group work.

Social group work as defined herein is applicable in any setting with any population whether it is perceived as being primarily concerned with corrective services for social dysfunctions or with "normal growth and development—socialization." It is neither the target population nor the "purpose" for which the social group worker is engaged that is the significant determinant of whether social group work is being practiced. The significant determinant is whether the three basic concerns are present in the consciousness of the worker and if he has explicated these concerns with the members of the group in developing the working agreement with them.

SOME HISTORICAL FACTORS

Reissman and Miller (1964, p. 29) characterize the intellectual atmosphere of the 40's and 50's as being taken over by the "psychiatric world view . . . which defined almost everything in psychological terms." All kinds of problems were reduced to psychological factors. Thus what Durkheim had cautioned sociologists against, namely the reduction of social facts and sociological phenomena into a psychological framework became the overwhelming orientation.

Social group work as a professional practice succumbed to the prevailing influences of the time. It was during the 40's and 50's that social group workers began to be found in social work settings that were strongly committed to the psychoanalytical conception of personality and to the therapeutic use of the social work methods.

Gisela Konopka (Hartford, 1964) describing the use of social group work in child guidance clinics and other institutional settings in 1946 noted that the social group worker needed to sharpen his psychiatric knowledge and diagnostic ability.

The role of the social group worker in treatment settings seemed to be greatly influenced by the hierarchical social structure of the psychiatric hospital in which the psychiatrist was preeminent. This influence is seen in the following statement, "Diagnostic goals for each individual as established by the worker supersedes group goals. . . . Membership is predetermined and diagnostically selected by the worker. . . . He (the worker) is characteristically directive and assumes a position of clinical preeminence and authority" (Papell and Rothman, 1966, pp. 66-67).

This view of the social group worker is placed in juxtaposition to that in the statement in "Group Work as We See It" (Hartford, 1964) published in 1939 by the Boys Clubs of America which saw the Group worker as "setting the stage and providing suitable environment for learning, expression, adjustment and social action based on his understanding of needs of individual members and sensing underlying social purposes of the group."

Social action and social change objectives appeared throughout most of the attempts during the 20's and 30's to define social group work as a method of social work practice.

It is not our intention to bring in the past as a prestigious reason for returning to the founding tradition. Rather it is to recall to our awareness that the early pioneers of social group work recognized the inexplicable interpenetration of the individual and society. It was this recognition that contributed to the emphasis on social action and social change objectives as being an essential component of social group work.

The concept of the interrelationship between the individual and society is equally valid today as it was then. Reissman and Miller note, "the blinders acquired during the age of psychiatry in the 40's and 50's still limit intense commitment and the search for far-reaching social change" (1964). That social work and social group work may still be hampered by "these blinders" seems to be axiomatic.

FRAME OF REFERENCE

The concept of social group work in its three essences is based on several important views of our "social reality." Man and society are opposite sides of the same coin. One cannot exist without the other. This inextricable relationship between the individual and society requires the social group worker to help the individual and the group to participate actively in the world around them. The literature has viewed this as "citizenship participation in a democracy," "fulfillment of social responsibility," "assuming responsibility for themselves and others" and "to take part in the decision-making process." Papell and Rothman (1966) designate this as the "social goal model." The unfortunate aspect of this designation is to highlight and isolate one of the three interrelated interdependent essences of social group work. The result is to create the impression that the social worker's attempts to help the individual and the group to play a part in those societal aspects which affect them is a unique one called "social action." It seems that social action has become "unique" as social group work incorporated inappropriate role models for professional practice.

Our view of the development of man's nature is based on the theoretical formulation of Charles Horton Cooley—namely, that man develops his basic human nature in constant interactions within a variety of groups—family, peers and neighborhood. We therefore see the individual and the group as being inextricably intertwined in the process of human development. We cannot therefore differentiate between what has been identified as "corrective" on one end of a continuum and "enhancement of growth and development" on the other. We are hard pressed to conceptualize when a "corrective group experience" does not enhance growth and development. Similarly, we do not find it very useful to designate "enhancement of growth and development" as not having elements of a "corrective experience."

The third view is that when a number of people come together to create a group, a social process is set into motion which creates unique group properties which can be utilized by the social group worker in helping the individuals to use the experience for a variety of personal psychosocial needs. It is our contention that these properties can only be found in a group in its particular form. It is the social group worker's skill in relating to individuals within the context of these group properties that is one of the major characteristics of the professional.

Whatever words we use to try to communicate the essential aspect of the helping process, we return to the "interpersonal relationship" that develops between the professional and the member as being at the core of the process. It follows then that the network of interpersonal relationships established among the participants in the group will materially increase the "power" of the helping process. This recognition of the multiple sources of "potentially helpful relationships" in the group creates a situation which Schwartz (1966) has called "a mutual aid society." The concept of "mutual aid" places the worker in the position in which he uses himself to facilitate the operation of the "potentially helpful relationships" so that they become actual helpful relationships. The worker does not bring to the group situation those potentials which do not exist in the group. Rather, he brings knowledge and skill to help actualize the potentials.

A diagram which tries to illustrate the total interrelationship of the individual, group and other systems (Figure 20-1) may be helpful.

The social group worker in making an assessment of what is happening at any given moment needs to scan simultaneously the possible meaning of the individual's behavior as it reflects or is indicative of his personality, his psychosocial development, his ways of coping with situations within the framework of what is happening in the group situation and how both the group and the individual are linked to other societal systems and how they interpenetrate with each other. It is only as he scans all of these areas that the social worker can make an assessment which encompasses the many factors in a situation. Thus his intervention may be more reflective of the "reality" and hopefully more effective in helping the individual.

Figure 20-1.

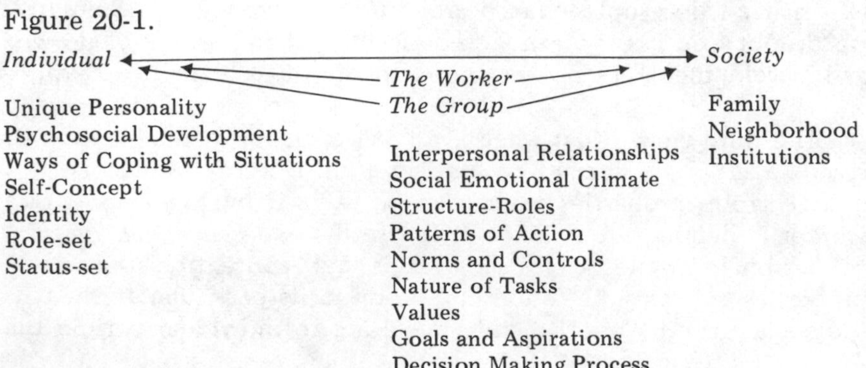

The conception of social group work requires the worker to utilize many frameworks in his assessing process. He needs to understand individual dynamics, social processes in groups, and sociocultural aspects of society. The utilization of any one framework alone may provide the worker with an incomplete and hence distorted assessment of what is happening.

A focus which tends to be limited to a concern with the worker in the group and his activities has led to the development of categories of group influence attempts. Scheidlinger delineates five categories: (1) activity-catharsis-mastery focus; (2) cognitive-informational focus; (3) interpersonal-socialization focus; (4) relationship-experiential focus; and (5) uncovering-introspective focus, all of which are not mutually exclusive nor concerned with the relationship of the individual and group in interaction with significant others (Scheidlinger, 1968). This conception is so narrow that it distorts the real meaning of working with people in groups. There is an underlying assumption about the worker in relation to the group that places too much emphasis on him and not nearly enough on the group members and the group as a whole as crucial contributors to the "helping power of the group."

The intersystemic framework of social group work has a number of important implications for the social worker.

One of these implications is related to the social worker's attitude and perception of people he works with in a group. It is not accidental that social group workers refer to people in groups as members and not clients or patients. There is a connotation to the concept client or patient which has a superordinate-subordinate relationship implication. This hierarchial status relationship places the person seeking help in a dependency position and the worker in a giving position. This is an unequal power relationship in which, whether in reality or fantasy, the social worker can attempt to exert control by either giving or withholding "help." He makes his "resources" available to the person seeking help on the condition that the person respond to him as having some "clinical pre-eminence or authority." He puts a "tax" on his help.

The "mutual aid" concept requires the social group worker to reaffirm his conviction that he is in a partnership relationship with the members of the group. Each participant in the partnership brings his assets and liabilities, his capacities and needs, his ability to give help and take help, his unique personality, his knowledge and skills, and places them at the disposal of the group. Thus, the social group worker must give up his desire to *control* either the process in the group or the individuals for "some goals he has developed" in favor of developing a *mutually acceptable* working agreement with the members of the group that will establish the framework for the group members and the social worker to enter into the relationship.

The social group worker, in this endeavor, as in all of his work with people, must be governed by a value system which stresses the inherent right of each person to self-fulfillment, the right of people to be self-determining, the obligation of a democratic society to ensure the constant maximization of opportunities for self-determination and for development of his fullest capacity.

The social group worker must believe in a process of growth and change and in the individual's inalienable right to participate in the decision-making processes which affect him within the group and within other systems. This requires the worker not to do for people that which they should be able to do for themselves. To do for them is to maintain power, control and dependency. To do with them is to share power, control and foster relatively independence.

The author has described a technique, called "confrontation with reality" (Goroff, 1967), in which he confronted the group members with contradictions in two areas of overt behavior—verbalization of desires and conduct. The confrontation in the here-and-now reality of the group resulted in some modifications of conduct more in keeping with the verbalized desires. A carry-over of the new behavior into the institutional setting resulted in responses which indicated to the group members the superiors in institution did not welcome the "new" behavior.

When this reaction was brought to the group, it became clear that the social worker had to intervene in the links between the group members and their superiors. After several weeks of discussions as to preferred strategies, the group members wanted the social worker to intervene on their behalf and the social worker wanted them to meet with the superintendent in a direct face-to-face discussion; the group members agreed to meet with the superintendent.

The social worker had to devise appropriate ways to try to help change patterns of behavior within the institution which were working against the purposes of the group experiences. He had to do it with the members rather than for the members.

Another implication concerns his firm belief in the fact that the basic power to help people in a group resides in the people in the group. People help one another through the process of working through a myriad of group-related and group-generated problems which they must continually resolve as they live in the social reality, here-and-now experience we call a group. Tropp (1968) said, "people can be helped to help each other: this is the heart of the matter and all else is commentary." For the social worker who has truly accepted this basic truth, there develops simultaneously a greater sense of security for himself in his work with people in groups, a feeling of humility as he *shares* in the process of people helping one another and possibly a sense of optimism as he realizes that the capacity for people to be helped in a group goes beyond those imposed by his limitations.

Increasingly, we find the concepts, "the advocate role," "the broker role" and "the activist role," being used in social work (Grosser, 1965). The intersystemic framework of social group work has within it these roles for the social worker.

The social group worker is required to become increasingly cognizant of the interplay of the other social system and the group. He must assess the structure and functions of the other system and identify both functional and dysfunctional consequences as they relate to the individuals in the group. The social worker's basic commitment to the wellbeing of the individual makes it a categorical imperative for him to attempt to effect changes which have dysfunctional consequences for the individual. In order to be effective in this role, the worker needs to develop the necessary knowledge to make the analysis and to formulate strategies necessary to eliminate those dysfunctional consequences. In this process, the social worker must remember that he is working with a group of people who have a stake in the outcome and therefore must be involved in appropriate ways to bring about the change.

Polsky develops a similar theme: "my central point of departure for the discussion of helping social systems is that they serve a function both in society and relative to client needs *and* the two functions are often not complementary. . . . I want to enlarge upon the idea of a system as functional or dysfunctional to its members and the subsystem. I want to approach the idea that in social work, rehabilitation must start with dysfunctional clients and a system functional to clients' dysfunctioning and that both have to change in order to effect a global functional resolution that answers both the positive needs of society as well as its clients. . . . Clients in helping systems need assistance in overcoming the rules that lock them into patient roles so that they can eventually begin to become ex-clients *within* the service system" (Polsky, 1968).

Failure to utilize the total framework for analysis will inevitably result in distorted and inappropriate assessments. We have a youngster whom we have diagnosed as being emotionally disturbed. The mere fact of such a diagnosis sets into motion a number of factors which may affect the people working with him. One of these may be what Merton (1968) called the "self-fulfilling prophecy" and Goffman (1961) called "looping—back onto the patient." In this situation, the child's behavior will be explained by his being "emotionally disturbed" and will provide further evidence of his emotional disturbance. The subsequent behavior of the people working with the child may contribute to the child behavior in such a manner as to in fact fulfill a prophecy.

Redl describes a classic example of this when he discusses a youngster whose behavior in a cottage was extremely difficult for the workers and the residents to cope with. He was highly disturbed and any attempt to work with him within the cottage failed. The staff was ready to conclude that this boy was beyond their capacity to help until the focus was changed from an exclusive reliance on his intrapsychic problems to looking at the individual within the context of the particular cottage. At this point, it became evident that for a variety of factors, namely the composition of the group, this youngster was misgrouped. A transfer to another cottage resulted in a noticeable change in his behavior (Redl, 1966).

The focus on the individual in isolation from the group resulted initially in a very discouraging prognosis. Viewing the individual within the context of the particular cottage resulted in a shift from the individual to the individual-in-interaction with a group of individuals and hence a different assessment, a modification of the treatment plan—shifting to another group and a more hopeful prognosis.

A focus on the individual in the group without considering the social cultural background will result in inappropriate assessments and hence ineffective strategies for intervention.

In the recent past, when in schools of social work human behavior was taught almost exclusively within the framework of psychoanalytical personality theory and ego psychology, it was rather common for students to make assessments of behavior within that framework. One student, working with a group of eight-year-old boys, made the assessment that one of the boys who didn't want to paint had been "poorly toilet-trained."

After we gathered a supply of old shirts for use as smocks and made them available to the boys, the youngster who had been "diagnosed" as "poorly toilet trained" became involved in painting, clay work and other messy work. The fact that the youngster was from a stable working-class family and came to the center directly from school was not taken into consideration. The student worker discovered that the boy had specific instructions from his mother not to get his "good school clothes" messy.

A focus on the genesis of behavior from outside of the group encounter may hinder the social worker in trying to deal with the particular behavior in the group. However by focussing on the behavior in the "here-and-now of the group" he can begin to try to effect changes by intervening within the appropriate group processes.

Maas (1966) describes how he attempted to utilize the group process in dealing with behavior in a group that was reflective of many attitudes which contributed to the problem of the adult patients in a psychiatric hospital. In this group of adult patients and their parents there developed the pattern in which the parents would address each other by the family name, but the adult patients would be called by their given name. The worker intervened in the normative pattern of the group by insisting that every member of the group address each other in a consistent manner, either all would be addressed by their family name or by their given name. This confronted the parents and the patients with the existence of a dual standard which reflected an attitude and a definition of the situation that was debilitating for both parents and patients.

The social worker's strategy in intervening in the group normative pattern had to take into account the effect that this would have on the interpersonal relationship of the group members outside of the group. To intervene without consideration of the possible reverberations outside the group for the participants does not meet the criteria of group work as viewed here.

A focus on the group without regard for the relationship the members have with the broader socio-cultural environs will provide an equally faulty assessment.

In a city school system, a group of junior high school boys have been referred by the guidance department for social group work treatment because of their exceedingly disruptive behavior.

The academic achievements of the boys are below grade level. They are seen as "dull normal in intelligence, emotionally immature, lacking adequate inner controls which tends to make them impulsive."

As the student worked with them, some very significant facts emerged. Much of the boys' behavior was triggered by being called upon to perform publicly tasks which were beyond them and therefore doomed them to public failure. These tasks included reading aloud and doing math problems on the blackboard. This meant that the student worker had to intervene within the school setting in order to eliminate the "triggering mechanism" because it was dysfunctional for the pupil, the class, the teacher and for the school in pursuing its educational goal.

The peer culture of the student body was at variance with the behavior of the boys in the group. Yet there were others in the school, who although not as disruptive as those referred, nevertheless did not fit into the overall "peer culture." This resulted in the recognition by the worker of the fallacy of the concept of a monolithic peer culture. There were numerous subsystems of peers within the school. How was this group linked to other subsystems? Was there a reference group with whom they identified?

A gang of high school students, a nonacademically oriented self-perpetuating "fraternity" was uncovered. This "fraternity" required a "rep" as a "hard-nose" as requirement for membership. The junior high school students were linked to this fraternity in their aspirations. Any potentially successful attempt to affect the junior high students must involve simultaneously efforts to change the high school "fraternity." As long as this particular reference group remains in its present form, the prognosis for change within the junior high school group is poor.

A careful analysis of the community revealed three basic subsystems which were developmental systems. They provided a "career track" for its members who entered the subsystems in elementary school and continued throughout their school career. These subsystems (Alissi, 1965) were identified through an examination of the current situation plus some historical information which revealed that these subsystems had persisted over a sufficient period of time for them to have become institutionalized.

The intersystemic frame of reference required the social worker to go beyond the individuals, the specific setting and look for an increasing complex of systemic interpenetration and linkage. The resulting strategies for intervention will involve a variety of groups in addition to the specific boys who were the initial focus of attention.

REFERENCES

ALISSI, A. S., 1965. "Social Influences in Group Values," *Social Work*, Vol. 10. No. 1.

GOFFMAN, E., 1961. *Asylums.* Garden City, N.Y.: Anchor Books.

GOROFF, N. N., 1967. "Confrontation with Reality: A Social Group Work Approach," *Mental Hygiene*, Vol. 51. No. 3.

GROSSER, C. F., 1965. "Community Development Programs Serving the Urban Poor," *Social Work*, Vol. 10. No. 3.

HARTFORD, M., 1964. "The Search for a Definition," *Working Papers Toward a Frame of Reference for Social Group Work.* New York: National Association of Social Workers.

MAAS, P., 1966. "Therapist-induced Crisis in Group Treatment," *Mental Hygiene*, Vol. 50, No. 1.

MERTON, R. K., 1957. *Social Theory and Social Structure*, Rev. Ed. Glencoe, Ill: Free Press.

——, 1968. *Social Theory and Social Structure*, Enl. Ed. New York: Free Press.

PAPELL, C. P., and B. ROTHMAN, 1966. "Social Group Work Models: Possession and Heritage," *Journal of Education for Social Work*, Vol. 2, No. 2.

POLSKY, H. W., 1968. "Systems as Patients: Client Needs and System Functions," *Council on Social Work Education* (mimeographed).

REDL, F., 1966. *When We Deal with Children.* New York: Free Press.

REISSMAN, F., and S. M. MILLER, 1964. "Social Change Versus the Psychiatric World View," *American Journal of Orthopsychiatry*, Vol. 34, No. 1.

SCHEIDLINGER, S., 1968. "Therapeutic Group Approaches in Community Mental Health," *Social Work*, Vol. 13, No. 2.

SCHWARTZ, W., 1966. "Some Notes on the Use of Groups in Social Work Practice" (mimeographed).

TROPP, E., 1968. "The Group: In Life and in Social Work," *Social Casework*, Vol. 49, No. 5.

Study Questions

1. How are goals and purposes determined in Schwartz's approach? What are the roles of the agency, the worker, and the clients in establishing the contract? To what extent does the worker represent the agency, the client, or himself in the process? How does this compare with Phillips's (Chapter 13 above) concept of agency function and the view that the worker functions as an "agent" of the agency? How does it compare with Tropp's (Chapter 15 above) humanistic approach?

2. In Schwartz's view, what part does the worker play in the internal division of labor of the "client-group system"? What specifically are the worker's functions within the system?

3. How are the worker's tasks distinguished from those of the clients? Compare Schwartz's concepts of parallel processes, mediation, demands for work, authority, intimacy, and power of specific purposes with Vinter's strategies for intervention and concepts of the worker as central person, symbol and spokesman, motivator and stimulator, and executive (Vinter, Chapter 17 above).

4. How do Schwartz's work phases—"tuning in," "beginnings," "work," and "transitions," and endings—differ from the treatment sequence described by Vinter? What differing skills are required to carry out these activities?

5. Schwartz suggests that instead of contemplating group processes, workers should learn to *move* in the group situation and to develop skills and perform operations needed to help people in groups. How then would workers go about incorporating knowledge and theory about small group processes in their work? What guidance is there on how group processes may be influenced to help the group and its members? Or can it be assumed that this will take place naturally? Similarly, how does the worker apply knowledge about programming as it might effectively influence group processes? What specifically are the interactional techniques and skills to be learned and performed?

6. How would the mediating approach outlined by Schwartz take on different dimensions as applied in such settings as settlements, public schools, hospitals, public welfare agencies, trade unions, residential treatment centers, prisons? How might these settings react differently to the mediating activities of the worker?

7. In 1977 (p. 1332), Schwartz wrote, "The interactionist description of client- worker system is as compelling for the worker-to-individual as for the worker-to-group relationship and it sets certain theoretical tasks for a generic definition of social work practice." What are the implications of this proposition? Does it imply that social workers should be held accountable in all of the relational systems in which they operate? What is seen as the social work function? Toward what ends are the mediating activities directed?

8. Compare Klein's view that techniques are not important and cannot be relied upon in working with groups for social work objectives with Edwin Thomas's (1971) view that behavioral approaches offer a variety of techniques and procedural guides for group work practice. To what degree, for example, would the use of such behavioral approaches as token economies, modeling,

behavioral rehearsal, systematic desensitization, and programmed instruction militate against Klein's notion of "freeing up" the members?

9. Unlike other authorities, Klein holds that workers can and do meet their own needs, growing and developing as part of the system and as "partners'. in the "group enterprise." At the same time, workers, in his view, should no longer be seen as agents or representatives of the agency, but as servants of the group and its members. What implications does this have in terms of current agency practices and procedures? Are there additional issues to be raised?

10. Can you give some practical examples of the differences between "harnessing" and "freeing" the energies inherent in the group? What does "limit setting" mean in this context? Describe the process whereby democratic values may be transmitted in the struggle to be free. In your view, what obstacles continue to stand in the way of exercising completely the right to self-determination?

11. According to the intersystemic approach described by Goroff, group work cannot deal with "reality" unless it simultaneously takes into account the interrelationships of variables concerning the individual, group relationships, and external linkages. What bodies of knowledge are available to further our understanding of these areas? What practice theory exists to guide interventions? Have any cause-effect relationships been established?

12. What is meant by the statement that the network of interpersonal relationships established within the group will materially increase the power of the helping process? Describe how this happens. To what extent should the worker intervene in these relationships to enhance further the helping potential? Can you give some practical examples of what it means for the worker to place his knowledge and skills at the disposal of the group?

Suggested Readings

GOROFF, N. N., 1967. "Confrontation with Reality: A Social Group Work Approach," *Human Hygiene*, Vol. 51, No. 3.

KLEIN, A. F., 1972. "The Struggle to be Free and Have Equal Opportunity," *Effective Groupwork*. New York: Association Press.

LEVY, C. S., 1963. "Decision-Making and Self-Determination," *Adult Leadership*, Vol. 12.

POLSKY, H. W., 1970. "Small-Scale System Analysis: Three Models for Social Work," in *Social System Prespectives in Residential Institutions*, H. W. Polsky, D. S. Clasher, and C. Goldberg, eds. East Lansing: Michigan State University Press.

SCHWARTZ, W., 1961. "The Social Worker in the Group," *The Social Welfare Forum, 1961*. New York: Columbia University Press.

——, 1962. "Towards a Strategy of Group Work Practice," *Social Service Review*, Vol. 36, No. 3.

——, and S. R. ZALBA, eds. 1971. *The Practice of Group Work*. New York: Columbia University Press.

——, 1977. "Social Group Work: The Interactionist Approach,' *Encyclopedia of Social Work*, 17th Issue, Vol. II. New York: National Association of Social Workers.

SHULMAN, L., 1968. *A Casebook of Social Work with Groups: The Mediating Model* New York: Council on Social Work Education.

——, 1969. "Social Work Skill: The Anatomy of a Helping Act," *Social Work Practice*, Selected Papers, Annual Forum of the National Conference on Social Welfare.

THOMAS, E., 1977. "Social Casework and Social Group Work: The Behavioral Modification Approach" *Encylopedia of Social Work*, 17th Issue, Vol. II. New York: National Association of Social Workers.

PART III
Related Applications

SECTION A

Social Work with Groups

Increasingly, the potentials of the small group experience are being utilized in social work as a component of practice in casework, community organization, social work administration, and other areas as well. The selections in this section illustrate how group work concepts have been applied differentially in related social work practice.

Generally, three alternatives may be pursued by social workers. First, they may look at the client basically in terms of their primary training, whether it be in casework or community organization, and seek to transpose concepts derived from their earlier training into the group situation. Often, the potential of group work is simply ignored in the search for other methods such as "group therapy," "group counseling," or "family group casework," which are seen to be more suitable.

A second approach calls for adopting a modified view of practice where group work concepts and techniques are applied to practice problems. Stempler's article describes such as approach. Utilizing Schwartz's interactional perspective, he demonstrates the applicability of social group work to work with the family treatment group.

A third, more eclectic approach incorporates "bits and pieces" of the specific group work techniques into a more integrated approach. This is perhaps best seen in community organization and administration, where the traditional influence of group work has been great. Abel's concept of the community group worker as an instructed advocate illustrates group work's contribution to the community organization process. Similarly, the significance of group work concepts in the administrative process was early recognized by Trecker. The excerpt from his work makes it clear that administrative problems are human and not technical in nature and that administrative functions and responsibilities can be enhanced through an understanding of group work.

21

A Group Work Approach to Family Group Treatment

Benj. L. Stempler is Clinical Social Worker, Jewish Family and Children's Bureau, Atlanta Jewish Federation, Atlanta, Georgia.

Benj. L. Stempler

As social work practice becomes more generic in nature, many of the techniques used in one modality of practice are often applicable to others. Such a relationship exists between the approaches used in family treatment and group work. Nathan Ackerman, a noted family therapist, illustrates this phenomenon in the following definition of family therapy:

> It is a procedure that makes use of a true group, a primary group; the sphere of intervention is not the isolated individual patient, but rather the family viewed as an organismic whole. . . . It deals with the relations between the psychosocial functions of the family unit and the emotional destiny of its members [Ackerman, 1967, p. 4].

Treatment of whole families in a group setting is geared toward helping the family to communicate:

> Family sessions offer new opportunities to many families to express and share in clearer and more direct ways what is actually going on within and among members. New and more satisfactory ways of communicating *as a group* provide corrective experiences [Mitchell, 1967, p. 114].

The treatment emphasis here is not confined to an intrapsychic examination, but is given in the context of the interactions between the members of the family. This concept is similar to the treatment focus outlined by William Schwartz in his definition of a model for group work: "The interactionists see the Social Work function as one of mediating the often troubled transactions between people and the various systems through which they carry on their relationships with

Reprinted from "A Group Work Approach to Family Group Treatment," by Benj. L. Stempler (*Social Casework*, March 1977), with permission of the *Family Service Association of America*, Publisher.

society" (Schwartz, 1971b, p. 1258). This principle would appear to be valid whether it is applied by the social group worker or by the family therapist to the work they do in their individual practice settings.

The intent of this article is to examine a family treatment case from the perspective of "the interactionist approach" to social group work. It will require viewing a family during the treatment process from the perspective of a family treatment model, and illustrating how the family group process evolved in a manner similar to that of the Schwartz group model. To demonstrate the applicability of techniques of group work to working with family treatment groups, the author will be

> . . .following this model [of] the Social Worker in the group [who] fashions his skills from the demands of four major *phases of work:* (1) his preparations; (2) his beginnings with the group; (3) substantive work on the problems that brought them together; and (4) the endings [Schwartz, 1971b, p. 1259].

This analysis is to demonstrate that by applying the principles of one modality to analysis of another, social workers widen their knowledge, raise their level of skills, and increase their professional competence as generic practitioners.

IDENTIFYING INFORMATION AND HISTORY

The family group began its formation more than ten years before family treatment began, by the encounter of Pablo F who was working as a kitchen boy, with Jose M, a chef, at the same hotel. Although Jose was twenty years Pablo's senior, they formed a paternal-filial friendship which led Jose to share his apartment with the younger man. Shortly thereafter, Pablo reluctantly entered into a common-law marriage with Maria T, once a childhood girlfriend. This relationship soon resulted in the birth of their first son, Pablocito.

The marital relationship was not a stable one and was compounded by Pablo's inability, lacking an education, to become a breadwinner. Pablo turned to alcohol and then to drugs. The relationship continued to be a stormy one, with many separations. Two more children were born, a girl, Maria, and a boy, Antonio. Although Pablo entered drug programs and psychotherapy, he clung to his addictions. Despite all, Pablo and Maria were legally married two years before family treatment was initiated.

The major event which caused the group to emerge as the author knew it, was a formal verbal agreement between Pablo and Jose, giving Pablocito, at age three, into Jose's permanent care; the boy was then brought up almost exclusively by Jose, along with help from Jose's mother and older sister (later deceased), and various female relatives of his household. Jose himself never married.

The author and a colleague were assigned by the Hunts Point Mental Health Clinic to begin a family treatment group with the combined family. Pablocito had been referred to the agency by his parochial school because of acting-out behavior in the third grade. It was decided that family treatment sessions would be held at either the M or F homes (rather than at the office) on a regular basis. Before the first session, Jose and Pablocito were informed of, and agreed to this arrangement, and were to invite the other members of the family to take part.

The meetings covered a span of four months, generally on a weekly basis. There were a total of nineteen full sessions, with both workers present at seventeen sessions. Each session lasted from one to one and one-half hours. In addition, there were individual contacts at the office with Jose, Pablo and his wife, and daughter Maria, and collateral contacts at the school with Pablocito's teacher.

Jose and Pablocito attended all the sessions. The other children and Mrs. F attended more than half. Pablocito's "cousin" Arthur (who was Jose's nephew), age fifteen, was asked to attend about six sessions (he was temporarily living in the M home with his parents and brother). Pablo attended only three sessions and then dropped out, leaving his family for a short while to live in Puerto Rico, and then returning but, remaining isolated within the family. The average number of people at the sessions was five, exclusive of the workers. Attendance varied, either because of illness or because of Pablo's refusal to allow certain members (particularly Maria, his daughter) of his household to attend regularly.

CULTURAL GROUP CHARACTERISTICS

Before the analysis of the family sessions as a group process, it is necessary to examine a few factors of Puerto Rican culture which will be seen as impinging directly on the family group. First, at the very heart of the Puerto Rican family is the concept of role. In this culture: "in family life a man tends to assume the more dominant role and the woman a more subordinate and dependent role . . ." (Spencer, Swinborne, and Shapiro, 1959, p. 57). When, as in the case of the F family, the man is not the provider, and they must rely on public assistance instead, there is usually a painful role reversal, which touches each family member profoundly. Emilicia Mizio sees the greatest impact of this on the marital group within the family:

> Some women may experience contempt for their husbands because they can no longer view them as *Machos.* A husband can be expected to strive to reassert his dominance, but in view of all the external pressures, he will often experience defeat and lose his sense of *dignidad* [pp. 76-83].

Another factor which often has the effect of creating reversals in normal family roles occurs in the parent-child relationship when

> . . . language acquisition may upset the defined roles within the Puerto Rican family. . . . Situations in which poorly educated parents must depend upon their children's greater knowledge of English may involve a painful role reversal [Fitzpatrick, 1971, p. 144].

What can result from this situation is competition between parents and children for both control and authority within the family, as well as the formation of subgroups operating independently, and often contrary, to the needs and goals of the family group as a whole.

A final factor, and perhaps the major one affecting the special formation of this family group, is the

> . . . practice known as *compadrazgo* (really "coparenthood"). . . . In Puerto Rico there is a fairly widespread custom of loaning or giving away a child to another family as a foster-child (*hijo de crianza*) . . . in New York, this foster-child pattern may have increasingly harmful effects and contribute to the child's confusion and the development of delinquency in the new environment [Spencer, Swinburne, and Shapiro, 1959, pp. 37, 40].

This practice almost exclusively involves the youngest child in the family, almost never the first-born male. Because the latter was the case in this family, the use of Jose M as *compadrazgo* has to be considered as having a unique impact on the whole nature of the family group, for to the Puerto Rican family member, "His confidence, his sense of security and identity are perceived in his relationship to others who are his family" (Fitzpatrick, 1971, p. 78).

PREPARATION FOR FAMILY TREATMENT

Knowledge of the cultural values of Puerto Rican families, as they apply to the historical evolution of this family group, enabled the workers to more easily enter into the first phase of the group process—tuning-in. The function of the worker at this stage (differing from the caseworker's methods of attempting to assess personalities) is to establish a preliminary empathy by

> . . . making tentative predictions about the terms of the encounter itself—the actions and reactions through which he and the members will deal with each other in the opening stages of the group experience. He does not, of course, ignore prior knowledge of either the class of clients or the personalities in the group; but he does try to make this knowledge operational by sensitizing and rehearsing his own responses within the expected framework of perceptions and feelings into which he is about to enter [Schwartz, 1971b, p. 1259].

Knowledge of the family group prior to joining it prepared the workers for their reactions to meeting with them about the problem of Pablocito's behavior. At the first meeting, Jose saw the child's difficulties as a school problem. Pablocito blamed his teacher, while Mrs. F felt it was because Pablo did not give him enough attention. Pablo blamed Jose for being too lax, and the younger children saw it as a means of getting attention. The workers responded by telling the family that they recognized their concern over the effect of Pablocito's behavior on the family group as a whole, and despite different views, they understood that the family wanted to know how to help Pablocito behave in a way that would make all of them proud of him. The family was expressing its anxieties regarding the workers' purpose in being there, each giving his or her impression of how they should offer assistance. This anxiety was to be expected, and the workers responded nonjudgmentally by stating that they saw each one's concern with the problem as affecting their functioning as a group. This first meeting was also the beginning of moving toward a contract, which is in keeping with Schwartz's statements about the phases of group life, "Each encounter has its own tuning-in, beginning, middle and end transitions" (Schwartz, 1971a, p. 13).

Another part of this tuning-in process concerns perceptions of how people communicate. Schwartz states that it is achieved, "in a kind of coded exchange that reveals only a small part of what they mean" (Schwartz, 1971b, p. 1259). Virginia Satir (1967), in *Conjoint Family Therapy*, further defines this concept:

> The word "communicate" is generally understood to refer to nonverbal as well as verbal behavior within a social context. Thus, "Communication" also includes all those symbols and clues used by persons in giving and receiving messages [p. 63].

As part of the preparation with the family group, the workers noted some of these means of communication, particularly the differences between the statements made and the nonverbal actions taking place in conjunction with them. During the course of the first three meetings, Pablocito stated that he loves his father, yet he sits at the other side of the room, near his mother, when his parents are both present. Pablo expressed his own affection for the boy, but actually sits apart not only from him, but from the entire family. Mrs. F said that she loves all her children equally, but she hugs and kisses only Pablocito, while ignoring the other children entirely, despite their overtures to her. Jose, who described his close friendship for Pablo, always made sure to seat himself close to Pablocito, and as far away from the boy's father as possible. Based upon this evidence of the family group's behavior, the workers were aware that much of what was verbally stated was not confirmed in nonverbal behavior; there were many disruptions, or "miscommunications" in how the family was operating as a group. It was also becoming clear that the family's initial reason for coming to the session was to deflect the school authorities and members of the community from perceiving them as responsible for Pablocito's acting-out behavior.

ESTABLISHING A BEGINNING CONTRACT

Once workers have tuned-in to what is happening and what is being expressed by the group, the next stage is to establish a beginning contract with them. Schwartz defines the tasks for the worker:

> (a) to make a clear and uncomplicated (unjargonized) statement of why he thinks they are there, of their stake in coming together and the agency's stake in serving them; (b) to describe his own part in the proceedings as clearly and simply as he can; (c) to reach for feedback, for their reactions to his formulation and how his formulation squares with theirs; and (d) to help them do whatever work is needed to develop together a working consensus or the terms on the contract and their frame of reference for being together [Schwartz, 1971a, p. 15].

While this model differs somewhat from the growth and systems models put forth by Satir (1967, pp. 179-80), which do not specifically call for this kind of contractual statement, the work with the family group described did make a statement of contract similar to that suggested by Schwartz. Thus, at the third meeting, the workers reminded the family that they were there because of Jose's request of the Mental Health Clinic to send somebody to help him learn how to improve Pablocito's behavior. The workers had asked all of the family to meet with them, because they believed that all of the family members had a stake in Pablocito: as a son, godchild, brother, or cousin. The workers pointed out that they wished to collaborate with the family in an attempt to find ways to help Pablocito deal more effectively with his school, his peers, and his family. This joint attempt could, in turn, serve to reduce the pain felt by all the family members due to Pablocito's present behavior.

The workers then paused and were silent, allowing each member of the family group to reflect on what was said and waiting for the feedback which soon followed. There was first some cross talk from the siblings, in which Maria said she did not care to help the child, while Antonio said he did. Cousin Arthur said he would like Pablocito to behave better, because he often is responsible for the boy whose behavior is more than he can stand sometimes. Jose agreed that even he sometimes cannot put up with this behavior. Mrs. F then said she believed that she has little influence on him because he does not live with her, but she wants to help in any way she can. Pablocito said he would like to stop being blamed for everything at school, and would like the workers to help him achieve this end. Finally, Pablo said that he does not see why he is needed here because Jose is really in charge of Pablocito. Jose then pointed out that they were all his family; even the two social workers are part of the family now, and all must work together to help Pablocito improve himself. The workers then explained that all were concerned over Pablocito's behavior, and although Jose has direct charge of him, Pablo, as his natural father, has a say and an influence on him, whether they live in the same house or not. Then it was agreed upon that each family member (including the workers) would work together to help Pablocito behave better. During the exchange, two things had occurred: first, a beginning agreement was being offered by the workers and reached for by the family group, each one in his own way; second, the workers were being accepted "into the family," a major achievement within Puerto Rican family culture, where the seeking of help from the mental health professional is often deemed as *loco* (Fitzpatrick, 1971, pp. 123-24).

In order to give the family a further frame of reference to begin working together, a form of behavior modification that they could all participate in was introduced. This system was based upon use of a time-out procedure with a reinforcement system:

> The time-out procedure involves temporary suspension of the subject's normal activity. . . . Simultaneous use of the time-out procedure and positive and negative reinforcements resulted in success in modifying behavior. . . . Tokens were to be used as reinforcements [Boisvert, 1974, pp. 43-47].

In choosing this system as a work tool, the workers were aware that

> . . . this method of modifying . . . behavior would have an impact if [family members] were clear about administering the method and able to be consistent, without allowing their ambivalence to interfere with the reinforcements and the time-out procedure [Boisvert, 1974, p. 46].

Using this tool as a means of binding the initial contract, all of the steps of the time-out reinforcement procedure were outlined, and each person's task explained. Jose is responsible for keeping a diary of Pablocito's behavior during the week. Each member of the family group is to report any exceptionally good or poor behavior on Pablocito's part, to Jose for inclusion in the diary, and to the group at the beginning of each meeting. Pablocito was given specific rules for how he can use the "tokens" he earns each week. The workers would arrange with his teacher that a weekly report be sent, indicating all outstanding and poor incidents of school behavior for inclusion in the diary. Finally, all were asked to agree that Pablocito receive no allowances except through this system, and all negative reinforcement would be recommended by Jose as the primary caring person, and agreed to by the group as a whole. Following discussion and questions from everyone, all agreed to their tasks, and to the whole plan itself. Introducing this tool also provided a necessary means for transition between the present and future meetings of the group. For, the worker, as Schwartz states, "recognizes, prepares for, and encourages the work between meetings; reaches for the material it yields; and calls attention to the task of maintaining continuity" (Schwartz, 1971b, p. 1261).

PROGRESSIVE THEMES IN GROUP TREATMENT

Work with the group is actually being "demanded," in a sense, from the very onset of the group process, much as the caseworker provides treatment from his first contact with his client. Similarly, just as treatment follows a series of steps or goals, work with the group goes through a progression of themes. The first of these is, "the search for common ground between the needs of clients and those of the systems they are required to negotiate" (Schwartz, 1971b, p. 1260). Such needs became apparent, early in the family group treatment. The group members strongly expressed their feelings about the school's rigid demands for pupils' behavior, and particularly about Pablocito's view that he was being singled out by his teacher for incidents he was not responsible for causing, although he was involved in them. The group saw it as unfair to always punish him, even when he did not instigate the problem in class. The workers responded by explaining that the school and even one class is a large system with many rules, and that the teachers are human; that it is a fact that Pablocito does more than his share of instigating trouble. Did it, therefore, not seem reasonable that if Pablocito were involved in a number of transgressions against class rules, then the teacher might not always be able to distinguish between what was and was not his fault? After some discussion, there was agreement on this point. The workers then offered that because people related to others based upon their past experiences of them, it would now require effort by Pablocito to change his image. The adults in the family could let the school personnel know, when they are sure, of times when Pablocito is not the cause of disruption in the class. The group was able to accept this reasoning after further discussion, and then turned to look at ways of expressing it to the teacher, using Jose as spokesman.

A second thematic part of getting work done is "detecting and challenging the obstacles to work as these obstacles arise" (Schwartz, 1971a, p. 16). Often in a family group, attempts to avoid discussion of painful areas hinders work on facing and overcoming that pain. Such was the case with the F and M family where, after several sessions, Jose continued to draw the group away from any attempt to discuss problems affecting the family because of Pablo's illness. At the sixth meeting, the workers challenged this behavior. Jose had once again brought a stop to any attempt to discuss family feelings about Pablo when he is drunk, by offering to show pictures of the family to the workers. They told him that they appreciated his concern for not wanting to cause the family pain, but that pain existed whether it was discussed or not. The workers then suggested asking Mrs. F and the children if they would not prefer to discuss their feelings about Pablo's drinking instead of everyone pretending it did not exist. After a rather lengthy silence, Antonio said, "I do not like it when papa drinks; then he is not nice to me." Then the other children and Mrs. F began to express their feelings of the effect of this problem on the family.

Another means for seeing that work goes on is in "the worker's responsibility for contributing ideas, facts, and values," because these data may be useful in the course of their work together (Schwartz, 1971b, p. 1260). Later, at the tenth meeting, when Jose was having difficulty in setting limits at home for Pablocito, the workers contributed to help him and the family move beyond this problem to a solution. Jose brought up the fact that although Pablocito had improved in school, he was showing new problems at home. He would not get up on time, would come in late from playing, and often fought against keeping to Jose's schedule. The workers pointed out that it is natural that Pablocito was using the home as a new outlet for his hyperactivity, because he was now controlling it in school. But, there was also a question of the need for him to understand why certain rules were made for him at home. Often, rules are not explained, so that children do not understand their purpose, and adults often make rules solely for their own convenience, without considering the feelings of the children. Jose then asked for advice on individual examples of which was which, based on what he was doing. The group were asked to give their views to him on this matter, and also to compare it to how things were done in the F home. . . . Later, Jose himself offered his own view as to which rules he saw as protective of Pablocito and which were arbitrary.

The workers found two other areas that became important to the work done with the family. Schwartz defines these areas as "lending his own vision and projecting his own feelings about the struggles in which they are engaged; and . . . defining the requirements and limits of the situation in which the client-worker system is set" (Schwartz, 1971a, p. 16). These tactics were often used jointly in the continuing attempt to keep the group "working." One example arose over making decisions on which negative reinforcements to choose in dealing with Pablocito's various deviations from the rules. Having been given Jose and Pablocito's explanation of how a bicycle came to be "borrowed," the workers were asked to decide on an appropriate punishment for the boy's actions. They told Jose and the family that they believed that this choice was not theirs to make. Rules had been established and agreed upon. Assessing punishment was a total group decision to make, based upon those rules, with Jose being charged with seeing that the penalty assessed is carried out. The workers pointed out that the family was perfectly capable of making this decision together, and their purpose was to help discuss all of the possibilities, but not to take the right of decision from the family. Jose replied that he wanted to "do the right thing." Pablocito expressed the feeling that unless the workers made the decision, it would not be fair. The workers said that it was not easy to make such decisions, they were aware of the pain that was involved, but also knew the family capable of deciding themselves and accepting their share in the decision. After a moment, Pablocito said "I want to say what I think my punishment should be. . . ."

Authority and intimacy were handled as an intricate part of everything the workers undertook with the family. Authority is the area "in which members are occupied with their relationship to the helping person" (Schwartz, 1971a, p. 9). Initially this relationship involved testing on both parts: the workers offered the rules, which were accepted, and then often had to deal with their own feelings of sharing the arbitration of those rules with the group. One of these rules was that no one could leave during the meeting without asking permission of the others. Toward the end of the family group treatment meetings such rules, that once were so strange to the family had become part and parcel of the process, and the workers were not so much "in charge," as they were subject to now-established mores of the group. For example, no one, including the workers, would dare interrupt another person while he spoke, without expecting everyone else to immediately defend the offended member.

The concept of intimacy, "in which members are concerned with their internal relationships and the problems of mutual aid" (Schwartz, 1971a, p. 9), is intricately bound to the concept of authority. It was much in evidence in the twelfth meeting, following Pablo's departure for Puerto Rico. Jose said, "Maria, you are so quiet." Mrs. F offered that Maria was behaving badly since Pablo left. Antonio said "She misses papa. I do not." Jose said, "I think she wants us to pay attention to her." Pablocito sulked and said "I do not want to share Jose with her." To which Jose replied "I am not yours to share. You are being selfish, Pablocito." When the group began to discuss Pablocito's selfishness, Jose went and picked up Maria and put her on his lap. Maria did not discuss Pablocito but involved herself in getting attention from Jose. Pablocito offered, "If it is okay, Maria can spend the weekend with me. And I promise not to fight with her as I usually do." Jose said Pablocito was very nice in making the offer, but should ask the others if it was okay with them. Then each one expressed his feelings about Maria spending the weekend.

TRANSITIONS AND TERMINATION

By the time it was necessary to consider termination of the group activities with the family, many transitions had taken place in the work activities. Schwartz notes that while an initial contract has to be established in order to begin the work, "Negotiation and renegotiation take place periodically, as they do in any relationship" (Schwartz, 1971a, pp. 15-16). In working together, the family moved from consideration of the problem of mediating Pablocito's behavior in school, to their relationships with him as part of the family, to how the family functioned together as a unit, to how each was affected and did affect him, and finally to which others in the family were in pain and how they, as a family unit, could act to reduce each individual's suffering.

These transitions and renegotiations, looked at from a family therapy systems view, are ways in which the family, with an identified patient such as Pablocito, reacts when the work begins to reduce this patient status. As Satir explains: "If one member of a family has pain, which is exhibited in symptoms, all members will, to some degree, react to that pain. They cannot *not* react" (Satir, 1967, p. 35). These transitions, when occurring in working with a family group, are means by which the family learns to communicate each individual's share of their pain, and then moves toward reducing it and coping with it.

Having moved through these previous stages of group development with the family, working together through each transition in the contract, the workers began to consider termination directly (because the group was time-limited from the outset and termination had been implied from the first meeting). As they did so, they discovered that despite the group's accomplishments,

> the conflict between the acknowledgment of improvement and movement away from social work help, and the fear of the loss of the worker's special attention and support of the group, leads to varied reactions to termination on the part of members [Northen, 1969, p. 229].

Schwartz elaborates on the forms these reactions may take, considering them as a series of stages the group goes through:

> an evasive period in which the prospect of ending is ignored and denied; a sullen angry stage in which hostile cues are both hidden and overt; a period of "mourning" in which the members are close to their complex feelings and are capable of intensive work on both the *authority* theme . . . and the *intimacy* theme . . . and, finally, the "graduation" effect, in which members show eagerness to try out new ways of working [Schwartz, 1971b, p. 1261].

Final work with the family group paralleled these stages, beginning with the first introduction of termination, at the fifteenth meeting, when the subject was virtually ignored. Excerpts from the sixteenth and seventeenth meetings give examples of how this process occurred in this group. Pablocito said he was being quiet because he had a headache. The worker remarked that this was becoming a real coincidence, having a headache each time we had our meeting. While the worker's concern was focused on his illness, the author noted that Maria was trying to start a fight with Antonio, which was drawing Mrs. F's attention away from the group. And Jose asked permission to leave so he could get aspirin for Pablocito and wash up. Pablocito, having just received his "tokens" for the week, blurted out to one of the workers, "I like you, I'm going to miss you." The worker replied that he would miss Pablocito too and everyone in the family very much. Jose added that he felt lost at the thought that the meetings would end; that the family needed more help in working out their problems; and that Maria in particular needed help, because she is having problems in school now. The workers pointed out that their help and advice were, at one point very important, but the family had shown that they are capable of making their own decisions; social workers cannot really do anything for people, unless they are willing to do for themselves. "You mean," said Pablocito, "that you helped me and Jose, and now we have to help Maria with what we have learned." The workers smiled and nodded affirmatively, not being able to say anything else at this point.

As the workers moved toward the final meeting, both discovered that they were experiencing their own sense of loss at ending the work with the family. Helen Northen states that "termination is viewed with ambivalence by almost all members of groups and by the social worker, for that matter" (Northen, 1969, p. 229).

In the final meeting, the workers resolved that despite their own ambivalence (the need to "hold on"), their feelings were positive about what had been accomplished: "Throughout this phase the worker must involve himself closely in the separation experience, sharing his own feelings directly with group members, while he retains his function . . ." (Schwartz, 1971b, pp. 1261-62). The workers shared their feelings with the family who expressed their own feelings of loss at the termination and their own newly achieved independence of functioning.

The worker who was staying with the agency made it clear that although there will be no further meetings, if any or all of the members of the family need to talk to someone, she would be available at the agency. The author added that he would miss the family (who knew he was leaving the agency), but he was happy to see what had changed over the four months; that although they were still in two households, they were really one family helping each other. Jose spoke for all of them, saying the workers would always be part of the family. He continued, saying "we are not afraid to talk to each other, or to listen to what each has to say. You have taught us that." The workers replied that "more important, you have learned that for yourselves." Maria and Pablocito rose and hugged each other. Antonio giggled at first and then joined them. Mrs. F rose and hugged all of the children. All the adults smiled warmly. Jose then asked if the workers would share a drink with them, as this was the last session together. When the workers accepted, the children asked if they could help and then, receiving permission to leave the room, went to get the glasses.

WORKER-GROUP RELATIONSHIP

The basis for the worker-group relationship was founded on the concept of the workers' ability to relate to the family group and understand their culture. They chose to combine the use of relationship treatment from casework theory, with the use of co-therapists as role model-leaders. According to Hank Walzer, use of a relationship treatment approach "provides a 'corrective emotional experience.' The client finds that the caseworker does not respond in the manner the client anticipates as a result of his earlier relationships experienced with parental figures" (Walzer, 1968, p. 300). The workers extended this approach by not reacting in ways similar to the family's experience with other psychologically oriented treatment persons. By taking on roles that combined a familial quality with the use of authority, consistent with Puerto Rican family cultural values, they gained acceptance as warm, interested, helping "members of the family." While the amount of acceptance did vary from individual to individual, the group trust that developed through creation of such a worker-group relationship was consistently high and correspondingly productive.

The maximization of worker-group rapport was equally dependent upon the use of co-therapists as role model-leaders. This approach was the logical choice because of the inconsistency of roles in the family that were contributing to confusion in the internal relationships between the members. The workers' function as co-leaders was to show a consistent male-female adult relationship to the family. As Ross V. Speck states:

> One of the tasks of the therapists is to become attuned to the family patterns, feelings, and mythology. This has been conceptualized as *becoming a member of the family system.* When this occurs, the therapists are accepted almost as members of the family, and the behavior of the family is no longer guarded or defensive, as it is likely to be when the family is meeting with strangers [Speck, 1967, p. 42].

By being warm, concerned, and authoritative, consistent with their understanding of the expectations of "father" and "mother" in the Puerto Rican family, the workers found that their presence contributed to opening up family communication, causing a kind of "parroting" of what they did. There was a notable increase in the kind and amount of intimacy that was shared by the family group, and in the quality of intimacy that developed, especially between Jose and Pablocito, and Mrs. F and all the children, by the time termination approached.

SUMMARY

The focus of this article has been an analysis of family treatment from a group work perspective. As such, its rationale has been to show that it is possible to examine the interaction between workers and group and the interaction within the family itself by application of a theoretical group framework to the evolution of a family treatment process. In this instance, Schwartz's "interactionist approach" was utilized, although other group frameworks, for example, developmental or social goals models would appear to be equally applicable.

The results of this analysis show that treatment can be examined and discussed from more than one point of view. By examining one modality from the perspective of another, theories of communications, behavior modification, and "experiential" casework are all naturally and permanently linked together as part of a total systems approach to working with the natural family group. Schwartz confirms this finding when he tells us:

> The work itself is beginning to persuade us that the idea of a common method is neither utopian nor premature. On the contrary, practitioners will inevitably fashion their group skills out of those they learned in their work with the individuals; and they will learn, in the process, the integral connections between the two [Schwartz, 1971a, p. 6].

By making an analysis of one modality from another modality's perspective, this article serves to emphasize the validity in the application of group theory to the family treatment process, and points out that social work methods should not be considered mutually exclusive of one another:

> In social work education, there is a mounting concern with the teaching of skills and the integration of those skills into a frame of reference that will encompass the patterns of worker activity within the individual interview, the family, the small group, and other systems [Schwartz, 1971b, p. 1262].

All systems of social work treatment can and should be viewed in this generic way, in order to improve the social worker's total range of skills, and in turn raise the standards of practice in the profession as a whole.

REFERENCES

ACKERMAN, N., 1967. "The Future of Family Psychotherapy," in *Expanding Theory and Practice in Family Therapy*, N. Ackerman, et al., eds. New York: Family Service Association of America.

BOISVERT, M. J., "Behavior Shaping as an Alternative to Psychotherapy," *Social Casework*, Vol. 55.

FITZPATRICK, J. P., 1971. *Puerto Rican Americans: The Meaning of Migration to the Mainland.* Englewood Cliffs, N.J.: Prentice-Hall.

MIZIO, E., 1974. "Impact of Existing Systems on the Puerto Rican Family," *Social Casework*, Vol. 55.

MITCHELL, C. B., 1967. "Problems and Principles in Family Therapy," in *Expanding Theory and Practice in Family Therapy*, N. Ackerman, et al., eds. New York: Family Service Association of America.

NORTHEN, H., 1969. *Social Work with Groups.* New York: Columbia University Press.

SATIR, V., 1967. *Conjoint Family Therapy.* Palo Alto, Cal.: Science and Behavior Books.

SCHWARTZ, W., 1971a. "On the Use of Groups in Social Work Practice," in *The Practice of Group Work*, W. Schwartz and S. R. Zalba, eds. New York: Columbia University Press.

——, 1971b. "Social Group Work: The Interactionist Approach," in *Encyclopedia of Social Work*, Vol. II. New York: National Association of Social Workers.

SPECK, R. V., 1967. "Family Therapy in the Home," in *Expanding Theory and Practice of Family Therapy*, N. Ackerman et al., eds. New York: Family Service Association of America.

SPENCER, K., O. SWINBURNE, and J. SHAPIRO, 1959. "Puerto Rican Newcomers: Guide to Puerto Rican Cultural Background," in *Socio-Cultural Elements in Casework.* New York: Council on Social Work Education.

WALZER, H., 1968. "Casework Treatment of the Repressed Parent," in *Differential Diagnosis and Treatment in Social Work*, F. S. Turner, ed. New York: Free Press.

22

Instructed Advocacy and Community Group Work

Paul Abels is Professor of Social Work and Associate Dean for Students, School of Applied Social Sciences, Case-Western Reserve University, Cleveland.

Paul Abels

An instructed advocate is a social worker whose advocacy is defined and limited by the group with which he works, and whose major task is to work with the community in its efforts to bring about environmental change.

Historically, people not able to find solutions to their problems have sought help from others. Where possible, they have attempted to set and limit the terms under which they would accept this help so that they could still maintain a maximum degree of autonomy. For example, the community in fourteenth-century Zaragoza, Spain, demanded oaths even of their new kings:

> We who are as worthy as you and could do more than you, elect you king on condition that you preserve our privileges and liberties, and that between you and us there shall be someone with power greater than yours (the law). If this shall not be so, we say no.

Similarly, the tasks for the instructed advocate are mutually defined by community and worker, and it is the agreed-upon "contract" that binds them together and helps determine their roles.

COMMUNITY GROUP WORK AS AN ENGAGEMENT PROCESS

We define our community as "interactions within a *Gestalt* of individuals and groups seeking to achieve security and physical safety, to derive support at times of stress, and to gain significance and autonomy."

From *Social Work Practice*, 1971, copyright © 1971, National Conference on Social Welfare; New York: Columbia University Press, by permission of the publisher.

Community group work is a social work process in which the worker helps the members learn ways of utilizing each other, the worker, and a broad range of resources as the means of working on community problems related to environmental change. The worker involves himself in actions which help the group achieve the specific goals it has set for itself as it is able to partialize and bring these into focus. He has four major goals: (1) to help the group achieve its purpose; (2) to help the group remain together as a unit long enough to achieve these purposes; (3) to enable its members to function in an autonomous manner; and (4) to help the group come to terms with its community (environment).

One key to this learning process seems to be the ability of the worker to help the community engage in change. Engagement consists of involvement in the change process; commitment to a certain goal and method of action; and movement in action toward accomplishment of the goal.

The start of a change process is choice—to seek help with a problem or not; to listen or not; to reveal himself or not—and this choice must remain the individual's. The choice that is made will often depend on the nature of the contact that is made between the individuals and the agent, and so involvement is related to the nature of the confrontation that takes place between the two. During the involvement process there is an attempt by the change agent to meet head-on the differences that may exist between the two so that they can become one, a working unit, a purposeful action unit.

There is an attempt to bridge the gap that arises between people so that some relationship or connection can be made between them. Relationship is the "bonds of feeling" communicated among the participants in the transaction.

Groups become involved when they are aware of some conflict which creates tension or stress enough that the group feels it must be modified. The initial task of the worker is to help the group clarify what its tension is related to. What does it wish changed? what are its goals?

Involvement. A number of authors have discussed some of the techniques which they feel are important in attempting to get people involved in the processes of change. Bruner has discussed the "discovery" concepts of learning, pointing out that people will become involved in the things that interest them, and that in fact this might be one of the strongest motivators for change (Bruner, 1966). Allied with this approach, Thelen suggests that the beginning of an educative experience is an encounter in which something happens to pique the interest of the person (Thelen, 1960). Bion (1961) suggests the "violation of expectations" as one way of involving people in change.

The key, however, seems to be the acceptance that something "different" must take place which can act as a catalyst for initial engagement. In addition, there must be human contact and a moving out to the individual in a way that bridges the differences that many people fear and expect will be present between them. What we are seeking here is contact which reflects a mutuality of concern and an unrestricted feeling of helpfulness from the total person, not just the "professional role." The thrust of many of the concerns of youth, encounter groups, communes, and "countercultures" maintains this striving for connections with people on a feeling level, the development of human bonds. During the involvement phase we come to realize that the factors influencing relations among members of the transaction will play an important part in the outcomes. There must be some joy in the relationships as well as in the accomplishments.

Commitment. The commitment phase is an attempt to move from mutual understanding to a "readiness," a partialization of the problem with some plan for next steps and a commitment or contract. It is a commitment to work, and requires the development of a work culture in the group.

The partialization of the problem around clarified needs permits working on the part of the problem that can be handled now. The planning is really a creative process that grows out of the integration of possibilities that are discussed. It should lead to a mutual commitment to take certain steps toward some specified goals. This mutual commitment is an initial "contract between the members and the workers' related to goals and means" (Abels, 1967). The goals are established, and a tentative grand strategy is worked out.

Movement in action. The commitment to goals and means is a start on the work process but precedes movement in action. Action is the public attack on the problem and depends on the ability to risk change, success, and defeat. Groups can learn to risk and to act, and this political process (decision-making and social interaction) can be practiced in the group. The worker and the group become an action unit directed at a target in an environment system.

Rational action requires the ability to cope with reality and to recognize and assess the rewards and costs in action and inaction and the group's ability to act. The worker's task is to help the group make this assessment.

The movement in action phase is a process of tactic exposition in two areas: the action tasks and the supportive tasks.

The action tasks consist of those public tactics (even if they are behind the scenes) which the group has decided to attempt or which are "reactions of the moment." These are primarily aimed at achieving the environmental change goals of the group and involve contacts outside the group.

The supportive tasks take place during the process of organization building. These include mediation among group members, role clarification and development, practice of action tasks, tactic development, and so on. They also include recruitment and publicity but are not directly related to primary goal achievement.

THE WORKER AS "INSTRUCTED" ADVOCATE

The need for advocacy seems most crucial during the action phase of the engagement process, and most particularly in pursuing action tasks. As action-oriented community groups are faced with confrontations with power groups which they feel they are not able to cope with, demands for new worker roles have evolved, and one such role is that of "instructed advocate." This role involves speaking and acting with, and on behalf of, an action unit in the context of a particular problem, and as a planned tactic. "Instructed" means that the group permits the worker to take this role and limits and directs its use.

It is important that when the role of instructed advocate is delegated to the worker and accepted by him there be a clear understanding of the reasons for doing so and its temporary nature. It is not seen as a style of operation but as a role to be used when needed. This role when linked to Schwartz's mediating roles extends the goal accomplishment potential of the worker-group system (Schwartz, 1961).

The mediating model has brought the worker and the group closer together, but another step is needed in the warp and woof of the worker-client relationship. The concept of mediator includes within it the idea of intercessor, someone who pleads on behalf of another, an instructed advocate if you will. This aspect of the role broadens the orientation of the mediator and permits the kind of action that is demanded by all groups, but particularly by adult, social-change-oriented groups.

The assumption by the worker of the role of instructed advocate or intercessor on behalf of the group is not meant to imply that he should direct the action of the group. We must distinguish between interceding as a technique with the enabling approach to be used when the needs of the group demand it, and being directive as a basic approach (as opposed to nondirective). It is possible to use democratic means to direct the group toward the worker's preconceived goals. Advocacy "kills" when it takes the decision-making process out of the hands of the group.

The decision as to when the instructed advocate role is needed is made, not in the light of worker purposes, but of the group's purpose. To insure this, the worker must be identified with the group and familiar with their goals and aspirations, their strengths, limitations, and potential. He is then in a position to assess quickly with them whether intercessor action to strengthen the current purpose of the group might satisfy their short-term needs but jeopardize the long-term needs. His actions as intercessor must be taken in light of both short-term and long-term needs, and must promote both. He can only do this if he is in tune with and identified with the needs of the group; and if the group is willing for him to assume this role. This action should be taken when there is group consensus, and when it does not violate the professional integrity of the worker or his contract with group or agency.

Additional factors influencing the worker's decision will be his view of the stress exerted on his group by external forces and the ability of the group to deal with these forces. Where the opposing forces are overwhelming aligned against the community change goal, and the goals are legitimate in terms of our professional values, then the role is also legitimate.

There are also critical points in the life of a group when instructed advocacy acts as a catalyst. The first public action of the group may be one such point, as would be any crisis situation. We need to reemphasize the need to advocate in public actions while not using this role internally when the group works on its supportive tasks. This is a rational use of advocacy.

During some phases of community action, group needs will lead to a call for help which can only find solution by instructed worker advocacy. The worker must be extremely careful in taking this step to reiterate to the group his reluctance to take action on their behalf into his own hands. But the luxury of waiting before taking important action until the group is powerful enough to carry it through by itself (without worker advocacy)is simply not acceptable to grassroots organizations, nor to our emerging profession.

REFERENCES

ABELS, P., 1967. "The Social Work Contract: Playing it Straight." Cleveland: National Association of Social Workers (mimeographed).

BION, W., 1961. *Experiences in Groups.* New York: Basic Books.

BRUNER, J. S., 1966. *Toward a Theory of Instruction.* Cambridge, Mass.: Harvard University Press.

SCHWARTZ, W., 1961. "The Social Worker in the Group," *The Social Welfare Forum, 1961.* New York: Columbia University Press.

THELEN, H., 1960. *Education and the Human Quest.* New York: Harper & Row.

23

Administration as a Group Process: Philosophy and Concepts

Harleigh B. Trecker is University Professor Emeritus, School of Social Work, University of Connecticut, West Hartford.

Harleigh B. Trecker

Our understanding of the nature of social work administration has evolved to the point that we now identify administration with *process* rather than *techniques;* we see administrative functions as *responsibilities widely distributed* in contrast with *authority centered in one individual;* and we place administration in its proper setting as *an inherent part of the whole social work process rather than merely a tool, adjunct, or facilitating device.* We are now at the point of examining and making specific that part of social work administration in which group processes are predominant.

Social welfare agencies are made up of various groups. Some of them are responsible for the conducting of programs and the rendering of services. Other groups take responsibility for planning and financing. A variety of groups are active as members, participants, or recipients of professional services. They may be called agency constituency or clientele. In large agencies a major share of the time of administrative personnel is devoted to work with these groups. There are definite and specific skills involved in giving leadership to groups. These skills are predicated upon basic understandings of persons in their group relationships. . . .

The professional worker is called upon to build, form, develop, and work with groups of several different kinds. Recruiting, selecting and orienting new staff, volunteers, and board members are continuing duties of administration. The conducting of group meetings and the training of others to plan and lead group discussions is another area of work. Maintaining records of group meetings and writing reports of group action come under the general heading of administration. Expert knowledge is required of the worker who

From *Group Process in Administration*, New York: Woman's Press, 1947, with permission of Follett Publishing Company.

must make judgments concerning when to refer a matter to a group; choice among groups to which it is to be referred and the timing of referral are important. Groups need help in making a plan and schedule for their work. They need suggestions on how their work relates to the work of other groups and the agency as a whole. These specific activities of administrative leadership support the belief that there is emerging a definable content, body of knowledge, and skill in the group aspects of administration.

As an incentive for the development of thinking in group process skills we have the cultural milieu of today. The collectivism and interdependence of modern society are no less evident in the modern social welfare agency. As agencies have grown in size and scope, specialization and departmentalization have come. Almost all the current complexities of contemporary society are reflected in our agencies. No one person can expect or be expected to know all that is required to make that agency operate effectively and efficiently. It takes the best thinking and the particularized effort of many individuals and groups to offer a program or service that meets community needs by means of the newest knowledge in professional practice. None of these individuals or groups can have more than a partial view of the agency unless efforts are made to relate their experience and function to one another. Coordination of effort which results in integration is one of the prime responsibilities of administration.

We are beginning to see that we cannot divorce the process of administration from the content of the agency program or service. The effect of administrative procedures is felt by those who work for the ends of the agency and by those who share in its program. The group approach is intimately related to our deepest beliefs about democracy as a process of group living. There is a certain underlying philosophy about the group approach to administration. When we think of the basic assumptions which must be made, several stand out very clearly:

All the groups in the agency are equally important parts of the whole. The concept of superior-inferior is eliminated, and in its place we substitute an equality of status based upon function. Staff, board, volunteers, members, constituents are related not by means of vertical higher-lower scales but by virtue of their function in the agency.

Participation in group life is essential if that group is to meet the needs of the members and develop a high enough group morale to carry responsibility. It is genuine participation, not mere listening, that is required if groups are to be significant.

Administrative authority is authority along with rather than over others. It is derived from consensus and voluntary choice of action rather than fiat or decree. This is authority which grows out of group intelligence; it is behavior which is conscious and controlled in its ultimate purposes.

The use of the group approach in administration calls for a reorganization of many of our habits and for new patterns of thinking. On a deeper psychological level it is certain that the ego satisfactions of the administrator are achieved on an entirely new basis. Individual accomplishments are subordinated to group accomplishments.

Different qualities of executive ability become apparent. Emphasis must be placed on skills in communication, the development of representative thinking, decentralization, and delegation of duties. The ultimate of skill resides in the continued enlargement of group awareness so that integration comes as a natural outcome of group effort. . . .

THE FUNCTION OF ADMINISTRATIVE LEADERSHIP AS AN ENABLING PROCESS

The task of administration is a multiple task. Though it is necessary to see it in its largest possible aspect it is also necessary to see the subfunctions. The literature of administration is helpful in identifying the chief jobs which make up the over-all administrative function. It is the duty of administration to determine the *broad area of service* in which the agency will work. *Specific purposes*, plus a reasonable scope, must also be worked out by administrative leadership. Beyond this it is required that we establish *policies* according to which we will operate. *Broad lines of organizational structure* must be erected. *Sound financial planning* is, of course, a basic function. None of these functions can be brought into a program bearing results without personnel to staff the operations, hence *staffing* is another specific job of administration. The duties unfold to include *business management*, *maintenance of physical properties* and *planning for a steady flow of supplies and materials. Community relationships* must be established and maintained both from the standpoint of public relations and, more important, from the standpoint of good community planning for services. Furthermore, all these functions require a *never-ceasing coordination* which becomes the chief means of arriving at *balanced, harmonious operations.*

Admittedly this list of functions places a heavy responsibility on the general process we call administration and on the workers we call administrators. As a list, however, it seems somewhat cold, lifeless, even mechanistic. This list of *what* is to be done by administration omits the more important and basic consideration of *how* to do what we know must be done. This omission is serious because it leaves out not only the process but also the people who make the process work. Perhaps it is valid to center special attention on the one primary function of administration which is basic to all the others: *It is the primary function of administration to provide leadership of a continuously helpful kind so that all persons engaged in the manifold workings of the agency may advance the agency to ever more significant service and accomplishment.* As we look into this a little further we see administrative leadership giving help to persons at certain key points.

First, we must help the constituency, the community, the board and the staff to discover focal points of community concern sufficiently compelling that they will call forth a maximum of cooperative effort. We give help at the points of objectives and motivations.

Second, we must help these same groups to develop a scheme of values which enables them to refine, select or choose those needs upon which they will place priority. The trivia of social agency administration frequently obscure the main jobs to be done. To avoid being trapped in trivia we must help people become able to recognize and work upon those things which are really important.

Third, we must help our groups by guiding, stimulating, even energizing them so that they will be able to feel within themselves a unity of integrated effort. To a great extent successful achievement in administrative leadership is made by those who are most able to imbue others with a desire to be a part of a collective effort.

Fourth, we must help our people to determine their skills, strengths, interests, and capacities so that they will be ably matched in responsibilities. When the members, staff, and board of an agency are working together at a peak of collaborative endeavor there is a maximum of personal security, because each has a part to play and each will make a contribution to the other so that all will benefit.

Fifth, we must constantly strengthen and cultivate the conditions necessary for cooperative effort. This means we shall see our first duty as that of helping people relate satisfactorily to one another because, without good personal relationships, free, frank, honest, and forthright, there can be little cooperation.

BASIC PRINCIPLES OF ADMINISTRATIVE LEADERSHIP WITH GROUPS

In a report from the field of education we discovered a definition of leadership which is applicable to the administrative situation:

> Leadership is that quality in an individual which enables him to affect the intentions and voluntary actions of another. . . . The best leadership comes out of a contributive pattern which encourages and provides opportunity for the contribution of each individual; decisions are fashioned out of the combined thinking of the group affected. . . . Once decisions have been made on the basis of intelligent interaction of the individuals in the group, then the leaders have the responsibility of implementation, reinterpretation, and administration [Spears and Meel, 1943].

Persons carrying administrative responsibility inevitably occupy a central role in the life of a social agency. It is dangerous to dwell upon the specific nature of their responsibilities without first stressing the comprehensive aspect of such work. The administrative leader must possess a dual or bifocal vision which enables him to see the persons for whom the agency exists and the persons working together to make the agency a reality. Planning, organizing, relating, and evaluating are, without this vision, apt to become routines or, worse, unreal abstractions. Administrative workers in social agencies are basically central persons around whom, through whom, and with whom others become intimately devoted to helping that agency reach its maximum of effectiveness.

Among the detailed responsibilities we see that the administrator must constantly seek to

1. motivate the group, encourage initiative, and draw from each group all that it has to give,
2. enlarge the channels of communication so that the flow of ideas between groups will be continuous and full
3. relate the different wills represented by the various groups which make up the agency
4. make groups feel their responsibility and widen the extent to which they are competent
5. organize the past experience of the group into a strong foundation so that progressive development may take place in the future
6. define the purposes of the program so that immediate and ultimate goals will be compatible and mutually supporting
7. open up new paths and new opportunities for the development of the individuals and groups in the total organization

It is interesting to speculate upon the proportion of time the administrator devotes to work with individuals and to work with groups. The evidence is still impressionistic; however, the very nature of the modern social agency as a multiple-group organism implies that leadership must be given to groups in an ever increasing proportion. In a time analysis of a working month at the Family Service Agency of the Los Angeles Area, professional workers in charge of the several district offices spent 32.7 per cent of their time in work with groups; 25.7 per cent of their time was given to meetings of district advisory committees and councils, case work development, joint board and staff committees and staff meetings related to administration; 7.5 per cent of their time was devoted to broader professional activities including participation in social planning groups and other programs related to the social work profession (Francis and Coombs, 1948).

It is our intention at this point to list prominent principles which may help the administrator in work with all the groups that make up the agency. These principles apply with reference to the board, the staff and the members: First, if we are to work with a group we must know something of its composition and background. This means knowledge and understanding of the individuals which make up the group, its meaning to them as members; and it means a willingness to help individuals become a significant part of the group. Second, if we are to be of assistance to a group we must help the members to define and understand their purpose and function in relation to the other groups which also carry a part of the load. Third, we must integrate these several groups so that harmonious interdependence results and each group supports and sustains the other to the end of agency unity. Fourth, we must achieve a personal balance with these groups weighing our time expenditure and thought concentration to the end of a functional equality. Fifth, we must give help with problems of group organization so that participation and distribution of responsibility will be widespread rather than centered in a few. Sixth, we have an educational task in helping leaders of groups plan and conduct group meetings so as to create and distribute satisfactions among all the members. Seventh, we must help these groups evaluate their work in relation to their responsibilities and in relation to the enduring purposes of the agency.

REFERENCES

FRANCIS, B. W., and G. F. COOMBS, 1948. *A Study of the Use of Professional Time.* Los Angeles: The Family Service of the Los Angeles Area.

SPEARS, H., and A. MIEL, 1943. *Leadership at Work.* Department of Supervisors and Directors of Instruction of the National Education Association.

Study Questions

1. Stempler states that although Schwartz's interactionist approach was used as his group work perspective in family treatment, other frameworks such as the developmental and social goals would be equally applicable. How would the analysis have proceeded had other orientations been used? To what degree, for example, do you think the developmental model (Tropp, Chapter 15 above) could be applied in family treatment? From a "social goals" perspective how might the analysis of group processes proceed? Would the worker have functioned differently?

2. How might Stempler's approach have been different had he adopted a problem-oriented approach such as is outlined by Vinter? How would the family group be viewed in terms of Vinter's treatment stages? Which of the worker's interventions might be described as direct, indirect or extra-group? On the other hand, how might the approach have been different had Northen's (1976) psychosocial orientation been used?

3. The role of the group in meeting community need was central in early thinking about community organization practice. As Newstetter (1948, p. 214) wrote: "Nothing that is allowed to go under the name of social work practice should permit or encourage 'individuals' to remain as mere individuals in the intergroup situation. It seems to me that the individual has no social significance apart from responsible group functioning; and that, except to its own members, the group has no social significance apart from responsible community functioning." To Newstetter the worker was an enabler in the area of intergroup relations. How does this differ from Abel's mediating instructed advocacy role? How does the goal formulation process outlined by Abel differ from the more traditional views? Who specifically are the recipients of the service? How does the contract modify the nature of the worker's involvement with community groups?

4. How does Abel's approach compare with current concepts of community organization practice? What particular group work concepts are evident in his approach? Can you think of other group work perspectives that would be equally adaptable to community work? How, for example, might one utilize the "social action" perspective of Sirls et al.? Goroff's intersystemic approach? Tompkins and Gallo's model of goal formulation? Would these approaches be essentially the same?

5. What do you think would be the role of the agency or organization in Abel's approach? What is meant by the statement that it is possible to use democratic means to direct the group toward the worker's preconceived goals?

6. How do Trecker's early concepts regarding administration as group process compare with contemporary concepts concerning group and organizational change? How, for example, does "organization development" conceive of the work group in organizations? Has the development of group work techniques and methods in administration kept pace with the development of a technology based on group dynamics and the "human relations" approach? To what extent are group methods consciously used in social work administration today?

Suggested Readings

ALISSI, A. S., 1969. "Social Work with Families in Group Service Agencies: An Overview", *Family Coordinator.* Vol. 18, No. 4.

CONE, J. D., and E. W. SLOOP, 1974. "Parents as Change Agents," in *The Group as Agent of Change,* A. Jacobs and W. W. Spradlin, eds. New York: Behavioral Publications.

COX, F. M., J. L. ERLICH, J. ROTHMAN, and J. E. TROPMAN, eds., 1970. *Strategies of Community Organization.* Itasca, Ill.: Peacock.

FRENCH, W., 1973. "Organization Development: Objectives, Assumptions and Strategies," in *Tomorrow's Organizations: Challenges and Strategies,* J. S. Jun and W. B. Storm, eds. Glenview, Ill: Scott, Foresman.

NEWSTETTER, W. I., 1948. "The Social Intergroup Work Process," *Proceeding of the National Conference of Social Work, 1947.* New York: Columbia University Press.

NORTHEN, H., 1976. "Psychosocial Practice in Small Groups," in *Theories of Social Work with Groups.* R. W. Roberts and H. Northen, eds. New York: Columbia University Press.

RESNICK, H., 1977. "Effecting Internal Change in Human Service Organizations," *Social Casework,* Vol. 58. No. 9.

ROTHMAN, J., 1970. "Three Models of Community Organization Practice," in *Strategies of Community Organization,* F. M. Cox, J. L. Erlich, J. Rothman and J. E. Tropman, eds. Itasca, Ill: Peacock.

SOMERS, M. L., 1965. "Group Process Within the Family Unit," in *The Family Is the Patient: The Group Approach to Treatment of Family Health Problems.* New York: National Association of Social Workers.

TRECKER, H. B., 1971. *Social Work Administration.* New York: Association Press.

SECTION B

Related Group Methods and Processes

Today we are witnessing a dramatic increase in the number and types of group methods being developed both within and outside the helping professions. Group workers need to be knowledgeable about how these approaches are applied by the various disciplines, for increasingly they are being called upon to render competent opinions regarding a wide range of approaches and procedures. At the same time, sound practice requires that group workers be familiar enough with the developing techniques and methods so that they may, where appropriate, use them to modify and improve their own practice. Particular attention is also being given to the self-help group, which has developed, independently of the profession, as a natural support group for people experiencing a variety of problems. The development of such groups has many implications. And again, group workers will need to assess the changing practices in light of their own work.

What are these new group approaches like? How can they be distinguished from one another? Where does social group work fit into the picture? These are the types of questions addressed in this section.

The chapter by this editor, written specifically for this volume, surveys the various group methods that have emerged and developed in the disciplines of medicine, counseling, psychology, and social work. In this larger context, it becomes evident that although the various perspectives on social group work share certain features with social work in general, often they more strongly reflect the ideas and practices of other disciplines. In his overview of self-help groups, Katz provides a beginning framework for differentiating among the various self-help efforts. While group work cannot ignore the potentials of such group experiences, Katz raises serious questions regarding the involvement of professionals in self-help groups.

24

Comparative Group Methods

Albert S. Alissi

Whatever else happens, the rapid expansion of radically different methods of working with groups is forcing us to re-examine our views regarding the significance of the small group experience to assess anew what is acceptable practice in the helping professions. It would appear that those long-fought-for principles and cherished values which have guided our work so much in the past must now somehow seek reaccreditation in a climate of vigorous methodological and ideological competition.

The current emphasis on emotional display, mutual touch, physical acting-out, and exhibition represents a greatly altered set of expectations of what people are encouraged to do in some groups. For example, the very need to lay down a rule that there be no physical fighting or breaking of furniture seems strange indeed when the group is composed of perfectly "healthy" adults. In one type of group (Ellis, 1970), a participant may be invited to have a "love experience" with another member of choice within the group. The two may also have five minutes of privacy to continue the experience on the condition they describe their activity in detail upon returning to the group. "Let it all hang out" seems to be the order of the day.

The customary role of the leader or therapist is also changing rapidly as leader-member distinctions are increasingly blurred. Gibb's TORI groups (Gibb and Gibb, 1970), for example, highlight the dysfunctional nature of role behavior in groups and insist that the leader should be free of any role demands, role obligations, role prescriptions, and role expectations. And in one Marathon group, a male and female co-therapist give testimony to genuine involvement and authenticity as they escalate their personal differences in the group to the point where a *physical* fight erupts between them—presumably to the therapeutic advantage of the group's members as onlookers (Fagan, Smith, and Timms, 1968).

Although progress has been uneven, generally the use of groups as a method of choice in working with people has achieved a new form of acceptance and respectability. This is evident in the bids for credit and competing claims for recognition that characterize the literature. In the field of medicine, for example, the initial uncertain acceptance of the work of such group therapists as Joseph Pratt, J. L.

Moreno, E. W. Lazell, L. Cody Marsh, and Trigant Burrow has changed drastically within recent years. Moreover, current authors have somewhat belatedly sought to trace the contributions of the traditional therapies of Adler, Horney, Sullivan, and others to the development of group methods of treatment.

To be sure, the evidence is not always convincing. Kanzer (1971), for example, in his review of the minutes of the Vienna Psychoanalytic Society, seems to be stretching a point with his claim that Freud's leadership of the society of early Viennesian analysis made him the "first psychoanalytic group leader." And Moreno (1969), who has been described as "a visionary of no less than cosmic dimensions," doubtless has been most influential through the years, although some will probably react with surprise to his claim that the encounter movement, existentialism, group dynamics, and sensitivity grew out of the Austrian encounter experience he himself described as far back as 1914. On the other hand, Dreikurs (1971, p. 21), who practiced "collective therapy" in Vienna in the 1920s, claims that Moreno's work there "had nothing to do with group psychotherapy as we understand it today." There are of course those who hold no such positive views regarding groups and who make no such claims. Hence Jung, true to the end, stated, "When a hundred clever heads join a group one big nincompoop is the result because every individual is trammeled by the otherness of the others" (Illing, 1963, p. 134).

The main focus here will be on describing the different methods of working with groups that are commonly employed in the field of medicine, counseling, psychology, and social work. Although the descriptions will help to compare and contrast alternative ways of working with groups, the basic intent is not to assess and evaluate their respective merits, but rather to highlight their prominent features. The necessity of a critical review cannot be denied, but there is a more immediate need to better understand the full range of group methods, for few if any writers have chosen to deal with the subject in a comprehensive manner.

For the group methodologist intent on conceptual clarity and organization, there are the usual frustrating problems of overlapping approaches, elusive assumptions, confusing terminologies, and inconsistent practices and techniques. Clearly, these problems will not be resolved here. First, no one has ever been able to capture the full essence of any human experience and formulate it into a model that serves as an exact replica of real life. There are perhaps as many if not more unrecognized forces at work that are overlooked as practice experiences are translated and systematized. Second, no approach is methodologically pure, for in human relations one can never separate the influences of the leader's personal style from the dictates of the method. Third, our tendency to treat alternative methods as though they were unstable entities is unreal, for techniques and methods are not only changing but are also shared and borrowed, often blurring distinctions between the approaches.

Although group methods may of course be categorized in different ways, the usefulness of the distinctions in the final analysis will depend on how closely they resemble reality. The decision to organize them according to disciplines, as was done here, merely forces us to recognize that the point of departure for the vast majority of group leaders will more than likely stem from their professional identifications.

MEDICAL CLINICAL APPROACHES

The group procedures that have characterized the medical-clinical field, in contrast to the usual accepted standards of the profession, have lacked specificity and standardization. No classification has as yet been developed that clearly explicates group methods and techniques in dealing with and "curing" medically recognized problems and symptom categories. Whereas a range of practitioners with varying kinds of training engage in group treatment in medical settings, it would appear that it is more often the conceptualizations and terminologies that are carefully guarded rather than the actual practice techniques that distinguish group psychotherapy from the others. On the advice that psychiatrists might think it presumptuous for lay therapists to describe their activities using medical terminology, Slavson some time ago avoided the use of the term "group psychotherapy," substituting the more broadly diffused term "group therapy" to describe his work (Spotnitz, 1961). Yet Slavson, perhaps more than anyone else, is responsible for the fact that in the United States group psychotherapy functioned as a brand of applied psychoanalysis (Anthony, 1971). In any case, in the field of group practice, one seldom hears any one accused of "practicing medicine without a license."

The varied medical approaches that characterize today's practice can be traced to the efforts of a relatively few pioneering group therapists (Corsini, 1957; Moreno, et al., 1966; J. L. Moreno and Z. T. Moreno, 1959; Lieberman, 1977).

Dr. Joseph Pratt (1907), a Boston internist, is generally acknowledge as the first to utilize group psychotherapy, although it was not clear that he was always aware of the potential curative powers residing in groups. In 1907 he conducted "thought control" classes of tuberculosis patients. These consisted of group sessions where patients received group recognition for individual progress towards health. Sessions were spotted with periods of relaxation and short inspirational lectures. Later his approach was extended to psychosomatic patients (Pratt, 1953). There was some criticism from the medical profession of Pratt's earlier work, which was sometimes confused with the Emmanuel Church Movement because Reverend Worcester—who had himself successfully helped people in groups—provided funds to help Pratt launch his "experiments" (Pinny, 1978).

Lazell (1921, 1930) used lectures, inspirational talks, selected readings, and analysis of psychoanalytic and popular literature with Dementia Pracox patients at St. Elizabeth Hospital in the 1920s. Similarly, L. Cody Marsh (1931) gave a series of thirty lectures dealing with hospital adjustment, growth, and development to psychotics at Kings Park Hospital. In the 1930s he used group singing, arts, and crafts and included similar methods with hospital personnel, relatives, and other members of the communities (1933). J. W. Klapman (1946) used a "didactic" group psychotherapy and developed a textbook of his lectures to be read by patients in conjunction with outside reading assignments. Anonymous case histories and autobiographies written by patients were also discussed.

The more psychoanalytically orientated approaches were advanced by such therapists as Trigant Burrow, Louis Wender, and Paul Schilder. Burrow (1927) introduced the term "group analysis" and later "phyloanalysis" to describe his early method, which stressed the importance of the "here-and-now," spontaneity, and immediacy and sought to bridge the gap between feelings and verbalization among his patients. Wender (1940) was perhaps the first to conduct psychoanalytically oriented groups in hospital settings during the 1930s. Combining individual and group therapies, he started seeing small single-sex groups of patients two or three times a week and worked intensively with group feelings, which were seen to be representative of family conflicts. Around the same time, Paul Schilder (1936) utilized psychoanalytic techniques in groups at Bellevue. He was among the first to share and justify his own personal ideology with the group and was in this sense very much a part of the group process. The technique, however, has never really caught on in group psychotherapy.

Some of the current clinical approaches will be described briefly under the following headings: Freudian Group Psychotherapy, Neo-Freudian Approaches, Activity Group Therapy, Tavistock, Group Psychotherapy, Adaptive Approaches, Psychodrama, Reality Therapy, Transactional Analysis, Behavioral Therapy in Groups, Existential Group Psychotherapy, Bio-energetic Therapy, Primal Scream,

Therapeutic Social Clubs and Communities, and Repressive-Inspirational Groups.

Freudian Group Psychotherapy

In the psychoanalytic tradition, groups of about eight to ten patients ranging from eighteen to sixty in age sit facing each other in a circle interacting primarily through discussion for the purpose of exploring and interpreting unconscious processes. Groups are usually self-perpetuating, with patients entering and leaving the group as they are deemed to be ready. The groups serve as a "control" on free association as resistances are interpreted by group members as well as the therapists. Members are encouraged to air past experiences as well as to focus on current disturbances in their relationships. Although therapists vary in their directiveness, the role of "doctor" is clearly understood.

Alexander Wolf ranks among the better known psychoanalysts to directly apply the principles of individual psychoanalysis to the group (Wolf and Schwartz, 1962, 1971). Antagonistic to the use of group dynamic concepts, he maintained that the group itself cannot be used as a means for resolving intrapsychic problems and at one time at least referred to his method as psychoanalysis *of* groups rather than psychoanalysis *in* groups. Wolf introduced the technique of "going around," which is a procedure where each member in turn free associates about the next member. He also introduced the "alternative session," whereby the group meets on occasion without the therapist present to continue psychotherapy relatively uninfluenced by the therapist. In contrast to Wolf, S. H. Foulkes (1948, 1957; Foulkes and Anthony, 1965), the noted British psychoanalyst, utilizes a method he calls "Group Analytic Psychotherapy," in which he incorporates field theory and group dynamic concepts. In his approach, the "doctor must be group oriented as well as individually oriented." The therapist is likened to a "conductor" functioning as a participant-observer unobtrusively directing, encouraging, and withdrawing from the group.

Neo-Freudian Approaches

Included within the analytic approaches are a variety of "schools" based on the traditional theories of Adler, Horney, Sullivan, and others that have resulted in currently recognized distinctive group therapies. Rudolf Dreikurs (1957), an Adlerian, has advanced a group method that recognizes the social nature of man's conflict and sees the group as ideally suited to highlight and reveal these conflicts and offer corrective influences. Inferiority feelings are most effectively counteracted as attitudes and values are directly affected within the group. The Group Analysis of Bohdan Wassell (1966) is perhaps the most explicit approach based on the theories of Karen Horney, where the goal of analysis is to mobilize and organize the patient's striving toward self-realization and full development as a human being. The therapist is a "conductor-participant," supporting and encouraging the group members' movement toward spontaneous self-expression and self-growth. Sidney Rose (1957) incorporates Horney's concept of the here-and-now and concentrates on the basic health strivings, which can be freed to develop into constructive integrating patterns as neurotic adaptations are worked through. George Goldman (1957) has applied Harry Stack Sullivan's theories to group psychotherapy. The therapist is a participant-observer of the human interaction who seeks to acquaint patients with the various processes and techniques they employ to minimize and avoid anxiety.

These distinctions seem to lose meaning in practice. Hyman Spotnitz (1961) indicated, for example, that he heard himself described as a follower of Freud, Alder, Sullivan, Rank, Stekel, T. Reik, W. Reich, and others, and that he was referred to as a follower of Carl Rogers before he had any knowledge of Rogers's concepts or procedures.

Activity Group Therapy

S. R. Slavson (1945) has contributed a form of group therapy based on psychoanalytic concepts, which he used primarily with disturbed children ranging from age seven to fifteen. Group members are carefully selected on the basis of their mutual therapeutic influences. The children are encouraged to utilize nonverbal forms of expression, participating at their own pace in a variety of activities: arts and crafts, cooking, going on trips, and so on. An extremely permissive group atmosphere is created, where children "act out their impulses, hostilities, and fantasies, even to the point of committing aggressive acts directed against the person of the 'therapist.' " The therapist has no particular role but seeks to meet the patient's conscious and unconscious needs in an unobtrusive manner. Latent aspects of children's behavior are interpreted in terms of psychoanalytic concepts. More recently, Slavson and Schiffer (1975) have pulled together theories and practices of group psychotherapy with children where activity group therapy is seen as one of a variety of methods including activity-interviews, group psychotherapy, play group therapy, and therapeutic play groups.

Tavistock

W. R. Bion (1959), the noted British psychoanalyst associated with the Tavistock Clinic, developed the theory that groups could best be described in terms of their prevailing emotional states or "basic assumption cultures." Individuals were seen to be functioning in terms of "valences," such as pairing, expressing a need for dependency, and "fight-flight." Group movement was seen as shifts from one emotional culture to another. In this method the therapist "establishes no rules or procedures and puts forth no agenda." He makes it clear from the start that he is not the group leader but is a participant observer more interested in observing and studying group tensions. The reactions created by his refusal to be drawn into active leadership provides the material for interpretation. Such groups are sometimes referred to as study groups or "S" groups, because the therapist or consultant is essentially concerned with alerting participants to ongoing group process to study and explore their experiences as members of a social unit. Interpretations are made concerning emotional states observed and are based on group rather than individual behavior.

Henry Ezriel (1950, 1952), a contemporary of Bion, also used an ahistorical approach and is in fact credited with having coined the expression "here-and-now," which so permeates the literature. In his view, patients will express themselves through three kinds of patient-therapist fantasized relationships: that which is required, that which is to be avoided, and that which is calamitous. Collectively, these eventuate in a common group tension, which emerges into a common group structure. In the usual format, the therapist identifies the common group structure, which is interpreted to the whole group, followed by individual interpretations of various avoided and anticipated calamitous relationships. The therapist, according to Ezriel, is "nothing but a passive projection screen except for his one active step of interpretation." For example,

> In one group, in which the majority of members remained in therapy for nine years and three for eleven years, the members at the end of therapy discussed the changes that had occurred in each person; they all agreed that, aside from being a decade older, Dr. Ezriel had not changed whatsoever. "That," states Dr. Ezriel, "is a good technique" [Yalom, 1970, p. 138].

Bion's basic assumptions, Ezriel's common group themes, and Whitaker and Lieberman's group focal conflicts are leading examples of "holistic" approaches insofar as they rely on assumptions about the unity of group themes. Leonard Horwitz (1977) offers a contrasting "group-centered" approach that does not pass over individuals in deducing group themes but inductively works through individual contributions as a step in a process that eventually leads to a focus on group themes.

Group Psychotherapy

Drawing from research studies and experiences of patients as well as group therapists, Irvin Yalom (1970) was able to identify different "curative factors," which represent the successful components of group therapy and assume varying importance depending upon group purposes, composition, stages of treatment, and so forth. The curative factors divide into ten categories: imparting information, instillation of hope, universality, altruism, the corrective recapitulation of the primary family group, development of socializing techniques, imitative behavior, interpersonal learning, group cohesiveness, and catharsis. The overall function of the therapist is to create and maintain a therapeutic atmosphere, which depends largely on the development of therapeutic resources in the group to facilitate the application of the curative factors. Utilizing specialized knowledge and techniques, the therapist functions both as a "technical expert" in creating and maintaining a therapeutic atmosphere and as a model-setting participant in influencing group norms and culture building. In keeping with the view that the patient's behavior in the group is an accurate representation of interpersonal behavior outside the group, Yalom emphasizes the ahistoric here-and-now approach.

Adaptive Approaches

Unlike the analytic approaches, James Johnson (1963), has advanced a form of group therapy that does not seek to uncover deep-seated conflicts or problems and other neurotic and psychotic illnesses. The approach is adaptive in that it is primarily aimed at affecting the social and psychological process where "emotional re-educational and re-learning experiences can occur." A group contract is essential in that it establishes an understanding regarding number of length of meetings, therapist's role, attendance, and the like. Johnson's approach also calls for the presence of a recorder—a co-worker who takes written notes of each meeting but who remains silent and otherwise does not participate in the group. Patients are carefully selected, and it is quite evident that goals are clearly explicated in advance of the therapy. The method is adaptable to a variety of diagnostic categories: personality disorders, neurosis, psychophysiological illnesses, and psychoses.

Psychodrama

Psychodrama represents just one of the many contributions of Moreno (1946, 1971; Moreno and Moreno, 1959; Moreno et al., 1966). Essentially psychodrama represents a method of learning through spontaneous enacting of a drama created and experienced by group members. Five major instruments are used: the *stage*, the *patient* or protagonist, the *director* therapist, the *staff* of therapeutic aides or auxiliary egos, and the *audience*. The stage is viewed as an extension of life where the protagonist takes roles reflecting present, past, or future situations and re-enacts them in the form of a spontaneous drama. The hallmark of psychodrama is spontaneity. Emotional material is re-enacted through the encouragement of the director with the assistance of reciprocal action of auxiliary egos, which act as therapeutic extensions of the therapist portraying real or imagined persons in the patient's life. The psychodrama usually begins with the "warm-up," which is an initial period in which members become acquainted with one another. Then, utilizing a variety of techniques, such as role reversals, doubling, and mirroring, attempts are made to enact the situation to arrive at a clear understanding of self and others. This is followed by a period of sharing with the audience to provide feedback (Blatner, 1973). Although psychodrama is most often used in conjunction with other group approaches, usually little control is placed on group composition. Sociodrama differs from psychodrama in that the former deals with group problems emphasizing social and community problems that are not necessarily related to the private personal problems of the individual members. In contrast to the spontaneity of the psychodrama, the sociodrama performers are given roles to play.

Reality Therapy

Reality therapy grew from a disenchantment with conventional psychiatric therapies. In the eyes of its primary theoretician, William Glasser (1965), a patient is not seen to be mentally ill but rather is seen to be acting irresponsibly because either or both of his basic needs—to love and be loved, and to feel worthwhile—are not being fulfilled. The three R's of reality, responsibility, and rightness underlie certain basic principles, which are followed to help people fulfill such needs. For example, there is a total involvement of the therapist in a relationship of love. Value judgements are offered. Realistic alternatives are sought. No excuses are accepted.

Characteristically, a total involvement of the therapist with the patient is sought; value judgment's are offered regarding individual behavior; there is an active search for realistic alternatives; there is a commitment to a plan; no excuses are accepted; and no punishments are given except for what are consequences of behavior. Although introduced primarily as a one-to-one method, reality therapy is often viewed as a group method, inasmuch as its principles are easily applied in groups. Typically, it is employed in schools, correctional settings, mental hospitals, half-way houses, and so forth.

Transactional Analysis

The transactional group method was originated in 1954 by Eric Berne, whose bestselling book *Games People Play* (1964) represented a significant departure from traditional views of psychotherapy. Basic to his theory is the existence of ego states within persons identified as the Parent, Adult, and Child, which are "experiential and behavioral realities" quite different from constructs such as ego, superego, and id. Characteristically, the Parent state reflects behavior copied from parents or authority figures; the Adult state is essentially a computer-type, objective data-processing function; while the Child state reflects behavior of the person's childhood. Any person is seen to reflect one of these three ego states at any given time. Structural analysis seeks to reveal how these three systems interact intrapsychiatrically, whereas transactional analysis focuses on analyzing transanctions that occur as various ego states within a person interact with ego states in others. Through the extensive use of diagrams, linkages between states are traced and misperceptions and misunderstandings are recognized. Berne analyzes "games" to understand further the patterned transactions that occur among people. In addition, scripts are conceptualized as a kind of unconscious plan based on fantasies, which act as a major force shaping a person's entire life (Berne, 1961).

In transactional analysis, group composition is heterogeneous. There are few, if any, membership requirements. Much of the group practice is contractual in nature; every member knows where he stands at any given point in time. Essentially, the contract is stated in terms as, "How will you know and how will we know when you get what you are coming to the group for?" Although the therapist does recognize group processes, the emphasis is on individuals' transactions within the group. Among the main therapeutic operations are interrogation, specification, confrontation, explanation, illustration, confirmation, interpretation, and crystallization (Berne, 1966).

Behavior Therapy in Groups

With the exception perhaps of Rogerian therapy, behavioral therapy ranks among the few approaches that have been subjected to controlled studies to test validity and effectiveness. Behavioral therapies, of course, rest on a pedagogical foundation which stresses the fact that the most productive focus for change resides within the individual in interaction with his current environment rather than on his ability to gain insight into the past. Arnold A. Lazarus (1961, 1968; Lazarus and Wilson, 1976) reported on the use of systematic desensitization in groups of patients presenting phobic complaints, frigidity, and impotence. His approach reflects direct transfer of individual-orientated procedures to groups of people with homogeneous problems. Therapy takes place primarily in but not by the group, as interactions are mainly between therapist and members. In contrast to these desensitization groups aimed at achieving specific and objective behavioral outcomes," assertiveness training groups" are increasingly being used to reduce maladaptive anxiety, which prevents people from expressing themselves honestly and spontaneously (Butler, 1965).

Spontaneous expression of basic feelings and emotions are encouraged to provide a "re-educative milieu for the extinctions of maladaptive social anxieties." A variety of methods are employed with basically homogeneous groups, including open and free discussion, role-playing, modeling procedures, behavior rehearsal, and relaxation training. The emphasis generally is directed toward adaptive constructive responses to life situations. Goldstein and Wolpe (1971) describe a group method where five to seven members are seen by two group therapists. Their groups are heterogeneous in sex and age but homogeneous in degree of psychological sophistication and intelligence. Patients are first seen in individual therapy. Five basic therapeutic interventions are used: feedback, modeling, behavior rehearsal, desensitization, and motivational stimulation and social reinforcement.

Existential Group Psychotherapy

The objective of existential psychology is the discovery of the authentic individual. To the existentialists (Buber, 1958; Hora, 1971; Bugental, 1965), group psychotherapy process could be viewed as consisting of a phase of self-discovery and increased self-understanding. Since the group is seen as an existential encounter, the content of the here-and-now is emphasized. The approach seeks to keep away from the habitual way of being of most people, which is to use others as objects. Participants learn to be aware of what they are experiencing and focus primarily on the experiential aspects of communications. Content is of secondary importance. For example, if one patient tells a dream, the group may focus not on the dream but on how and when it was told. It follows that the therapists must be free from artificiality, technicity, and preconceived theoretic dogmatism. There is in this sense a transcendence of the need for technique.

Viktor Frankl (1967) has developed a method of analyzing existence he calls *logotherapy.* Whereas existential analysis represents a kind of diagnosis, logotherapy is a treatment strategy that seeks to create a sense of meaning for the suffering a patient is experiencing. Uniquely, there is no attempt to remove symptoms or deep-seated causes of symptoms. Instead, logotherapy treats the spiritual dimensions of man, helping him to assume a certain freedom and new responsibility to reorient his values regarding his previous problematic behavior. The technique of dereflection seeks to ignore difficult problems, substituting positive alternatives. Paradoxical intention is a technique where the patient deliberately tries to produce the undesired behavior to bring about a reorientation to the problem.

Bioenergetic Therapy

As espoused by Alexander Lowen (1958, 1967, 1971), Bio-energetic therapy approaches problems of human personality through direct involvement of the body in psychoanalytic processes. The method seeks to mobilize body energy through breathing and movement to express feeling and release repressed emotions. The physical work with the body allows direct physical contact between patient and therapist. Although some writers emphasize ways in which group members may facilitate physical release and analytical discussion, it is questionable whether this is in fact a group method.

Primal Scream

Similarly, primal group therapy represents a significant departure from conventional methods, which, according to its originator, Arthur Janov (1970), has 100 percent success with nonpsychotic patients. Indeed, it is claimed that in a relatively short time not only do symptoms disappear, but personality, self-concepts, and even body chemistry undergo lasting changes. Basically the theory holds that primal pain grows in childhood when basic needs and feelings are denied, causing the child to split himself away from unfilled needs and to adopt a facade to please others. The primal scene represents an accumulation of past hurts that have built up to a point which forces the child into a neurotic state. Neurosis is therefore the symbolizing of primal pain, which is a protective shell for the real self against intolerable hurting. Layers of defenses need to be stripped away to express the primal pain and to be freed of the neurotic blocks. Through a series of techniques of working with a patient lying on his back on the floor, the primal experience is recreated through a variety of breathing and screaming techniques. Changes occur with the draining off of psychic pain and the occurrence of psychoanalytic insights.

Primal groups have often been used as a follow-up activity for patients who have had individual therapy. They function mainly to stimulate group participants into new primals. Group size is usually restricted to six or eight patients. There is relatively little interaction as the members vie to "be on the floor" at one and the same time. There is, however, some discussion and sharing of feelings following group sessions. Additional uses for groups in primal experiences are being explored (Freundlich, 1976).

Therapeutic Social Clubs and Communities

In the 1940s Juasha Bierer (1962a; 1962b), the English psychiatrist, encouraged the formation of social clubs made up of patients who were recently discharged from mental institutions. Functioning under the accepted rules of parliamentary procedure, officers were elected, dues collected, and group structures were created to increase patients' skills in social participation. Bierer's philosophy has an impact on current psychiatric thinking, especially in the development of the concept of the "therapeutic community" advanced by Maxwell Jones (1953). Basically, this approach implies the optimal use of the entire milieu for the improvement of the patient's condition within social democratic structures. Less time is spent on individual interviewing and more on group and community meetings, where patients verbalize their feelings freely. In a sense, all end up needing therapy—patients for their problems, and staff to help them "cope with patients' increasing strength and refusal to be led" (Rosenbaum, 1965).

Repressive-Inspirational Groups

The term "repressive-inspirational" has been used extensively to refer to nonanalytic methods of working with groups (Thomas, 1943). Among these the efforts of a variety of self-help groups composed of neurotics, psychotics, alcoholics, drug addicts, obese persons, former criminals, gamblers, and others have been most successful. Characteristically, these groups rely heavily on a supportive subculture as a natural response to common problems. The development of strong group identification, esprit de corps, emotional acceptance, social support, and the sharing of mutual experiences are all critical dimensions in this approach. Among the better-known self-help groups are AA, Daytop, Gamblers Anonymous, and Low's "Will Training." Although these groups are more often self-directed, the preoccupation with "curing" places them among the medical/clinical approaches.

GROUP COUNSELING AND GUIDANCE

Group counseling is not easily separated from the case conference method and group guidance. It seems to have begun with Dr. Richard Allen's (1931) early use of groups in public schools in Providence, Rhode Island, during the 1930s. In his view, group counseling was used to "arouse interests in current educational, vocational and social problems, to develop social attitudes, and to build up a background of occupational information."

It was Allen's practice to establish relationships with students over an extended time period. The case conference method provided the means for students to discuss their personal and social relationships and deal with common problems. Cases were presented to the group to illustrate problems, and each student compared himself with the case discussed. Group members were encouraged to consider the impact of their behavior on others before taking action. The leader never expressed approval or disapproval and did not give any personal opinions. Most contemporary group counselors do not structure their group session around specific cases in this way. Today, group guidance refers primarily to a class or educational experience aimed at imparting educational and vocational information, while group counseling is a group experience emphasizing personal exploration and change. Both are practiced most often in educational settings with relatively normal individuals referred to as clients, counsellees, or students.

Various forms of group counseling will be described as follows: Developmental, Goal-Directed, Problem-Solving, Adlcrian-Teleoanalytic, Functional, Group-Centered, and Family Group Counseling.

Developmental Approaches

Clarence Mahler (1969) defines group counseling as a social experience that deals with the developmental problems and attitudes of individuals in a secure environment. Basically, the concerns and problems encountered are centered on "the developmental growth tasks" of members rather than on pathological blocks and distortions of reality. The chief goal is to develop relationships that will enable the counselor to meet the important developmental needs of students and help in the identity-seeking processes. Groups vary in size, degree of voluntary participation, and openness of membership. Meeting with the groups as often as three times a week, the counselor develops and uses a variety of exercises, experiences, and techniques to facilitate involvement. In contrast to group discussion, Mahler's group counseling pays particular attention to the feelings, thoughts, and beliefs of members.

Goal-Directed Methods

Merle Ohlsen (1970) provides a goal-directed approach to group counseling that is concerned with helping reasonably healthy people solve their problems and apply what is learned in their daily lives. In his view, it is essential that specific goals be developed as early as possible for each client. There should be a commitment by clients to discuss their problems openly, to change their behavior based on mutual expectations, and to help others to change their behavior as well. Ohlsen maintains that counselors should be free to accept for counseling only those who he reasonably feels can be helped. The group counselor is responsible for developing and maintaining effective treatment relationships in accordance with mutually specified expectations and goals. Therapeutic potential is realized best when clients are committed to change, when they act responsibly in maintaining a therapeutic climate that fosters acceptance, attraction, feelings of belonging, trust, and acceptance of group norms.

Problem-Solving Approach

Bernard Kinnick (1971) has presented a problem-solving approach where discussion is utilized as an essential feature of the group experience. The primary purpose is to help the student learn the necessary skills to improve his ability to solve his own problems through experience in group deliberation. The method is used with normal but "troubled" individuals. Counselees are helped to achieve increased maturity and sociality, acceptance of reality, adaptability, and responsibility for self. Participants select their own problem areas to be discussed and share information, knowledge, and ideas according to the problem-solving norms of the group. An essential aspect of this method is the leader's democratic group-centered style and the creation of a friendly atmosphere. The method seeks to foster positive human relations, helping students to gain understanding of and respect for each others feelings, needs, and viewpoints.

Adlerian (Teleoanalytic) Counseling

Adler's individual psychology has become the basis of a group method of counseling employed by Rudolph Dreikurs and Manford Sonstegard (1968), which is referred to as Adlerian teleoanalytic family counseling. The method is used in a number of centers for parent education and childrearing throughout the country. It is also being used by school counselors in dealing with various school-related problems of children. According to this view, man is seen as a social being whose every action has a purpose. He is "wholistic" in nature. The teleological concept emphasize self-determination, while strong desires for belonging put a premium on social relationships. The principal phases of treatment include developing relationships, analysis, interpretation, and re-education. Uniquely, the group counseling method is used in a public hearing type of setting. This self-disclosure in open settings and lack of "abuse of privacy" represents an area of learning where all sessions are "training" sessions.

In family group counseling, a number of persons are participants in addition to the family members. Interpersonal dynamics are exposed and explained to all participants. Suggestions are offered for dealing with problems. Children are counseled before groups of parents. Parents' problems in turn may be discussed before other parents, neighbors, teachers, and clergy to "change prevailing concepts of community."

In children's groups, directive techniques are used to control behavior. In the main, the natural or logical consequences of the child's behavior is seen as a sufficient reinforcement schedule to correct behavior. Groups are open in membership but are usually limited to ten to twelve children. Intimate feelings and conflicts are aired within the group, and an effort is made to affect attitudes and values. In group interactions, each child expresses his goals, intentions, and social orientation.

Functional Approach

George Gazda (1968, 1976) has advanced an eclectic approach to counseling based on principles of learning from behavioral therapists. Group counseling is done basically with normal persons where there are a variety of concerns "which are not delimitating to the point requiring personality change." The group is organized to facilitate improved personal adjustment where group interaction provides the opportunity to learn and unlearn certain attitudes and behavior. Counseling focuses on conscious thought and behavior, permissiveness, orientation to reality, catharisis, mutual trust, caring, acceptance, and support. The counselor also assists in the process of generalizing the client's anxiety-producing expression, assuming an anonymous role which generally represents other significant persons. One unique technique is the use of "trial" groups to test out group compositions prior to final grouping. The method has been used in dealing with reading difficulties, peer group conflicts, interpersonal differences, underachievers, and marital problems.

Group-Centered Counseling

The Rogerian school of nondirective, client-centered therapy has formed the basis for a group-centered counseling method advanced by Nicholas Hobbs (1951). The use of techniques seems to be of least importance in this method. There is an implicit confidence in the capacity of individuals to grow toward self-actualization health and homeostatis. The nondirective school emphasizes, moreover, that every individual has a drive toward health, growth, and personality maturation. The emphasis is on the "client" rather than the "patient." According to this approach, the individual who tests his needs in a group will find that he can get from others the things he wants only when he has developed a relationship with them that will stimulate them to give him what he needs. Through his actions, the counselor serves as a catalyst who conveys a quality of congruence, a sense of confidence and acceptance of the ability of the client with the help of the group to resolve his own problems.

According to Hobbs, the counselor cannot be "both mentor and therapist." He requires nothing of the client other than that he work out his own solutions to his problems. Similarly, Gordon (1964) points out that people fear being changed, influenced, evaluated, or rejected. Giving information and making interpretations enhance these fears, whereas the ability to listen with understanding is essential to convey acceptance. Group leaders do, however, serve a linking function relating the various contributions of members to each other. Walter Lifton's (1968) approach calls for a more active leadership both in teaching needed group roles and in labeling behaviors to help provide group members with cues to use as they take on new roles.

Family Group Counseling

Fullmer (1971) has advanced a method of group counseling termed "family group counseling," which is a procedure based on the assumption that a person's behavior is a reflection of his family relationships. Basically, the purpose of the method is to utilize the family patterns to bring about new forms of behavior among individuals with school-related problems. On the premise that behavior is formed within the family relationships, various combinations of families are brought together in an effort to utilize the power of the family to generate new behavior. Counselors seek to modify behavior through group processes, changing patterns of reinforcement through interrupting, intervening, and influencing all action taken in family group consultation. Individual behavior is learned in the family group and "exported" into the social system. Fullmer found this to be an effective method of training group counselors.

PSYCHOLOGICAL SELF-AWARENESS

Contemporary group methods have been dominated by the rapid growth and development of a range of new and dramatic methods alternately labeled as sensitivity training, encounter groups, sensory awareness, and marathons. Collectively, these developments are seen to make up the human potential movement, inasmuch as they are designed to enhance personal functioning through self-awareness.

Earlier influences on the development of sensitivity and encounter groups stemmed directly from the work of Leland Bradford, Ronald Lippitt, and Kenneth Benne (1964; Back, 1973). It was largely an outcome of an action research effort conducted under the direction of Kurt Lewin for the Connecticut State Interracial Commission in training leadership for combating racial and religious prejudices in communities. This led to the creation of the National Training Laboratories in 1947. Lewin's concept of creating "here-and-now" data, analyzing it, and using feedback are among some of the basic essentials that have continued through to the present.

In earlier years those who were most active were social psychologists and field theorists interested in group processes, group dynamics, and behavioral skills. Their focus was on helping people to understand groups better and improve the ways in which they worked in groups. Later, clinical psychologists, industrial psychologists, and psychiatrists were attracted to sensitivity training, and the goals shifted to a more individualized orientation. Today sensitivity training more often refers to that part of the group involvement which stresses personal growth and self-actualization.

Although they may vary considerably, the more prominent group methods discussed here generally share this emphasis. More often, all are aimed at providing opportunities for basically healthy people to engage in new and different relationships, to learn experientially new sources of satisfaction and personal enhancement. Among the methods to be considered are: Laboratory Methods and T groups; Group Relations Conferences and S groups; Encounter Groups; Marathons; Sensory Awareness; Gestalt Therapy Groups; and *est* groups.

Laboratory Methods and T Groups

In general, the laboratory method can be viewed as a self-study process often used by organizations where the focus is on "expanded consciousness" and more effective personal functioning in groups and organizations. Characteristically, it takes people out of their usual environment, away from their day-to-day preoccupations, to interact in conference with others. The method stresses expanded consciousness, a spirit of inquiry, authenticity in interpersonal relations, and collaborative conception of authority. Goals of laboratory training such as are related to understanding group processes and developing skills in dealing with organizational behavior are incidental to the sensitivity experience (Golembiewski and Blumberg, 1970; Lakin, 1972).

Sensitivity training may be viewed as a more specific aspect of the laboratory method, which deals directly with personal and interpersonal matters and only indirectly with group processes and organizational concerns. Sensitivity training is not usually seen as therapy, although, as it is more difficult to distinguish between normal and psychiatric populations, the methods have been applied increasingly in group psychotherapy.

Although used in many ways, the T group or "Training Group" is often used as a single sensitivity training group experience lasting over a period of a few hours as a part of a larger laboratory conference, which includes other kinds of "meetings" as well. The group, usually composed of ten to fifteen persons, provides for unstructured learning opportunities. The role of the trainer is not to provide the group with any structure or agenda but to help the group learn from immediate interpersonal experiences. The members' reactions to the ambiguous unstructured situation provide the main data for learning. The techniques of the trainer include role-playing, guided group fantasies, confrontation, and feedback.

Gesard Eagon (1970), outlined the major variables operative in groups organized for interpersonal growth and established a methodology for a particular kind of sensitivity training group he termed "contract-interpersonal-growth group." Basically, the contract group differs from the traditional T group in that there is a high degree of visibility of structure as opposed to ambiguity. Participants are very much involved in understanding what the experience is all about, in the determination of goals, structure, and so on. The leader promotes the contract by "modeling the behavior called for by the contract" as a leader-member. He is a prime example of self-disclosure and self-examination, and characteristically expresses his own feelings in the group.

Jack and Lorrain Gibb (1970) have developed a form of growth group experience that emphasizes role freedom. TORI refers to the individual need for trust, openness, realization, and interdependence. The group experience seeks to meet these basic needs. A basic concept is that the most effective leader is the person who is able to enter the group in a "role-free" manner. The TORI leader seeks to respond spontaneously without consciously censoring or filtering his responses to be helpful, relevant, supportive, confronting, or effective. The goal is to be a truly personal person, free of role demands and expectations.

Group Relations Conference and S Groups

In many ways the Group Relations Conference parallels the laboratory method. First developed by A. K. Rice (1975), an organizational consultant with the Tavistock Institute in London, the conference was seen as a learning model designed to provide opportunities and construct situations where members could study their own behavior as it happened. Staff developed a program and set patterns of behavior, which encouraged experimentation by reducing the need for members to resort to conventional defenses against dealing with their interpersonal hostilities and rivalries. Hence, the ways in which anxiety is generated, acted out, or controlled becomes part of the learning experience.

"S" groups, or Study Groups, are to the Group Relations Conference what the T groups are to Laboratory Training. Consisting of about eight to twelve members, led by a staff consultant, the emphasis is on examining and understanding group processes. The task of the consultant, unlike the trainer, is to interpret group behavior to the group. In the conference, a series of study groups are offered, along with the "large group" conference membership, intergroup exercises, lectures, and application groups to consider the relevance of conference learning to normal situations.

Carl Goldberg (1970) has described a variation of sensitivity training called the process group, which is a direct modification of the Tavistock Group Relations Conference. Process groups are used to help people become aware and and appreciative of attitudes and behaviors they normally experience as dysfunctional. The leader or consultant focuses heavily on the "group mentality" (Bion, 1959) and observes and makes statements indicative of the unconscious passions being experienced. Psychodrama, exercises, and games are used to increase personal awareness and resolve conflicts. In contrast to therapy groups, process groups are usually short-term group experiences. A greater emphasis is placed on alerting participants to feelings of uncertainty, frustration, anger, alienation, anxiety, and other discomforts growing out of the group interaction.

Encounter Groups

There is considerable variation among encounter group approaches, although all who conduct such groups appear to agree that personal growth, change, and deeply felt experiences are more important than the study of group process or anything else that smacks of theory (Schultz, 1971; Solomon and Berzon, 1972; Buckhout, 1971). Encounter groups focus on personal growth rather than therapy, although the distinction between the two is blurred. Burton states, for example:

> Those whom society labeled "average" or "normal" frequently resented their being placed in that existential limbo, resented the fact that their alienation, their loneliness, their despair, and their anxiety were ignored *because* they were normal. The normal have at times even produced symptoms to gain the center of the stage—the existential neurosis—but the entire question of the meaning of the flowering symptom is now a complex and confused one. A psychic symptom is today no longer a symptom but a sign that life lacks joy [1970, p. 9].

The primary emphasis in encounter groups is on confrontation. Groups consist of about six to twelve members meeting together regularly, with the focus on self-disclosure, self-revelation, and perceptual feedback. Group structure is at a minimum, and sensory awareness techniques are utilized. Rules emphasize spontaneity, honest reaction (rather than understanding), concentration on the "here-and-now," and feedback. In short, the aim is to provide unprogrammed, spontaneous contact without "countering" or maneuvering, filtering, or distorting.

Albert Ellis (1970) in his experimentation with various kinds of encounter group methods developed what he calls the "Rational Encounter Group," an approach that is a more structured experience deliberately weighted to emphasize cognitive as well as emotional involvement. It differs from other encounter methods in that it treats disturbed patients as well as normal persons. Members are encouraged to interact at intimate interactional levels. Ground rules are quite free, permitting everything short of inflicting physical harm on one another. The leader's confrontation tactics are quite apparent as the group is encouraged to "smoke out anyone who does not bring up any problem for detailed discussion."

Marathons

The goals of marathon groups seem in many instances to be personal change rather than group training, and for this reason they may be seen as one of the group therapies (Ruitenbeek, 1970, 1971; Kilman and Sotile, 1976). The marathon group is distinguished mainly in terms of its time-extended session and represents a radical departure from traditional approaches. In its standard form, groups meet nonstop for periods of twenty-four hours or longer. Characteristically, the leaders' orientations are found to differ considerably, and co-leaders are used quite often in the marathon, which helps relieve strain on the workers and add to creativity.

The psychological intimacy which comes with constant interaction provides unique opportunities for honest encounters where subjective truths are shared. The orientation is basically ahistorical. According to George Bach (1966), marathonians should want to bring about personal change before they are admitted into groups. Certain rules are employed during the marathon, such as remaining together throughout the experience, maintaining confidentiality, focusing on the here-and-now, and so forth. Elizabeth Mintz (1971) has shown how physical fatigue exerts a definite influence on the group functioning of the members. The method also generates considerable interpersonal feeling, which may be continued outside the group.

Gestalt Therapy

The goal of Gestalt Therapy (Perls, 1969; Levitsky and Perls,

1971; Ruitenbeek, 1970; Fagan and Shepherd, 1970) is to help people break through their psychic impasses or "incomplete gestalts" by becoming more completely aware of themselves in the present moment. Based on a growth-oriented rather than a sickness-oriented model, clients are helped to become aware of the *what* and *how* of their existence. Self-awareness is seen as a powerful force helping persons to take more responsibility for themselves, mobilize their energies, and achieve genuine contact with others. The strong emphasis on the here-and-now and on confrontation places it among the nonanalytic existential forms of treatment.

As Frederick Perls, the acknowledged leader of the gestalt approaches, states,

> Any time you use the words *now* and *how* and become aware of this you grow. Each time you use the question why, you diminish in stature. You bother yourself with false, unnecessary information. You only feed the computer, the intellect. And the intellect is the whore of intelligence. It's a drag on your life [Ruitenbeek, 1970, p. 145].

Gestalt techniques conform to certain well-recognized guidelines and rules. Communication occurs in the "I-Thou" framework where "no gossiping" is permitted. Similarly, direct "I" language is used to increase attention on one's own behavior. Clients take responsibility for themselves and are discouraged from "helping," advising others, or imputing meaning to behavior. Among gestalt games are dialogues between the "top dog" and "underdog" parts of oneself, imagining and boasting about secrets, and rehearsing social roles. In dream work, individuals re-experience all parts of the dream, the objects as well as the persons.

Although feedback is used, the method generally makes little use of group processes. Most often, the group's structure resembles a "broken wagon wheel," where interactions are directed primarily to the therapist. Also, the individual being treated is often placed in the "hot seat," with the group acting as an audience for individual work.

Recent attention has been given to a more focused use of groups in gestalt therapy. Erving and Miriam Polster (1974) have described experiments in reaching out to natural groups such as "indigenous" coffeehouse audiences utilizing large group "encounter" meetings to stimulate individual creativity and personal awareness. Joseph Zinker (1977) has developed a set of principles to govern gestalt group processes. He stresses the need to maintain attention on the moment-to-moment experiences of the group as a whole; to develop group awareness as well as individual awareness; to sustain active contact between participants; and to introduce experiments in encouraging interactional experiences.

Sensory Awareness Groups

Pioneered largely by Bernard Gunther (1968) at Esalen, sensory awareness is a method for reorienting the individual to his earlier, freer life state prior to the acculturation that shaped, restricted, and otherwise influenced the individual's ability to discriminate his sensory awareness. The goal is to reawaken and fully develop the organism in all its senses to rediscover the joy of being. A variety of sensory experiences are programmed for members, which focus on learning to relax, experiencing and becoming aware of the sources of tensions, identifying bodily aspects of the tensions, and "letting go," that is, to experience the tension fully without trying to avoid it. The leader takes a fairly active role giving instructions, demonstrating, and assisting members to experience. Group "games" are introduced to accent interpersonal relations and provide for shared reactions to experiences. Usually this method is not viewed as a separate treatment in group method but rather is used as an adjunct to the other group methods used in education, work, religious groups, and so forth.

est Groups

Erhard Seminar Training (Greene, 1976; R. March, 1975) is yet another method that has entered the pop-psychological movement. Originated by Werner Erhard, a former encyclopedia salesman, *est* seems to represent an admixture of ideas from Scientology, Mind Dynamics, Silva Mind Control, Zen, Transcendental Meditation, Hypnosis, Rolfing, the Bible, Esalen, and others. In general, *est* training is aimed at helping people rid themselves of faulty belief systems and misconceptions about themselves and to get "it"—that is, to experience life's ups and downs to the fullest. Hand-picked trainers conduct a variety of training programs, such as the *est* Standard Training, which consists of sixty hours of training directed at no fewer than 250 people gathered in a hotel ballroom without bodily comforts and diversions of any kind. Utilizing confronting authoritarian tactics, the trainer lectures (gives data) to stimulate the sharing of beliefs and information (sharing) and providing meditative exercises (the process). *est* is staffed primarily by volunteers, *est* graduates, who spend a considerable amount of time recruiting people for training programs throughout the country. An advisory board of respected psychologists, psychiatrists, and well-known personalities advise Erhard, who is the acknowledged guru of *est* and the head of the corporation.

SOCIAL WORK APPROACHES

Social group work ranks among the earliest practical efforts to realize the potentials inherent in the small group experience to achieve socially desirable ends. Tracing its origins to the early social reform movements, which arose to combat the dehumanizing influences of the Industrial Revolution, it sought to help people improve their social conditions as well as their personal lives. The early principles of citizen involvement, democratic participation and association, social action, cultural pluralism, personal growth, and social development were all important in the development of the group work method. Although priorities given to such values varied over the years, the sense of social commitment persists, accounting for social group work's uniqueness among the group methods considered above.

To be sure, caseworkers as well as community organizers employ group methods in their work with families, task-centered groups, and committees. Also, "generic" models of practice are being advanced, which tend to diffuse traditional distinctions between methods and integrate them into comprehensive practice models. Increasingly, references to "social group work" are giving way to the more generic emphasis on "social work with groups." Yet social group work's long-standing commitment to developing a viable group method has produced a wealth of experience that could come only from such a specialized focus. And it is this specialized body of experience with groups that has enhanced social work's credibility in offering professional services to people in groups.

Within recent years, differing views of social group workers have been identified and conceptually refined, resulting in heightened attention to distinctive "approaches," "models," and "theories" of practice (Roberts and Northen, 1976). Although it is not altogether clear how the conceptual frameworks reflect actual practice, some of the distinctive categories may be briefly described under the following headings: Traditional Group Work Approaches—Developmental, Social Action, Functional; Remedial Approaches; Interactional Approaches; and Emerging Generic Models.

Traditional Social Group Approaches

Perhaps the most significant characteristic of the traditional group approach is the dual emphasis placed on helping people to enhance their own well-being and to participate in societal processes that eventuate in changing social conditions for the common good. Hence, while a group's experiences are designed to help facilitate the normal growth and development of its members, to actualize individual potentials and provide constructive educational and recreational opportunities, the small group is simultaneously viewed as the primarily vehicle for inculcating democratic values, social consciousness, and social responsibility and for providing opportunities to participate in social action efforts to bring about change. In traditional group work the worker functions as an "agent of the agency" to advance agency-determined goals and objectives. The worker utilizes a variety of interpersonal and programming skills to influence group processes and democratically help the individuals and the group as a whole to achieve commonly determined goals (Newstetter et al., 1938; Coyle, 1948; Wilson and Ryland, 1949; Kaiser, 1959; Konopka, 1963; Middleman, 1968; Klein, 1970; Trecker, 1972).

The traditional orientation is clearly represented in the *Developmental* approach described by Emmanuel Tropp (1969, 1977). Basically, this view holds that the most effective means for achieving social growth is through participation in self-directing groups, where members have opportunities to achieve common group goals and objectives. The model focuses on two principal goals: first, to help people enhance their social functioning by engaging with others in the pursuit of mutual interests and concerns, and second, to help groups find ways to achieve purposes more effectively and responsibly. The group is taken to be the primary unit of service by the worker, who is the primary helping agent. Members are helped to arrive at meaningful group goals based on common interests, concerns, or life circumstances. The group in turn is helped to use interpersonal resources most effectively to achieve these goals. And in the process matured social functioning and individual self-actualization are promoted. Throughout, clients are seen to be free, responsible, and capable of self-realization. The approach is humanistic—one human relating to another; developmental—people continually moving forward; and, phenomological—focusing on the "here-and-now" realities. Insofar as the group medium is seen by Tropp to be humanistic, there is little room left for the study-diagnosis-treatment processing of people.

The *Social Action* approach, with its emphasis on social change and reform, constitutes another established traditional orientation. Social group work goals include the enhancement of individual social functioning through group experience, the development of mature functioning groups and the involvement of such groups in actions aimed at social betterment. There has been concern that the emphasis on action for social betterment has been neglected. As Sirls, et al.

(1967) put it, "Social group work, in practice, cannot be considered social group work unless the members of the group have the opportunity and are encouraged to work to bring about change in their social environment" (p. 5).

Although the position stressed the responsibility of the group worker to help bring about change in the community and society, it did not neglect individual functioning either developmentally or remedially. Examples of this kind of effort may be found in work with block clubs, where the groups can be used as a force for overcoming feelings of powerless, hopelessness, and despair. This is achieved through effective group action, which enhances self-esteem while at the same time dealing with concrete environmental problems (Vattano, 1972). Other group workers have, in a similar vein, helped to organize wards of patients in hospitals to take action to change their own living conditions for the better (Jacobs, 1964). In the process of carrying out a common social action, dramatic individual changes often occur, which are in every sense therapeutic for the individual participant.

The *Functional* approach constitutes still another contribution to mainstream group work. Based largely on the writings of Helen Phillips (1954, 1957) and the "functional" school of social work, this approach places great emphasis on the need for a "clearly defined and agreed upon social purpose," which represents a blend of professional social work purposes, societal sanctions and approval, and agency or organization purposes. The agency function as structured to reflect societal values, goals, and direction is utilized as the chief dynamic in the provision of service. Drawing on Otto Rank's concept of the human will as a creative organizing force on people's lives, the individual himself is seen to be an active participant in promoting his own growth and development. Emphasis is also given to the use of the "present moment," which is the pivotal point where the worker interacts with the group to help members use their present relationships to learn from the past and plan actively for the future. The functional approach places responsibility on the worker to free individuals and the group to select the nature for change and growth. Members are helped to take responsibility for their own choices, to assess results, and to use their assessment for further action and growth. Group members are also helped to use the group process in identifying and working toward achieving group goals. Key social work skills as outlined by Phillips include the following: skill in use of agency function; skill in communicating feelings; skill in use of time to exploit the present reality for group use; and skill in the use of group relationship (Ryder, 1976).

Remedial Approaches

Alternately referred to as "rehabilitative" or "treatment" models, remedial approaches focus primarily on helping individuals cope with problems of psychological, social, and cultural adjustment. They are based largely on the medical or clinical approaches where the emphasis is placed on study, diagnosing, and treating clients who are experiencing problems of adjustment in their personal and social relationships. The individual is viewed as the primary target for change, which is accomplished through carefully selected group experiences. The worker is seen as a change agent who is responsible for guiding the group through treatment stages that take place in and through the group. The group is both the means and the context for change. In this model, the agency is perceived clearly as a treatment setting in which groups are formed to treat individuals in accordance with specific treatment objectives. Psychoanalytic concepts figured prominently in some of the earlier writings of Redl (1944), Slavson (1943), Scheidlinger (1956), Sloan (1953), Fisher (1949), Konopka (1952), and Garland and Frey (1970). The more recent influence of social role theory, sociobehavioral theory, and ego psychology are evident in the work of Robert Vinter (1965, 1967) and his associates from the University of Michigan. According to Vinter, who is most often identified with the remedial approach, "treatment goals" are critical. His practice principles stress the need for the worker to develop specific goals for each individual in the group, which are in turn related to group goals. In addition, the worker helps the group develop appropriate values, norms, and so on in accordance with the worker's treatment objectives.

Charles Garvin and Paul Glasser (1977) have advanced an *Organizational* model, which builds on the preventative and rehabilitative practice principles. The individual is seen as the primary focus of change, although environmental changes with and through the group is also sought. Goals are developed in more or less precise operational terms and are explicated through the use of contracts. Basic to this approach is the placing of the individual not only in the context of the group but also in the social environment. Two ideal functional types of organizations are identified where people being served as seen to be in "transition" or in "social conflict." These types are further subdivided into subfunctions: social transition, including anomie reduction and socialization, and social conflict, including social control and resocialization. The worker, who is viewed as a mediator, carries out assessment, planning, executing, and evaluating of stages of treatment. Intervention consists of assessment and selection of targets, strategies, and techniques, which are used differentially in each of the organizational contexts.

Interactional Approach

Still another major approach in group work practice dominates the current scene. William Schwartz (1976, 1977; Schwartz and Zalba, 1971) has developed the theoretical rationale for an interactional model of practice based largely on social system concepts and field theory. In his view, social group work is practiced relative to the different social systems in which the worker engages as part of some kind of social service. The worker functions in terms of a kind of "triangular array of interacting forces," operating between the individual client, the group, and the larger social system. In contrast to some of the other methods, the worker does not predetermine goals for group intervention. Instead, goals are arrived at mutually through the use of the contract. The chief force for change comes from the group, which is seen as a "mutual aid" society. In the interactional model, the worker is neither an enabler nor a change agent, but a mediator or resource person helping individuals and groups negotiate the complex social systems in which they are implicated.

Emerging Generic Models

With increased interest in conceptualizing practice models, some writers have stressed certain underlying features of group work practice that have been recognized as ongoing components of practice. Mary Louise Somers (1976), for example, points out how *problem-solving* characterizes the varying formulations of social group work practice. Whether the focus is on the individual or on society, problem-solving serves as a unifying force over a span of some fifty years. Hence, whereas the early problem-solving activities were turned to citizen participation, education, personal growth through participation, and social responsibility, the same kind of problem-solving was later turned to deal with personal conflicts and problems.

Similarly, a socialization model has been described by Elizabeth McBroom (1976) as an "inevitable component of all theories of social work with groups and of practice based on those theories." According to the socialization model, the worker functions as an agent of socialization, teaching, modeling, and assisting in the learning of effective social roles. Clients, on the other hand, are expected to internalize newly learned expectations, modify self-conceptions, take on new roles, and be actively motivated to participate in social process.

Drawing upon a symbolic interactionist perspective, the critical factor is seen to be the emergence of the social self growing out of the interaction between the individual and significant others. Viewed as a lifelong process, this model can be applied at all stages in the life cycle.

Still another theoretical approach is described by Helen Northen (1976), who emphasizes the psychosocial aspects of social work practice drawing heavily from Hollis's psychosocial therapeutic view of casework as well as from mainstream group work. Its basic concepts can be traced to psychoanalytically oriented ego psychology, knowledge of problem-solving, and the dynamic theories of interdependence of individuals, small groups, and community networks. Insofar as the emphasis takes into account both psychological and social forces and interactions between individuals, small groups, and the larger environment, the approach is systems-oriented. The main overall focus of this approach is on enhancing psychosocial functioning, which encompasses prevention and enhancement as well as restoration or rehabilitation. Based on a psychosocial diagnosis of individuals, families, and groups in the context of their social situations, a treatment plan is developed that spells out persons to be served and the modes of treatment to be given. Full and active participation of clients throughout this process is essential. Treatment is differentiated according to individual needs and the nature and functioning of groups. The small growth-oriented group is deemed to be an appropriate unit of service to the degree that client needs can be met through interaction with others.

Changing social work practice in the 1960s helped stimulate additional methods in social work that seek to integrate individual and group approaches into more generic models. Garvin and his associates (1976) have written about a *task-centered social treatment* model, derived from Reid and Epstein's casework model, which is equally adaptable to both individuals and groups. The focus of help is on working on a "task" that reflects the clients' immediate desire to achieve some goals as well as the need to find means to alleviate the larger problem. Help is usually brief and time-limited, with interventions directed at alleviating only those specific problems mutually contracted for by the clients and the worker. A research monitoring process is also employed, serving as a basis for progressive modifications of the model. Drawing from Vinter, three types of interventions are utilized to help members accomplish their tasks: direct, indirect, and extragroup.

Time-limited crises intervention (Parad, 1965; Strickler and Allgeyer, 1976; Parad, Selby, and Quinlan, 1976) constitutes another generic approach where theoretical notions about individual crises are carried over to families and groups. Two goals are pursued in this model: first, to minimize negative consequences of disruptive stress, and second, to help affected persons mobilize psychological, interpersonal, and social resources to cope adaptively with the effects of stress. The aim is actively to influence the psychosocial functioning of individuals, families, and small groups during periods of acute disequilibrium. A warm, emphathic "reach and find" approach is used by the worker to help a wide range of families and natural or formed groups wherever individuals are experiencing crises in one form or another. Because of time limitations, the group process is usually accelerated, with the worker taking on a directive role "cutting through resistances" to maintain a goal-oriented focus and helping members find solutions within tight time limitations.

However one chooses to differentiate among social group work methods, clearly knowledge, goals, and techniques are often commonly shared with medical, counseling, and psychological self-awareness approaches. Some of the similarities are based on adherence to similar psychoanalytic, behavior-modification, or existential orientations. Others stem from commonly emphasized goals, such as self-actualization, socialization, development, problem-solving, or therapy. Finally, techniques from psychodrama, Tavistock, gestalt, transactional analysis, sensitivity training, encounter, and others have been selectively incorporated into some social group work practice.

The degree to which this has occurred, however, may not be so easily determined, for it is as true today as in the past that the day-to-day work of group workers generally goes unreported in the literature. Thus, while model-building has a place in the development of practice, it is not clear just what benefits will be derived as models are continually refined in the absence of a careful examination of what is actually done in practice.

REFERENCES

ALLEN, R., 1931. "A Group Guidance Curriculum in the Senior High School," *Education*, Vol. 52.

ANTHONY, E. J., 1971. "The History of Psychotherapy," in *Comprehensive Group Psychotherapy*, H. I. Kaplan and B. J. Sadock, Eds. Baltimore: Williams & Wilkins.

BACH, G. R., 1966. "The Marathon Group: Intensive Practice of Intimate Interaction," *Psychological Reports*, Vol. 18.

BACK, K. W., 1973. *Beyond Words: The Story of Sensitivity Training and the Encounter Movement*. Baltimore: Penguin Books.

BENNE, K. D., 1964. "History of the T Group in the Laboratory Setting", in *T Group Theory and the Laboratory Method*, L. P. Bradford, J. R. Gibb, and K. D. Benne, eds. New York: Wiley.

BERNE, E., 1961. *Transactional Analysis in Psychotherapy: A Systematic Individual and Social Psychiatry.* New York: Grove Press.

——, 1964. *Games People Play: The Psychology of Human Relations.* New York: Grove Press.

——, *1966. Principles of Group Treatment.* New York: Oxford University Press.

BIERER, J., 1962a, "The Day Hospital: Therapy in a Guided Democracy," *Mental Hospital,* Vol. 13.

——, ed., 1962b. *Therapeutic Social Clubs.* London: H. K. Lewis.

BLATNER, H. A., 1973. *Acting-In: Practical Applications of Psychodramatic Methods.* New York: Springer.

BION, W. R., 1959. *Experience in Groups.* New York: Basic Books.

BUBER, M., 1958. *I-Thou.* New York: Scribner's.

BUCKHOUT, R., et al., 1971. "The Encounter Group Boom," in *Toward Social Change: A Handbook of Those Who Will,* R. Buckhout and 81 concerned Berkeley Students, eds. New York: Harper & Row.

BUGENTAL, J. F. T., 1965. *The Search for Authenticity: An Existential Analytic Approach to Psychotherapy.* New York: Holt, Rinehart & Winston.

BURROW, T., 1927. "The Group Method of Analysis," *The Psychoanalytic Review,* Vol. 14, No. 3.

BURTON, A., ed., 1970. *Encounter: The Theory and Practice of Encounter Groups.* San Francisco: Jossey-Bass.

BUTLER, P. E., 1965. "Techniques of Assertive Training in Groups," *International Journal of Group Psychotherapy,* Vol. 26, No. 3.

CORSINI, R., 1957. *Methods of Groups Psychotherapy.* New York: McGraw-Hill.

COYLE, G. L., 1948. *Group Work with American Youth.* New York: Harper & Brothers.

DREIKURS, R., 1957. "Group Psychotherapy from the Point of View of Adlerian Psychology," *International Journal of Group Psychotherapy,* Vol. 12, No. 4.

——, 1971. "Early Experiments with Group Psychotherapy: A Historical Review," in *Group Therapy Today: Styles, Methods, and Techniques,* H. M. Ruitenbeek, ed. New York: Atherton Press.

——, and R. CORSINI, 1954. "Twenty Years of Group Psychotherapy," *American Journal of Psychiatry* Vol. 110, No. 2.

——, and M. SONSTEGARD, 1968, "The Adlerian on Teleoanalytic Approach," in *Basic Approaches to Group Psychotherapy and Group Counseling,* G. M. Gazda, ed. Springfield, Ill.: Charles C. Thomas.

EAGON, G., 1970. *Encounter: Growth Processes for Interpersonal Growth.* Belmont, Cal.: Brooks/Cole, Wadsworth.

ELLIS, A., 1970. "A Weekend of Rational Encounter," in *Encounter: The Theory and Practice of Encounter Groups,* A. Burton, ed. San Francisco: Jossey-Bass.

EZRIEL, H., 1950. "A Psychoanalytic Approach to Group Treatment," *British Journal of Medical Psychology*, Vol. 23.

——, 1952. "Notes on Psychoanalytic Group Therapy: Interpretation and Research," *Psychiatry*, Vol. 15, No 2.

FAGAN, J., and I. L. SHEPHERD, 1970. *What Is Gestalt Therapy?* New York: Harper & Row.

——, R. D. SMITH, and R. J. TIMMS, 1968. "Three Views of an Incident at a Marathon," *Voices*, Vol. 4, No. 3.

FISHER, R., 1949. "Contributions of Group Work in Psychiatric Hospitals," *The Group*, Vol. 12, No. 1.

FOULKES, S. H., 1948. *Introduction to Group-Analytic Psychotherapy*. London: William Heinemann.

——, 1965. *Therapeutic Group Analysis.* New York: International Universities Press.

—— and E. J. ANTHONY, 1957. *Group Psychotherapy: The Psychoanalytic Approach.* London: Penguin Books.

FRANKL, V. E., 1967. *Psychotherapy and Existentialism, Selected Papers on Logotherapy.* New York: Simon & Schuster.

FREUNDLICH, D., 1976. "Primal Experience Groups: A Flexible Structure," *International Journal of Group Psychotherapy*, Vol. 26, No. 1.

FULLMER, D. W., 1971. *Counseling: Group Theory and System.* Scranton, Pa.: International Textbook.

GARLAND, J., and L. A. FREY, 1970. "Applications of Stages of Group Development to Groups in Psychiatric Settings," in *Further Exploration in Group Work*, S. Bernstein, ed. Boston: Boston University School of Social Work.

GARVIN, C. H., and P. D. GLASSER, 1977. "Social Group Work: The Organizational and Environmental Approach," *Encyclopedia of Social Work*, Vol. II. New York: National Association of Social Workers.

——, W. REID, and L. EPSTEIN, 1976. "A Task-Centered Approach," in *Theories of Social Work with Groups*, R. W. Roberts and H. Northen, eds. New York: Columbia University Press.

GAZDA, G. M., 1968. "A Functional Approach to Group Counseling," in *Basic Approaches to Group Psychotherapy and Group Counseling*, G. M. Gazda, ed. Springfield, Ill.: Charles C. Thomas.

——, 1976. *Theories and Methods of Group Counseling in the Schools.* Springfield, Ill.: Charles C. Thomas.

GIBB, J. R., and L. M. GIBB, 1970. "Role Freedom in a TORI Group," in *Encounter, A. Burton, ed. San Francisco: Jossey-Bass.*

GLASSER, W., 1965. *Reality Therapy: A New Approach to Psychiatry.* New York: Harper & Row.

——, 1969. *Schools Without Failure.* New York: Harper & Row.

GOLDBERG, C., 1970. *Encounter Group Sensitivity and Training Experience.* New York: Science House.

GOLDMAN, G., 1957. "Some Applications of Harry Stack Sullivan's Theories to Group Psychotherapy," *International Journal of Group Psychotherapy*, Vol. 7, No. 4.

GOLDSTEIN, A., and J. WOLPE, 1971. "Behavior Therapy in Groups," in *Comprehensive Group Psychotherapy*, H. I. Kaplan and B. J. Sadock, eds. Baltimore: Williams & Wilkins.

GOLEMBIEWSKI, R., and A. BLUMBERG, eds., 1970. *Sensitivity Training and the Laboratory Approach.* Itasca, Ill.: Peacock.

GORDON, T., 1964. "The Functioning of the Group-Centered Leader," in *Perspectives on the Group Process.* C. G. Kemp, ed. Boston: Houghton Mifflin.

GREENE, W., 1975. *est: 4 Days to Make Your Life Work.* New York: Pocket Books.

GUNTHER, B., 1968. *Sense Relaxation.* New York: Collier Books.

HOBBS, N., 1951. "Group-Centered Psychotherapy," in *Client-Centered Therapy*, C. Rogers, ed. Boston: Houghton Mifflin.

HORA, T., 1971. "Existential Psychiatry and Group Psychotherapy: Basic Principles," in *Comprehensive Group Psychotherapy*, H. I. Kaplan and B. J. Sadock, eds. Baltimore: Williams & Wilkins.

HORWITZ, L., 1977. "A Group Centered Approach to Group Psychotherapy," *International Journal of Group Psychotherapy*, Vol. 27, No. 4.

ILLING, H. A., 1963. "C. G. Jung on the Present Trends in Group Psychotherapy," in *Group Psychotherapy and Group Function*, M. Rosenbaum and M. Berger, eds. New York: Basic Books.

JACOBS, J. O., 1964. "Social Action as Therapy in a Mental Hospital,"' *Social Work*, Vol. 9, No. 1.

JANOV, A., 1970. *The Primal Scream.* New York: Putnam's.

JOHNSON, J., 1963. *Group Therapy: A Practical Approach.* New York: McGraw-Hill.

JONES, M., 1953. *The Therapeutic Community: A New Treatment Method in Psychiatry.* New York: Basic Books.

KAISER, C., 1959. "The Social Group Work Process," in *The Social Group Work Method in Social Work Education*, Vol. XI: *Curriculum Study*, M. Murphy, ed. New York: Council on Social Education.

KANZER, M., 1971. "Freud: The First Psychoanalytic Group Leader," in *Comprehensive Group Psychotherapy*, I. Kaplan and B. J. Sadock, eds. Baltimore: Williams & Wilkins.

KILMAN, P., and W. SOTILE, 1976. "The Marathon Encounter Group: A Review of the Outcome Literature," *Psychological Bulletin*, Vol. 83.

KINNICK, B. C., 1971. "Group Discussion and Group Counseling Applied to Student Problem Solving," in *Group Guidance and Counseling in the Schools: Selected Readings*, J. C. Hansen and S. H. Cramer, eds. New York: Appleton-Century-Crofts.

KLAPMAN, J. W., 1946. *Group Psychotherapy.* New York: Grune & Stratton.

KLEIN, A. F., 1970. *Social Work Through Group Process.* Albany: State University of New York at Albany.

KONOPKA, G., 1952. "The Role of the Group Worker in the Psychiatric Setting," *American Journal of Orthopsychiatry*, Vol. 22, No. 1.

——, 1963. *Social Group Work: A Helping Process.* Englewood Cliffs, N.J.: Prentice-Hall.

LAKIN, M., 1972. *Interpersonal Encounter: Theory and Practice in Sensitivety Training.* New York: McGraw-Hill.

LAZARUS, A. A., 1961. "Group Therapy of Phobic Disorders by Systematic Desensitization," *Journal of Abnormal and Social Psychology*, Vol. 63, No. 3.

——, 1968. "Behavior Therapy in Groups," in *Basic Approaches to Group Psychotherapy and Group Counseling.* Springfield, Ill.: Charles C. Thomas.

—— and G. T. WILSON, 1976. in *The Therapist's Handbook: Treatment Methods of Mental Disorders*, B. B. Wolman, ed. New York: Van Nostrand.

LAZELL, E. W., 1921. "The Group Treatment of Dementia Praecox," *Psychoanalytic Review*, Vol. 8.

——, 1930. "Group Psychiatric Treatment of Dementian Praecox by Lectures in Mental Re-Education," *U.S. Veterans Bureau Medical Bulletin*, Vol. 8.

LEVITSKY, A., and F. PERLS, 1971. "The Rules and Games of Gestalt Therapy," in *Group Therapy Today: Styles, Methods and Techniques.* H. M. Ruitenbeek, ed. New York: Atherton Press.

LIEBERMAN, M. A., 1977. "Problems of Integrating Traditional Group Therapies with New Forms," *International Journal of Group Psychotherapy*, Vol. 27, No. 1.

LIFTON, W. M., 1968. "Group-Centered Counseling," in *Basic Approaches to Group Psychotherapy and Group Counseling*, G. M. Gazda, ed. Springfield, Ill.: Charles C. Thomas.

LOWEN, A., 1958. *Physical Dynamics of Character Structures.* New York: Grune & Stratton.

——, 1967. *The Betrayal of the Body.* New York: Macmillan.

——, 1971. "Bio-energetic Group Therapy," in *Group Therapy Today: Styles, Methods, and Techniques.* New York: Atherton Press.

MAHLER, C. A., 1969. *Group Counseling in the Schools.* Boston: Houghton Mifflin.

MARCH, R., 1975. "I Am the Cause of My World," *Psychology Today.* Vol. 9.

MARSH, L. C., 1931. "Group Treatment of Psychotics by Psychological Equivalent of the Revival," *Mental Hygiene*, Vol. 15, No. 2.

——, 1933. "Experience in Group Treatment of Patients at Worcester State Hospital." *Mental Hygiene*, Vol. 17, No. 3.

McBROOM, E., 1976. "Socialization Through Small Groups," in *Theories of Social Work with Groups*, R. W. Roberts and H. Northen, eds. New York: Columbia University Press.

MIDDLEMAN, R. R., 1968. *The Non-Verbal Method of Working with Groups.* New York: Association Press.

MINTZ, E. E., 1971. "Time-Extended Marathon Groups," in *Group Therapy Today: Styles, Methods, and Techniques,* H. M. Ruitenbeek, ed. New York: Atherton Press.

MORENO, J. L., 1971. "Psychodrama," *Comprehensive Group Psychotherapy,* H. I. Kaplan and B. J. Sadock, eds. Baltimore: Williams & Wilkins.

——, 1946. *Psychodrama.* New York: Beacon House.

——, 1969. "The Viennese Origins of the Encounter Movement: Paving the Way for Existentialism, Group Psychotherapy and Psychodrama," *Group Psychotherapy, Psychodrama, Sociometry,* Vol. 22, Nos. 1–2.

—— and Z. T. MORENO, 1959. *Psychodrama.* New York: Beacon House.

MORENO, J. L., et al., eds., 1966. *The International Handbook of Psychotherapy.* New York: Philosophical Library.

NORTHEN, H., 1976. "Psychosocial Practice in Small Groups," in *Theories of Social Work with Groups,* R. W. Roberts and H. Northen, eds. New York: Columbia University Press.

NEWSTETTER, W., M. J. FELDSTEIN, and T. M. NEWCOMB, 1938. *Group Adjustment: A Study in Experimental Sociology.* Cleveland: School of Applied Social Services, Western Reserve University.

OHLSEN, M. M., 1970. *Group Counseling.* New York: Holt, Rinehart & Winston.

PARAD, H. J., 1965. *Crises Intervention: Selected Readings.* New York: Family Service Association of America.

——, L. SELBY, and J. QUINLAN, 1976. "Crises Intervention with Families and Groups," in *Theories of Social Work with Groups,* R. W. Roberts and H. Northen, eds. New York: Columbia University Press.

PERLS, F. S., 1969. *Gestalt Therapy Verbation.* Lafayette, Cal: Real People Press.

PHILLIPS, H., 1954. "What Is Group Work Skill?" *The Group,* Vol. 16, No. 5.

——, 1957. *Essentials of Social Group Work Skill.* New York: Association Press.

PINNY, E. L., 1978. "The Beginning of Group Psychotherapy: Joseph Pratt, M. D., and the Reverend Dr. Elmwood Worcester," *International Journal of Group Psychotherapy,* Vol. 28.

POLSTER, E., and M. POLSTER, 1974. *Gestalt Therapy Integrated: Contours of Theory and Practice.* New York: Vantage Books.

PRATT, J. H., 1907. "The Class Method of Treating Consumption in the Homes of the Poor," *Journal of American Medical Association,* Vol. 49.

——, 1953. "The Use of Dejerine's Methods in the Treatment of Common Neurosis by Group Psychotherapy," *Bulletin of the New England Medical Center,* Vol. 15.

REDL, F., 1944. "Diagnostic Group Work," *American Journal of Orthopsychiatry,* Vol. 14. No. 1.

REID, W. J. and L. EPSTEIN, eds., 1977. *Task-Centered Practice.* New York: Columbia University Press.

RICE, A. K., 1975. "Learning for Leadership," in *Group Relations Reader,* A. D. Coleman and W. H. Bexton, eds. Sausalito, Cal.: Grex.

ROBERTS, R. W., and H. NORTHEN, eds., 1976. *Theories of Social Work with Groups.* New York: Columbia University Press.

ROSE, S., 1957. "Horney Concepts in Group Psychotherapy," *International Journal of Group Psychotherapy*, Vol. 7, No. 4.

ROSENBAUM, M., 1965. "Group Psychotherapy and Psychodrama," in *Handbook of Clinical Psychology.* New York: McGraw-Hill.

RUITENBEEK, H., 1970. *The New Group Therapies.* New York: Avon Books.

——, 1971. *Group Therapy Today: Styles, Methods and Techniques.* New York: Atherton Press.

RYDER, E. L., 1976. "A Functional Approach," in *Theories of Social Work with Groups,* R. W. Roberts and H. Northen, eds. New York: Columbia University Press.

SCHEIDLINGER, S., 1956. "Social Group Work and Group Psychotherapy," *Social Work,* Vol. 1, No. 3.

SCHILDER, P., 1936. "The Analysis of Ideologies as a Psychotherapeutic Method, Especially in Group Treatment," *American Journal of Psychiatry,* Vol. 93, No. 3.

SCHULTZ, W. C., 1971. *Here Comes Everyone: Bodymind and Encounter Culture.* New York: Harper & Row.

SCHWARTZ, W., 1976. "Between Client and System: The Mediating Function," in *Theories of Social Work with Groups,* R. W. Roberts and H. Northen, eds. New York: Columbia University Press.

——, 1977. "Social Group Work: Interactionist Approach," *Encyclopedia of Social Work,* Vol. II. New York: National Association of Social Workers.

—— and S. R. ZALBA, eds., 1971. *The Practice of Group Work.* New York: Columbia University Press.

SILLS, M., J. RUBENSTEIN, and E. MYERSON, and A. KLEIN, 1967. "Group Work Revisited: A Statement of Position," *The Jewish Social Work Forum,* Vol. 4, No. 2.

SLAVSON, S. R., 1943. *An Introduction to Group Therapy.* New York: Commonwealth Fund.

——, 1945. *An Introduction to Group Therapy.* New York: International Universities Press.

—— and M. SCHIFFER, 1975. *Group Psychotherapies for Children: A Textbook.* New York: International Universities Press.

SLOAN, M. B., 1953. "The Special Contribution of Therapeutic Group Work in a Psychiatric Setting," *The Group,* Vol. 15, No. 4.

SOLOMON, L. N., and B. BERZON, eds., 1972. *New Perspectives on Encounter Groups.* San Francisco: Jossey-Bass.

SOMERS, M. L., 1976. "Problem Solving in Small Groups," in *Theories of*

Social Work with Groups, R. W. Roberts and H. Northen, eds. New York: Columbia University Press.

SPONTNITZ, H., 1961. *The Couch and the Circle: A Story of Group Psychotherapy.* New York: Knopf.

STRICKLER, M., and J. ALLGEYER, 1976. "The Crises Group: A New Application of Crises Theory," *Social Work*, Vol. 12, No. 3.

THOMAS, G. W., 1943. "Group Psychotherapy: Review of the Present Literature," *Psychosomatic Medicine*, Vol. 5, No. 166.

TRECKER, H. B., 1972. *Social Group Work: Principals and Practices.* New York: Association Press.

TROPP, E., 1969. *A Humanistic Foundation for Group Work Practice.* New York: Selected Academic Readings.

——, 1977. "The Developmental Approach," *Encyclopedia of Social Work*, Vol. II. New York: National Association of Social Workers.

VATTANO, A. J., 1972. "Power to the People: Self-Help Groups," *Social Work* Vol. 17, No. 4.

VINTER, R. D., 1965. "Social Group Work," *Encyclopedia of Social Work.* New York: National Association of Social Workers.

——, ed., 1967. *Readings in Group Practice.* Ann Arbor, Mich.: Campus Publications.

WASSELL, B., 1966. *Group Analysis.* New York: Citadel Press.

WENDER, L., 1940. "Group Psychotherapy: Study of Its Application," *Psychiatric Quarterly*, Vol. 14, No. 4.

WILSON, G., and G. RYLAND, 1949. *Social Group Work Practice.* Cambridge, Mass.: Riverside Press.

WOLF, A., and E. K. SCHWARTZ, 1962. *Psychoanalysis in Groups.* New York: Grune & Stratton.

——, 1971. "Psychoanalysis in Groups," in *Comprehensive Group Psychotherapy*, H. I. Kaplan and B. J. Sadock, eds. Baltimore: Williams & Wilkins.

YALOM, I. D., 1970. *The Theory and Practice of Group Psychotherapy*, New York: Basic Books.

ZINKER, J., 1977. *Creative Process in Gestalt Therapy.* New York: Brunner/Mazel.

25

Self-Help Groups and the Professional Community

Alfred H. Katz is Professor of Public Health and Social Welfare, School of Public Health, University of California, Los Angeles.

Alfred H. Katz

To one who has been interested in self-help phenomena and their relationship to social welfare and health services for many years, the recent surge of professional interest in them is striking and gratifying. Professionals in various fields and disciplines are now discovering the potentials and potency of self-help forms of care and treatment, and coming to realize that "natural" or "spontaneous" support systems have unique values in offering an alternative or adjunct form of helping to the formalized structures of professional agencies and practitioners. Research, which for many years had hardly looked into these phenomena, has now begun to consider different aspects of self-help groups—their history, operations, structure, dynamics; their effects upon member participants and on the professional community. Hardly an issue of a professional journal in social work, psychology, psychiatry, nursing, or other fields appears without some discussion, specialized or general, of self-help groups.

The reasons for this surge of interest are manifold and interactive, but not hard to define. They represent, first, social movement factors arising in response to the perceived failures, exclusions, and discrimination of the larger society: the failure of its institutions to provide nurturance and social support for the needy, the stigmatized, the socially isolated or nonconformist. Then there are professional developments—a convergence of research, practice, and theory in education, psychology, sociology, and medicine—all of which have produced telling evidence for the importance, the value, the indispensability of involving the consumer, the client, the pupil, the patient in his own learning or relearning, and in contributing to decisions about his own destiny. These convergences have resulted in the rediscovery of the self-help form, those natural support systems of peers, relatives, kith and kin, and the like-minded which have existed immemorially but are now especially necessary and salient in a time of much social fragmentation, loss of relatedness, and alienation.

The recent flowering of self-help groups and of professional interest in them, then, is all to the good, but I have several cautions and caveats to convey to those whose interest in them has arisen more recently. My first caution lies in the area of definition; I suggest that in thinking about self-help groups we must be especially self-conscious and sensitive to the social role of professionals and to its implicit elements of social control. To this burgeoning new field there may be applied that tendency in American life which we have come to refer to as co-optation, or, "If you can't lick 'em, join 'em," or, more subtly, "control 'em." We have seen this phenomenon arise in regard to the youth culture, especially in its easily commercialized aspects, such as clothing, music, and food. It would be a tragedy if, arising from a sense of frustration about the possibilities of system change—that is, change in the particular agencies or institutions in which we work—we were to go overboard about the potentials represented by self-help groups on the one hand, or to look on them as merely some form of extension of professionalized service on the other. If from the best motives in the world we look on self-help groups as a kind of adjunct to the professional services that we have tried patiently to construct over the years, and that for whatever reasons target populations do not greet with hosannas of praise or universally use, then it is perhaps natural for us to seek to be the arbiters of *who should join and use self-help groups*, and even of what self-help groups do and how. That this is not a fictitious danger may be gauged by a few quotations from a paper given at the American Orthopsychiatric Association by Dr. Thomas Powell of the University of Michigan School of Social Welfare. In discussing the relationship of professionals to self-help groups Dr. Powell states:

> With a client for whom it is important to remain involved with the dominant community and continued treatment with the professional, it is important [for the professional] to weigh carefully the probable effect of affiliation with groups, such as Synanon or various patient liberation groups. Likewise affiliation with a group, such as the Gay Liberation Front (depending on the extent of politicization in the local group), may also tip the balance in favor of opposition to participation in larger community activities including formal human service agencies [1975, p. 3].

In other words, Dr. Powell believes that professionals should decide for clients whether or not they should participate in self-help groups in which they might be interested. The analysis in his paper is careful, compassionate, and professional in the best sense, and *his* cautions include the possibility that for a client to participate in self-help groups may "magnify the difference" or otherwise "tip the balance" against the client's participation in mainstream "larger community activities." Powell goes on: "Membership in a group like Parents Anonymous, given its built-in feature of a professional sponsor, is likely to strengthen whatever existing inclination there is to participate in treatment" (p. 4). In other words, if a self-help group *does* intensify the likelihood that a particular client will then seek out or participate in professionalized services, then participation in that self-help group is viewed as good and useful. Dr. Powell is thus arrogating to the professional the responsibility for making life decisions for clients in support of values or behaviors which the professionals judge as useful or constructive for the client. It does not take much sophistication to understand that such a suggestion contravenes quite precisely the very definition of self-help groups, as well as the impulses that led some people to have formed them in the first place and others to join them. These are purely and simply impulses for finding in the like-minded forms of support and nurturance otherwise lacking "in the larger community," including the institutionalized panoply of professional services.

DEFINITION AND ATTRIBUTES OF SELF-HELP GROUPS

Perhaps it will advance this discussion and clarify the picture to quote the definition of self-help groups that Eugene Bender and I employ in our book:

> Self-help groups are voluntary, small group structures for mutual aid and the accomplishment of a special purpose. They are usually formed by peers who have come together for mutual assistance in satisfying a common need, overcoming a common handicap or life-disrupting problem, and bringing about desired social and/or personal change. The initiators and members of such groups perceive that their needs are not, or cannot be, met by or through existing social institutions. Self-help groups emphasize face-to-face social interactions and the assumption of personal responsibility by members. They often provide material assistance, as well as emotional support; they are frequently "cause"-oriented, and promulgate an ideology or values through which members may attain an enhanced sense of personal identity [Katz and Bender, 1976].

Please note that self-help groups have several characteristic attributes that flow from this definition:

1. They are patterned small-group or face-to-face interactions.
2. They are spontaneous in origin.
3. They may have a variety of functions and characteristics.
4. There is personal participation. Mere formal membership or financial support (as in belonging to and contributing to a conservation or neighborhood improvement group) does not define the individual as a true member or participant.
5. The groups supply a reference group, a point of connection and identification with others, a baseline for activity, a source of ego reinforcement, a value system by which the individual's tasks, joys, sorrows, accomplishments, and frustrations can be evaluated and dealt with.
6. The members agree upon and engage in some actions.
7. Typically, self-help groups start from a condition of powerlessness. No matter what they may later achieve, their initial resources are always limited, and the exercise and control of power are not among their objectives.

DIFFERENCES AMONG GROUPS

These attributes point to a second caution: self-help groups are not all the same. They need to be differentially evaluated and analyzed in order to be understood by professionals, and enthusiasm for them may be tempered thereby. A couple of years ago *Social Work* published a rather rhapsodical article by Dr. Anthony Vattano (1972), which made some rhetorical claims for self-help groups, and in effect put them all in the same box, as representing a form of countercultural protest and a political stance which Vattano broadly classed as "power to the people." But such a claim does not stand a moment's analysis, for example, of the philosophy, values, or internal operations of groups like Alcoholics Anonymous (AA) or Recovery, Inc., two of the largest, most influential, and, in many respects, most useful of the self-help groups organized to serve special categories of needy people. Investigation would have convinced Dr. Vattano that the aim of groups like AA (and its many spin-off "anonymous" groups, such as Narcotics Anonymous, Overeaters Anonymous, Gamblers Anonymous, etc.) is exactly that of assisting their members to conform to the values of the dominant, middle-class society. Their members are viewed as being outside the mainstream of that society because of their particular addiction or behavior problem. To suggest that groups whose major aim is to keep an alcoholic dry, to help obese persons overcome a compulsive food addiction, or to give emotional support to persons who define themselves as "nervous" (the Recovery member) are exponents of "power to the people' is to distort the evidence; the aims of such groups are clearly those of adapting to, and not challenging the values of, the dominant society. As such, in my opinion, they do useful work, but they should hardly be confused with the Black Panthers or Maoist cells.

No, the analysis needs to be sharper than this. We first have to understand the phenomena with which we are dealing in their many-sidedness, and to develop some taxonomies for ordering and classifying them, before we can usefully discuss any of their aspects—whether it be their relationships with professionals, their probable future, their relationship to the "organized society," and so on. In our book (1976), we attempt a fivefold classification of self-help groups as follows:

1. *Groups that are primarily focused on self-fulfillment or personal growth.* These are often referred to by themselves and others as "therapeutic" (as in the American Federation of Therapeutic Self-Help Clubs). A good example of this type of self-help group is "Recovery, Inc."

2. *Groups that are primarily focused on social advocacy.* We use this term rather than the more usual "social action" because it is broader. Advocacy includes agitating and education directed at existing institutions, professionals, the public; confrontation, muckraking, and social crusading. It can be both on behalf of broad issues, such as legislation, the creation of new services, change in the policies of existing institutions, and so on, or it can be on behalf of individuals, families, or other small groups. Typically, such groups as welfare rights organizations and the Committee for the Rights of the Disabled use both kinds of advocacy.

3. *Groups whose primary focus is to create alternative patterns for living.* Group solidarity provides a foundation for society's changing social institutions and attitudes. These groups may start new living and working alternatives of their own. Individual growth and self-fulfillment are obtained in the process, but are not the primary group goals. Examples are Women's Liberation, Gay Liberation, Operation Bootstrap, many communes.

4. *"Outcast haven" or "rock bottom" groups.* These groups provide a refuge for the desperate attempting to secure personal protection from the pressures of life and society, and thereby save themselves from mental or physical decline. This type of group involves total commitment in a living-in arrangement (a sheltered environment), with close, if not twenty-four-hour-a-day, supervision by peers or persons who have successfully grappled with similar problems of their own. An example of this type of group is the

X-Kalay Foundation in Vancouver, British Columbia, and, in its beginning, but in our view not at present, the Synanon Foundation.

5. "*Mixed*" *types.* We resorted to this variant because some groups did not fit neatly into any of the above, such as Parents Without Partners and some groups of former prisoners.

When viewing self-help groups through even this primitive classification scheme it becomes apparent that they cannot be forced into a single box like "power to the people" or any other simplistic categorization. In fact, analysis and study of them need to pursue, in our opinion, a number of dimensions which we have only briefly touched on in the book, but which, it seems to us, hold suggestive implications both for their relationships with professionals and for research. Among the dimensions that need consideration and study is, first, that of the groups' ideology. Do they, for example, have a belief in God or a higher power, on which their adherents ultimately depend for the solution of their problem behavior? Many self-help groups, particularly AA and its spin-offs, do have such a philosophy, and it is characteristic of these groups that they maintain a tight control over members, expect frequent participation in meetings, and regular consultation with a "sponsor" or "buddy" more experienced than themselves. Such groups believe, in fact, that the problem behavior is never "cured" but may only be controlled through close involvement with the group. In practice, without relying on the notion of a higher power, and without as well worked-out a set of procedures and rituals as is found in AA and its imitators, Synanon has a similar approach. Anyone who has visited or participated in Synanon activities knows that an underlying belief is that "once a Synanon member, always a Synanon member"; members are not encouraged to "split" or outgrow the sheltering self-help group. In fact, this kind of self-help group often assumes a messianic and universalistic character; it proselytizes actively and sees itself as providing a truly alternative and total way of living. This dimension, then, of the kind and extent of philosophy or ideology, and the consequent tightness of social control of members, is a very important one to keep in mind in considering how to work with particular self-help groups; or in thinking about the degree to which their members may attain liberated self-awareness and social competence.

The importance of ideology as an influence upon structure, group life, and member adaptations is observable among communes or "intentional communities," as social scientists like to call them. Those communes endure which have a strong ideology as a binding tie. Examples are the Hutterite and other religious groups which live communally and therefore have rules of behavior, procedures, and internal system-maintaining regulations, but which are found much less frequently in the rapidly appearing and equally rapidly disappearing rural and urban communes formed by the alienated or disaffected or by proponents of particular life styles in our population.

So, professionals do have to take into account these specifying, differentiating characteristics, the presence or otherwise of ideology, and of system-maintaining regulatory procedures and behaviors in attempting to understand these groups as organizations *sui generis*, and in understanding as well their potential meaning and helpfulness to clients, and also, more broadly, in speculating about their probable future and durability as social institutions.

DEPENDENCY

A point that often troubles professionals about self-help groups is their perceived role in promoting, maintaining, intensifying, or prolonging dependency. About this there are both general and specific things to say. Dependency on others is of course as natural to the human species as breathing or metabolizing one's food. Such dependency on those to whom one is, or can feel, close is lifelong and constructive; effects of the lack of reliable interpersonal supports on which to depend are documented in the annals of human misery that social workers daily compile. And the securing or extension of reliable support systems is one of the latent but obvious motives people have in establishing and joining self-help groups, even though the manifest motives may be to obtain concrete services or engage in social action.

Here again, differential analysis is required in order to understand that in their concrete particularities various self-help groups approach the problem of dependency in different ways. To take a striking example, that of organizations of former drug addicts, Synanon, as we have seen, socializes its members to believe that affiliation with it is indeed a lifelong affair. But other organizations of former addicts and "refuge haven" self-help groups, such as X-Kalay in Canada which in other respects is close to the Synanon model, approach the matter of lifelong affiliation quite differently. They not only encourage independence and their members' growth to the point that they no longer need the continuous sheltering environment provided by the group, but they have ingenious graduation or *rites de passage* ceremonies to mark the coming of age, as it were, of member participants, their reentry or entry into the wider social world. In self-help groups which do not involve such a total commitment or life style—Parents Without Partners is an example—the question of prolonged dependency for their members does not really arise.

The whole complex question of the role of professionals vis-à-vis self-help groups, then, merits much further thought. In my opinion, the first requirement for professionals is to understand that these groups are a natural phenomenon, that they are here to stay, as a permanent and probably growing feature of the social landscape; that they can provide for many people who themselves choose to go that way a resource for life support and sometimes life change that has qualities different in kind from and in some ways transcending those available from professional sources. Among these, to repeat, are opportunities for peer support, for identity establishment, for personal change and self-validation, as well as for simple socialization and an array of concrete benefits. They achieve these through group contacts and group life that simulate "real" life—the stuff of living social reality—in ways that professional relationships and contacts can never duplicate. Above all they offer the status of reciprocal equality in social relationships. Whatever else we may think about professionalism, it can never really supply a climate or status of egalitarianism. Professional relationships always imply and carry the burden of super- and subordination, of "authority," while in the self-help group the relationship is a horizontal one between equals and peers—peers in the possession of a common problem, but also peers in the possession of a common social status. As I have written elsewhere (Katz, 1970), professionals have many contributions to make, arising out of their training, their personal sense of justice and their sensitivity, their technical skills, their anxiety to do good in the world. It would be a mistake to regard self-help groups as operating in exactly the same way and in the same universe of assumptions as professionals, for in that way we would tend to regard them as mere untrained and therefore presumptuous competitors and would see them as mainly a threat or danger. There is plenty of work to do in this world to help needy people, and self-help groups for some time have been doing it, often with success, sometimes with professional support and understanding, often without it. Professionals should have humility and open-mindedness, learn what they can about and from them, cooperate with them when they can, but should not regard the groups either as panaceas or nostrums for every social ill, or as undisciplined, threatening rivals.

What professionals can occasionally contribute to self-help groups is expertise in the form of knowledge and resources of all kinds; professional knowledge regarding effective programmatic approaches, sources of funding and political strategies. Sometimes this may take the form of teaching or consultation or even supervision, but it is clear, harking back to that hoary social work principle of self-determination—much more honored in the breach than in the observance—that professionals in no way can dominate self-help groups and that they should only intervene in them when asked. If they are instrumental in their initial creation, then professionals should withdraw gracefully from the scene as early as possible. If an individual social worker wishes to be a member of a self-help group, he should be just that, expect no special status, and relate to its other members on a basis of equality.

That there are gains for "clients," members of the community, the disenfranchised and dispossessed, the stigmatized and needy in affiliation with these new or rediscovered forms for mutual aid and caring in social life seems to me indisputable. That some of them can occasionally undertake and accomplish larger effects upon the social environment, upon social policy, that they can be factors in system change to bring about more human living conditions for all, I also do not doubt. But in order to accomplish the latter, it is clear that they cannot go it alone, that they need friendly support, understanding, and friends and potential allies. I include in the latter group the most concerned and flexible, the least bureaucratically minded, among professionals—those whose greatest commitments are not to professional or personal status and to system maintenance but to human welfare and the full flowering of human potential.

REFERENCES

KATZ, A. H., 1970. "Self-Help Organizations and Volunteer Participation in Social Welfare," *Social Work*, Vol. 15, No. 1.

—— and E. BENDER, 1976. *The Strength in Us.* New York: Franklin Watts.

POWELL, T. J., 1975. "The Use of Self-Help Groups as Supportive Reference Communities," paper presented at annual meeting of the American Orthopsychiatric Association.

VATTANO, A. J., 1972. "Power to the People: Self-Help Groups," *Social Work*, Vol. 17, No. 4.

Study Questions

1. How would you distinguish among the various group methods as they are applied within the fields of medicine, psychology, counseling, and social work? What comparisons can you make between and among the methods themselves? How do they differ in terms of history, philosophies and values, theories and research, settings, claims, major practice principles, levels of professionalism, and variations and extensions?

2. Is there a unified social group work method? Do the varied group work perspectives reflect a common "social work content"? How similar or different are they relative to each other and to the methods used in related disciplines? What, if anything, is unique about social group work?

3. Based on your understanding of social work knowledge, values, commitments, and practice experience, how would you specifically distinguish between group work and psychological self-awareness approaches such as T groups, marathon sensitivity groups, and the like? How does group work compare with medical approaches? with the various counseling methods? (See Konopka, 1978.)

4. What relevance do the psychological self-awareness methods have for social work generally and social group work specifically? How can they contribute to our theoretical understanding of groups and add to our technical skills? How, for example, can T group experience and sensitivity training be specifically applied to social work? What specific social work skills can be sharpened and developed further through more collaboration and study?

5. What "hard" evidence do we have from research regarding the impact of different group experiences on participants? What are some of the problems encountered in trying to demonstrate the effectiveness of group services?

6. What kinds of ethical issues have been raised as criticisms of some of the new group methods? What are perceived to be "casualties" that result from some group experiences? What are their sources? What are some of the ways to deal with the personal and interpersonal sources of group casualties? Should group leaders, for example, take it as their responsibility to define the potential hazards that may befall persons entering group treatment? Have screening methods been sufficiently developed to protect effectively those who are most vulnerable? What specific guidelines would you suggest to protect participants from unethical practices?

7. Galinsky and Schopler (1977) state that in developing reasonable peer group controls, it would probably be better to have too many rather than too few rules as long as they are not harsh or coercive in character? How would this issue be viewed by proponents of the different social group work perspectives?

8. Katz welcomes the recent interest in self-help groups and the increased recognition of their unique value as a natural support system for people in need. What is your view of the questions he raises concerning social work's approach to self-help groups? Is professional involvement compatible with the self-help concept? Should professionals play a role in determining whether or not clients should participate in such groups? Does the taxonomy developed by Katz provide a basis for differentiating expectations and assessing the potential impact

of group experiences on participants? Does it suggest any additional roles for social workers?

9. If the strength of the self-help group is derived from its place as a natural responsive phenomenon, can the helping professions find ways to incorporate certain of its features into their practice? Do you agree with Katz that professional relationships, by definition, militate against attaining reciprocal equality in social relationships? Is the concept of "mutual aid society" therefore unattainable? On the other hand, is it conceivable that indigenous leaders may emerge in self-help groups, taking on leadership functions that can threaten natural peer group support? What about the use of volunteers in this process?

10. Is there any danger that self-help programs may come to be accepted as substitutes for the expansion of professional services to minorities and powerless groups? How effective has the self-help movement been in dealing with the larger social issues in society?

Suggested Readings

ANDERSON, J. D., 1975. "Human Relations Training and Group Work," *Social Work*, Vol. 20, No. 3.

CROGHAN, L. M., 1974. "Encounter Groups and the Necessity for Ethical Guidelines," *Journal of Clinical Psychology*, Vol. 30, No. 4.

EDENFIELD, W. H., and R. D. MYRICK, 1973. "The Effect of Group Sensitivity Experience on Learning Facilitative Verbal Responses," *Small Group Behavior*, Vol. 4, No. 2.

GALINSKY, M. J., and J. H. SCHOPLER, 1977. "Warning: Groups May Be Dangerous," *Social Work*, Vol. 22, No. 2.

GARTNER, A., and F. RIESSMAN, 1977. *Self-Help in the Human Services*, San Francisco: Jossey-Bass.

JERTSON, J. M., 1975. "Self-Help Groups," *Social Work*, Vol. 20, No. 2.

KATZ, A. H., 1970. "Self-Help Organizations and Volunteer Participants in Social Welfare," *Social Work*, Vol. 15., No. 1.

——, 1977. "Self-Help Groups," *Encyclopedia of Social Work*, 17th Issue, Vol. 2. New York: National Association of Social Workers.

KONOPKA, G., 1978. "The Significance of Social Group Work Based on Ethical Values," *Social Work with Groups*, Vol. 1, No. 2.

LIEBERMAN, M. A., I. D. YALOM and M. B. MILES, 1973. *Encounter Groups: First Facts*. New York: Basic Books.

MANTELL, J. E., et al., 1976. "Social Work and Self-Help Groups," *Health and Social Work*, Vol. 1, No. 1.

POWELL, T. J., 1975. "The Use of Self-Help Groups as Supportive Reference Communities," *American Journal of Orthopsychiatry*, Vol. 45, No. 5.

REDDY, W. B., 1970. "Sensitivity Training on Group Psychotherapy: The Need for Adequate Screening," *The International Journal of Group Psychotherapy*, Vol. 20.

Index

Index